... Sulzer,

With the Compliments of
the Author.

Presented
to Library
Ohio Northern University
by
John E. Osbor
+
Emile Carbonnel

THE AMERICAN
MERCHANT MARINE

THE AMERICAN
MERCHANT MARINE

ITS HISTORY AND ROMANCE
FROM 1620 TO 1902

BY

WINTHROP L. MARVIN

NEW YORK
CHARLES SCRIBNER'S SONS
1910

TO

THE AUTHOR OF "THE NAVAL WAR OF 1812"

A STANCH FRIEND OF THE AMERICAN SHIP
AND THE AMERICAN SAILOR

THEODORE ROOSEVELT

𝔓𝔯𝔢𝔰𝔦𝔡𝔢𝔫𝔱 𝔬𝔣 𝔱𝔥𝔢 𝔘𝔫𝔦𝔱𝔢𝔡 𝔖𝔱𝔞𝔱𝔢𝔰

INTRODUCTION

THE war navy of the United States has had many, the merchant navy few, historians. Yet the two services are joined by an intimate relationship: they are indispensable the one to the other; they have the same brave, vigorous traditions, and for many years they were cherished with equal pride by the people of the nation whose flag they bore to victory. Now our war fleet, after a period of neglect and decline, has again grown strong and prosperous, while our merchant fleet on the high seas has shrunk to a mere shadow of its ancient greatness. It is in the firm belief that the renaissance of the merchant navy also will come — indeed, is already near at hand — that this volume has been written.

There is abundant proof of a quickening of American interest in maritime affairs. For this, our fighting navy, its noble ships, and the dazzling sea triumphs of the Spanish War are chiefly responsible. The United States possesses one of the four most formidable war fleets in the world, but our merchant vessels are so few in number that they convey less than one-tenth of our own sea-borne commerce, and almost none of that of other nations. When the American people once realize the grotesque disparity between the two divisions of the national marine, they will not rest until the same overwhelming power which forced a heedless Congress to build our first steel cruisers and armor-clads has compelled it to clear the way for the creation of an adequate fleet of swift mail ships and heavy freighters. A nation which is reaching out for the commercial mastery of the world cannot long suffer nine-tenths of its own ocean-carrying to be monopolized by its foreign rivals. This is a situation which must appeal to the shrewd Yankee sense of humor, as well as to the Yankee passion of patriotism.

It is the declared purpose of this volume to present both the romance and the history of the American merchant marine. The picturesque aspect of our ocean adventure is not less important than the economic and political. No heroes of the Iliad or the Crusades were bolder than the merchant navigators of the young republic. Our national independence was really won and maintained for us upon the sea by the splendid constancy, valor, and skill of the armed crews of our trading ships, whalers, and fishermen, who in the Revolution were almost as numerous as, and far more effective than, the entire army of Washington. Again, in the Civil War it was the sea power of the Union, composed largely of merchant ships, and four-fifths of merchant officers and sailors, which swung the balance against the seceding States. Even in our short conflict with Spain, the merchant fleet proved a reserve ready and indispensable.

Yankee privateers, Yankee packets, Yankee clippers, sail the seas no longer, but their fame endures and their exploits stand unequalled. More of the romance of the ocean than landsmen know has survived a half-century of steam navigation. Modern liners have a picturesqueness of their own in the long sweep of their steel bulwarks, and the broad wake whitening astern as they drive onward twenty knots an hour. Nor has lofty canvas vanished altogether from the salt breeze, for this very year 1902 has seen the launching of the greatest sailing vessel ever fashioned in America.

Fortunately, the merchant marine of the United States means more than that portion of our fleet engaged in foreign commerce, or shipbuilding and seamanship would have become almost lost arts to the people long pre-eminent in both. The coast and the Great Lake traffic has grown with the growth of the country while our deep-sea ships have been disappearing. Separate chapters of this volume are devoted to these active and thriving interests, as well as to the whalemen and the fishermen, — for they are all alike our toilers of the deep, and their place and part in the American merchant marine are officially recognized by the National Government.

A word personal: This work is the outcome of twenty years of such study as the student gives to the theme that lies nearest to his heart — of study supplemented by constant observation of the sea, its ships, and the ebb and flow of its commerce. The author, out of this experience, has reached some positive convictions of his own, but it has been his honest effort to make these pages interesting and informing rather than controversial. As to the causes that have destroyed all but a fragment of our ocean fleet, it is impossible for any American who knows them to speak or write without deep feeling — impossible, certainly, to the first of his race in a long New England line who has not been either shipowner or seaman.

WINTHROP LIPPITT MARVIN.

Boston, September, 1902.

CONTENTS

CHAPTER I

THE COLONY SHIPS

CHAPTER II

OLD RIGS AND MODELS

CHAPTER III

AFTER THE REVOLUTION

CHAPTER IV

THE FIRST SWIFT GROWTH. 1789–1800

CHAPTER V

A Celebrated Voyage

CHAPTER VI

The Merchant Navigators

CHAPTER VII

Impressment and Embargo.   1801–15

CHAPTER VIII

The Yankee Whalemen

CHAPTER IX

Reciprocity on the Sea. 1816–30

CHAPTER X

A New–World Venice

CHAPTER XI

The Incoming of Steam. 1831–45

CONTENTS

CHAPTER XII

MAIL SHIPS AND CLIPPERS. 1846-60

CHAPTER XIII

THE DEEP-SEA FISHERIES

CHAPTER XIV

WAR AND ITS RUIN. 1861–75

CHAPTER XV

OUR COASTWISE CARRIERS

CHAPTER XVI

NEARING LOW-WATER MARK. 1876–90

THE AMERICAN MERCHANT MARINE

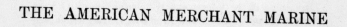

THE AMERICAN MERCHANT MARINE

CHAPTER I

THE COLONY SHIPS

Early Americans, Shipbuilders and Seamen First of all — Wealth of Ship Timber — British Meddling with Colonial Sea Trade — Vital Work of the Privateers of the Revolution — Far More Effective than the Continental Navy — Our Great Debt to the Sailors of 1775–1783

FORTUNATE is that race whose veins hold the salt of the sea, for in its soul there is sure to be genius for adventure. The founders of the American colonies were shipbuilders and sailors, both by inheritance and by environment. The English of New England, Pennsylvania, Maryland, Virginia, and the Carolinas, the Dutch of New York, and the Swedes of Delaware, were all sprung from the world's best seafaring stock. Moreover, the conditions of their pioneer life in the New World were such as to intensify the racial instinct. Without exception the early settlements clung close to the ocean. It was the one sure source of their food until the gathering of the first uncertain harvest. It was their road toward home and their safe refuge, if need be, from an overwhelming onset of the red savages. So it is not strange that the sea and its affairs dominated the thoughts of the first Americans, and that they scarcely waited to raise rude shelter above their heads before the dark, forbidding wilderness which stretched all along

1

the coast began to be notched here and there by busy shipyards.

This most ancient of American industries is as old as Jamestown and older than Plymouth. The ill-fated Popham colony launched in 1607, at the mouth of the Kennebec, "a faire pinnace of thirty tons," the "Virginia," which safely crossed the Atlantic. But the first decked vessel was built on the Hudson by the redoubtable Adrian Block of New Amsterdam, in the summer of 1614. The first seagoing ship of Massachusetts was the half-trader, half-fighter, "Blessing of the Bay," built on the Mystic at Medford the year after the coming of the Puritan colonists to Salem and Boston. Governor John Winthrop deserves, perhaps, to be called the father of American maritime policy, for with sturdy ambition and independence he wrote: "The general fear of want of foreign commodities, now our money was gone and that things were like to go well in England, set us on work to provide shipping of our own." The governor had a lieutenant after his own heart in the famous Puritan divine, the Rev. Hugh Peters, who built at Salem, in 1641, a prodigious ship of three hundred tons! When we read in Hume that toward the close of the sixteenth century only 217 of the 1232 vessels owned in Great Britain were of over eighty tons' burden, and that there were not five which exceeded two hundred tons, and remember that the "Mayflower" of 1620 was of only one hundred and eighty tons, we can realize something of the courage of this devout scholar of Trinity College, who sought to foster the trade as well as to save the souls of his Salem parishioners, and went home to hold up the hands of Cromwell, and finally to die on the gibbet at Charing Cross, a martyr of the Restoration.

But the New World work of Hugh Peters lived after him. He helped to give Salem its characteristic impress as a famous source of maritime adventure, and more than this, as Winthrop testifies, when he built his three-hundred-

ton ship "the inhabitants of Boston, stirred up by his
example, set upon the building of another at Boston of
one hundred and fifty tons." For more than two hundred
years Massachusetts Bay continued to pour out an innumerable fleet of wooden shipping. In 1641 Edward Banks
of Plymouth launched a bark of fifty tons, and the
Pilgrim Fathers, with a worldly shrewdness not always
attributed to them, enforced regulations for care and
thoroughness in shipbuilding. In their enactments they
insisted under heavy penalties that nothing should be
" defective or amiss in any materials or workmanship."[1] For
more than two centuries Massachusetts craft lived up to
the enviable reputation wrought by this Pilgrim foresight.

Hutchinson's record declares that as early as 1676 there
hailed from Boston and ports in the neighborhood thirty
ships of between one hundred and two hundred and fifty
tons fit for the voyage to Europe, two hundred of between
fifty and one hundred tons, and five hundred smaller vessels. Meanwhile the Dutch at New Amsterdam, which
had lately become New York, were almost as active as their
New England neighbors. The Puritan port, however, was
still foremost in all America in maritime development. In
1700 Boston possessed 194 seagoing ships, while New York
had 124. Two years before, Lord Bellamont, colonial governor, wrote in admiration of the adventurous New England spirit, " I believe I may venture to say there are more
good vessels belonging to the town of Boston than to all
Scotland and Ireland, unless one should reckon the small
craft, such as herring boats."

In those primitive years the sea was still the best and
surest highway between the colonies. The chief towns
were still on the edge of the ocean or on navigable rivers.
For passenger or freight transportation from Massachusetts
to New York or alongshore to Virginia the main reliance was
the handy ketch or pinnace. And this habit of the colonies

[1] Ancient Laws and Charter of Massachusetts Bay.

was also the habit of the small neighborhoods. So far as was possible the farmhouses were set near the water, and a boat rode at anchor by the door, to convey the goodman and his family to Sunday meeting. Roads through the wilderness were few and bad, and menaced perhaps by prowling Indians. But on stream or sea the colonists felt themselves secure. Their stout shallops had nothing to fear from the fragile bark canoes of the red men. Thus a great part of the population was inured to the sea, and very many even of the farmers were half farmers and half fishermen.

The settlers of New England and New York were quick to discover the reciprocal advantages of West Indian commerce. Those sunny, languorous islands of the South produced the sugar which our Northern acres would not grow, and offered in return an eager market for the early colonial staples, dried fish, lumber, and rum. In spite of English, French, and Spanish prohibitions a thriving trade arose. Nor were the colonial merchants and mariners content even with this West Indian traffic. They built ships and freighted them for Spain, Portugal, and the Mediterranean, and often sold not cargo only but the ship itself. For in the very first century of American maritime enterprise, the colonial vessels had an established fame for durability and cheapness. Colonial shipbuilders found a market for their handiwork both in Britain and on the Continent. Of 1332 vessels borne on the archives in the State House at Boston as built between 1674 and 1714, 239 were disposed of to foreign owners.

But these early ventures were not always prosperous. The perils of the ocean were far greater then than they are now. The coasts were not lighted, charted, and buoyed. The West Indies swarmed with pirates who sailed to the north for plunder when prizes failed them at home. And the largest of the merchant ships of the seventeenth century would not now be trusted for a summer voyage alongshore. They were crude and feeble craft at best, and their safety was impaired by the keen scarcity and almost prohibitive cost of proper metal fastenings. Very early in the colonial annals sad records of disaster begin to appear. In 1647, the people of New Haven, having suffered from reverses in trade and industry, sought to retrieve themselves by building a one-hundred-and-fifty-ton ship and freighting it for England. The vessel sailed away manned by the best and bravest of the town, but one slow month followed another and no tidings came of its arrival overseas. All New Haven was distraught, until one day, as a chronicler of the time relates it : —

"After a great thunder storm about an hour before sunset, a ship of like dimensions, with her canvas and colors abroad, appeared in the air coming up the harbor against the wind for the space of an hour. Many, says the Rev. Mr. Pierpont, were drawn to behold this great work of God, yea, the very children cried out, 'There is a brave ship.' When so near that a man might hurl a stone on board, her main top seemed blown off, then her mizzen top; then her masting seemed blown away by the board; she overset, and so vanished into a smoky cloud. The vision was given, in the opinion of the beholders, that they might understand the tragic end of the ship and their friends."

Against the gloomy background of the trackless forests under whose edge the first white settlements huddled, these frequent stories of wreck and death in the colonial annals have a pathos all their own. Between the fierce savages and the cruel sea, there need be small wonder that even the most devout of the colonists were sometimes tempted to cry out that Providence had forsaken them in the strange New World. This New Haven story shows that our coasts had their wraith-ship long before the " Palatine " first glowed on the frightened gaze of the people of Block Island.[1]

[1] The "Palatine," a German emigrant ship, was wrecked and burned on Block Island in the eighteenth century. For many years afterward a strange

Already when New York, Boston, and Philadelphia were founded, the forests of old England had begun to fail, and there was a great dearth of wood for shipbuilding. But here on the coasts of America the material was convenient and almost inexhaustible. A colonist of 1642, writing of shipbuilding, says, "we being much encouraged herein by reason of the plenty and excellence of our timber for that purpose." The primeval forest covering the land to the high-water mark from the Bay of Fundy southward was full of noble white oak-trees which excited the enthusiasm of the first explorers. Though their trunks were from three to eight feet thick, these oaks rose to a height of sixty to eighty feet. The trunks themselves were usually straight, but the limbs and branches furnished the crooked timber so requisite for shipbuilding. This white oak is heavy, but it is tough, elastic, durable. So abundant was it that the early builders often put nothing but the heart of oak into their ships, sawing off the outer, softer, and less enduring material.

Another wood of great value to shipbuilders was and still is the yellow pine or pitch pine of the Southern seaboard. This is an admirable material for planking and ceiling the oak frames of ships. It is hard and strong; and with the gradual shrinkage of the oak forests it came into great favor with the northern shipyards. A third material in which America was fortunate was the light, straight white pine. This is the best of all woods for masts, spars, and deck planking. The British Admiralty was quick to recognize the immense importance of the lofty white pine-trees of America. In the early patents granted to the colonies the long, straight trunks were

light, looming out of the sea from time to time, was known as "the Palatine Light" by the islanders. Whittier makes this the theme of one of his poems:

"And the wise Sound skippers, though skies be fine,
Reef their sails when they see the sign
Of the blazing wreck of the Palatine."

reserved as the king's property, and it was the practice to send a royal surveyor into the woods to mark with a broad arrow the finest trees, which were thus imperatively set aside for naval use. The king claimed as a rule every tree two feet and more in diameter, and a heavy fine was the penalty for the bold fellow who ignored the king's prerogative. Parliament granted bounties to encourage the importation of mast timber into Britain, and it is said that before the Revolution about fifty shiploads of American white pine-trees were annually sent out of Portland, Me., Portsmouth, N. H., or the neighboring ports to hold aloft the swelling canvas of the royal line-of-battleships and frigates. In the year 1768 thirty-six-inch American masts were valued at £153 each, delivered at the king's yards in England. A hundred years earlier naval officers had begun to sound a warning of the disappearance of English oak. Its price in 1663 had doubled in fifty years, and consequently an English-built oak ship cost very much more than an oak ship constructed in the colonies. The versatile John Evelyn, fervent Royalist, and one of the earliest of England's distinctively literary men, devoted his pen for forty years to arousing his countrymen to the need of providing the material of England's "wooden walls." His persistency bore fruit in a general planting of oak-trees all over the kingdom, and particularly in the royal forests. It requires from one hundred to two hundred and fifty years to grow oak suitable for heavy naval construction. Thus, thanks to Evelyn, England's renewed oak supply began to mature just as the American Revolution threw English builders back on their island's own resources. Lord Melville in 1810 declared of the fleets of the era of Nelson and Napoleon that "the vast quantities of great timber consumed by our navy during the present reign were chiefly the produce of the plantations made between the Restoration and the end of the seventeenth century."

Although New England and New York built the earliest American ships and the greater number of them, there were some active shipyards in the colonial era on the Delaware River and Chesapeake Bay, and in the first half of the eighteenth century there began to be building in the Carolinas. Those Southern States were fortunate not only in their immense stores of tar, pitch, and turpentine, but in a great variety of fine timber. Their live oak was superior to even the white oak of the North, and before the Revolution it had come into eager demand for high-class ship construction. This early record of American shipbuilding for the year 1769, from Lord Sheffield's Review of American Commerce, shows how widely the industry had then come to be distributed: —

Colonies.	Vessels Built.	Tonnage.
New Hampshire	45	2,452
Massachusetts	137	8,013
Rhode Island	39	1,428
Connecticut	50	1,542
New York	19	955
New Jersey	4	83
Pennsylvania	22	1,469
Maryland	20	1,344
Virginia	27	1,269
North Carolina	12	607
South Carolina	12	789
Georgia	2	50
Total in 1769	389	20,001
" " 1770		20,610
" " 1771		24,068
" " 1772		26,544

In all the colonies from the very first, shipbuilding was a favored and protected industry. For one thing, the immigration of ship carpenters was actively encouraged, with such good results that in 1724 the Thames builders made public protest that their trade was being destroyed by the departure of their best workmen for America. As early as 1639 New England began to exempt shipwrights from the compulsory military service which men of other callings rendered. Between the lurking Indians on the one hand and the French, Spaniards, and pirates at sea on the other, the hardy fellows of the shipyards could ill be spared, and their exemption is vivid proof of the extraordinary importance which colonial legislators attached to the art of the vessel-builder. Under such friendly shelter shipbuilding in new America flourished, of course, beyond all other industries. It very soon began to excite the lively interest and keen jealousy of the mother land. Sir Joshua Child, a typical seventeenth-century British economist, once chairman of the great East India Company, wrote indignantly in 1668 in his Discourse on Trade that "Of all the American plantations His Majesty has none so apt for the building of ships as New England; nor none comparably so qualified for the breeding of seamen, not only by reason of the natural industry of the people, but principally by reason of their cod and mackerel fisheries, and in my opinion there is nothing more prejudicial and in prospect more dangerous to any mother kingdom than the increase of shipping in her colonies, plantations, or provinces."

A century before Lord North this selfish view of the American colonies as dangerous rivals to be kept poor and weak at any cost had already begun to color English legislation. An Act of Parliament in 1661, aimed frankly at smothering the colonial trade, defined the colonial products which could lawfully be transported, and two years later it was proclaimed that "no commodity of the growth, production, or manufacture of Europe shall be imported into the British plantations, but such as are laden and put on board in England, Wales, or Berwick-on-Tweed, and in English-built shipping whereof the master and three-fourths of the crew are English." The plain purpose of such a restriction was to prevent American shipowners from conducting their own direct trade with the Continent. Nor was this all. English jealousy struck, also, at the prosperous American carrying trade to and from the West Indies. As the historian [1] of the British merchant marine frankly says, the Act of 4 George III., chapter xv., "combined with various conditions taken from the Navigation Laws, requiring heavy duties on numerous articles imported into the colonies from the countries that produced them or from anywhere else except Great Britain, and prohibiting the importation of sugar from the colonies except in British bottoms, necessarily aroused the indignation of the American colonists and sowed the seeds of future rebellion."

These were particularly exasperating laws because they struck at poor men who ran great hazards in their arduous calling. The West India trade was conducted chiefly in small and inexpensive craft. A whole neighborhood in New England or New York or Pennsylvania or Virginia or the Carolinas would combine to build a little vessel and to freight it for the sugar islands. The shipwrights would give their skilled labor. The farmers would bring their corn, flour, tobacco, or horses; the woodsmen would contribute their lumber. Such a vessel fully laden would represent very little actual money, but a great deal of hard toil and stern self-denial. The failure of the enterprise meant penury, if not actual ruin, for a whole community. There were the risks of the sea, the uncharted Southern reefs, the fog, the hurricane, and, worst of all, the ferocious pirates who were the plague of the Spanish Main in the earlier half of the eighteenth century. The lucky vessel that escaped all these perils had still another deadly enemy in the cruiser or customs officer of the king, and many a weather-beaten craft returning well laden was seized right in her home harbor and carried off before the eyes of her poor, co-operative owners, who could only stand by in helpless grief and fury at this wasting of their hard labor of the year. Well does Lindsay denounce the "narrow-minded politicians" who thus sacrificed both the colonists

[1] Lindsay's "Merchant Shipping," vol. ii.

and themselves, for "the extinction of the French and Spanish shipping trade caused, as its natural result, a serious diminution of the direct carrying trade between England and the North American colonies, and this again, depriving them of their accustomed market, prevented their being any longer able to consume British manufactures to the same extent as formerly, or even to discharge debts due to creditors in England. Hence an effect not anticipated; in that the Americans, forming associations to dispense with English manufactures, were led to resort to native industry and thus to lay the foundation of a permanent rivalry, the end of which cannot now be conjectured. In short, a national American spirit was evoked, highly antagonistic to British interests."

This is all true. Except as they exasperated the colonists, these ingeniously restrictive British acts, which numbered thirty in a hundred and twenty years, were unavailing. The merchant ships and the sailors of America steadily increased, until at the breaking out of the Revolution there were more people in Northern New England — Maine and New Hampshire — engaged in shipbuilding and in navigation, than there were in agriculture, and Massachusetts was said to own one seagoing vessel for every hundred of its inhabitants.[1] Here was a latent sea power of the first importance. The merchant ships of the colonies, hastily fitted as privateers, were an active factor in the struggle for independence. It must be remembered that the merchant vessel of that day, large or small, usually went to sea armed for its own protection, and that far larger crews than would really be required for the ordinary ship's work were carried to man the guns and swivels against pirates or national enemies. Thus, old records note the clearing from Boston for Carolina of a sixty-ton vessel with ten men, or twice as many as such a craft would now carry; the clearing for Jamaica of a larger ship with one hundred

[1] David A. Wells' "Our Merchant Marine."

and forty men and fourteen guns; the sailing for Barbadoes of a one-hundred-and-fifty-ton vessel with eighteen men, as many as would now be found aboard a thousand-ton ship, and the sailing of a two-hundred-ton vessel with twenty men for Nevis. The merchant seaman of the eighteenth century was compelled not only to know how to "hand, reef, and steer," but to be expert in the use of great guns, and of musket, pike, and cutlass. Of course such men were ready when the war came. There was no more commerce. British cruisers put an end to that. The slow vessels of the colonies were laid up in port; the swift ones were sent a-privateering.

The American people owe a vast debt of honor to the private armed ships of the Revolution. The Continental Navy was, in the main, a poor experiment. At no time was it a formidable factor in the war. Its ships were for the most part small and weak; its crews ill disciplined; its commanders distinguished more for personal intrepidity than for the professional skill and wisdom which could come only from long naval experience. John Paul Jones won his most famous victory in a French-built ship, and our only American-built frigate which came out of the war with a brilliant reputation was the swift and beautiful "Alliance," launched at Salisbury Point on the Merrimac and so shamefully mishandled in the battle of the "Bon Homme Richard" and the "Serapis," by the traitor and madman, Landais. Indeed, the "Alliance" was almost our only frigate which came out of the Revolution in any way whatever. Nearly all of our other regular ships were destroyed or captured in the course of the war by the overwhelming British squadrons. The thirty Continental cruisers of 1776 had shrunk in 1781 to nine, carrying one hundred and sixty-four guns. But in the same year the American privateers, converted out of merchantmen, and managed by individual shipowners, numbered four hundred and forty-nine, mounting in all 6,735 guns. The American

privateers of 1775–83 captured or destroyed three times
as many of the enemy's ships as did our frigates and
sloops-of-war.[1]

The audacity of the Yankee privateersmen was astounding. Paul Jones met some of them right on the British
coast, whither they had gone before him. They hung like
hawks in the Irish Channel and the North Sea, and the
wrath and fear which they aroused were far greater than
the results of any of our land victories. Silas Deane, one
of Franklin's fellow-Commissioners to Paris, wrote home
to the Marine Committee of Congress in 1777 that the
exploits of our many privateers and few cruisers "effectually alarmed England, prevented the great fair at Chester,
occasioned insurance to rise, and even deterred the English merchants from shipping goods in English vessels at
any rate of insurance; so that in a few weeks forty French
ships were loaded in London on freight, — an instance
never before known." So frightened were the merchants
that they demanded naval protection for the linen ships
crossing from Ireland to England. " In no former war,"
mournfully declared an English newspaper of the period,
" not even in any of the wars with France and Spain, were
the linen vessels from Ireland to England escorted by warships." In this year, 1777, the year of Bennington and
Saratoga, the men at sea in our merchant vessels transformed into privateers almost equalled the strength of the
Continental army under the immediate command of Washington.[2] They scoured the Atlantic from the Orkneys to
Yucatan. A letter written home from Grenada in 1777
gives a graphic idea, from the British standpoint, of the
havoc of these privateers: "Everything continues exceedingly dear, and we are happy if we can get anything for
money, by reason of the quantity of vessels taken by the

[1] Maclay's " A History of American Privateers."
[2] " During the campaign of 1777 the army of Washington had never
exceeded 11,000 men." John Fiske's " The American Revolution," vol. ii.

Americans. A fleet of vessels came from Ireland a few days ago. From sixty vessels that departed from Ireland not above twenty-five arrived in this and neighboring islands, the others, it is thought, being all taken by American privateers. God knows if this American war continues much longer, we shall all die of hunger. There was a ship from Africa with four hundred and fifty negroes, some thousand weight of gold dust and a great many elephant teeth — the whole cargo being computed to be worth twenty thousand pounds — also taken by an American privateer, a brig mounting fourteen cannon."

Parliament in 1778 began a special inquiry into American depredations on British commerce. Alderman Woodbridge testified at the bar of the House of Lords that " the number of ships lost by capture or destroyed by American privateers since the commencement of the war was seven hundred and thirty-three, of which, after deducting for those retaken and restored, there remained five hundred and fifty-nine." Another witness declared that the losses suffered by British merchants from the American privateers amounted to "at least two million pounds sterling" in October last (1777) and that "by this time they could not be less than two million two hundred thousand pounds." From July, 1775, to December, 1777, American shipowners had received commissions for one hundred and seventy-four of their idle ships as privateers. These vessels mounted 1,836 cannon and their crews comprised from nine to ten thousand sailors. New Hampshire, with only twenty miles of seacoast and one port, Portsmouth, had sent out eight privateers before the end of 1777; rich and patriotic Massachusetts, fifty-three; Rhode Island, six; Connecticut, twenty-two; New York, though her great port was held by the British, seven; Pennsylvania, thirteen; Maryland, twenty-one; South Carolina, six, and North Carolina, three. For this hazardous but profitable work the best ships in the American merchant fleet were chosen. Already, almost a hundred years before the development of the astonishing Yankee clippers, our shipwrights had begun to produce a class of vessels of superior speed, and our seamen were famous for their hardihood. Later in the war vessels were designed and built especially for privateering, but the smart merchantmen which put to sea with their ugly rows of teeth from 1775 to 1777 were, most of them, able to run away from the king's cruisers.

Some of these early privateers were extraordinarily successful. Several of them took as many as twenty British prizes in a single voyage, and one is said to have taken twenty-eight prizes. Of course this was exceptional luck. It was due to getting into the track of a West India convoy, or hovering off Halifax or the Gulf of St. Lawrence in the path of supply ships and transports. While the war enriched some American shipowners, it impoverished others. Not all privateers came home with wealth and glory. A large number never came at all. Many of these vessels, built for the uses of peace, were overloaded with guns and overpressed with lofty canvas, and they sailed and were never after heard from. Twenty-two vessels with more than a thousand men are said to have vanished in this way from the Massachusetts town of Newburyport, on the Merrimac, during the Revolution.

No mere greed of gain animated the owners of our private armed ships in the War for Independence. Indeed, merchant vessels though these were, they held a semi-public, national character. They were as a rule swifter than our few regular warships, and often better fitted and found. They were, of course, very much more numerous, and they were often called on to perform difficult tasks for the Continental government. They carried our envoys to and fro between our coasts and Europe. They conveyed despatches, and kept France and our other friends on the Continent informed of the temper of our people and the actual progress of the war. They transported specie and brought to us time and time again the arms, ammunition, and supplies so indispensable to the patriot army. If we had depended on our navy alone for all this service afloat in the Revolution, we should have leaned upon a breaking reed.

It proved to be great good fortune for the colonists that England's selfish laws had not stifled the maritime genius of the American people, or driven them from the sea which was their heritage. The large and active merchant fleet of the colonies, transformed, as could easily be done in those days, into a fighting and commerce-destroying fleet, was a warlike factor without which our freedom might not have been won. Saratoga was the turning-point of the war. But it was not until after Saratoga that the French squadrons and the French regiments came to our aid. During those two critical years, from 1775 to 1777, it was chiefly the armed merchant ships, the privateers, which kept our communication with Europe open, and thus made it possible to impress the Continent with the belief that the American colonies had staked all on their fight for liberty and would not be denied.

Of course the havoc wrought to commerce by the Revolution was not all on one side. There were many British privateers, besides scores of the king's cruisers, at sea, watching our coasts and the main highways of our trade. The American food fisheries were severely harried; the whale fishery for the time being was destroyed, and in all throughout the war nine hundred American merchant vessels were captured by our powerful enemy.[1] Some of the Yankee privateers, too confident or venturesome, also fell into British hands. Their crews and the crews of American merchant prizes were treated in England with the utmost severity. As American representative at the French Court, Benjamin Franklin exercised a general authority over our maritime affairs in Europe. His great

---

[1] John Fiske's "The American Revolution."

heart was torn by the suffering of the sailor-captives. English prisons of the eighteenth century were harsh places at best, but an especial malignity seemed to be manifested by guards and attendants toward those unfortunates who happened to be Americans. Some of them were even transported, as if they had been felons, to the poisonous coast of Africa and the remote East Indies. Many others were impressed into British ships-of-war and compelled to fight against their country. To whalemen the alternatives were offered of entering men-of-war or joining British whaleships, and there were several British vessels in the South Seas manned entirely by Americans who had thus escaped the grim necessity of training guns on their brethren.

On the other hand, the French ports were full of English sailors captured by American privateers or cruisers. Franklin endeavored to arrange a regular system of exchange, which would set both Americans and Britons at liberty. He sent a communication to Lord Stormont inquiring whether a hundred prisoners of the sloop-of-war " Reprisal " could not be exchanged for a hundred American captives in the dungeons of Plymouth or Portsmouth. The question was ignored. Franklin sent a second letter. The answer came, " The King's ambassador receives no applications from rebels unless they come to implore His Majesty's mercy." [1]   Such was the spirit, a fit heritage of the harsh navigation acts, with which England waged this war on American ships and American seamen. Technically the British position was that the Americans were not ordinary prisoners of war but traitors. That was why the men from our captured ships were kept penniless in their English prisons, hungry and cold, why they were abused by petty tyrants, and denied the privilege of writing letters to acquaint their friends at home of their misfortune.

[1] "Benjamin Franklin." By John T. Morse, Jr., in American Statesmen Series.

Franklin's efforts to relieve them were persistent but unsuccessful, although he was aided by several humane Englishmen. Even when Franklin released five hundred British sailors who gave a solemn pledge in writing to free, each, one American prisoner in return, nothing came of it. Hundreds of our sailors died in prison, and others survived with a bitter memory of wrong that gave a keen edge to the subsequent rivalry between the British marine and the ships of the new republic.

CHAPTER II

OLD RIGS AND MODELS

The "Mayflower" a Typical Seventeenth-Century Merchantman —
Her Rig and Dimensions — The Incoming of the Yankee Schooner
— Brig, Snow, Brigantine, and Ketch — Crude Gear and Cumbering Artillery — Skilful Shipwrights of the New World

SAVE for vague tradition and a few rude engravings, there is little knowledge now obtainable as to the models or rigs of the American merchant craft of the years before the Revolution. It is not at all necessary to assume that the vessels in which the trade with Europe or alongshore was conducted a hundred and fifty or two hundred years ago were the misshapen, even grotesque, hulks that have come down to us in the scanty marine pictures of the period. The best artistic genius of the seventeenth and eighteenth centuries did not look to the sea for its inspiration. As for the book illustrators of the old time, if they were as clumsy in drawing ships as they were in portraying men, houses, and other familiar objects, it is not surprising that there is a popular delusion that the art of naval architecture made very little progress between Noah's ark and the " Mayflower."

As a matter of fact, when the Dutch and English settlers first came to the shores of the New World, shipbuilding in the Old World was already a respectable science. It was very quickly and successfully transplanted to America. Out of the vast mass of Pilgrim literature a recent writer, Dr. Azel Ames, in " The Mayflower and her Log," has managed to compile a volume which gives a very good idea of the hull, spars, sails, equipment, and crew of a typical merchant ship of the early part of the seventeenth century. The "Mayflower" was not technically an American vessel. She was English-built, but her voyages to Plymouth and to Salem have identified her with the American colonies, and she was doubtless just such a ship as the earliest settlers constructed when they came to launch vessels of their own.

The "Mayflower" is known from Bradford's diary to have been of about one hundred and eighty tons' burden, or less than one-half of the tonnage of an ordinary three-masted coasting schooner of the present day. She was undoubtedly from ninety to one hundred feet long, and twenty-four or twenty-five feet wide. Her three masts carried, on the fore and main, two square sails, one above another, a lower sail, or course, and a topsail, and on the mizzen a triangular lateen sail, instead of the gaff-spanker and square topsail, which did not come into general use on a ship's third and smallest mast for more than a century afterward. On her steep bowsprit the "Mayflower" spread not the familiar jibs, but probably a spritsail, hung from a spritsail yard. The spritsail and the lateen sail were crude contrivances, but in other respects the "Mayflower" was rigged substantially as is a ship or bark of to-day, save that the square canvas on each mast was divided into only two great and rather unwieldy sails, instead of being split up into lower sail, topsail, topgallantsail and royal. The old mariners had not learned that this subdivision meant a lessened weight aloft and a gain in time and safety.

As to her hull, the "Mayflower" must have been undeniably an awkward craft, judged by our modern standards. And yet it must not be forgotten that she made her return passage from Plymouth to London in ballast, urged by the "brave west winds" in thirty-one days, which would be a satisfactory voyage now for a steel two-thousand-ton skysail-yarder. It is clear that however ungainly the "Mayflower" may have seemed above the water-line, her under-water body was draughted by a man who knew his trade. One vicious characteristic of these old vessels was the proneness of their builders to erect a steep cabin at one end and an almost equally steep forecastle — well named — at the other, to the impairment always of the symmetry of the ship and often of her strength and seaworthiness. In order to avoid lifting the centre of gravity and thus making a vessel "crank," these towering upper works were constructed of flimsy material, which strained and opened in a seaway, and made cabin and forecastle uninhabitable, even if the stout body of the ship held well together. Thus Bradford writes of the "Mayflower": "They met with many contrary winds and fierce storms, with which their ship was shrewdly shaken and her upper works made very leaky." It was these upper works which gave the hundred-and-eighty-ton "Mayflower" the height above water of a modern ship of a thousand tons. It was the lofty range of cabins which explains how so small a craft could carry a hundred passengers.

But of course the height of the old-fashioned cabins and forecastle and the resistance which they offered proved a great drag in strong, contrary winds. Thus the "Mayflower," sailing from England on Sept. 6, 1620, made such wretched work of beating against the prevalent westerly gales that she did not sight Cape Cod until November 10, a weary nine weeks' passage. The practical wit of Yankee builders very early began to scale down the unsightly upper works with which oldtime ships were overloaded. Such things as state cabins and storied forecastles did not accord with the shrewd spirit of a pioneer democracy. It was very soon discovered that the colonial ship, stripped of this top-hamper, not only sailed faster but carried sail more stiffly and kept cargo and passengers drier than the tall-pooped vessels of Europe.

But the greatest gift of American shipyards to the merchant fleet of the era before the Revolution was that incomparable craft, the schooner. Up to the early years of the eighteenth century, the square rig was the unvarying characteristic of all vessels having more than one mast. Even the little ketches in which the first American coasting trade and fisheries were carried on were often square-rigged craft, pure and simple, having one tall mast with two or more crossed yards set well back from the bow toward amidships, and a smaller mast, also with square sails, nearer the stern. This square rig is so much more complex and expensive and requires so much more cordage, difficult to handle on a narrow deck, that it is easy to understand why the ketch of the Old World design gradually vanished from our waters before the all-conquering New World schooner.

The origin of this distinctively Yankee type is one of the cherished traditions of New England. In the year 1713 or 1714 Captain Andrew Robinson, of Gloucester, built a vessel of two masts, bearing on each a fore-and-aft sail set from a gaff and boom, with a jib forward. The model was sharp; the vessel was designed, as Gloucester craft ever have been, for speed as well as for seaworthiness. As the unique two-master was launched, she glided so swiftly and gracefully over the water that an enthusiastic spectator cried, "See how she scoons!"[1] Thereupon worthy Captain Robinson, who had been puzzled to find a name for his odd craft, instantly replied, "A schooner let her be!" This word, which had reference at the outset only to the peculiar qualities of Captain Robinson's hull-model, came by natural and easy transfer to characterize the two-masted fore-and-aft rig, which was destined to stand for a century and a half as the favorite and distinctive rig of American waters.

[1] "Scoon" in the eighteenth century was a word popularly used to describe the skipping of a flat stone over the water when thrown by a strong and skilful hand.

The schooner proved to be peculiarly adapted to the requirements of New World navigation. Our many rivers and estuaries, where the wind tended to draw up or down the channel, involved a great amount of beating to windward in relatively short "tacks." For such service the schooner was superior to the square-rigger of two or three masts. Moreover, the schooner, requiring fewer "hands," was more economical as well as more efficient. The schooner rig was a great boon to merchants and seamen. The excellent qualities of this Yankee device were promptly recognized in Europe, where it has long been a familiar sight all along shore between the Baltic and the Bay of Biscay. But it is in America that the schooner has been brought to its greatest and best development, in the monster five, six, and seven masters, carrying dead-weight cargoes of from four to seven thousand tons.

For many years after 1713, however, the American schooner represented a compromise. The prevailing type was the so-called topsail schooner, carrying the Robinson fore-and-aft foresail and mainsail, but bearing on the foremast a lower and a topsail and sometimes a topgallant yard, and thus combining the good qualities of the fore-and-aft and square rig. It was the topsail schooners which were the favorite privateers of the Revolution and the War of 1812. Later they sailed to every quarter of the world in peaceful commerce. This graceful and convenient topsail schooner rig has now become extinct on the coast of the United States, but it still survives in the maritime provinces of Canada. Its great advantage was that in a head wind the square topsail and topgallantsail could be snugly furled, the yards sharply "braced up," and the vessel steered closely to windward under fore-and-aft canvas; while the moment the breeze became free and fair the gaskets could be cast off and the square canvas sheeted home, with perhaps a great balloon-like square foresail added.

Ever since 1713 Gloucester has been the peculiar home of the schooner, and this is now and long has been the unvarying rig of her unrivalled fleet of deep-sea fishermen. The first entry of a schooner in Boston's commerce occurs in 1716, — the "Mayflower," Captain James Manson, from North Carolina.[1]   As Captain Andrew Robinson was a direct descendant of John Robinson who preached to the Pilgrims at Leyden, it is conjectured that this "Mayflower" was the first schooner, the original Gloucester craft.   Be this as it may, her useful successors are numbered by the thousands, and old Captain Robinson deserves a place of honor with the benefactors of mankind.

The schooner became in the later half of the eighteenth century the favorite rig for all American merchant vessels between fifty and one hundred and fifty tons, but a schooner of upwards of one hundred tons was then reckoned a rather large one, when there were not many full-rigged ships of three hundred.   A cleverly executed colored print[2] of Boston Harbor, about 1730 or 1740, much prized by antiquarians, shows types of all the vessels of the period, but only one schooner, and she a very small one, is included.   The full-rigged ship of this era is depicted as carrying a spritsail yard on the bowsprit and a lateen sail on the mizzenmast, after the fashion of the "Mayflower" of more than a hundred years before. But above the lateen sail is a square mizzen topsail, and there is a notable reduction in the upper works, although the tall stern is crowned by a stately lantern.   One other vessel almost as characteristically American as the schooner is conspicuous in this old engraving.   It is the so-called hermaphrodite brig, a two-masted vessel, square-rigged on the foremast and schooner-rigged on the main, thus combining very handsomely the advantages of the two types.   The name hermaphrodite brig of late years has

[1] Boston Records, vol. xxix., page 231.
[2] The Carintham Print, so called.

come to be shortened to brigantine, but the brigantine of the eighteenth century was a different and distinct rig. It had a large fore-and-aft mainsail, but instead of a gaff topsail it bore a square topsail set on light yards.

Another craft which figures prominently in the marine records of the eighteenth and the early years of the nineteenth century was the snow. The only difference, however, between a snow and a full-rigged brig (that is, a two-masted vessel, square-rigged on both masts) was that the snow had its spanker hoisted on a trysail mast instead of on the mainmast proper. This was really a trivial detail, not to be distinguished at a distance and scarcely perceptible at all to landsmen. But those old sailors were great sticklers for correctness in their professional vocabulary.

Of all forms of square rig, the bark of late years has been the most familiar, — with its fore and main masts rigged like a ship, its mizzenmast like a schooner. But the bark is infrequently mentioned in the nautical annals of the eighteenth century. Ships, snows, brigs, brigantines, ketches, schooners, sloops, are the prevalent terms of marine definition. The day of the bark came afterward. Neither ships nor anything else in those old years spread very lofty canvas. The ordinary trading vessel crossed no yards above topgallant; the royal was the mark of a man-of-war, and the audacious Yankee skysail had not yet lifted above the blue horizon. Sails were still of hemp, dark colored, stiff, and unwieldy. Hemp cables were in universal use, and light and strong steel rigging was far distant. The mariners of that day hove in anchors by rude windlasses and main strength. The lofty single topsails, the best sails in a ship, were mast-headed by sheer weight of brawn, and reefed, if need be, by the perilous toil of many numbed and groping fingers. A vessel of three hundred tons would carry as many men before the mast as a ship of three thousand in

these days of double topsails and topgallantsails, steam
hoisting engines, patent blocks, and ingenious purchases.
Cannon, generally of small calibre, fours or sixes, were
an essential part of the equipment of every good merchantman.   Their carriages obstructed the clear decks which a
sailor loves, and interfered with the quick handling of the
mast-gear.   In a severe storm the guns were dangerous
because of their weight and their liability to break their
lashings.   Many a good ship was lost because of her cumbrous but indispensable artillery.

The poverty of the colonists drove them to some desperate expedients.   In 1770 an English journal notes the
arrival in the Thames of the "Newbury," Captain Rose,
from Newbury in New England, "a raft of timber in the
form of a ship, which came from Newbury to soundings
in twenty-six days," — an incredibly swift passage for a
mere mass of logs and planking.   The "Newbury" was
one of several craft built in this fashion on the Merrimac
for a Mr. Levy, and known as "Jew's rafts."   One or
two of the queer vessels were never heard from after they
sailed, and the hazardous business of sending these rafts
to Europe was abandoned.   But it was not an uncommon
occurrence years afterward to sail one of these rude vessels
down to the West Indies, where there was always a sharp
demand for good American pine lumber.

Before the Revolution it looked as if America would
secure the monopoly of furnishing new tonnage for the
British mercantile marine.   Colonial-built craft were not
only cheap but good and strong.   Already a reputation
for speed and handiness was being established by these
American vessels.   Nor is this at all surprising when the
circumstances are considered.   From the very first the
colonies had held out especial inducements to shipwrights
and ship carpenters.   They were even offered immunity
from military service.   The result was that year by year
very many of the most intelligent and ambitious of the

shipbuilders of England and Holland came to seek their fortunes in the New World. In the winter of 1724–25 the shipwrights of London complained to the Lords of Trade "that in the eight years ending in 1720 they were informed that there were 700 sail of ships built in New England, and in the years since as many if not more, and that the New England trade had drawn over so many working shipwrights that there are not enough left here (in London) to carry on the work." Therefore, the English shipwrights asked that colonial-built ships be excluded from all trade except that with Great Britain and her colonies, or that the colonists be forbidden to build ships above a certain size.

Of course no such policy as this could be adopted. It would simply hasten insurrection. In 1769, in spite of the jealousy of English shipyards, the colonies built and launched 389 vessels, 113 of them square-rigged, and 276 sloops and schooners.[1] These sloops and schooners, by the way, after the custom of the time, carried, most of them, square topsails. It was a great fleet to put afloat in a single year, but the annual waste then from wreck and other casualties of the sea was far larger, relatively, than it is at present. A small ship, well built and well equipped, is perhaps as safe as a great one, but the builders of the seventeenth and eighteenth centuries, although they were clever men at their profession, did not have the tools and machinery for working their excellent and abundant wood which modern practical science has made available. Ship for ship, the older vessels were not so strong as the wooden vessels of the nineteenth century.

The scarcity and high cost of metal fastenings confined the early builders to relatively light materials. Moreover, the high sterns, the clumsy forecastles, and the drooping bows, which American common-sense finally managed to abolish or reduce, were long a grave source of weakness.

[1] Journal of House of Commons, 1792, page 357.

It is probable that very few of the old ships could pass the rigid marine inspection of to-day and secure insurance from careful underwriters. But small, feeble, scantily equipped, and crudely rigged as were these old merchantmen, the majority of them managed to make safe and profitable voyages. The more one studies the ancient models, the greater admiration grows for the patience, the courage, and the seamanlike skill of the mariners who, all their lives through, fought in these frail craft the fierce gales and giant surges of the North Atlantic.

CHAPTER III

AFTER THE REVOLUTION

American Vessels shut out of British Trade — Helplessness of Our
Unprotected Shipping — A Few Bold Voyages to the far East —
The " Empress of China " and the " Experiment " — More Loss
than Profit — The Demand for National Encouragement

THE years between the treaty of peace in 1783 and the
setting up of the first Federal government under the Constitution in 1789 — " the critical period of American history," as Dr. John Fiske well calls it — were years of
struggle and discouragement for the American merchant
marine, as well as for all other interests of the young
country, free and independent but not yet compacted into
a nation. Privateering had kept the Yankee maritime
spirit alive throughout the war, and this immediately began
to manifest itself in more adventurous voyages than the
colonists had ever known. Such a prompt revival of a
form of activity which had caused England acute concern
before the war and was largely responsible for her defeat,
aroused the intense wrath of the English Tories. They
set themselves to devising plans to choke the ambition of
the young sea power of the West. In one point our ocean-
carrying trade was very vulnerable.

Before the Revolution colonial vessels as British craft
had built up an important commerce with the British West
India islands. The American colonies and these southern
islands were natural customers, the one of the other. The
colonies had an abundance of the products of the temperate
zone, — corn, dried fish, lumber, horses, and cattle, — which
could be exchanged to advantage for the West Indian sugar,

coffee, cotton, rum, and indigo. Before the war the
colonial trade with the British West Indies amounted to
$17,000,000 or $18,000,000 a year. But when the colonists
won their independence, their merchant ships, of course,
lost their British nationality and became foreign ships,
which were forbidden under heavy penalties to visit the
British West India possessions. Pitt, the younger of the
name, now Chancellor of the Exchequer, endeavored to
introduce the principle of reciprocity into West India commerce. But he was unsuccessful. The British shipowners
arose in furious remonstrance. An Order in Council of
July, 1783, proclaimed that hereafter the trade of the
British West Indies must be carried on in British ships,
owned and manned by British subjects. This was a deliberate blow at the shipowners and shipbuilders of America.
It banished American vessels from a rich and important
trade, but grave as were its effects upon our marine, the
results to the British islands themselves were far more
terrible. Between 1780 and 1787, fifteen thousand slaves
died from sheer starvation,[1] because the American brigs
and schooners no longer brought them dried fish and corn,
and their own crops had been wasted by hurricanes.

A writer of the time declared that " The Ministry sup-
pose they have now put a finishing stroke to the building
and increase of American vessels," and it was added that
three hundred sail of West Indiamen, already afloat, would
be destroyed by this discrimination. It is estimated that
when the Revolution began one third of the seagoing
merchant ships which flew the British flag were of American construction. They could be built more cheaply in
this country, for the material was abundant all along the
Atlantic seaboard, and the wages of labor were not much
higher than Old World wages. A white oak vessel before
1775 cost perhaps $24 a ton in New England, and a live-

---

[1] Professor James Russell Soley, " The Maritime Interests of America," in
"The United States of America," edited by Professor Nathaniel S. Shaler.

oak ship about $38 a ton. But in Old England or on the Continent an oak ship could not be built for less than $50 a ton.

Excitable Britons, in 1783 and afterward, saw in their imagination their country's shipyards transferred to the Merrimac, the Hudson, and the Delaware, and king's frigates launched by Yankee hands at Boston, New York, or Philadelphia. To save British shipbuilding from what seemed to be sure ruin, the British government straightway refused British shipowners the privilege of purchasing vessels built in America. As a further protection, an Order in Council restricted the American products which could lawfully be imported into England in American ships to such crude materials as pitch, tar, turpentine, and indigo, and masts and bowsprits from our forests. Moreover, it was insisted that American ships should bring to England only the products of the particular States in which their owners resided. In view of the distracted condition of the American States of that day, this stipulation was certainly sardonic.

But British post-bellum hostility to our merchant shipping reached its height in the extraordinary pamphlet of Lord Sheffield, who coolly argued that the Barbary pirates, preying on the defenceless commerce of the United States, were really a blessing to Great Britain. Franklin wrote that London merchants had cynically declared that "if there were no Algiers, it would be worth England's while to build one!" In 1783 and for some years afterward Americans had no reply to make to this insolence. England could proclaim and enforce any hostile policy toward our ships and sailors which she happened to choose. We could make no consistent and effective retaliation, for no strong central government had yet been established.

In 1785 New York imposed a double duty on goods imported in British ships. Massachusetts and New Hampshire adopted navigation acts, forbidding British ships to carry goods out of, and imposing a stiff duty on goods which they might bring into, our harbors. Rhode Island did the same thing. But these helter-skelter measures failed of their purpose. British ships and British goods still came into the ports of the States which had enacted no such laws, and American ships lay idle at their moorings. No general Navigation Act could be passed by the feeble and inharmonious Continental Congress. The merchants of Boston, then, as ten years before, distinguished for ardent patriotism, met in Faneuil Hall on April 16, 1785, and pledged themselves not to buy goods from the British merchants, factors, and agents who were seeking to monopolize the import and shipping trade, and "not to sell or let to them warehouses, shops, houses, or any other place for the sale of their goods." This seems to have had salutary local results, for in July, 1785, there was not a single British merchantman in the harbor of Boston.

Meanwhile the sectional jealousy of the South continued to tie the hands of the Continental lawmakers. The Southern leaders, with the honorable exception of a few broader men like the gallant Moultrie, Governor of South Carolina, professed to fear that if any advantage were given to American over British ships, the American vessels, chiefly owned in the North, would charge monopolistic rates for exporting Southern cotton, rice, and tobacco. The brief fragments of the political debates of those early years which still survive are not cheerful or inspiring reading. Sectional prejudice was strong, and national patriotism as it is now known was often conspicuous by its absence. In the Virginia Assembly, an interesting individual known as the "warrior parson" openly suggested "whether it would not be better to encourage the British rather than the Eastern marine." But it is some comfort to observe that this fellow was roundly hissed by the other lawmakers.

Neither hostility abroad nor contumely at home, however, could daunt the bold spirit of the American merchants and mariners of this period. Crowded out of the important trade with Great Britain and her colonies, they looked for new seas to conquer. In February, 1784, the ship "Empress of China," Captain Greene, sailed from New York for Canton, and returned in May of the year following, after a round voyage of fourteen months and twenty-seven days. A London journal of March, 1785, had remarked that "The Americans have given up all thought of a China trade, which can never be carried on to advantage without some settlement in the East Indies." In December, 1785, a courageous merchant, destined to be famous, Elias Hasket Derby of Salem, sent his "Grand Turk," under Captain West, on the first voyage from New England to the Isle of France, India, and China. Soon teas direct from beyond the Cape of Good Hope began to be advertised in the newspapers of New York and Boston, and on November 20, 1788, two ships, the "Hercules" and "Omphale,"—shipowners of that day delighted in classic names,—were loading at the latter port for the Isle of France and India, and "anybody wishing to adventure to that part of the world may have an opportunity of sending goods on freight." So by the indomitable force of Yankee enterprise the long monopoly of the East India Company had been broken.

Within five years after the "Empress of China" finished her pioneer voyage, the shipowners of New England and New York had many vessels in the trade with the far, strange countries bordering on the Indian and Western Pacific Oceans. Some of these craft, of course, were very small,—incredibly small judged by our modern standards. One of the most famous of them was a little eighty-ton sloop, the "Experiment," built at Albany and commanded by a bold and resourceful mariner, Stewart Dean, who had been a privateersman in the Revolution. This singu-

larly well-named vessel was no larger or more seaworthy
than any ordinary Hudson River sloop of the present day,
freighting bricks from Haverstraw to Manhattan. Captain
Stewart Dean and his good mate, John Whitten, were
audacious sailors to venture in such a cockleshell to the
other side of the world. It is even asserted[1] that the
"Experiment" was the real pioneer in our Canton trade,
— that she anticipated the "Empress of China." But it
is certain that Captain Dean went out from New York to
Canton, that he returned to New York after an excellent
passage of four months and twelve days, — a voyage which
modern two-thousand-ton clippers have not always excelled, — and that he brought back all of the fifteen men
and boys who composed his crew, "having had no sickness
whatever during his absence from the United States."
This little eighty-ton sloop of the eighteenth century had
to face not only the typhoons of the eastern seas, but the
even more treacherous pirates whose swift proas swarmed
in the waters of the Malay archipelago. They had no
terrors, however, for stout old Stewart Dean. Behind
his Lilliputian bulwarks he mounted six carriage guns,
and his fifteen men and boys had plenty of muskets,
boarding pikes, and cutlasses. Indeed, the valiant spirit
of the captain of this odd little old East Indiaman went
even further, for an eye-witness of her arrival from Canton
has left a record that the sloop hauled into the wharf, on
her return to New York, in regular frigate fashion ;
"martial music and the boatswain's whistle were heard on
board, with all the pomp and circumstance of war."

Nowadays a seaman would be adjudged mad who took
an eighty-ton river sloop off soundings. Not a few of the
other first ventures in the East India trade were conducted
in vessels scarcely larger or more seaworthy than the
"Experiment." The truth was that the Revolution had
left the country desperately poor. As Daniel Webster

[1] Coggeshall's "Historical Sketch of Commerce and Navigation," page 53.

said in one of his famous speeches years afterward, the period which followed the peace of 1783 was a "period of depression and distress on the Atlantic coast, such as the people had hardly felt during the sharpest crisis of the war itself. Shipowners, shipbuilders, mechanics, all were destitute of employment, and some of them were destitute of bread." It was the sharp demand of absolute necessity, therefore, which drove our ships and our sailors to the uttermost parts of the earth. Of course, many of the early vessels were hastily built and ill provided. But even this was not the worst of it. An American ship, large or small, was then an Ishmael of the ocean. It had a flag, but nothing else. There was no government to protect it, there were no consuls to guard its interests in the alien ports which it entered, no line-of-battleships or frigates to shield the peaceful merchantman with their rows of shotted guns. The English, French, or Dutch traders in the East were sheltered by a recognized nationality and an active naval force, but the American mariners had nothing to depend on but their own cool courage, their breadth of canvas, and the swiftness of their keels. It is difficult to know which to admire the more, — the pluck of the Boston, New York, and Salem merchants who freighted ships for those inhospitable seas, or the hardihood of the masters and men who executed their commissions. An American vessel, outward bound for India or China, was, in the first place, subject to the risk of being robbed of her best sailors by the press-gang of an English frigate almost before she had lost sight of Cape Cod or the Navesink Highlands. Then in the latitude of the Bahamas there began a peril of surprise and seizure by pirates which lasted all the way around the Cape of Good Hope to the harbor gates of Bombay, Calcutta, or Canton. Pirates of those days lived strictly up to the grim maxim that "dead men tell no tales." Capture meant almost inevitably the extinction of every living soul on board. But safe in an eastern port the Yankee mariner found his trials not ended but simply altered. Every ingenious resource of tonnage and customs taxation that merciless jealousy could contrive was brought to bear against him, and his ship was confiscated and he and his owners ruined on the slightest pretext of irregularity.

It is not strange, therefore, that there were more losing than winning voyages, and that in spite of the vigor and perseverance of individual shipowners, American ocean carrying as a whole did not thrive. As late as 1789, our entire merchant fleet, registered for foreign commerce, was only 123,893 tons, while Great Britain [1] had a fleet of 94,110 tons, or almost as large as our own, engaged in American ocean-carrying alone. This was a very unsatisfactory condition. There was no lack of personal initiative. We had the most ambitious merchants and the boldest sailors in the world. We had cheap timber, skilled mechanics, deep and spacious harbors. Our forests, farms, and fisheries supplied materials for profitable outward cargoes. The seafaring and trading spirit, always strong in our race, had been intensified by the new self-confidence which followed a victorious war. But the American merchant shipping in the main did not increase. It had a hard fight against foreign shipping in our own trade and our own waters. What the shipbuilders, shipowners, and seamen needed was some reasonable measure of national protection and encouragement.

[1] H. C. Adams's "Taxation in the United States," p. 42.

CHAPTER IV

THE FIRST SWIFT GROWTH. 1789–1800

Protection for Shipping the Earliest Act of the Federal Congress in
1789 — The Atlantic, the Coastwise, and the East Indian Trade
all included — Immediate Response of our Shipowners and Seamen — A Wonderful Upspringing of Marine Activity — Bold
Merchants and Bolder Masters — A Fivefold Growth by 1800 —
The Barbary Corsairs and our Shameful Tribute — French Depredations and an Ocean War — The Robbery of "Impressment"

AMERICAN statesmen, merchants, and sailors of the first
decade of peace and independence after the Revolution
knew precisely what was needed to spread the white sails
of our ships on every sea, but it was not until the machinery
of national government was set in motion that this potent
influence could be applied. As early as 1785, sturdy John
Adams, who understood the trade of ocean-carrying, wrote
from the Court of St. James in patriotic rage at the helplessness of American shipowners, "This being the state of
things, you may depend upon it the commerce of America
will have no relief at present, nor in my opinion ever,
until the United States shall have generally passed navigation acts, and if this measure is not adopted, we shall
be derided, and the more we suffer the more will our
calamities be laughed at."

The first Congress under the new Federal Constitution,
which met in April, 1789, found before it strenuous appeals for legislative encouragement for American shipping
in the foreign trade. A memorial from the merchants
and shipowners of Baltimore with true prophetic insight
stated: "Your petitioners, on whichever side they may

turn their eyes, see reason to believe that the United States may soon become as powerful in shipping as any nation in the world. . . . Permit us to add that for want of national protection and encouragement, our shipping, that great source of strength and riches, has fallen into decay and involved thousands in the utmost distress." It was in response to the widespread and intense public feeling, of which this Baltimore memorial was a token, that within two days after the assembling of the first Congress, James Madison, of Virginia, though a free trader himself, brought into the House bills for protective duties on foreign merchandise and foreign ships.[1]

It is a memorable fact that the very first real Act of the first Congress of the United States contained vigorous provisions for the protection of the American merchant marine. This was the famous law, passed, appropriately enough, on July 4, 1789, which frankly proclaimed its purpose in its preamble: "Whereas, it is necessary for the support of the government, for the discharge of the debts of the United States, and the encouragement and protection of manufactures, that duties be laid on goods, wares, and merchandise imported." Thus this first law of the fathers of the republic was specifically a protective tariff Act, but it aimed to give American shipowners and seamen the same consideration which it bestowed upon American manufacturers and mechanics. This purpose was accomplished by the simple but effective expedient of allowing a discount of ten per cent of the tariff duties upon imports brought to this country in ships built and owned by American citizens.

It was taking a leaf out of British practice, but it is impossible to read the debates upon this significant legislation without realizing that there was something more in the mind of Congress than a mere wish to retaliate against hostile British navigation acts. There was a deliberate

[1] Henry Hall's "American Navigation."

and earnest desire to build up a great American merchant fleet, and to do this by invoking all the power of the newly created national government. Of course, this feeling was stronger in some States and among some public men than it was in and among others. The South, which had relatively few ships and few sailors, was rather lukewarm, though there were some Southern leaders like Jefferson and Madison who took a broad and truly national view of our maritime resources. In the manufacturing and commercial States of the North, however, the demand for protection for the American ship was wellnigh unanimous, and, taking the whole country over, no work of the first Congress won more cordial approval than those sections of the law which drew about our merchant marine the sheltering arm of the national government.

Those early statesmen were not content to give American shipowners a general protection of ten per cent of the customs duties on foreign goods imported in American vessels. This would perhaps suffice to gain control of the greater part of the carrying trade with Europe. But Washington, Hamilton, Jefferson, and Madison looked beyond the North Atlantic, and sought for their adventurous countrymen a larger share in the romantic commerce of the Far East. The daring keels of New York, Boston, and Salem navigators had already found their way thither. In 1789 there were forty New England vessels engaged in trade beyond the Cape of Good Hope. But this traffic was still precarious. Loss was more frequent than profit, and the brave men who faced the hazards of those distant seas believed that they had a peculiar right to national assistance. Congress promptly and gladly recognized their claim.

Tea was then the chief article of import from the East Indies. The same Act which gave American ships a general advantage of ten per cent of the customs duties on their homeward cargoes provided another and a very important discrimination in favor of American vessels in the new India and China trade. If tea was imported in American ships direct from those Eastern countries, it paid a duty of six cents a pound for Bohea, ten cents for Souchong, twenty cents for Hyson, and twelve cents for all other green varieties. But tea imported in a foreign ship was forced to pay a duty of fifteen cents a pound for Bohea, twenty-two cents for Souchong, forty-five cents for Hyson, and twenty-seven cents for the other varieties, — an increased rate, considerably more than double.

Nor was this all. The rich and powerful European East India companies brought large quantities of tea home to Great Britain and the Continent, whence it could be transshipped to America. These companies were, of course, determined to keep American vessels out of the direct trade with the East. But Congress was still more stoutly determined that they should not be excluded, and that we should have a great East India fleet of our own. Therefore, to persuade American merchants to send their own ships for their own cargoes, President Washington's lawmakers imposed a duty of eight, thirteen, sixteen, and twenty-six cents a pound on all teas which even American vessels might bring from the East India Company warehouses in Europe, — a rate higher than if they were brought direct around the Cape of Good Hope.

This was stalwart legislation for the development of an East India commerce carried beneath the Stars and Stripes. Of course, it was immediately effective. On a cargo of one hundred thousand pounds of assorted teas an American ship coming from China or India would pay duties of $12,200, or, with the general ten per cent discount, of $10,980; while a foreign ship making the same voyage would be compelled to pay $27,800 into the Federal Treasury. The inevitable result was that no foreign vessels came into an American harbor with freights from the East, and this most noble and valuable of all branches of ocean trade was absolutely secured to American ship-owners. A report of the American Institute of the city of New York stated in 1828 that "such and so complete has been this security that your committee believes that there has not been a single pound of tea imported since the passage of the law in question which has not been imported in an American bottom."

But not even the ten per cent discrimination in customs duties and the special East India arrangement satisfied the desire of the first Congress to give every possible protection to American merchant ships. The third Act of this Congress, dated July 20, 1789, allowed American-built ships owned by American citizens to enter our ports with the payment of tonnage duties of six cents a ton, but demanded thirty cents a ton from American-built ships owned by foreigners, and fifty cents a ton from ships built as well as owned abroad. This gave our own vessels launched from our own yards an inestimable advantage in the carrying of American commerce. At the same time it was provided that American vessels in the coasting trade should pay the tonnage duty only once a year, while foreign craft which sought admission to this trade should pay it at every entry. It was not until 1817, twenty-eight years afterward, that our coastwise traffic was absolutely closed to foreign vessels, but the legislation of 1789 really established the policy of reserving this purely American trade for American carriers, — a protective policy which, adhered to till the present moment, has given us the greatest and most efficient coastwise shipping in the world.

The Tariff and Navigation Act of 1789 was amended by Congress in the year 1794, and made still more energetic. Protective duties on foreign merchandise as originally imposed had proved inadequate. They were increased, — for the ruling spirit of the founders of the new nation was vigorously protectionist At the same time the method of encouraging the merchant marine by discriminating duties was changed. In place of the ten per cent discount in the duties on imports brought in American vessels, ten per cent was added to the tariff rates when the goods were imported in foreign vessels. The principle of the discriminating duty in favor of American shipowners was not altered, but the advantage was now secured without reducing the protection which the tariff rates gave to American producers in general.

There was also prompt legislation in the interests of American seamen. The new Act, passed in 1790, was distinctly in advance of the practice of the time. It guarded very carefully the employment of sailors, stipulating that they should have the benefit of a written contract defining the voyage and the rate of wages. If the shipping articles or agreement which the law required were not executed, the shipmaster would not have full control of his men, and could be compelled to give them the highest rates of pay, for which the ship itself was held liable. A master abandoning American seamen in a foreign country was subjected to severe punishment. On the other hand, and equitably, if the seamen who had signed articles deserted their ship they could be made to forfeit their wages and be brought back under compulsion. This early shipping legislation showed a shrewd knowledge of the sailor and his weaknesses, and of the master and his great power and responsibility. It held the balance of justice even between master and man. To this day American seamen's regulations are based in the main on the sound principles established in 1790. For many years thereafter American ships were celebrated for the high character of their crews and for their superior discipline.

Between 1789 and 1828 Congress [1] passed no fewer than fifty tariff or other laws intended directly or indirectly to protect American shipbuilding and shipowning. The maritime enterprise of the Atlantic seaboard responded

[1] Report of a Committee of the American Institute of New York, 1828.

magnificently to this powerful encouragement. American merchant shipping registered for the foreign trade which on Dec. 31, 1789, had been only 123,893 tons,[1] rose at once to 346,254 tons in 1790, to 363,110 tons in 1791, and to 411,438 tons in 1792. As Mr. H. C. Adams says in "Taxation in the United States," "The growth of American shipping from 1789 to 1807 is without parallel in the history of the commercial world." In 1789, when the protective law was passed, English shipowners were not only carrying almost all of their country's trade, but had 94,110 tons of ships, or a fleet three-fourths as large as our own, engaged in our own commerce. In 1792, according to Mr. Adams, they still had many vessels in our trade, but in 1794 their participation in our carrying had fallen away to 37,058 and in 1796 to 19,669 tons. In 1796, by the record of the Bureau of Navigation, the American fleet registered for foreign commerce amounted to 576,733 tons.

At this period almost the whole population of the United States was still to be found within the boundaries of the thirteen original States, along the coast from New Hampshire to Georgia. The unfolding of the great West had scarcely begun. Kentucky was not admitted to the Union until 1792; Tennessee, until 1796. Not only did most of the American people live within reach of the ocean, but the ocean everywhere seemed to be the nearest, the most natural, and the most inviting field of adventure. It was true then of many more American towns than tide-encircled Boston that "Each street leads downward to the sea." Down those streets went most of the young men who had dreams in their heads and iron in their blood, and they always found ships waiting. The years between 1789 and 1828 were the golden age of American seaborne commerce. A far greater tonnage came afterward in the days of the clipper ships, and the actual money value of

[1] Report of the United States Commissioner of Navigation for 1900.

the country's trade in that old time does not now loom to large proportions. But relative to population the American people have never since owned so much seagoing tonnage as they possessed when Jefferson or Madison was President. They had in 1807 12.54 cubic feet of shipping in the foreign trade for every inhabitant, and in 1810 13.43 feet. In 1855, at the high-water mark of the clipper era, they had a per capita shipping of only 8.63 feet. It is now scarcely one cubic foot.

In the year 1789, before the national policy of ship protection by discriminating customs and tonnage duties was adopted, the 123,893 tons of American shipping carried only 17.5 per cent of our imports and thirty per cent of our exports. Foreign vessels, chiefly British, enjoyed the lion's share of our own commerce. But in 1790, under the impulse of the new policy, American ships carried forty-one per cent of our imports and forty per cent of our exports, and in 1791, fifty-eight and fifty-two per cent. By 1794 foreign vessels had been almost completely driven out of American trade, and no less than ninety-one per cent of our imports and eighty-six per cent of our exports were conveyed in our own ships by our own sailor-citizens.

It is to this era that there belong the famous voyages of the "Columbia" to the northwest coast, the first American ship to circumnavigate the globe; of the "Massachusetts," the largest merchantman yet built on this Continent, to Java and China; of the "Hope" to the isles of Oceanica and the North Pacific, and of many more ventures less celebrated but not less meritorious. Massachusetts took the lead in this noble maritime activity, but Pennsylvania and New York followed not far behind. The duties on tonnage collected in the three great commercial States from Oct. 1, 1789, to Sept. 30, 1790, the first full year of the new national policy of encouragement to the shipping interests, show something of the energy with which

American merchants of that day responded to the favorable legislation of the new Federal government. Those tonnage duties represented in Massachusetts 197,368 tons of shipping; in Pennsylvania, 109,918 tons; in New York, 92,114 tons.

A Boston newspaper[1] of Oct. 27, 1791, gives this stirring glimpse of the commercial activity of the New England capital: "Upwards of seventy sail of vessels sailed from this port on Monday last for all parts of the world. Among them was the ship 'Margaret,' James Magee, Esq., Commander, bound on a voyage of observation and enterprise to the northwest coast of this Continent. This vessel is copper-bottomed, and is said to be the best provided of any one that ever sailed from this port."

In May of 1790 the ship "Federalist," at New York from Canton, had brought news of the safe arrival of the "Columbia" on the northwest coast, and in midsummer of that year the "Columbia" herself had appeared in Boston Harbor, firing a salute as she passed the Castle and another as she swung to her moorings, bringing a modest cargo of China teas for which she had exchanged her Indian furs, and opening a magical vista of adventure and wealth to the daring sailors and keen merchants of Boston and New York. Before the "Margaret" got to sea, Captain James Ingraham in the brig "Hope," a craft no larger than a modern pilot boat, had cleared for the northwest coast and China, and in April, 1791, he discovered two islands of what is now known as the Marquesas group in the mid-Pacific, just south of the Equator. He called these islands Washington and Adams, good patriotic names which they still retain.

All this time an increasing fleet of American ships and brigs was regularly swinging back and forth in the more prosaic but important trade between our ports and Europe, carrying out lumber, fish, and all manner of agricultural

[1] The "Independent Chronicle."

staples, and bringing back silks and wines from Bordeaux, salt from Cadiz, general manufactures from Liverpool and Bristol, and hemp, duck, and iron from the Baltic. The West Indies swarmed with our brigs, schooners, and sloops. Any enterprising man alongshore who could get together enough of his own and his neighbor's products to fill a little fifty or sixty ton craft felt himself competent to sail for the sugar islands. As an old writer humorously describes it: "The Yankees knew the way to the West Indies a good while ago; they knew more ways than one. Their coasting vessels knew the way, without quadrant or Practical Navigator. Their skippers kept their reckoning with chalk on a shingle, which they stowed away in the binnacle; and by way of observation they held up a hand to the sun. When they got him over four fingers they knew they were straight for Hole-in-the-Wall; three fingers gave them their course to the Double-headed-shot Keys, and two carried them down to Barbadoes!"

Of course, the longer voyages to the East Indies and China, which the new Federal law so powerfully encouraged, demanded more elaborate preparation. One of the earlier ventures, as has been stated, was made in a Hudson River sloop of eighty tons. But as our merchants became more familiar with the trade and its conditions, and especially as their profits increased, they employed new and strong full-rigged ships, four or five times the size of the little "Experiment." These vessels invariably carried large crews and mounted from six to twenty cannon. Their masters were as a rule picked men, of approved integrity and judgment. They must be prime sailors, and they must be a great deal more. There were no telegraph cables in those old years, or for many years after. The mails were slow and uncertain.

The captain of an East Indiaman must have the training of the counting-room as well as of the quarter-deck. He must be a merchant, familiar with the machinery of trade, and capable of driving an advantageous bargain, of selling an entire cargo in a strange, distant land, and purchasing another. Above all, he must be absolutely faithful to his employers' interests. It was the practice of merchants at that time to conduct their own trade in their own ships, and they often sent out in a long-voyage vessel their personal representative, the supercargo, who was expected to transact their business for them. But if the captain was a man of long service, he was quite as often intrusted with the fortunes of the entire voyage, which was certain to last a year and might last two or three years. For East Indiamen necessarily sailed with very liberal, roving commissions. It did not always happen that American ships went directly out to the East. They sometimes made first the Isle of France, or, as it is now known, Mauritius, in the Indian Ocean just east of Madagascar, then a prosperous French colony with a cultivated and delightful society. There, in the Isle of France, the original home freight would be disposed of and another cargo secured. So when an East Indiaman finally returned she might have had four or five different ladings, and every one of these important exchanges would have to be determined upon and handled without counsel from home by the master, or by the supercargo, if it happened that one were carried.

There was a glamour of romance about this distant commerce. The homeward freights were not heavy and commonplace, but costly tea, silks, and spices, or coffee, sugar, indigo, or nankeens. The merchants who brought these eastern wares home in their own ships would sell what they could in our own ports, and send the rest to Hamburg, or other cities of North Europe, using the proceeds to buy European manufactured goods as a nucleus for the cargoes of their outward-bound East Indiamen. If the chances of profit were great, so were the hazards. A merchant might be enriched or ruined by a single voyage. This was playing for high stakes; it demanded a certain audacious inflexibility of temper. It was no trade for nervous men. The calm, square countenances of the old East India merchants, which look down from the stiff portraits they have left us, betoken regular lives and good digestion. They were men who could stand on the pierhead and watch with clear and steady eyes the looming topsails of the "Mercury" coming in from Canton, or the "Pilgrim" from Bombay, with a perfect realization that when the ship hauled alongside, and the captain made his report, they would know whether they should build a fine new house or confess themselves bankrupt.

The pride of the country in its ships and sailors during those first years of the Federal experiment was one of the influences which compacted a group of discordant States into a nation. It is true that a certain sectional jealousy disclosed itself in the deliberations of Congress. The South was fearful and resentful of the advantages which discriminating tariff and tonnage duties would give to New York, Pennsylvania, and New England. But this unworthy antagonism was smothered by Southern men like Jefferson, who, as Secretary of State in 1791, produced a remarkable argument for protection to our ocean-carrying and our fisheries. Jefferson went into an elaborate calculation of what the United States had been losing by its dependence on foreign shipowners. He argued, on the basis of the figures of 1790, that Great Britain, carrying two-fifths of the $25,000,000 exports of the United States, or $10,000,000, received in freight and insurance twenty-two and one half per cent, or $2,250,000, in a year of peace. In a year of war Jefferson estimated that these British charges on our commerce would be advanced by war hazards to $5,500,000.

This difference between peace and war for freights and insurance was $3,250,000; and this large sum, so Jefferson urged, represented the tax on our agriculture occasioned by British wars and our dependence on British bottoms. "In every term of seven years," he said, "we pay three times $3,250,000, or $9,750,000, which, averaged on the years of peace and war, is annually $1,392,857 more than if we had our own shipping." Jefferson, in his plea for some measure of protection to save our shipping from being driven off the seas, had argued with an admirable breadth of vision that: "The loss of seamen unnoticed would be followed by other losses in a long train. If we have no seamen, our ships will be useless, consequently our ship timber, iron, and hemp; our shipbuilding will be at an end; ship carpenters will go over to other nations; our young men have no call to the sea; our products, carried in foreign bottoms, be saddled with war-freight and insurance in time of war, — and the history of the last hundred years shows that the nation which is our carrier has three years of war for every four years of peace."

President Washington's views of the wisdom of a protective policy toward our maritime interests were quite as pronounced as those of his distinguished fellow-Virginian, the Secretary of State. This is sufficiently disclosed in some communications which he sent to Congress for its information and guidance in 1794, the year in which the discrimination in import duties on goods brought by American ships was changed and strengthened. Though these communications were not Washington's own words, they unquestionably conveyed his sentiments. One of them read: "To force shipbuilding is to establish shipyards; is to form magazines; to multiply useful hands; to produce artists and workmen of every kind who may be found at once for the peaceful speculations of commerce and for the terrible wants of war. . . . For a navigating people to purchase its marine afloat would be a strange speculation, as the marine would always be dependent on the merchants furnishing them. Placing, as a reserve, with a foreign nation or in a foreign shipyard, the carpenters, blacksmiths, calkers, sail-makers, and the vessels of a nation, would be a singular commercial combination. We must, therefore, build them for ourselves."

These old arguments suggest some of the considerations which moved the fathers of the republic in the shaping and enforcing of our early maritime policy. Whatever may be said for or against the economic soundness of the views of Washington, Jefferson, and their colleagues, it is undeniable that their policy won an immediate and brilliant success. Here is the record of the growth of American shipping in the foreign trade during the first twelve years of the protective law, the last twelve years of the eighteenth century: —

TONNAGE AND FOREIGN TRADE, 1789-1800.

Year.	Shipping.	Total Foreign Commerce.	Proportion carried in American Ships.		
			Imports.	Exports.	Combined Imports and Exports.
1789	123,893		17.5	30.0	23.6
1790	346,254		41.0	40.0	40.5
1791	363,110	$48,212,041	58.0	52.0	55.9
1792	411,438	52,253,098	67.0	61.0	64.0
1793	367,734	57,209,572	82.0	77.0	79.5
1794	438,863	67,643,725	91.0	86.0	88.5
1795	529,471	117,746,140	92.0	88.0	90.0
1796	576,733	140,010,789	94.0	90.0	92.0
1797	597,777	126,674,116	92.0	88.0	90.0
1798	603,376	129,879,111	91.0	87.0	89.0
1799	657,142	157,734,670	90.0	87.0	88.5
1800	667,107	162,224,548	91.0	87.0	89.0

The growth of the American merchant fleet, as these Treasury returns for twelve years show it, was notably regular and constant. In only one year was there a falling off in tonnage, — in 1793 as compared with 1792. This was due chiefly to a cause which was destined to harass our seamen at intervals for many years afterward. It was the depredations of the Barbary corsairs of the Mediterranean. As early as 1785 the Dey of Algiers had begun his piratical work. He had learned that a new maritime nation existed in the West, a nation with many merchant ships but no warships, and he proceeded in his character-istic way to lay it under contribution. On July 25, 1785, one of his pirate craft seized the Boston schooner "Maria," Captain Isaac Stevens, near the Straits of Gibraltar. Five days later the Philadelphia ship "Dauphin," Captain Richard O'Brien, was also captured. The crews of the two vessels, twenty-one men in all, were held in cruel slavery in Algiers with the hope that their sufferings would bring a heavy ransom.

The relation which the civilized Powers of Europe then held toward the nests of sea robbers in Algiers, Morocco, Tunis, and Tripoli is absolutely incredible to men of the twentieth century. These Mohammedan corsairs were deliberately protected in their inhuman work by the great Christian nations of Europe, that they might prey upon the ships and sailors and destroy the trade of the weaker nations.

The spirit of the time found frank if cynical expression in a speech of Lord Sheffield in Parliament in 1784: "It is not probable that the American States will have a very free trade in the Mediterranean. It will not be to the interest of any of the great maritime Powers to protect them from the Barbary States. If they know their inter-ests, they will not encourage the Americans to be carriers. That the Barbary States are advantageous to maritime Powers is certain."

Lord Sheffield in these words merely proclaimed the real temper of the British statesmanship of the period. For a time little Portugal, waging single-handed a war with the Barbary pirates, proved to be our friend and pro-tector, for the Portuguese cruisers kept the pirate ships shut up in the Mediterranean. But the British agent at Algiers arranged a twelve months' truce between the Dey and Portugal. This was done without authority. The real motive of it appears in the words which the British emissary at Algiers wrote into the agreement, that "the Portuguese government should not afford protection to any nation against Algerian cruisers." The blow was aimed at the United States. It fell with prompt severity. There was no chance to warn American merchantmen, many of which were in the vicinity of the Straits of Gibraltar. Immediately a corsair squadron of three xebecs and one brig darted out into the Atlantic, and in one cruise captured ten American merchant ships, and threw one hundred American seamen into bondage often worse than death.

This was too much for even the patience of a Congress some of whose members had been pusillanimous enough to plead that a naval fleet able to protect our commerce was "another menace to our republican institutions," and that "older and more powerful nations bought the friendship of Algiers, and we might do the same, or we might subsidize some of the European naval powers to protect our trade!"

It need not be said that this shameful cowardice found no mercy from the soldier-President, George Washington. He insisted before both Houses of Congress that "to an active, external commerce the protection of a naval force is indispensable," and again that "to secure respect to a neutral flag requires a naval force organized and ready to vindicate it from insult or aggression." Congress had already authorized the building of six frigates, three of forty-four and three of thirty-six guns. One of the three forty-fours afterward became the famous "Constitution." But before these ships could be completed, a treaty was arranged with the Dey of Algiers which bound the United States to give him about a million dollars in money and presents. We had not yet learned that it was cheaper to pay these piratical powers in iron than in silver or gold.

This disgraceful tribute to the corsair chief of Algiers

was delivered, although there seems to have been some delay about it. A newspaper of 1798 records: "Portsmouth, Jan. 20, 1798. On Thursday morning, about sunrise, a gun was discharged from the frigate 'Crescent' as a signal for getting under way, and at 10 A.M. she cleared the harbor with a fine leading breeze. Our best wishes follow Captain Newman, his officers and men. May they arrive in safety at the place of their destination, and present to the Dey of Algiers one of the finest specimens of elegant naval architecture which was ever borne on the Piscataqua's waters. The 'Crescent' is a present from the United States to the Dey as a compensation for delay in not fulfilling our treaty obligations in proper time. Richard O'Brien, Esq., who was ten years a prisoner at Algiers, took passage in the above frigate, and is to reside at Algiers as Consul-General of the United States to all the Barbary States. The 'Crescent' has many valuable presents for the Dey, and when she sailed was supposed to be worth at least three hundred thousand dollars. Twenty-six barrels of dollars constituted a part of her cargo. It is worthy of remark that the captain, chief of the officers, and many of the privates of the 'Crescent' frigate have been prisoners at Algiers."

Americans of to-day will read with astonishment that their country could ever have been guilty of this base weakness. There was peculiar irony in the fact that this fine frigate, launched at a time when we had only two or three frigates of our own, was sent to the Dey officered and manned in part by American sailors whom he had already robbed and enslaved, and, as the final touch of bitter humiliation, the "Crescent" sailed from the New England river whose free tides had borne a few years before the brave keels of John Paul Jones's "Ranger" and "America."[1]

---

[1] In the "Ranger," sloop-of-war, of eighteen guns, Jones captured, off Carrickfergus, Ireland, in 1778, the British sloop-of-war "Drake," of twenty

This tribute of a dollar-laden warship was wholly ineffective. It did not even placate the greedy potentate of Algiers, and it did inspire the other Barbary States to forays of their own upon our commerce. The total number of American vessels captured by the corsairs was not large, though the sufferings of their crews under their Moslem taskmasters were terrible. It was the sharp rise in insurance rates because of these outrages which for a time checked the growth of our merchant marine. American ships did not dare to venture into the Mediterranean, and any voyage over a course between Gibraltar and the Madeiras was fraught with peril.

A new and very much more formidable foe was now to cross the path of the American merchant sailor. Our old ally, France, in the upheaval which followed the Reign of Terror, forgot all about her protestations of friendship and began to outdo England in depredations on our apparently unprotected commerce. American vessels were subject to seizure on suspicion of trading with British ports. In fact, they were seized on no pretext whatever by French picaroons miscalled privateers which hovered thickly in West Indian waters, especially in the neighborhood of Guadeloupe. French greed, French jealousy of our active marine and French hatred of England, combined to bring our West India trade to ruin. In 1794 a list was published of thirty-eight American vessels which had been captured on the high seas and carried into French ports by French warships and privateers for confiscation, although we were then at peace with France and all the world.

Several years of negotiation and protest availed nothing, and finally the United States government decided to try a sterner course. In May, 1798, our alongshore cruisers

guns. The "America," our first seventy-four-gun ship of the line, was built for Commodore Jones at Portsmouth, and he superintended its construction. But this noble vessel was presented to France, to replace a ship accidentally destroyed in our service.

were ordered to capture any French vessels which might be found interfering with American commerce. On July 7, 1798, our government took a step further. It abrogated all its treaties with France and directed our naval commanders first to seize French vessels near our seaboard, and next to attack them wherever found. The President was authorized to build more frigates and to commission privateers.

Thus our brief, real, though unacknowledged war with France came into being. A considerable fleet of frigates and sloops-of-war, which we had built or purchased, was ordered to the West India station. It was in this war that the "Constitution," then a new ship in her first year out of a Boston shipyard, made her first cruise. But the laurels of the war were won by the "Constitution's" sister frigate, the thirty-six-gun "Constellation." Off St. Kitts on Feb. 9, 1799, the "Constellation" fell in with the French frigate "Insurgent," also of thirty-six guns, and captured her in an hour and a quarter of desperate fighting. A year later, on Feb. 2, 1800, the "Constellation," commanded as in her first action by Captain Thomas Truxtun, had a battle by night with the French forty-gun frigate "Vengeance," a larger and heavier ship. The Frenchman was thoroughly beaten, but not captured, after having lost half of the crew killed and wounded. This was one of the bloodiest battles in naval history. When the "Boston" some months later defeated and took the "Berceau," the French government concluded that it had had enough of war with the Americans. Besides the regular cruisers, France lost to us eighty-four armed vessels mounting more than five hundred guns. On Feb. 3, 1801, a treaty of peace with France was ratified by the Senate, and after two and a half years the war which had never been formally declared was formally ended.

The West Indies was the chief theatre of this strife with the French republic. It was the purpose of the Directory to force our vessels out of their profitable trade with the West India islands. Thanks to the vigilance and firmness of President Adams, this selfish project failed. But the mere fact of the war and its influence upon insurance rates and general commerce seemed for the time being to retard the growth of the American merchant marine in foreign trade. Our fleet gained only about ten thousand tons between 1799 and 1800. Under the circumstances, it was signal proof of the pluck and perseverance of Yankee shipowners and seamen that it should have shown any increase at all.

Perhaps the greatest and most enduring result of the ocean war with France was its demonstration of the intimate relationship of a merchant marine and a fighting navy. The one needs the other, and a merchant marine also furnishes the resources out of which a navy can be created. But for our spirited resistance France in 1798 would have first destroyed our West India carrying, and then turned her cruisers and privateers loose upon our coastwise trade and our profitable traffic with the ports of Britain and North Europe. It was necessary to strike at once a hard blow in self-defence. Our government did it so successfully that in spite of the war our exports increased from $51,294,000 in 1797 to $78,665,000 in 1799, and between 1797 and 1800 the national revenue from customs grew about fifty per cent. France began to realize that the United States was a useful friend and a dangerous enemy. Henceforth, she was less aggressive and unjust toward our merchant ships and sailors than was England.

While our merchant tonnage, which had increased fivefold between 1789 and 1800, demanded the protection of a regular war fleet, it also provided a naval reserve of vital importance. Eight of the twenty-two vessels which composed the seagoing navy of the United States, at the end of 1798, were purchased merchantmen, and the officers and seamen were almost without exception drawn from the merchant service. Immediately after the Revolution the surviving vessels of the Continental navy were dismantled or sold, and the brave officers and men who had kept the starred flag afloat throughout the shifting fortunes of the war were all dismissed and scattered. The task of constructing a Federal navy, under the Constitution, therefore, involved creating it from the beginning. The twenty-four-gun ship "Ganges," the first United States man-of-war sent to sea by the Federal government, was an old-fashioned, deep-waisted merchantman, bought for the national service and armed with a somewhat heavier battery than she had carried as a trader. Her commander was the redoubtable Richard Dale, John Paul Jones's first lieutenant in the "Bon Homme Richard."

Transforming a merchant sailor into a man-o'-warsman was an easier matter in the last years of the eighteenth century than it would be to-day. At that time all important merchant vessels mounted cannon, usually six or nine pounders, for protection against small privateers or pirates. The crews of these merchant vessels were, of course, less numerous than those of national ships and less smartly disciplined. Some merchant captains paid a great deal of attention to drilling their men; others very little. It depended on the temperament of the master, and the nature of his voyage. But the majority of able-bodied deep-water sailors of a hundred years ago knew how to serve great guns and to handle boarding pikes and muskets. The "Constitution" on her first cruise in the War of 1812, when she brilliantly outmanœuvred Commodore Broke's squadron and later captured the "Guerrière," was manned by a crew of young merchant sailors who had been aboard the frigate only a few weeks. Many of them had "never been on an armed vessel before,"[1] and one hundred had actually joined the ship as she was on the point of sailing.

[1] Official Report of Captain Isaac Hull.

The swift growth of American merchant tonnage in the years following 1789 gave the country a splendid reserve of brave and hardy men to fight its battles. Much of the best brain and sinew of the young nation turned to the sea. Even then, in the infancy of the republic, thorough-bred American sailors had begun to be famed for superior physique and intelligence. That is one explanation of the system of impressment which the English practised with increasing severity as their own seamen were exhausted by the terrible demands of the Napoleonic wars. Nelson's ships at the Nile and elsewhere were filled with men of all nations recruited wherever the press-gangs could find them. Active, well-trained American sailors were prizes all the more valuable, because they spoke and understood the English language. There is a tradition that Nelson's own barge crew on the "Victory" at Trafalgar, made up of men picked for their skill or strength, was composed chiefly of Yankee tars pressed out of merchant vessels. Certain it is that there were then thousands of American seamen in the British navy rendering the king a most involuntary service.

Of course, in the beginning of impressment, during the period from 1793 onward, British naval officers who boarded and searched our merchant vessels professed that they sought only British subjects, who, on the theory of "once an Englishman always an Englishman," could rightfully be compelled to serve in the ships of the Crown. But the physical resemblance between American and British sailors was very close. It was not always that even their speech would distinguish the one from the other. As a matter of fact, the British boarding officers took the men whom they happened to fancy, without much regard to their real nationality, and many an American ship was put into deadly peril, and many a voyage was ruined by the forcible removal of the most robust and important members of the American crew.

This habit of stealing men from beneath the flag of their country, and compelling them to risk their lives for a flag they loathed, is in large degree responsible for the strangely persistent hatred of Great Britain, which is to be found to this day in the coast villages of Long Island and New England, among people of the purest Anglo-American stock. Theirs is not a race-antipathy; it must be traced back to a deep sense of personal wrong. This hatred is not discoverable, or at any rate it is not so intense, in inland communities.

There was one factor in the last decade of the eighteenth century which relieved the tension between America and Britain. It was the celebrated Jay treaty of commerce, negotiated in 1794, but not given full effect until 1797. This sounded a great deal more favorable than it really was, for it ostensibly provided that "there shall be between all the dominions of His Majesty in Europe and the territories of the United States a reciprocal and perfect liberty of commerce and navigation." But there was, in fact, no such reciprocity, no such liberty. The regulations of the treaty covering the West India trade were unacceptable to Americans, and our ships gained a scarcely improved footing in British waters. The real advantage of the treaty was that any commercial treaty whatever with Great Britain at that time served to allay fears of a commercial war. It gave our shipowning merchants something to stand on. It satisfied the commercial interests of both countries that the feud between the young republic and the mother land was not implacable and everlasting, and that they would continue to trade as they had traded before the violent separation.

This assurance was very important, because Great Britain in all mercantile affairs stood for vastly more than it does now to America. It was not only the chief market for our products, but the indispensable source of all kinds of manufactured goods, and the traffic between our own and British ports was by all odds the largest and most active branch of our ocean-carrying. Imperfect though it was, the Jay treaty continued to regulate commerce and navigation between the United States and British ports until 1807.

CHAPTER V

A CELEBRATED VOYAGE

From Boston to the Northwest Coast — A New Commerce opened by the "Columbia" and "Lady Washington" — Furs for China and Tea for Home — First to circumnavigate the Globe — The "Columbia's" Second Venture — Her Meeting with Vancouver and Discovery of the Columbia River — How Oregon was won for the United States

FOR a true understanding of the spirit which grasped the helm and loosed the sails of the early American merchant marine, we must look to something more than the mere statistical records of trade and tonnage. What manner of men these old merchants and seamen were, what they dared, and what they achieved, can best be learned by a study of individual voyages. Perhaps the most famous venture which an American merchant ship ever undertook, and certainly the most memorable in its consequences, was the voyage of the ship "Columbia" of Boston to the far and savage Northwest coast in 1787.

All of old Oregon Territory, including what are now the States of Oregon, Washington, and Idaho, was then a terra incognita. Many nations laid vague claim to the region, — Spain because her navigators discovered it, Britain because Francis Drake had sailed along the coast in 1579, Russia because Bering had mapped the North Pacific and prepared for the opening in 1771 of the export fur-trade from Oregon to China. But these Powers had no real foothold on the land. Over the whole region a mystery rested. There was a tradition that somewhere along the coast between Latitude 43° and Latitude 47° a great river, celebrated in Bryant's sonorous line "Where rolls the Oregon," poured its broad tide down into the heaving sea.

Toward the close of our Revolution a greater navigator than Bering was exploring the lonely isles and sombre shores of the North Pacific. It was Captain Cook, for whom even then such feeling was cherished that Franklin, our Minister to Paris and Marine Superintendent abroad, issued in 1779 a special order to Continental cruisers which Americans have always been proud to remember, that "in whatsoever part of the sea they might meet the great discoverer, Captain Cook, they were to forget the temporary quarrel in which they were fighting, and not merely suffer him to pass unmolested but offer him every aid and service in their power, since it would ill beseem Americans to lift their hands against one who had earned the reverence and gratitude of all mankind." [1]

With Captain Cook there sailed a young American seaman, John Ledyard, who published a journal and a chart of the voyage in Hartford in 1783. Ledyard is supposed to have been the first American to urge the importance of the Northwest fur-trade. He convinced Robert Morris of the practicability of the venture, but the merchants of New York were sceptical, and in Great Britain and on the Continent the young enthusiast met very little more success, although he won the sympathy of John Paul Jones and Thomas Jefferson.

But in the counting-rooms of Boston there were the keenest eyes and the boldest hearts of all. Joseph Barrell, a distinguished Boston merchant, had as a clerk an interesting and brilliant young man, not long from Harvard, — Charles Bulfinch, who had not yet entered on the profession of architecture that made him famous. The young man and the older one had heard of Ledyard's book, and they had read Cook's own journal of his third voyage, published

[1] John Fiske, "The American Revolution," vol. ii.

in 1784, which told of the warm and beautiful skins of the sea-otter, purchased from Indians on the Northwest coast for beads and a few other trinkets, and sold by the Russians to the Chinese for from $75 to $100 each. In 1787, Mr. Barrell, moved by the enthusiasm of his young friend, resolved to fit out an expedition for the Northwest country. Four others joined Messrs. Barrell and Bulfinch in their audacious venture, — Samuel Brown, merchant, John Derby, shipmaster, of Salem, who had carried to England the first news of the battle of Lexington, Captain Crowell Hatch of Cambridge, and John Marden Pintard of Pintard & Co., of New York. These six subscribed fifty thousand dollars, a sum equivalent to half a million as capital is now counted. The next step was to find a suitable ship. Choice fell upon a vessel already old as ships' lives go, launched in 1773, before the Revolution. But the "Columbia" was built by mechanics of famous skill, on the North River, Scituate, a little stream now sand-choked and insignificant, of which it is difficult to imagine in these days that its shores have launched more than a thousand seagoing ships. The "Columbia," or "Columbia Rediviva," as she was often afterward known, was a substantial, two-decked square-sterned craft of two hundred and thirteen tons, rather a small vessel even for that period, with three square-rigged masts, and a defensive armament of ten cannon.

As consort to the "Columbia," and a tender for collecting furs in the inlets and among the islands, a smaller craft, the "Lady Washington," was purchased, — a sloop of ninety tons, about as large and seaworthy as the sloops which are now freighting stone from Cape Ann to Boston Harbor. A medal struck at the time shows the "Lady Washington" to be a sturdy, solid, not ungraceful vessel, hoisting on her tall single mast a huge mainsail, three narrow jibs, and, as was then customary, a lofty square topsail. A rig more unfit for deep-sea voyaging could scarcely be devised.

The captains and officers of both the ship and the sloop were selected with as much care as if their charges had been men-of-war of the government. The commander of the "Columbia" and commodore of the expedition was John Kendrick of Wareham, an experienced mariner, forty-five years old. For the sloop, Captain Robert Gray of Boston, a friend of Kendrick and an officer in the Revolutionary navy, was chosen. Gray was descended from Pilgrim stock, and proved to be a man of extraordinary force of character. The success of the enterprise was really due to him; it was he who soon assumed the actual leadership. On the "Columbia," the first officer was Simeon Woodruff, who had sailed with Cook on his last voyage to the Pacific. The second officer was Joseph Ingraham; the third, Robert Haswell of Hull, an accomplished young man and a skilful artist, whose pen and pencil have left an admirable record of the expedition. There were also on the "Columbia" a fourth mate, a clerk, a surgeon, and an astronomer, or schoolmaster.

The vessels were very carefully overhauled and equipped for their long and perilous journey. Mr. Barrell's confidence in the North River shipwrights was not misplaced. Besides the regular ship stores the "Columbia" and "Lady Washington" carried a cargo of hardware, tools, utensils, buttons, toys, beads, etc., to be bartered for furs with the Indians. The unusual character of the expedition was frankly recognized by the merchants and the authorities of Massachusetts. Both State and Federal governments granted especial sea letters to the captains, and hundreds of medals signalizing the enterprise were put aboard for distribution wherever the vessels touched. Years afterward some of these medals and cents and half-cents of the State of Massachusetts were to be found in the wake of the "Columbia" among the Spaniards of South America, the Kanakas of Hawaii, and the Indians of Oregon.

Amid a great demonstration from the Boston wharves,

the "Columbia" and "Lady Washington" took their departure on Sept. 30, 1787, in order to have a summer passage around Cape Horn. Minute directions had been given to the commanders. They were enjoined to treat the Indians justly, and to have no more to do with the Spaniards than they could help. The furs gathered on the Northwest coast were to be taken across the Pacific to China and exchanged there for a cargo of teas for Boston.

Instead of steering straight for the Horn, the "Columbia" and her tender called at the Cape Verde Islands and tarried there so long that trouble arose among the officers. Woodruff, Cook's comrade, a most important man for the expedition, and Roberts, the surgeon, left the ship. This was an inauspicious beginning. But Kendrick and Gray were not dismayed by it or by the growing lateness of the season. They sailed from the Cape Verdes, stopped at the Falkland Islands, and sailed again on Feb. 28, 1788, for their battle around the dreaded Horn. The winds were wild, the seas mountainous. The little sloop had her decks swept. It is a miracle that she survived at all, for even the "Columbia" was thrown on her beam ends and almost dismasted. In a hurricane in April the ship and the sloop lost each other in the roar and blackness. It was bitter cold, with the first blasts of the Cape Horn winter, and officers and crews were almost exhausted.

But there was too much Yankee grit for any turning back. Each captain held his course. On April 14, 1788, Gray in the "Lady Washington" found himself squarely within the Pacific, amid softening weather. In June he caught the northeast trade winds, and on August 2 made the coast near Cape Mendocino. The sailors were weary and scurvy-stricken after their long voyage of almost a year from Boston. Although the Indians seemed hospitable, their innate treachery was quickly disclosed. Near Cape Lookout the captain's black boy quarrelled with the natives and was stabbed to death. A sharp fight followed. Some of the

Indians were shot and killed, and Gray named the site of the tragedy " Murderers' Harbor." Their worst peril, after all, lay not on the sea, but on the shore.

On August 16, the " Lady Washington" reached the rendezvous at Nootka Sound, the headquarters of the fur-trade. A week later a ship under short canvas crawled wearily in. It was the "Columbia," with her crew disabled by scurvy, that curse of the sea before tinned vegetables were known and the value of lime juice was discovered. Two of the "Columbia's" men had died, and the others were so weakened that the ship's topgallantmasts were sent down and her topsails reefed. Only under this snug rig could the "Columbia" be handled by her suffering company. This was no unusual experience in distant voyaging. Between the scurvy and the yellow fever, which was then rampant in tropical America, poor Jack's hard life was not worth insuring.

The "Columbia" and "Lady Washington" had consumed a year in making a voyage easily made nowadays in six months by modern sailing vessels which are by no means clippers. One cause of their slowness may have been the rapid growth of weeds and barnacles on their bottoms in the waters of warm latitudes. Deep-sea vessels were not so regularly coppered in 1787 as they were years afterward, and between our own Atlantic coast and Oregon there was really no civilized port where American ships could safely undergo the process of careening by which hulls were then cleaned and tightened.

The winter of 1788-89 was passed by the "Columbia" and "Lady Washington" in the propitious shelter of Friendly Cove, Nootka Sound. A large house was built on shore, and here the two crews made themselves at home and exulted in the change from the cramped quarters of shipboard to the boundless reaches of the forest. But a keen watch was kept on land and at the moorings against a surprise by the fickle savages. James Fenimore Cooper, in his " Afloat

and Ashore," that graphic autobiography of a fine type of
the American merchant sailor, Miles Wallingford, tells a
grim story of what happened to traders on the northwest
coast who could not see the covetousness and cruelty behind
the smug features of the Northwest Indians. While some
of the men of Kendrick and Gray stood guard, the rest
worked with rude forges to convert their store of iron into
chisels and other useful implements for barter with the
natives. So the long winter wore on. In the spring each
chisel was worth at first a skin of otter. But later the wily
red hunters demanded seven or eight chisels for one skin, and
got them. Of course, a vessel of the size of the "Columbia"
could not procure a cargo of furs at any one place.
The "Lady Washington," smaller, of lighter draught,
and more easily handled, made short cruises alongshore,
penetrating the inlets and visiting one by one all the accessible Indian villages. Her beads and buttons, her tools
and trinkets, were exchanged for skins as fast as these
could be gathered. When the sloop was well laden, she
would return to the "Columbia," transship her furry freight,
receive more barter goods, and proceed to search for more
Indian settlements.

So this unique trade went on until the "Columbia" had
secured a respectable cargo of the fine furs which the
Chinese prized, as they do to-day. Then the two captains exchanged ships, Kendrick taking the "Lady Washington" and Gray the "Columbia." On July 30, 1789,
while, all unknown to these intrepid sailor-traders, the first
Federal Congress under the Constitution was legislating
for the protection of American ships and American commerce, the "Columbia" bade farewell to the shadowy
waters of the northwest coast, and set her course southwest across the wide Pacific. As was the custom then,
the ship called at Hawaii for rest and provisions, and
then sailed for Canton, the great port of Southern China.
The furs were sold, but they did not bring the full price

anticipated. The proceeds were used, according to the owners' instructions, to purchase a cargo of tea for Boston. On Jan. 26, 1790, before Captain Gray had finished his business and gone to sea, Captain Kendrick arrived at Macao with the " Lady Washington." The little craft had had an evil time in the long passage over, and reached port in shattered condition. The Pacific has often belied its name.

But the " Columbia " and her consort did not fall in with each other. The ship sailed on Feb. 12, 1790, for Boston, calling at St. Helena and Ascension. On Aug. 10, 1790, having logged nearly fifty thousand miles, the " Columbia" stood in by Boston Light, and steered up the harbor, welcomed by artillery salutes and a great crowd of rejoicing citizens. Going out *via* Cape Horn and returning *via* the Cape of Good Hope, the " Columbia" had circumnavigated the globe. The New England capital was proud of the ship and her achievement. Governor Hancock gave a dinner to the officers and owners of the " Columbia." More conspicuous than Gray himself at this celebration was his cabin boy, Attoo, a young Hawaiian prince, the first of his race ever seen in Massachusetts.

This famous voyage was more fruitful in fame than in gain.[1] It brought so little profit to the owners that two of them, Messrs. Derby and Pintard, sold out to the other four. Mr. Barrell, Mr. Bulfinch, Mr. Brown, and Captain Hatch were not disheartened. They prepared the " Columbia " at once for a second venture. The vessel was put into the hands of Boston shipwrights, and given new masts and yards and an entirely new equipment. Captain Gray sailed on Sept. 28, 1790, only seven weeks after his return from Canton. He bore instructions to treat the Indians kindly, not to trade with the Spaniards "for a single farthing," and to offer no insult to foreigners and to

[1] " The Ship 'Columbia' and the Discovery of Oregon," by Edward G. Porter, "New England Magazine," June, 1892.

receive none "without showing the becoming spirit of a free, independent American." Gray scarcely needed such admonition. And his officers were of the same prudent but indomitable type. Young Haswell sailed with him as first mate. The carpenter of the "Columbia" was Samuel Yendell of the North End, who had served on a frigate in the Revolutionary War, and after the return of the "Columbia" was destined to help to build the stout hull of the "Constitution." Yendell is remembered as the last survivor of the crew of the "Columbia," dying in 1861, aged ninety-one. He was a kinsman of Governor William Eustis Russell of Massachusetts.

On this voyage the "Columbia" did not stop at the dreamy Cape Verdes, where it is always afternoon. She touched at the uninviting Falkland Islands, once more doubled Cape Horn, this time in the favorable season, and on June 4, 1791, anchored at Clayoquet on the northwest coast, — a harbor which fur-traders frequented. The "Columbia" had consumed eight months from port to port, — a very long passage, but really three months shorter than the first one. This was an exciting and tragic summer on the coast. Trade was a matter of keen diplomacy. Many times the ship and sloop were threatened by the Indians. On August 12, three seamen, who bore the good New England names of Caswell, Barnes, and Folger, were murdered by the natives while in the jolly-boat very near the "Columbia." The Indians almost captured the "Lady Washington." They did, indeed, swarm on to the deck of the sloop, and their leader grabbed the key of the arms chest, exclaiming, "Key is mine, and sloop is mine, too." But Kendrick, a man of quick resource, drove the savages overboard and saved his vessel.

Kendrick's young son Solomon was killed and scalped by a native. The father, however, with most admirable self-control, refused to retaliate upon the assassin, but turned the savage over to his own chief for punishment, believing that this would best serve the ends of justice and assure the safety of white men on the coast. The "Lady Washington" crossed the North Pacific once more to Macao, and was there transformed into the handier rig of a brigantine. This brave little vessel was the first to display the American flag in Japan, but she was warned away and sternly refused the right to trade there. It was not until more than sixty years later that an American war squadron succeeded in opening this hermit nation to the commerce of the world.

At Clayoquet Captain Gray, thanks to the skill of Samuel Yendell, built a new consort, the sloop "Adventure." Just then the natives conspired to destroy the "Columbia" and her crew. But their plot was discovered by Attoo, the Hawaiian prince, to whom the Indians had appealed for aid. They offered to make him a great chief if he would wet the ship's powder. Though Attoo's skin was brown, he was a firm friend of the white men. The "Adventure" was completed and launched, and she proved to be a very successful craft, swift enough to outsail the larger "Columbia."

But Gray was thinking of something else than furs. He had the instinct of the true explorer. He had heard, as had all other strangers on the coast, of the mysterious great river which was the gateway to the ownership of Oregon. When opportunity offered, he sailed in search of it. On April 29, 1792, far out at sea, the Yankee captain saw the unwonted spectacle of three ships-of-war in company in those waters where anything except the modest fur-traders or a prowling Spanish cruiser was never beheld. These three ships were the squadron of George Vancouver, the British navigator, who had sailed with Captain Cook on his second and third voyages, and now commanded an expedition of his own, sent out to execute the terms of the Nootka convention with Spain, and to examine the coast to the northward.

When Gray's ship and Vancouver's had spoken each other, and the accustomed maritime civilities had been exchanged, the British commodore remarked that he had made no discoveries as yet, and asked the American if he had done anything in that direction. Gray frankly replied that he had found in Latitude 46.°10 what seemed to be the long-sought great river of Oregon, and that for nine days he had endeavored to cross the bar and enter the channel, but had found the swirling current too strong. He intended, however, to make another attempt under fairer conditions.

To this modest report of the New Englander, Vancouver loftily replied that that river must have been the opening passed by him two days before, but that it was a small river only. "Not considering this opening worthy of more attention," wrote Vancouver in his journal, "I continued our pursuit to the Northwest."

A little less superciliousness, and Great Britain might have gained incontestable title to the entire Oregon country. More than either Yankee or Briton dreamed of hung upon this chance meeting in the Northern sea. The stake was really the fate of an empire.

Captain Gray was as good as his word. He kept on to the southeast. On May 7, 1792, he discovered a harbor which he called Bulfinch Harbor in Latitude 46.°58. This has rightly come to be known as Gray's Harbor, after the brave navigator whose keel first furrowed it and whose anchor first plunged into its waters. Here the "Columbia" was furiously attacked by the Indians, but she beat off their war canoes by clever use of her guns. Sunrise of May 11 brought Captain Gray's great river straight before him. The wind was fair and strong, and very proudly the "Columbia" with all sail set ran inside the breakers. Gray steered up a large, fresh-water river for ten miles. There were Indian villages along the shores, and the "Columbia" passed several days in trading with the natives and procuring water. Then Gray ran up the river fifteen miles farther, "and doubted not that it was navigable upwards of a hundred miles." Sailing down again to the sea, Gray buried coins under a pine-tree on the bold headland which forms one wall of the mouth of the Columbia. This headland he called Cape Hancock; the low spit on the opposite side, Point Adams, after the two great men of Massachusetts.

On May 19, 1792, Captain Gray landed with his crew and formally named the great river Columbia. On the next day he put to sea, and returned to his trading. When he had secured his cargo of furs, he sold the tender "Adventure" to the Spaniards at Nootka, and sailed in September, 1792, for Canton and home. The "Columbia" reached Macao leaking. Her furs were forwarded to Canton and sold. Captain Gray purchased a cargo of tea, sugar, chinaware, and curios, and cleared on Feb. 3, 1793, for the United States. In the Straits of Sunda the "Columbia" met a British war fleet escorting Lord Macartney, Ambassador to Pekin, — the same proud ambassador who a few months later sailed up the Pei Ho in a gorgeous junk flying a banner inscribed in Chinese characters all unknown to him, "Tribute-bearer to the Emperor from the King of England." Captain Gray took despatches from Lord Macartney for St. Helena, touched there, stood on through the trade winds and reached Boston on July 29, 1793, ending the "Columbia's" second voyage of circumnavigation.

It has been claimed for many men before and since Marcus Whitman that they saved Oregon to the United States. But surely the earliest and most compelling title to this distinction is that of Captain Robert Gray of Boston and the good ship "Columbia." They gave us the great river by the powerful right of discovery, and the great river dominated the region through which it ran. The voyage of the "Columbia" was plainly and undeniably the first step which won for the United States a grip on the Oregon territory that no diplomatic casuistry and no arrogant bluster could shake. Twelve years after Gray sailed into the great river and named it for his ship and claimed it for his flag and country, Lewis and Clark's hardy band of overland explorers crossed the "Shining Mountains," entered upon the upper Columbia, and floated down to the sea. Seven years later still, John Jacob Astor, of New York, founded Astoria, the first town in Oregon. The owners of the "Columbia" never realized their dream of golden profits. As so often happens, other and later comers reaped what the pioneers had sown. But those sagacious Boston merchants did render a great and noble service to their country, and the fame of their courage and foresight and the name of their ship will live on as long as history endures.

What were the hazards of the sea in those old years, what the fate which confronted adventurous sailors, is vividly shown in the lives of the brave men who were conspicuous in the "Columbia's" voyages. Captain Gray, more fortunate than his comrades, closed his eyes in peace in his own native land. After his return from his greatest voyage, he continued to follow the sea, commanded several other vessels, and died in Charleston, S. C., in 1806. Captain Kendrick never returned to his pleasant Wareham home, where the substantial house which he built for his wife and children and the shade trees which he planted are still standing, his only memorial. After opening a valuable trade in sandalwood, Kendrick was killed in the Hawaiian Islands. An English captain, firing a salute in his honor, by some dreadful mischance charged a gun with round and grape shot, which slew Kendrick and two boys on his own quarterdeck. Ingraham, second officer of the "Columbia," became an officer in the United States Navy and perished when the cruiser "Pickering" went down with all on board in the great equinoctial gale of September, 1800, during our

ocean war with France. Haswell, the accomplished young
third and first officer of the "Columbia," sailed for the
Pacific in 1801 and perished while returning. The "Lady
Washington" also never saw Boston again. After having conquered the perils of Cape Horn, and four times
crossed the wide Pacific, she was lost in the Straits of
Malacca. But her share in the great work had been
done.

CHAPTER VI

THE MERCHANT NAVIGATORS

America's First Great East Indiaman — The "Massachusetts" and her Interesting but Ill-Starred Voyage — Groping down the Coast of Africa — A Rotten Ship and an Unsalable Cargo — Captain Delano and his Exploits in Many Seas — Captain Richard Cleveland — In a Cockleshell to the Cape of Good Hope — In Another across the Wide Pacific — A Trading Voyage around the World — Thirty-Five-Fold Profit in Seven Years — Cleveland's Last Voyage in Astor's "Beaver" — Vigor and Resourcefulness of the Old Master Mariners

REAL Homeric figures were the old shipmasters, in their disdain of danger and their large way of looking out upon the world. Some of them have left us vivid accounts of their life experiences, and these homely volumes show the fine blending of simplicity and dignity which adorns the memoirs of General Grant. They were men of action and without literary pretensions, although American merchant captains of the best type were well educated as education then went. It was a pleasure to them and a profit to their country when they sat down in the calm evening of life and wrote their reminiscences. These master seamen of the young republic were as truly pioneers as their kinsmen who with axe and rifle on their backs were at the same time pouring through the passes of the Alleghanies to subdue the West. But there was this difference between them, — that the sea pioneers sailed out on a life which broadened their minds and mellowed their sympathies by contact with humankind all over the world, while the land pioneers became for the time being hermits in the wilderness. It was inevitable that of two sons who left their father's home together, — the one for the ocean, the other for the frontier, — the sailor son should twenty years later be intellectually the larger man, because he had had the more varied and interesting experiences. Seamen then were almost the only wide and constant travellers. They were in an especial sense the eyes and ears of the nation.

This is what makes so enjoyable even now such narratives as Captain Amasa Delano, or Captain Richard J. Cleveland, or Captain George Coggeshall has left us. Far better than any formal history these personal recollections show why American seamen succeeded, and how their country's merchant flag was made familiar in every strange corner of the globe.

It was Captain Delano's fortune to sail on the "Massachusetts" in her memorable voyage to the East. A six-hundred-ton ship would now be considered insignificant. There is not one full-rigged ship so small as six hundred tons in the present American merchant service. But when this vessel was launched at Quincy, Boston Harbor, in September, 1789, it was an event of national importance, for the "Massachusetts" was the greatest merchantman which had yet been built in the United States. After the Revolutionary War, two officers of the Continental Army, with their love of adventure unsated, had found their way to China. One of them was Major Samuel Shaw, who had been aide-de-camp to General Knox, Washington's Chief of Artillery. His comrade was Captain Randall. They seem to have cherished an ambition to create an American East India company, in competition with the vast concerns which monopolized the Asiatic trade of Europe. This Oriental traffic then employed the largest merchant ships in the world. Some of them were of a thousand tons and upward. They were built, equipped, and armed like regular men-of-war.

The "Massachusetts," which was the outcome of the

aspiring dreams of Shaw and Randall, was, therefore, the earliest first-class American East Indiaman. No trade in which our people had hitherto engaged had required a vessel of her tonnage. Her general design is said to have been taken from the "New Triumph," an English Indiaman at Canton in 1788, but the "Massachusetts" was built on reduced dimensions.

The "Massachusetts" was a two-decked ship, with a length of keel of one hundred and sixteen feet and a breadth of beam of thirty-six feet. She was smaller than most of the barks now used in the sugar and coffee trade from the West Indies and South America, and not very much larger than the average three-masted coasting schooner of to-day. There are four and five masted schooners now afloat which would each make three or four of the "Massachusetts." But in 1789 this new East Indiaman was a colossus, and conservative shipowners all alongshore stood aghast at the presumption of her builders.

The "Massachusetts" was a beautiful ship. She could not well be otherwise, for her lines were draughted by Captain William Hackett, of Amesbury on the Merrimac, who had built the "Alliance" frigate, the swiftest and most successful of American cruisers in the Revolution. Before and after her launching, the "Massachusetts" won the enthusiastic praise of all who beheld her. Captain Delano, who was on board when she was launched, hoisted her first colors, and went out as her second officer, says that she " excited a considerable sensation in the commercial part of the community. Parties of people in every rank in society frequently came on board of her to gratify their curiosity and express their admiration." Among these enthusiastic visitors were the officers of five French men-of-war, then lying in Boston Harbor, and Captain John Linzee of the British frigate " Penelope." Captain Linzee, whose compliments seem to have counted more with Delano and his comrades than the plaudits of the " parley-

voos," pronounced the "Massachusetts" "as perfect a
model as the state of the art would then permit."

So notable was the ship and so interesting was her
voyage that "hundreds of applications" for stations on
board of her "were made by persons of the best character."
Delano regarded himself as fortunate in securing his berth
as second officer. He and the three other mates had all
commanded ships in foreign service, but they were glad
to hold a subordinate post in a voyage of such national
consequence. The captain of the "Massachusetts," Job
Prince, was a merchant as well as a seaman.

According to our modern notions the vessel was
grotesquely over-officered and over-manned. Besides her
four mates she carried a purser, surgeon, several midshipmen, carpenter, boatswain, gunner, and sixty-seven men
before the mast. Nowadays a bark of six hundred tons
in the foreign trade carries two mates, a cook, and six or
eight seamen; a six-hundred-ton three-masted schooner
often not more than four seamen. But the "Massachusetts,"
like all other Indiamen, mounted a battery of cannon, and
required extra men to handle them.

Though this voyage was undertaken with the brightest
of auspices, it had a melancholy ending. It proved that
the Americans of 1789 were only apprentices in East India
commerce, and poor apprentices at that. Their great and
costly ship was improperly built and unwisely laden. The
model of the "Massachusetts" was faultless; and so was
the handiwork of the skilled North River mechanics who
sixteen years before had launched the famous "Columbia."
But through either haste or some fatal miscalculation the
master builder wrought this great and beautiful ship out
of white oak timber newly cut and wholly unseasoned!
There is no better material for ships than the white oak
of Atlantic America, save perhaps the live oak of the
same region. But it must be carefully prepared before-
hand. The frame and planking of the "Massachusetts"

were of "green wood," and before she had finished her first voyage this noble fabric was rotten.[1]

Moreover, the cargo was wrongly selected and foolishly stowed. Much of it consisted of "green" masts and spars, taken on board in winter, covered with ice and mud, and stowed away in the lower hold. Several hundred barrels of beef were also placed in this hold, and then the lower deck hatches were caulked down, hermetically sealing the whole body of the ship below them. The "Massachusetts" sailed on March 31, 1790. She made an ordinary passage, reaching Macao on September 30 and Canton a few days later. When the lower hold was opened, it was found that the close air and the fiery tropics had completely destroyed that Yankee beef, and the whole interior of the ship was in a woful state of decay — so little did the old merchants know of loading ships for six-month voyages.

In view of the importance of the "Massachusetts," it is astonishing to learn from Delano's narrative that she went to sea without a chronometer and without a single officer who could work a lunar observation! This compelled her to creep down the coast of Africa, feeling her way along, as it were, by the discolored water. She tried to sight the Cape Verde Islands to correct her reckoning, but missed them, and standing too far back toward the east came near bringing up on the inhospitable sands of South Africa. But the worst miscalculation of all was the missing of Java Head, that great landmark of East India voyagers. This blunder compelled the "Massachusetts" to make at least fifteen extra degrees of "easting," and cost her about three weeks' time. If a great ship like the "Massachusetts" was sent out so ill provided with the instruments of navigation, it is inexplicable how the small ships of poorer owners ever found their way around the Cape of Good Hope and through the labyrinths of the East Indian archipelago. The detailed story of this voyage and

[1] "Voyages and Travels," by Amasa Delano, page 23.

other voyages heightens our wonder at the pluck and resource of American deep-sea mariners of a century ago.

But brave though these men undeniably were, many of them were intensely superstitious. The " Massachusetts " shipped three different crews before she got away from Boston. A celebrated soothsayer, Moll Pitcher of Lynn, had prophesied that the " Massachusetts " would be lost with all on board. At this news the first crew bolted for the shore, and so did the second. It is worthy of record that the third crew, which stood by the ship in spite of the Lynn raven's croakings, was composed chiefly of native American seamen, nearly all of them New Englanders.

The " Massachusetts " carried out as a passenger her principal owner, Major Shaw, who bore a commission as American Consul for India and China, the first we ever had to the eastward of the Cape of Good Hope.[1]   This fact gave the ship a semi-public character, but it made no market for her freight in Batavia, the first port entered. The " Massachusetts " was compelled to steer on to Canton. She weathered a terrible typhoon — " tuffoon, " Delano spells it — in the China Sea, and on arriving at the great Chinese port, then the chief centre of Eastern trade, found that her cargo " would not sell for anything." So the voyage ended in failure. The " Massachusetts, " despite the quick decay of her " green " timbers, was keenly admired by the English, Dutch, and other European shipmasters at Batavia and Canton, and was acknowledged to be " the handsomest vessel in the two ports." It happened that the Danish East India Company at Canton needed a ship to replace one of its vessels which had been dismasted in the typhoon, and Major Shaw sold the " Massachusetts " to the Danes for $65,000. Delano, who had hoisted the stars and stripes over his beloved ship as she slipped off the ways at Quincy, now hauled down the colors for the last time. Officers and crew were set adrift to make their

[1] " Voyages and Travels, " Delano, page 38.

way home as best they could. Major Shaw himself died on the return passage and was buried at sea off the Cape of Good Hope. So vanished the dream of an American East India company.

This ambitious but futile voyage is worth recalling to bring into the sharper relief the real success which finally crowned the efforts of our mariners and merchants. When the "Massachusetts" arrived at Macao, she found there before her the ship "Washington" of Providence, Captain Jonathan Donnison. Other ships had reached the East even earlier, and still others followed. Captain Cleveland, who lay three months at Calcutta in the winter of 1799–1800, says in his journal that during those three months "no less than twelve ships were laden with the produce and manufactures of Hindostan for the United States."

The decisive factor which in the end made these East India voyages prosperous was not so much the shrewdness of the merchants who owned the ships as the nautical and commercial aptitude of the men who commanded them. Every capable officer of those times looked forward to becoming a merchant himself. Long before our trade gained a foothold in the East, our seamanship had won a superior reputation. Delano's own experience as his narrative describes it is an excellent case in point. No sooner was he released from his second mate's post by the sale of the "Massachusetts" than he was engaged to superintend the repairs of the Danish Indiaman, which had been dismasted and otherwise roughly handled in the typhoon. Although the Chinese had no hard timber, iron, or copper of the proper kind, Delano accomplished this task to the satisfaction of the Danish East India Company, which seems to have assumed that the work was beyond the capacity of its own officers. Like many other thorough-going American seamen of the period, Delano could build a ship as well as he could sail one. Having completely refitted the Dane, Delano turned it over to some of his

6

comrades of the " Massachusetts, " while he himself entered another and a very different service.

Commodore John McClure, a British explorer, happened to touch at Macao while Delano was there. His squadron had lost several officers, and he gave the American a lieutenancy on his flagship, the "Panther." This was a large responsibility. The "Panther" was an armed ship of the India Marine, and her officers were, of course, all Britons, who were at first disposed to resent taking their orders from an American merchant seaman. But this tension did not last long. The British officers found that their Yankee friend was a master of his profession, and Delano was soon able to record that "I was more happy than I had ever been in any service or with any set of officers before."

It was an arduous and important work which Commodore McClure had undertaken. His expedition was sent out to explore and map the then unknown, reef-studded waters of the Pelew Islands, New Guinea, New Holland, the Spice Islands, and others. The squadron sailed from Bombay bearing the commission of the English East India Company, and it was ruled by regular naval discipline. Delano remained with Commodore McClure for two years. The expedition was remarkably successful. It explored and charted the course which had been set out for it, and it also visited the Philippine and Sooloo archipelago. The idea never occurred to this Yankee commander of a British survey ship that his country's flag would sometime wave over the most populous and fertile realm which he beheld in his Pacific voyaging.

McClure's expedition was as hazardous as Captain Cook's. Its course lay among bristling coral rocks and savages who knew only enough of white men to bear them a mortal hatred. Time and time again McClure and his officers barely escaped the fate of Captain Cook, who was murdered in 1779 by the fierce natives of Hawaii. Indeed, on the coast of New Guinea the surgeon of the "Panther" was killed in a boat alongside. Not all the discipline and armament of a ship-of-war could save him from the black warriors, whose battle-axes fell like a stroke of lightning.

Delano settled at Canton with the English government for his two years of service, and then sailed in the ship "Eliza" for Europe. But the wars caused the ship to be detained at the Isle of France, or Mauritius, and Captain Delano bought a large Dutch Indiaman of fourteen hundred tons and sixty guns, crossed to India, and engaged in trade along the coast. Returning to the United States, he built a small ship of two hundred tons, the "Perseverance," and sailed from Boston on Nov. 10, 1799, for Cape Horn and the Pacific Ocean. He visited the island of Juan Fernandez, recaptured in a bloody combat a Spanish ship which had been seized by her negro slaves, explored the Galapagos Islands, which he describes at length, went on to Hawaii and to Canton, and thence returned home, circumnavigating the globe. Once again Delano fitted out his well-named "Perseverance" for a voyage to the South Sea and the northwest coast of America. He traded at New Holland and Van Dieman's Land and sailed across the South Pacific to Peru, and across again to Canton. Then he swung once more around the Cape of Good Hope to Boston. The last voyage which he records carried him to St. Bartholomew in the West Indies, where the "Perseverance" was seized by the Swedish officials for some technical infraction of law, but Captain Delano escaped by boldly running the batteries.

This career of an American shipmaster of a century ago is summarized here not because it is extraordinary, for it is not, but because Amasa Delano happened to leave a narrative of his lifework which illustrates in a straightforward way the experiences of hundreds of American shipmasters. Neither his perils nor his achievements surpassed those of his comrades. His wanderings were as eventful as those of Ulysses, but they were just the life which might have been expected by any stout-hearted Yankee lad who a hundred years ago sailed out of one of our ports for deep-sea voyaging. Without suspecting it those brave fellows were weaving an epic of their own.

Another of these bold merchant navigators of the old time was Captain Richard J. Cleveland, a kinsman in an earlier generation of ex-President Grover Cleveland. Richard Cleveland was born two years before the Revolution in the town of Salem, Mass. Both heritage and environment impelled a Salem boy of that day to turn to the sea for his career. At fourteen Richard entered the counting-room of the great merchant, Elias Hasket Derby, as a clerk. This was the customary beginning. Youths of promise were carefully trained to methods of business before they were sent out to learn the rough trade of the sea. At eighteen Cleveland made his first voyage as captain's clerk to Nathaniel Silsbee, his senior in Mr. Derby's counting-room. Captain Silsbee was not twenty years old when he sailed to the Cape of Good Hope and the Isle of France. His chief mate, Charles Derby, was but nineteen, and Cleveland, who became second mate, was a year younger. This voyage, conducted by mere boys, returned to the owner four or five times the amount of the original capital. Those were days of quick fortunes or quick ruin. Captain Silsbee, one of the most remarkable merchant navigators of New England, left his quarterdeck years later to sit in his own counting-room as the head of a great and famous firm, and to become United States Senator from Massachusetts.

Under such tutelage the young Salem sailor grew to manhood. In 1797, when Cleveland had already made one voyage as commander, he found himself at Havre temporarily without a ship. There he resolved upon a venture which for either maritime or mercantile audacity has scarcely an equal in the annals of trade. He bought on two years' credit a little coasting sloop, a mere cockleshell, and started on a voyage around the Cape of Good Hope to the Isle of France, that Mecca of Yankee East Indian navigators. The sloop was blown ashore before she could gain an offing, but, nothing daunted, Cleveland hauled her off and patched her up, and set sail a second time, with a smart Nantucket lad as mate, a cook, one sailor, and two boys. Well did a London journal observe that " surely never before was there an Indiaman with such a cargo and such a crew." Rats gnawed the water casks, and Cleveland was compelled to run in to the Cape of Good Hope to re-fill them. He arrived there on March 21, 1798, three months out from Havre, a rather long passage, which Captain Cleveland with the instinctive pride of the Salem mariner attributes to " very unfavorable winds." A less resolute spirit would have found the true cause in his flimsy cockleshell, which was fitter for a canal than for the tremendous swing of the waves of the South Atlantic. So small and fragile was this craft, so boyish her master and mate, and so improbable Cleveland's story, that the British admiral at Cape Town was strongly tempted to seize the whole daring company as French spies. But no pretext could be found to do this, and finally the admiral offered to buy the little sloop for $5,000, considerably more than she was worth or than Cleveland had expected to receive in the Isle of France, his destination. The sloop was taken into the British service and sent to sea in charge of a naval lieutenant. As might have been expected, she went straight to the port of missing ships, and was never afterward heard from.

Captain Cleveland made a profit of a few thousands on this mad voyage, the first of his independent ventures. In August, 1798, he took passage in a Baltimore brig for Batavia, and went thence to Canton, resolved on entering the fur-trade with the northwest coast of America. His capital would not suffice to purchase and equip a vessel of adequate size. It had taken $50,000 of Boston money

eleven years before to fit out the pioneer "Columbia."
Moreover, the northeast monsoon was roaring down from
inhospitable Formosa. So Captain Cleveland repeated
his Havre experience. He secured another small sloop
better adapted than a small square-rigged vessel for working to windward, gathered a crew of "as accomplished
villains as ever disgraced any country," — they were chiefly
runaways from European men-of-war and Indiamen, — and
sailed from Canton on Jan. 10, 1799, giving a wide berth
to the fleet off Macao, "lest some of his men might be
reclaimed by the ships from which they had deserted." [1]

For three weeks the sloop beat up in boisterous weather
against the monsoon, constantly swept by the seas, until the
crew, worn out by work and exposure, broke into open
mutiny. It was a terrible situation, — a crowd of angry
and murderous renegades forward, and aft the iron-nerved
young captain, and a few men who remained loyal. The
stage of this marine drama was a reeling deck perhaps
twenty feet wide and fifty long. Cleveland had two four-
pounders, mere popguns. But he loaded these with grape-
shot, armed each of his retainers with a musket and brace
of pistols, and grimly warned the mutineers that if they
passed the main hatch they would be blown into eternity.
For a whole day the sloop sailed thus, a howling, blas-
pheming gang of cutthroats, threatening Captain Cleveland
with destruction, and yet afraid to face the open-mouthed
guns by which there stood men with lighted matches.
Finally Cleveland put the worst of the mutineers ashore,
and sailed on without them. On February 10, he weathered
the north point of Formosa, and on March 30 anchored in
Norfolk Sound. The voyage of that tiny craft across
five thousand miles of the wintry North Pacific was an
appalling test of human endurance. The watch on deck
never escaped a drenching, and there was neither warm
food nor dry clothing for the exhausted men when they

[1] "Voyages of a Merchant Navigator," edited by H. W. S. Cleveland.

went below, for the same seas which poured over them smothered the galley fire.

Cleveland took the precaution of building a bulwark all around the sloop so that the treacherous Northwest Indians should not discover the weakness of the little ship and her company. He frequently met war canoes longer than his own vessel. Once the sloop went aground on a reef, but floated with the rising tide before the savages could discover her misfortune. After two months of trading and incessant watchfulness Cleveland gathered about two thousand of the cherished otter skins. Then he returned to China *via* the Hawaiian Islands, arriving at Whampoa on Sept. 15, 1799, with a fur cargo valued at $60,000. Cleveland sold his sloop, but went in her as a passenger with a cargo of teas to Calcutta, dodging in the Malacca Straits a Malay proa-fleet manned by a thousand pirates.

At Calcutta Captain Cleveland embarked in a third small-boat adventure. He bought a twenty-five-ton pilot boat and sailed in her across the Indian Ocean to the Isle of France. Old Commodore Biddle, who himself knew the meaning of bravery and seamanship, wrote to Captain Cleveland years after : " Your voyages from Havre to the Cape of Good Hope, from Canton to the northwest coast, and from Calcutta to the Isle of France, could have been undertaken and performed by none other than a New England man. They reflect credit upon the American name and character."

But these cockleshell voyages, bold and spectacular though they were, were really only the preliminaries to the serious work of Captain Cleveland's lifetime. He had met in Port Louis a remarkable man, William Shaler, who years afterward won wide fame as Consul-General at Algiers. The two friends went from the Isle of France to Europe in a Danish Indiaman, and at Hamburg purchased a fast American brig, the " Lelia Byrd " of Portsmouth, Virginia, one hundred and seventy-five tons' burden. They

tossed a copper for the captaincy. It fell to Mr. Shaler.
Together these young and brilliant men then set out on
a romantic voyage around the world, taking as a guest a
Polish nobleman, the Count de Rouissillon, who had
been Kosciusko's aide-de-camp and was living in exile at
Hamburg.

For two and a half years this voyage lasted. At Valparaiso Cleveland and his comrades were detained and
imprisoned by the Spanish authorities who made a practice
of robbing American merchant ships that were rash enough
to enter their unfriendly waters. Escaping from Valparaiso, the " Lelia Byrd " steered northward for Mexico.
Rouissillon was left at San Blas in charge of a quantity
of goods, and the brig went on to San Diego, California.
Here the Spaniards and the Yankees clashed again, and
Cleveland was compelled to fight his way out of the harbor, silencing the Spanish fort very handsomely with his
six three-pounder guns. Thirty years afterward, Richard
H. Dana, visiting the coast on the voyage immortalized in
"Two Years Before the Mast," found that San Diego and
the neighboring ports and missions still had a lively
memory of Cleveland's exploit. From California the brig
crossed over to Hawaii, taking the first horses ever seen
in the Sandwich Islands. These quadrupeds were viewed
with fear and reverence by the natives, who had never
seen an animal larger than a pig. The "Lelia Byrd"
reached Canton on Aug. 29, 1803. Here Cleveland left
the brig to his partner Shaler, and sailed as a passenger in
the ship " Alert " for Boston.

What the sailor's calling then meant in separation from
home and all news of home is vividly shown in Cleveland's
experience. He reached Boston on May 13, 1804, after an
absence of " seven and a half long years," as he writes in
his journal. His father, a seaman like himself, had died
two years before the belated tidings came to the son at
Canton. In those seven and a half years young Cleve-

land had twice circumnavigated the globe, he had performed three of the most audacious small-ship voyages on record, he had started from Havre with a capital of $2,000, and now came back to Salem with $70,000, — a thirty-five-fold increase in seven years. Seventy thousand dollars was then a fortune, when a Salem merchant who had accumulated a million was reckoned the richest man in the United States. Captain Cleveland gave up the sea forever, as he believed, and retired to an estate in Lancaster.

But the enterprises of his partner Shaler went ill, and their gallant and lovable comrade, Rouissillon, found in far-away Mexico the death which he had courted in vain on the battlefields of Poland. So Captain Cleveland went down to the sea again. He purchased a Baltimore clipper schooner, the "Aspasia," of one hundred and seventy tons, and sailed from New York in the summer of 1806 for the Pacific. Off the Brazil coast the "Aspasia" was dismasted. At Rio Janeiro, Cleveland re-rigged her as a brig, with the comment that "nothing can be so unwieldy, unsafe, and uncomfortable as so large a vessel rigged as a schooner." What would this old-time mariner say now of schooners of two thousand tons which could almost swing his "Aspasia" at their davits? Cleveland chartered a Portuguese ship at Rio Janeiro, and, turning the "Aspasia" over to his first mate, sailed in the "Telemaco" for Havana. But the ship was seized off Martinique by Admiral Cochrane's squadron, on one of the flimsiest of the pretexts through which the British were then harrying neutral commerce; and as the "Aspasia" and her cargo were also a total loss homeward bound, Captain Cleveland met a crushing double disaster.

After several futile efforts to recruit his fortunes, Cleveland, in the winter of 1809-10, sailed in the schooner "Maria" for Naples. It had been proclaimed by Napoleon that Naples was again open to the commerce of the world. But when thirty or more American vessels had entered the trap, it was sprung upon them. The ships were seized, and they and their cargoes confiscated. Thus were the neutral merchants and seamen of America plundered on either side of the world. For several years Cleveland stayed in Europe engaged in trading and shipping under several flags and to many ports. Here he remained during the War of 1812, and then, coming home, made an East India voyage in the ship "Exeter."

Captain Cleveland's last voyage and perhaps his most important occurred in 1817, when he persuaded John Jacob Astor of New York to send him out in command of the "Beaver" to Chile. This favorite ship of Mr. Astor, (mentioned in Irving's " Astoria ") had just been repaired and was valued with her cargo at nearly $200,000, a sum which nobody in America save Mr. Astor could then risk on a single voyage. Spanish greed again wrecked American enterprise. The " Beaver " was seized as soon as she reached the Chilean coast, and released only after some vigorous threats from one of our men-of-war and some ingenious diplomacy of Captain Cleveland. But the main purpose of the voyage was ruined.

Captain Cleveland never accumulated great wealth. He seems to have had far more than his rightful share of the frowns of fortune, but an indomitable Yankee pluck sustained him to the end of his active career. It is a proud record that in all his arduous service he lost but three men out of his many crews, — two by fever in the East Indies and one by a fall from a masthead. Moreover, although most of his voyages were very long ones, he was never compelled to put his men on short allowance of food or water, and his ships were never visited by the scurvy, — that scourge of old deep-sea navigation. In a time when the use and even the abuse of alcoholic stimulants were almost universal, Captain Cleveland never drank a glass of wine or liquor of any kind, and he never used tobacco. American shipmasters were always more temperate as a rule than

their comrades of other nations, but in the early years of
the nineteenth century total abstainers on shipboard were
few and far between. Captain Cleveland died in 1860 at the
ripe age of eighty-seven. As his long life had witnessed
the brilliant expansion of American merchant shipping,
so it saw in its last years the beginning of the melancholy
decline.

Nowadays when a merchant captain makes port in Montevideo, Sydney, or Yokohama, he has but to step up to the
cable office to find instructions from his owners almost as
minute as they might hand to one of their clerks in the
next room. The ocean telegraph controls the captain like
a magic tow-line, and leaves him responsible, in the main,
for nothing but the safe navigation of his ship. And the
elaborate charting of even the most distant seas, the
multiplication of lighthouses, beacons, and buoys, the improvement in nautical instruments, and the introduction
of steam have made the art of navigation very much easier
and more exact than it was when Cleveland, Delano, and
their comrades knew and practised it. The modern shipmaster does not need to be a merchant; he does not need to
be an explorer; he does not need to be either a fighting man
or a diplomatist. It is enough if he is a sailor pure and
simple. But the old masters were compelled to be all these
things. From the time the ship got under way until she
swung alongside her owner's wharf again on her return, the
captain was the most absolute of monarchs. His word
was law to his ship's company, and the whole fate of the
voyage was in his keeping.

It was the custom for a long time to allow to the master
a certain space in the ship for goods of his own. He was
not only permitted but encouraged to make his own mercantile ventures, — the theory, of course, being that if he
had a direct personal interest in the ship and her voyage, he
would be more likely to be faithful and vigilant. So a
captain's importance was not to be measured by his salary.

That, indeed, was often a minor factor.   If he were a shrewd and thrifty man, the profit of his own personal speculations would far exceed the wages of his professional service. Thus the old-time captains were enabled liberally to provide for their families, and at the same time to make a start toward becoming shipowners themselves.   To this day this ancient custom survives in the American merchant service to the extent at least of allowing and encouraging the master of a Maine or New York sailing ship to possess a share in the vessel known as the "captain's interest."   In the service of the steam lines, however, the captain of a ship, as a rule, is an employee of the corporation, and nothing more.

But the salary of a modern steamer captain is far greater than the wages of any shipmaster of the last years of the eighteenth and the early years of the nineteenth century. Congress, in 1794, fixed the pay of a captain in the naval service at $75 a month, or $900 a year, and many of the best merchant captains of the period eagerly sought even the commission of a lieutenant who received $40 a month, or somewhat less than $500 a year.   Now a naval captain is paid $4,000 a year; the merchant captain of a first-class ocean liner, $5,000; the captain of a large steamer or important sailing ship, from $1,500 upward.

There are good men in all these services.   In courage and fidelity there has been no falling off among American ship captains since the time of the old merchant navigators. The great fundamental qualities of the race have not changed.   If modern captains are less versatile than the old, it is simply because their calling, like so many other callings, has under modern conditions become more highly specialized, and because there is now not so wide a range of demands upon their skill and judgment.

CHAPTER VII

IMPRESSMENT AND EMBARGO. 1801-15

Jefferson's Cautious Course — Playing War with the Barbary Pirates — Preble fights in Earnest — England, France, and the "Rule of 1756" — Decrees and Orders in Council launched against our Neutral Merchantmen — Yankee Seamen kidnapped into the British Fleet — The "Leander" and the "Richard" — the "Leopard" and the "Chesapeake" — Our Retaliation in the Embargo of 1807 — More Harmful to Us than to Our Enemies — Napoleon's Trap sprung on American Vessels — The Day of Retribution — War declared against Great Britain — Brilliant Work of Armed Merchant Ships as Privateers — Impressment shot to Pieces — Our Tonnage, 1801-15

To the American sailor of a hundred years ago the characteristic perils of the sea — far greater then than now — must have often seemed only the minor dangers of his calling. His chief risk came not from the fury of the elements, but from the arrogance, greed, or treachery of mankind. The early years of the nineteenth century, from the close of our naval war with France, in 1801, to the close of our second war with England, in 1815, were a period of almost barbaric lawlessness upon the ocean.

International obligations, maritime rules and customs, were trampled under foot in the long, fierce death-grapple of Napoleon Bonaparte and the British government. The United States held aloof from this combat, which was probably wise, but it won the contempt as well as the hatred of both combatants by its obvious unreadiness to assert its neutral rights and especially to protect its sailor-citizens. Washington had believed in a strong seagoing navy; so had Adams.   When Jefferson became President, the fine fleet of frigates and sloops which the brief war with France had given us was reduced to a skeleton, and the national defence was committed to a preposterous flotilla of smooth-water gunboats, which accorded more nearly than our stout thirty-eights and forty-fours with Jefferson's ideas of democratic simplicity.   These craft proved worthless in the War of 1812.   They were so light of draught as to be unseaworthy; so cramped that life aboard was torment to their officers and crews; so overloaded with their one or two heavy guns that quickness or precision of fire was impossible.   Practical sailors everywhere derided this odd armada of the sage of Monticello, and England and France quickly recognized that a merchant marine thus protected was not protected at all.

Nor were these great wrestling giants the only eager foes of American commerce in the troublous first decade of the last century.   Tribute of money, guns, powder, naval stores, and even complete warships had failed to appease the Dey of Algiers, and had inflamed the jealousy of the sea-thieves of the other Barbary States.   Tunis demanded her share, and when she received it, Jessuf Karamauli, Bashaw of Tripoli, sent an impudent demand to President Adams.   The reply was not satisfactory.   On May 14, 1801, the Bashaw cut down the flagstaff of the American consulate, thus declaring war in characteristic Turkish fashion upon the United States.   A swarm of corsairs was at once let loose upon the American merchant ships bound to and from the north shore of the Mediterranean, while two cruisers of considerable force were sent to seize American vessels at the Straits of Gibraltar, or even outside in the Atlantic.

A keen surprise awaited these over-greedy Tripolitans. As they lay at Gibraltar on July 1, 1801, watching, like two hawks, for the white wings of unsuspecting Yankee traders, four Yankee ships came in, but not just the vessels for which the Turks were looking. They were the stately forty-four-gun frigate "President," the thirty-six-gun "Philadelphia," the thirty-two-gun "Essex," and the twelve-gun schooner "Enterprise," sailing under the broad pennant of Paul Jones's old lieutenant, Commodore Richard Dale. The "Philadelphia" was ordered to blockade the two corsairs. She kept so merciless a watch that the Tripolitan admiral, a renegade Scotchman, despaired of escape, dismantled his ships, and stole away in boats with his robber crews across the Straits and overland to Tripoli.

Commodore Dale's squadron had been sent out in May from home, when war was seen to be probable, if not inevitable. But President Jefferson's love of "strict construction" had tied the hands of the fighting executive of the "Bon Homme Richard." Jefferson saw that he must do something to save American merchant ships from seizure, and their crews from the awful fate of Moorish slavery. It appealed to his thrift that as Madison, his Secretary of State, had shrewdly argued, the frigates were part of the peace establishment, and "the expense of sending them abroad would not be much larger than the cost of keeping them at home." But Jefferson's horror of war was exceeded only by his worship of the Constitution. He believed that the power to make war was a prerogative of Congress, and that without formal declaration a state of war could not exist, though a Turkish despot hewed down forty flagstaffs and filled his dungeons with the crews of plundered American ships. Brave old Dale was thereupon ordered not to make war or to take a prisoner, but to content himself with a "spirited defence." When the "Enterprise" captured a Tripolitan polacre, the pirate craft was neither kept nor destroyed. Her guns were thrown overboard, and she was left to find her way back to Tripoli to refit and sail on another cruise against Yankee merchantmen.

This was interpreted as "a defensive act and no violation of the orders of the President." But how it must have fretted the stout soul of the fighting commodore!

Dale's squadron was strong enough to afford much protection to American commerce, if it had not been hampered by these restrictions. Jefferson's prudence accorded ill with the bold and enterprising spirit of his country's merchant marine. These orders to Commodore Dale were the first token that American merchants and sailors could look for no effective support to their government so long as Jefferson controlled it. These orders were the earliest of a series of grave blunders in our maritime policy, of which the embargo of 1807 was the chief and most memorable example.

Congress, in 1801, realized that the war with the African corsairs must be pushed more vigorously than Jefferson had permitted. An Act was passed not declaring war, but giving the President express authority to maintain a squadron in the Mediterranean, and to seize and destroy the ships and property of the Barbary Powers. More frigates were sent out. Commodore Dale, whose orders had brought him home in December, 1801, was succeeded by Commodore Morris. Still the conduct of the war remained over-cautious. American merchantmen, bound into or out of the Mediterranean, were given convoy between Gibraltar and Leghorn, or Malta. A few corsairs were captured or blockaded. But no direct attack was made on Tripoli. In 1803 Morris was recalled.

Commodore Preble, who relieved him, was almost an ideal leader for this difficult service. His officers and crew had a chance to learn his metal soon after his flagship arrived in the Mediterranean. The "Constitution" fell in with a strange ship one black night in the Straits of Gibraltar. Preble's hail was evasively replied to, while both ships adroitly manœuvred for the weather gage. Preble now shouted, —

"I hail you for the last time. If you don't answer, I'll fire into you. What ship is that?"

Back came the words, —

"His Britannic Majesty's eighty-four-gun ship-of-the-line 'Donegal.' Send a boat on board!"

This was a situation in which many an officer would have flinched. Not so this Yankee commodore. In quick reply he thundered, —

"This is the United States forty-four-gun ship 'Constitution,' Captain Edward Preble, and I'll be —— if I send a boat on board any ship. Blow your matches, boys!"

Preble had no need to fire, but he stood by the stranger all night, and when day broke, he discovered that she was not the great "Donegal" after all, but the thirty-two-gun British frigate "Maidstone," which, caught unprepared by the "Constitution's" swift approach, had resorted to a marine stratagem to gain time to get her men to their battle-stations. But the incident warmed the hearts of the "Constitution's" crew toward their strange, gruff commander.

Preble struck right at the pirate nest itself. On his way to Tripoli he visited Tangiers, and frightened the Emperor of Morocco into surrendering his American prisoners. Then Preble did with the "Constitution" what no frigate was supposed to be able to endure. He steered right into the harbor of Tripoli, deliberately shortened sail, with the men on the yards, and opened his broadsides at short range on the formidable batteries, mounting one hundred and fifteen heavy guns and manned by twenty-five thousand Turkish soldiers. This was the work of a line-of-battleship, but the "Constitution" performed it as safely and successfully as she did everything else she undertook.

This blockade and bombardment of Tripoli lasted several months. It was arduous and perilous duty, and it was illuminated by some of the most famous deeds of heroism

7

in all the records of the sea service of the United States. The exploit of Decatur in burning the wrecked and captured "Philadelphia," the noble self-sacrifice of Somers, the desperate hand-to-hand fighting with the Turkish gunboats, the terrific gunnery of the "Constitution," brought the proud Bashaw to terms. "These Americans fight like lions," he exclaimed. He signified his desire for peace, and on June 3, 1805, he signed a treaty relinquishing all claim of tribute from the United States. Meanwhile British "diplomacy" had been encouraging another Barbary despot, the Bey of Tunis, to declare war upon American commerce. On Aug. 1, 1805, Captain John Rodgers and a squadron of thirteen sail appeared off Tunis, and gave the astonished Bey thirty-six hours to accept terms of peace. They were promptly accepted. Not until the War of 1812 offered British agents another chance to employ their peculiar methods with the Barbary Powers, was American commerce again seriously harassed in the Mediterranean.

The cost of this distant war had been heavy, but it was worth every dollar of it in increased security to our ocean-carrying, and increased experience to our naval officers and men. The contest with the Barbary pirates was the hard school which trained the captains and lieutenants of our victorious frigates and sloops of 1812–15, and for the time being American merchantmen were safe from the Turkish rovers. This relief was all the more welcome because of the vastly more powerful enemies with whom they were now forced to contend.

England and France had been at war with each other almost continuously since 1793. The rise of Napoleon gave the struggle an intensity, almost a ferocity, scarcely equalled since the Middle Ages. Both combatants seized every device, lawful or unlawful, that promised injury to the warlike or commercial resources of the other. In this baleful rivalry, from which the United States was destined to be the sharpest sufferer, England took the initiative by her enforcement of a principle known as the "Rule of 1756." It was the general eighteenth-century custom to treat the trade of a colony as the absolute monopoly of the mother-land. England, France, Spain, and other countries which had colonies in the West or East Indies, or elsewhere, forbade the carrying of merchandise to their colonies under any other flag than their own, or the carrying of foreign merchandise to their colonies under even their own flag. Moreover, the products of these colonies could not be exported to foreign countries unless they were first brought to the mother country. So long as the colony-holding nations had merchant ships of their own and access to the sea, this exclusive policy was practicable. But it happened that in 1756, during that mighty struggle known in America as the French and Indian, or the Old French War, France, through repeated defeats, lost so many of her warships that she could no longer protect her merchant ships, and thereby lost the means of trading with her colonies. She could neither carry her goods to them nor bring their goods to Europe. In this extremity France opened her ports under certain limitations to neutral ships, and thus saved her colonies and herself from the commercial paralysis which would otherwise have followed England's absolute supremacy at sea.

When the neutral vessels of Spain, Portugal, and Holland accepted the French invitation and entered the ports of the French colonies, England saw that she must crush this neutral trade, or lose much of the advantage of her hard-won ocean victories. Her cruisers were ordered to seize these neutral ships. They did so, and the Admiralty Court justified the seizure on the opportune though original plea that the neutral vessels had become French by adoption. In other words,[1] the "Rule of 1756," as the British courts expounded it, is that "a neutral has no

---

[1] "A History of the American People," by John Bach McMaster, vol. iii.

right to deliver a belligerent from the pressure of his enemies' hostilities by trading with his colonies in time of war in a manner not allowed in time of peace."

This Admiralty judgment was destined half a century later to fall with crushing force upon the merchants and seamen of America. It was the foundation of all the savagely retaliatory orders and decrees of the Napoleonic wars. The British government did not enforce the "Rule of 1756" against France, when she became our ally in our War for Independence. It did not then seem worth the while. But in 1793, when France declared war on England and opened French colonial ports to neutral carriers, England immediately bound herself by a treaty with Russia to prevent all neutral trade with France. France retaliated by hostile orders against neutral commerce with England. Thus there were set grinding those two tremendous millstones which in the two following decades spent their main strength upon the American merchant marine.

Even in 1793 the United States was the foremost neutral carrier. Both British and French cruisers began to seize our ships for engaging in a trade which our own law and our interpretation of international law held perfectly legitimate. More than a hundred American ships were under seizure in France in 1793. Congress in retaliation imposed in 1794 the first embargo.[1] It ran for thirty days, and was renewed for another thirty days. Even more vigorous measures were pending when Congress resolved to try peaceful negotiation instead of war. Chief-Justice Jay was sent as minister extraordinary to England, and the famous commercial treaty which bears his name was the outcome. This treaty softened but did not wholly transform England's hostile policy toward our trade and shipping.

[1] Von Holst, "Constitutional and Political History of the United States," vol. i.

As the military genius of Napoleon began to make
France more and more master of Continental Europe,
England's enforcement of the "Rule of 1756" became
more and more severe. In 1799 a British Order in
Council added the colonies of Holland and Spain to the
black list of this rule, and forbade neutral ships, including, of course, American ships, to sail from these colonies
direct to the mother State. War prices for colonial
products soon began to run so high on the Continent that
this prohibited trade — unjustly prohibited, our people
thought — offered irresistible attractions to American
shipowners. They had a right to bring goods from the
Dutch and Spanish colonies to the United States. The
Order in Council did not forbid this. They had also a
right, which the Order in Council did not touch, to re-ex-
port the same goods from their own country to Holland
or Spain. Immediately a large trade sprang up in the
importation of Dutch and Spanish West Indian goods and
their re-exportation to Europe. England saw with chagrin
that the Yankee ships were evading her Order in Council,
and defeating her purpose to destroy the commerce of her
enemies.

English cruisers, if not English courts, were equal to the
emergency. An American ship, the "Polly," bound from
Marblehead to Bilboa, was seized and tried before the High
Court of Admiralty in 1800 on a charge that her cargo
consisted of Havana sugar and Caracas cocoa, destined for
a port in Spain. The owners of the "Polly" admitted
that her cargo came from the Spanish West Indies, and
was being carried to Spain. But they showed that the
goods had been landed and entered at the Custom House
at Marblehead, that the duties had been paid, the ship
repaired, a new insurance effected, a new clearance
secured, and a new voyage begun. The court held that
this was honest importation, and the "Polly" and her
cargo were released.

But the next Yankee ship was not so fortunate, nor was her case exactly parallel. She was the "Mercury," bound from Havana to Charleston, and was searched by a British privateer. As the trade between Havana and Charleston was not prohibited, she was allowed to go on her way rejoicing. But the "Mercury" stopped at Charleston just long enough to get clearance papers for Hamburg. Then she sailed again, and not far off the Carolina coast unluckily fell in with the same privateer. The Lords Commissioners who heard the "Mercury's" case condemned her on the ground that her stop at Charleston was only a pretence, and that the voyage was really direct, and therefore under the ban of the Order in Council. In a third case the British authorities in 1801 held that actually landing goods and paying duty in a foreign country broke the continuity of a voyage and legalized the trade.

This seemed to be sound law and sound sense. But in the intensifying pressure of the Napoleonic wars, both were soon to be forgotten. The treaty of Amiens brought a year or two of peace to distracted Europe. In 1803, however, France and England again sprang at each other's throats, and direct trade between an enemy's colonies and the enemy herself was once more forbidden to American shipowners. The indirect process of importation and re-exportation was still open to them. They assumed [1] that English law of 1800 and 1801 would be English law of 1803 and 1804, and they had the formal judgment of the king, the advocate-general, and the High Court of Admiralty, that landing goods in a neutral country and paying the duty broke the continuity of a voyage and made it legitimate.

American shipowners were soon to have a new realization of the grim exigencies of European politics. The war which began in 1803 was the War of Austerlitz and

[1] McMaster's "History of the American People," vol. iii.

Trafalgar. France, victorious on land, was crushed at sea. She lost her merchant ships as well as her ships of war, but her privateers played havoc with British traders. The result was the quick transfer to neutral flags of the bulk of the commerce of the North Atlantic, and as the United States was almost the only important neutral, ours became the lion's share. It was a harvest time with American shipowners. "In two years," says McMaster, "almost the whole carrying trade of Europe was in their hands. The merchant flag of every belligerent save England disappeared from the sea. France and Holland absolutely ceased to trade under their flags. Spain for a while continued to transport specie and bullion in her own ships, protected by her men-of-war. But this, too, she soon gave up, and by 1806 the dollars of Mexico and the ingots of Peru were brought to her shores in American bottoms. It was under our flag that the sugar trade was carried on with Cuba; that coffee was exported from Caracas and hides and indigo from South America. From Vera Cruz, from Carthagena, from La Plata, from the French colonies in the Antilles, from Cayenne, from Dutch Guiana, from the Isles of France and Reunion, from Batavia and Manila, great fleets of American merchantmen sailed for the United States, there to neutralize the voyage and thence go on to Europe. They filled the warehouses at Cadiz and Antwerp to overflowing. They glutted the markets of Embden and Lisbon, Hamburg and Copenhagen, with the produce of the West Indies and the fabrics of the East, and bringing back the products of the looms and forges of Germany to the New World, drove out the manufactures of Yorkshire, Manchester, and Birmingham."

But over this great maritime trade hung by its storied thread the sword of Damocles. Britain hated our swarming ships with a double hatred, — first, because they threatened her pre-eminence on the seas, and, second, because their activity saved the colonies of her foes from ruin and starvation. Yet, according to the reaffirmed judgment of the highest of British tribunals, this American trade was perfectly legitimate. But it must be crushed, in the interests of the British Empire, and especially of the British navy and British shipowners. This determination once made, a way was soon found to enforce it. The British government began by proclaiming in January, 1804, a blockade of the French West Indian colonies of Guadeloupe and Martinique. This instantly condemned our thriving traffic with these sugar islands. It was followed by a blockade of the Dutch colony of Curaçoa, and in August, 1804, our ships were shut out of central European ports by a proclamation covering the Straits of Dover and the English Channel.

Now, however, a still more potent agency was to be invoked. English law was deliberately to be reversed to suit the wishes and interests of the government. A description has already been given of the trial and acquittal of the "Polly" of Marblehead. In May, 1804, an almost exactly parallel case came before the Lords Commissioners of Admiralty Appeal. It was that of the ship "Essex," of Salem, Marblehead's nearest neighbor. This vessel had been seized on a voyage to Havana. She had come out from Barcelona in Spain to Salem, had landed her cargo there exactly as the "Polly" had done at Marblehead, had given bonds for the payment of the duty, had undergone repairs, and then had received the same cargo and cleared for Havana. The details were almost identical with those of the voyage of the "Polly;" the principle was absolutely the same. The two cases were tried in the same court before the same judge. The owners of the "Essex" and American merchants generally expected the same favorable judgment.

Imagine the surprise and consternation which ran along the seaboard when news came that the British court had condemned the "Essex." The judge, ignoring his former decisions, had laid emphasis on the intent of the owners. He insisted that the cargo was never bought for the American market, but that it was purchased in Spain for export to Cuba in defiance of the Order in Council. Several other American ships speedily met the fate of the "Essex," and hundreds were liable to seizure and confiscation if they fell into the clutches of the British cruisers. To many American merchants and shipowners this extraordinary decision in the case of the "Essex" meant instant ruin. Projected voyages were abandoned, cargoes sold at a loss, and ships laid up or diverted to less profitable service. Here and there an owner, richer or bolder than the others, sent his ships to sea as if the Admiralty decision never had been made. Some ran safely to their destination, but not all were so fortunate.

Monroe wrote to the Secretary of Foreign Affairs in September, 1805, that fifty-six ships, condemned by this decision, were known to have been carried into the ports of England, and as many more into the British West Indian colonies. Protests and memorials from the robbed and angry people of the seaport towns began to pour in upon Congress. They were directed not merely against the principle established by the seizure of the "Essex," but against the fraudulent blockades, the insolent treatment of neutral flags, the impressment of seamen, and the other details of the general policy of English and French maritime warfare, which had become too savage to be borne. It was significant that many of these protests suggested war as a final remedy, although they came from seaboard communities which would have to bear most of the burden and suffer most of the loss of such a conflict.

America's grievance was twofold. Both England and France stole our ships, but England also stole our sailors. Impressment was an old and familiar outrage in 1805. American protests were treated with derision by British

boarding officers and with contempt by the British government.   As belligerents the British had the right to stop
and search neutral merchantmen on the high seas; having
thus got on board of American vessels, they asserted the
right to impress all of the seamen who were or had been
British subjects.   Time and time again Great Britain
refused to make impressment the subject of negotiation.
Our government endeavored to save its sailors by issu-
ing to them certificates of citizenship, or papers of protection.   Some of these papers were doubtless bestowed
upon aliens, who did not deserve them, but they failed to
protect native Americans.   Finally our government sta-
tioned an agent in London to receive and report the
protests of American citizens held under duress in the
British service, and to procure their release.   But even
this plan was only slightly successful.   The cruel discipline of the British navy wreaked vengeance upon American seamen who endeavored to communicate with their
government or their friends.   "The detection of an attempt
to notify an American Consul of the presence of Americans
on board an English ship," says McMaster, "was sure to
be followed by a brutal flogging."   When the American
agent, Silas Talbot, in 1797, took out writs of *habeas
corpus* to rescue Americans from the British squadron in
Jamaica, the Vice-Admiral, Sir Hyde Parker, commanded
his officers to ignore this time-honored expedient of British
civil law.

In 1806 and 1807, as the files of the State Department
show, there were six thousand American seamen serving
against their will in the British fleet.   These were the
men who had been able to declare themselves; how many
there were who could not or dared not make their iden-
tity known can only be conjectured.   This detention of
American seamen from their homes and their country was
not for one cruise only or one year, but often for many
cruises and many years.   The poor fellows would reach

English dockyards after long and weary service, and would see their ship go out of commission, but that meant no relief for them. They would immediately be transferred to an outward-bound ship, without a chance to set foot on shore, and would be forced to sail again on a cruise of two or three years' duration. Meanwhile, the father, mother, wife, or children at home in America would be deprived of a strong man's support, and could not even know whether he were living or numbered with the myriad sailor-dead of storm and battle.

It seems incredible now, but in 1805 and afterward our merchant vessels were stopped and robbed by British ships of war right in our home waters. Two frigates, the "Cambrian" and "Leander," virtually blockaded the port of New York. One of the "Leander's" midshipmen was Basil Hall, afterward celebrated as an author. He has left a lively description of the way in which these frigates played the bully at the gates of the chief port of America: —

"Every morning at daybreak we set about arresting the progress of all the vessels we saw, firing off guns to the right and left to make every ship that was running in heave to or wait until we had leisure to send a boat on board to see, in our lingo, what she was made of. I have frequently known a dozen and sometimes a couple of dozen ships lying a league or two off the port, losing their fair wind, their tide, and, worse than all, their market for many hours, sometimes the whole day, before our search was completed."

Not only the ship's papers but private letters were opened and examined by the boarding parties of these swaggering frigates. If the faintest pretext offered, the ships were seized and sent to Halifax for condemnation. The presence of these frigates off New York was an insult to the whole country, but it was borne with what now seems to be disgraceful patience or feebleness until one spring evening, April 25, 1806, when the sloop "Richard" from Brandywine for New York, coming up two miles from Sandy Hook Light and a quarter of a mile from the beach, was fired on by the "Leander." One shot fell just ahead; the other flew right over. At this stern summons the coaster immediately hove to. But a third shot at this moment struck the taffrail and cut off the head of the man at the helm, John Pierce, brother of the captain.

When the "Richard" next morning reached New York, she kindled a flame like that which blazed up out of the red snow of the Boston massacre. Poor Pierce's mangled body was laid in state in City Hall, and was soon surrounded by thousands of citizens, cursing Great Britain and demanding vengeance. The funeral was made a great public demonstration. The boats of the frigates were chased out of the bay when they came in for supplies, and a few British officers on shore were driven into hiding. The grand jury indicted[1] the captain of the "Leander" for murder. New York's rage was repeated in every town and village where the tragedy of the "Richard" was told. On May 3 President Jefferson not unwillingly issued a proclamation closing the ports and harbors of America forever to the frigates and their commanders, and ordering the arrest of Captain Whitby, wherever he might be found in United States jurisdiction.

The slaying of this humble Yankee sailor was a bad day's work for the British navy and the British government. It did more than all the years of impressment to shock the whole American people into realizing that such an attack upon an American merchant vessel was an attack upon the integrity and honor of the nation. These things were only dimly perceived in the early years of the nineteenth century. Patriotism was not then the passion which it has since become.

Just as the murder of Pierce had focussed attention

[1] "History of the United States," by Henry Adams, vol. iii.

everywhere in this country on the American ship and the American sailor, the British government, in May, 1806, issued a new Order in Council, which dealt one more sharp blow at our ocean-carrying. This order proclaimed a blockade of the whole coast of Europe between the river Elbe and the port of Brest. The coast between Ostend and the Seine had already been blockaded, and neutral ships were forbidden to enter there on any condition. They could enter the other ports between the Elbe and Brest only if they carried neutral or British cargoes. This filled American merchants and shipowners with a fear of worse things to come. They did not have long to wait. Napoleon was crushing Prussia as he would an eggshell. On Oct. 14, 1806, he won the victory of Jena, and a few days later he made his triumphal entry into Berlin. Here, in the capital of his conquered foe, he dated, on Nov. 21, 1806, a famous decree which fell like a thunderbolt upon American commerce.

This Berlin decree was Napoleon's characteristic retaliation for the British Order in Council. It declared a blockade of the whole coast of England, Ireland, Scotland, and Wales, though Napoleon knew that he had no navy to enforce it. It was a paper blockade, but it made American ships which touched at ports in England the lawful prey of French privateers. Such ships were forbidden to enter any port or colony of France. All intercourse with the British Isles was absolutely prohibited, and neutral ships endeavoring to evade the decree were condemned to confiscation. Neutral ships in Napoleon's mind meant American ships, for the United States was the only nation having a merchant fleet that had not been drawn into the maëlstrom of the great European war.

Meanwhile, Congress had not been inactive. As early as February, 1806, Jefferson's friend Nicholson had introduced a Non-Importation Bill, aimed to strike England for her persistent warfare on American commerce. This bill prohibited the importation of British manufactures which might be procured of other nations or produced at home, — leather, brass, woollens, silk, glass, silver and plated ware, paper, etc. The debate over this bill was a memorable contest. It disclosed a strange line of division. The South, which had few ships and few sailors, figured as the eager champion of our merchant marine, and aggressive action was strenuously opposed by shipowning New England.

This would be incomprehensible but for the peculiar conditions of party politics. America, in 1806, was still intensely provincial. Her people, without realizing it, were divided not so much over purely American affairs as over the tremendous war in Europe. Jefferson's weakness for France made his fellow-Republicans virtually a French party, while the law of contraries and a large and potent mercantile interest made the Federalists admirers of everything English and fierce haters of the "upstart" Napoleon.

Thus it happened that the agricultural South was eager to protect the American ship, even to the extremity of commercial non-intercourse, while the trading North looked supinely on and seemed willing that its ships should be seized and its men impressed, if only it were not wholly denied the right to sail the seas for dollars. On neither side was there disinterested statesmanship. It was not a proud era in our national history. The time had come to fight for "free trade and sailors' rights." But the Republican party would not fight; it would only proclaim and legislate. The Federalist party, badly smitten with Anglomania, would do neither.

Nicholson's Non-Importation Bill was promptly passed. It was not to take effect, however, until toward the close of 1806. But it did not swerve the British government by a single hair's breadth. Another Order in Council proclaimed that "no vessels shall be permitted to trade from one port to another, both of which ports shall belong to or be in the possession of France or her allies." As Napoleon now dominated all of the Continent except Sweden, this new order meant in practice that American ships could no longer engage in European carrying. Now it was Napoleon's turn to grind the hapless American shipowner. He dated his Milan decree on December 17 from another of his conquered capitals. This directed the confiscation of all neutral ships which accepted British protection and paid British duties. It was a sharp dilemma which the American shipowner now found before him. If he complied with the Order in Council he collided with the Milan decree, and made himself liable to seizure by a French cruiser. If he ignored the Order in Council, a British cruiser would capture, and British courts condemn him. What trade, then, was safe for an American ship?

But worse still was coming. The American Non-Importation Act had scarcely gone into operation when, in December, 1807,[1] London newspapers brought tidings of another blow at American commerce. It was a royal proclamation of October 17, requiring all British officers to enforce the right of impressment to its full extent against neutral merchant ships. This was England's answer to our long years of protest. President Jefferson recognized that the Non-Importation Act was too mild a remedy for the new and critical situation.

The latest English packets had brought startling tidings that still more savage attacks upon American commerce were in contemplation. Jefferson called his Cabinet together on December 17, and submitted a message, urging Congress to authorize a complete embargo upon American shipping in the foreign trade. If he could not protect American ships and sailors on the high seas, he could, at least, he thought, save them by keeping them

---

[1] The Non-Importation Act was postponed for a year in its practical effect, pending efforts at negotiation in London.

at home. In this famous embargo message Jefferson said: —

"The British regulations had before reduced us to a direct voyage to a single port of their enemies, and it is now believed they will interdict all commerce whatever with them. A proclamation, too, of that government (not officially, indeed, communicated to us, yet so given out to the public as to become a rule of action with them), seems to have shut the door on all negotiation with us, except as to the single aggression on the Chesapeake. The sum of these mutual enterprises on our national rights is that France and her allies, reserving for future consideration the prohibiting our carrying anything to the British territories, have virtually done it by restraining our bringing a return cargo from them; and Great Britain, after prohibiting a great proportion of our commerce with France and her allies, is now believed to have prohibited the whole. The whole world is thus laid under interdict by these two nations, and our own vessels, their cargoes, and crews, are to be taken by the one or the other for whatever place they may be destined out of our limits. If, therefore, on leaving our harbors, we are certainly to lose them, is it not better as to vessels, cargoes, and seamen, to keep them at home?"

This acute line of reasoning won Congress at once. John Quincy Adams lost his seat in the Senate for deserting his party to sustain Jefferson. "The President has recommended this measure on his high responsibility," said Mr. Adams, in words that have survived the years. "I would not consider, I would not deliberate, I would act."[1] The reluctant spirit of New England had been better reflected by Josiah Quincy some time earlier, when he begged the House to remember that the ocean could not be abandoned by his people, "of whom thousands

[1] "Thomas Jefferson," by John T. Morse, Jr., in American Statesmen Series.

would rather see a boat-hook than all the sheep-crooks in
the world." "Concerning the land of which the gentleman from Virginia and the one from North Carolina think
so much, they think very little. It is, in fact, to them
only a shelter from the storm, a perch on which they
build their eyrie and hide their mate and their young,
while they skim the surface, or hunt in the deep." This
was an apt tribute to the indomitable seafarers not of New
England only, but of the whole coast-line. Such pleas
could not prevail, however, against Jefferson's sugges-
tion that an embargo was essential to the saving of the
sailors themselves. He sent his message to Congress on
Dec. 18, 1807. On December 22 the embargo had passed
both houses.

This is one of the most interesting and important Acts
of the American Congress. It was a war measure, or a
measure which should never be resorted to save in anticipation of war. But Jefferson pressed it upon the country
as an alternative to the war which he abhorred. At first
it was immensely popular. The national feeling against
England, kindled by the murder of the "Richard's"
helmsman, was blown to high fury by the "Leopard's"
attack on the "Chesapeake." That occurred on June 22,
1807, off Hampton Roads. The "Chesapeake," which
had just gone to sea on a new cruise, was in no condition to fight, and was surprised and easily overwhelmed
by her heavier antagonist. Of the four deserters from
the British navy taken out of the "Chesapeake" after she
surrendered, three were known to be American citizens.
It was bad enough to have our merchant ships robbed of
their sailors, but to have a national frigate thus insulted
was far deeper humiliation. To the mass of the people
it looked like a deliberate British attempt to break the
national spirit utterly by an aggravated case of the hateful practice of impressment.

If President Jefferson, in the summer of 1807, had

called on Congress to declare war, he would have had a united nation to sustain him. That was the fateful moment. But he let the dread responsibility fall on his successor, Madison, while he busied himself about his safer and easier embargo. The measure was very crudely drawn. Congress had to begin at once to amend and strengthen it. It originally forbade the departure of registered merchant vessels of the United States for any foreign port. But it did not prohibit the coastwise trade from one American port to another. Shrewd coasting skippers immediately took advantage of this to pretend to be blown off the coast and to deliver at Havana, Fort de France, or Surinam, a cargo loaded for Charleston or New Orleans. A supplementary Embargo Act in January forbade coasters to sail, unless bonds had been given to twice the value of ship and cargo, that the goods should be discharged in the United States. Whalers and fishermen were compelled to give bonds to four times their value, and even petty river craft and boats were forced to furnish security that they would not engage in foreign commerce.

American shipping registered for foreign trade fell off sharply from 848,307 tons in 1807 to 769,054 tons in 1808.[1] The loss would have been greater still but for the fact that hundreds of American vessels were absent on foreign voyages when the embargo was passed. Their owners did not wish to bring them home and lay them up in idleness, — for once in an American port they could not go to sea. So they remained abroad, trading from one foreign country to another. Here, in our own waters, in spite of constant evasions, the embargo soon produced a cruel paralysis. The foreign commerce of the United States fell off in 1808 from $246,000,000 to $79,000,000. A British traveller, who visited New York in this same year, described it as like a city stricken by pestilence.

[1] Report of the United States Commissioner of Navigation for 1900.

"The port, indeed, was full of ships," he wrote, "but they were dismantled and laid up; their decks were cleared, their hatches fastened down, and scarcely a sailor was to be found on board. Not a box, bale, cask, barrel, or package was to be seen upon the wharves. Many of the counting-houses were shut up or advertised to be let, and the few solitary merchants, clerks, and porters, and laborers that were to be seen, were walking about with their hands in their pockets. The coffee-houses were almost empty; the streets near the waterside were almost deserted; the grass had begun to grow upon the wharves."

All this paralysis of American trade failed to affect perfidious Albion. Napoleon praised it as "a great and courageous sacrifice," but the merchants of New York, Philadelphia, Baltimore, and Boston looked for some positive profit in the sacrifice, and looked in vain. Soon there began to be murmurings, soon notes of emphatic remonstrance. In Boston a hundred sailors marched in procession to the State House, demanding work or bread. In Philadelphia there was a similar demonstration. In New York the idle tars were fed at the expense of the city, and held under naval discipline. One hundred Massachusetts towns adopted resolutions against the embargo. The Massachusetts Legislature denounced it as unconstitutional. So bitter did the New England hatred of the embargo grow, that General Dearborn was ordered to be ready to put down insurrection. The coast was patrolled by men-of-war and revenue cutters. At Newburyport in Massachusetts, Bath in Maine, and other Northern ports, loaded vessels literally fought their way to sea. The collector and deputy collector at Boston resigned, rather than enforce the obnoxious law. Many other collectors were removed for lack of zeal.

An ingenious Force Act was passed a year after the passage of the embargo. It intensified the popular wrath. McMaster says of this law that "every lad who went out for a day's fishing might have his boat stopped and his lunch-bag searched by any collector who hated his father." The embargo was defied with greater shrewdness and greater determination. Goods were smuggled up the coast to Passamaquoddy Bay in small boats, for export through the British Provinces to England. They were spirited across the Georgia-Florida frontier. A lively illicit trade sprang up between Vermont and Canada. Not until 1809, however, did the Federalists in Congress feel strong enough to attack the embargo and move its repeal. After much debate the embargo was withdrawn in the spring of 1809, and a Non-Intercourse Act was substituted. American tonnage registered for foreign voyages had actually increased from 769,054 in 1808 to 910,059 in 1809,[1] but a great part of this tonnage must have been unemployed and waiting the lapse of the embargo.

The lifting of this ban upon our ocean trade was like the end of a long nightmare to the people of the seaboard. All the way from Maine to Georgia there was frank rejoicing. The Repeal Bill received on March 1 the signature of President Jefferson, whose executive career was closing, and the embargo ended for the most part on March 15. "On that day," says McMaster, "it ceased to be necessary for captains of coasters to load their ships under the eye of an officer of the revenue, and to give bonds that their cargoes would really be landed in the United States. On that day the fishing boats that went out of the Narrows for bluefish and haddock or down the Delaware in search of shad; the market boats that supplied the stalls in New York and Philadelphia; the craft that sailed the waters of bays and rivers, sounds and lakes not adjacent to foreign soil, were free to do so without a clearance. On that day trade was again revived with every foreign port save those of France and England, their colonies, dependencies, and places actually under their flags. With such ports

[1] Report of the United States Commissioner of Navigation for 1900.

there was to be non-intercourse. Nothing could be carried to them. Nothing could be brought away. To go to them was, indeed, a great temptation. The law, therefore, provided that no vessel should clear for any port, foreign or domestic, until a bond had been given that it would not be engaged during the voyage in trade, direct or indirect, with the forbidden places. Should France revoke her decrees, or Great Britain her Orders in Council, the law might be suspended, and trade renewed by proclamation of the President. The law was to continue in force until the end of the next session of Congress, and no longer. At that time, too, the Act laying the embargo, the three supplementary Acts, and the Force Act were all to expire. The day for beginning the next session had just been fixed as the fourth Monday in May. To the hopeful, therefore, it seemed not unlikely that before the leaves were again falling, the streets of the great seaports would once more be noisy with the rumble of loaded carts; that the Exchange would once more resound with the hum of busy merchants; that the books of the coffee-houses, so long unused, would once more be opened for the reports of captains and supercargoes, and that the neutral flag of the United States would once more be seen in the ports of every civilized nation on the globe."

But these bright hopes of reviving commerce were destined to fade away like a mirage. The embargo, indeed, was an acknowledged failure. It was abandoned. In its place, however, came forward the Non-Intercourse Act, and there was no relaxation in the fierce hostility of England and France toward the merchant ships of the republic. The English Minister at Washington did promise that the Orders in Council would be recalled on June 10, 1809, if the United States would renew its trade with His Majesty's dominions. But the Minister, Erskine, was not authorized to make this pledge, and when his government heard of it, it disavowed and recalled him. President

Madison had issued his proclamation, that after June 10 American ships would be free to trade with England and her colonies. Many ships had loaded, and some had gone to sea. England had cancelled some of her Orders in Council, but she had done so only to issue others, blockading the coasts of Holland, France, and Northern Italy. Congress, before it adjourned, now substituted for the Non-Intercourse Act a measure known as Macon's Bill No. 2, which allowed American ships to trade for the time being with any port in the world, but empowered President Madison, "In case either Great Britain or France shall, before the third day of March next, so revoke or modify her edicts as that they shall cease to violate the neutral commerce of the United States," to cut off all intercourse with the persistently hostile power.

Once again, as with the Embargo and the Non-Intercourse Act, America was doomed to cruel disappointment. Neither England nor France cared anything for the paper manifestoes of a young nation that had no line-of-battle-ships. Napoleon, in fact, set a deliberate trap for the swift American merchant ships whose cargoes he coveted. Thiers says [1] that the emperor wrote to the abject Prussian government: "Let the American ships enter your ports. Seize them afterward. You shall deliver the cargoes to me, and I will take them in part payment of the Prussian war debt."

This astonishing proposition was carried out to the letter, and hundreds of unsuspecting American ships became the spoil of international brigandage. In the summer of 1809 and the winter of 1810, when it seemed as if the diplomatic struggle for free trade and sailors' rights might win a peaceful triumph, a great and noble fleet of American merchantmen, long pent up in harbor, loosed sail and sped over the Atlantic. These ships were freighted with a full lading of American produce, and

[1] Thiers, xii. 50.

followed by the fervent hopes and prayers of a multitude of people, merchants, tradesmen, mariners, who saw a chance to recruit the fortunes almost ruined by hateful embargo and non-intercourse. It is one of the bitter memories of the old sea towns from New England southward, that very few of these gallant vessels ever returned. The snare was spread, though neither the waiting ones at home nor the brave ones who trod the stout decks knew it.

Some of these ships steered for the Bay of Biscay, some for the Mediterranean, some for the North Sea, some for the Baltic. On the Baltic vessels the bolt of fate promptly fell. They were seized by Danish privateers, and taken in for condemnation.[1] When John Quincy Adams, the new Minister to Russia, arrived at Christiansand in Norway, Sept. 20, 1809, he found there thirty masters of American vessels, who had thus been robbed of ship and cargo. This was done by desire of Napoleon and order of Davoust. Mr. Adams declared that fifty American vessels, valued at $4,000,000 or $5,000,000, had been confiscated in Norway and Denmark. Many others were seized in Holland and Prussia. Napoleon, pretending to retaliate for the Non-Intercourse Act, which had never injured French shipping, ordered that American vessels in the ports of France, Spain, and Italy be sequestered and sold.

The blow was terrible in its suddenness and completeness. Napoleon estimated the value of his American booty at $2,000,000 in Antwerp, $2,400,000 in Holland, and $1,600,000 in Spain, but in this $6,000,000, the seizures of American ships in Denmark, Hamburg, France, and Italy are not included. A report by the American Consul in Paris to the American Minister, Armstrong, stated that between April, 1809, and April, 1810, fifty-one American ships had been seized in the ports of France,

[1] "History of the United States," by Henry Adams, vol. v.

forty-four in the ports of Spain, twenty-eight in Naples, and eleven in the ports of Holland. These one hundred and thirty-four American ships at $30,000 each — they were probably worth much more — represented a value of $4,000,000. For the $10,000,000 of which Napoleon thus robbed American shipowners and merchants, France twenty years afterward paid $5,000,000 indemnity. But it was too late and too inadequate to restore our despoiled shipping.

It is an instructive, if melancholy fact, that the year 1810 stands as the high water mark of the American merchant marine in foreign trade, as measured by the ratio of tonnage to population. In that year there were registered for deep-sea carrying 984,269 tons of American vessels,[1] the largest total yet attained. Not again until 1843, when the country had three times as many people as it had in 1810, was this merchant tonnage equalled or exceeded. Our deep-sea fleet of 1810 was larger by 164,000 tons than our registered fleet of 1900.

The effect of Napoleon's treachery and greed became instantly apparent. The 984,269 tons of 1810 shrank in 1811 to 768,852. Of course, the impending war with England, and the reluctance of merchants to launch new ships in place of lost ones, contributed to this reduction, but a great part of the more than 200,000 tons cut off from the American register between 1810 and 1811 represents the robber-work of the French government.

It is one of the delicious ironies of history that the helpless and despised American merchant ships which Napoleon and his pro-consuls plundered, proved to be one of the potent agencies which at last drew him to his doom. When at his command American vessels were seized and condemned in Denmark and Norway, the survivors fled further up the Baltic, or the Arctic, and sought asylum in Kronstadt, or Archangel, free ports of the White Czar.

---

[1] Report of United States Commissioner of Navigation.

Napoleon demanded that Alexander exclude these Yankee craft, — they were British smugglers in disguise, and unworthy of Russian hospitality.   But Alexander had saved sufficient spirit from Austerlitz and Friedland to demur to this request.   He would not exclude the American ships. He told Minister Adams: "Our attachment to the United States is obstinate, — more obstinate than you are aware of."   He even admitted American products on favorable terms which discriminated against French products.   Napoleon in rage recalled his Minister, and prepared for vengeance, while the Russian harbors filled with grateful American merchantmen.   As Adams, the historian, says,[1] the American merchant marine was "the rock on which Napoleon's destiny split; for the quarrels which in the summer of 1811 became violent between France and the two independent Baltic Powers — Russia and Sweden — were chiefly due to those omnipresent American ships, which throve under pillage and challenged confiscation."

In August of 1810, Napoleon, through the famous letter of Cadore, had pretended to revoke his Berlin and Milan decrees, and the assurance seemed so complete that President Madison actually issued a proclamation accepting the repeal as valid and convincing.   But once more the United States was shamefully tricked by the desperate gamesters of Europe.   Before the proclamation was six weeks old, news came that American vessels were being sequestered at Bordeaux.

Meanwhile, America and England were plainly drifting toward war.   The London government had ignored the overture or the warning of the Macon legislation, and early in November, 1810, Secretary Gallatin gave formal three months' notice that commercial intercourse with Great Britain would cease, as required by this Act of Congress.   Two British frigates, the "Guerrière" and

---

[1] "History of the United States," by Henry Adams, vol. v.

"Melampus," appeared off Sandy Hook, and resumed the exasperating work of the "Cambrian" and "Leander." They stopped and searched American merchant vessels, maltreated and impressed their seamen, and seized all craft bound to French ports in Europe or the colonies. Meek and long-suffering Thomas Jefferson was no longer President of the United States. Madison's Secretary of the Navy sent Commodore John Rodgers, in the forty-four-gun frigate "President," to watch this insulting blockade of the chief port of a neutral nation. On May 16, 1811, south of New York, at sundown, Rodgers spoke a war vessel which he took in the gathering dusk to be the "Guerrière." He hailed, and received in return an evasive reply and a round shot in his mainmast. The "President's" crew was at quarters; a quick, straight Yankee broadside streamed out of the open ports. After fifteen minutes' firing the British ship was silenced with thirty-two men killed and wounded. The stranger proved to be not the "Guerrière," — she was left for the "President's" sister, "Constitution," — but the twenty-gun ship sloop "Little Belt." The fight was due to a misunderstanding, but it warmed the Yankee blood; it was accepted by the people as honest vengeance for the "Chesapeake."

Once more, in the spring of 1812, Congress resorted to an embargo, but this time it was no blank charge; the gun was shotted. This third embargo was meant frankly as a preparation for war. Madison told the British Minister that though "embargo was not war," the United States was undoubtedly justified in resorting to the extreme measure, for Great Britain was actually waging war on us, and within a month had seized eighteen vessels of a value of fifteen hundred thousand dollars. Congress, in April, laid the embargo for ninety days. It kept American ships in our own ports and saved them from capture, while a swift pilot craft was sent to warn American merchantmen in North Europe that war was impending, and that they must hurry home or lie up abroad in some neutral harbor.

The American sailor's turn had come. This was his battle. President Madison's embargo of June 1 laid all its stress upon British violations of our flag on the high seas, and British robbery of our ships and seamen. This grievance, the insulting presence of British cruisers in our home waters, the exasperating "paper blockades," and the Orders in Council were the counts in the indictment on which Congress acted. This second War for Independence was undertaken primarily for the protection of the American merchant marine. On June 18, 1812, the war declaration was formally passed by Congress, and signed by the President. That was a memorable June. Just the day before, all unknown, a new British Ministry, impressed by the gathering portents of American wrath, had rescinded the Orders in Council. Two days later Napoleon published the first bulletin of his Grand Army, and prepared for that awful march to Moscow. He sought revenge upon the Czar, one of whose crimes was the befriending of American merchantmen. Thus the ships and sailors of the Western republic bore a real and great though inadvertent part in the shattering of Napoleon's empire.

That United States war declaration of June, 1812, was delayed about five years too long for the honor of the nation and the welfare of the merchant shipping for which the war was chiefly fought. The embargo of 1807 had proved worse than worthless. It had probably saved some of our sailors from the press-gangs, but it sent them to the poorhouses instead. It had ruined many of our merchants, and had benumbed the seafaring instinct of the people. It is estimated[1] that the embargo cost 55,000 sailors aggregate wages of $20,000,000 in fifteen months, and 100,000 mechanics and laborers $36,000,000 more in a single year.

[1] "History of the People of the United States," by McMaster, vol. iii.

The ships lost $12,000,000 in net earnings. The national customs revenue shrank from $16,000,000 to a few thousands. One observer declares that 80,000 New England families were $100 poorer in 1809 than in the previous year, because the goods they produced could find no foreign market. The town of Portland, Me., set its share of the loss at $700,000. Thirteen hundred men were imprisoned in New York in 1809 "for no other crime than being ruined by the embargo."

On the other hand, this expedient inflicted very little injury on England or France. The goods which they could not procure from us they now attempted to produce in their own colonies. The American embargo was a genuine blessing to the British merchant marine, which throve as ours dwindled. President Jefferson believed that he was thwarting and angering his country's enemies; he was really playing their own game. Never since 1809 has the word "embargo" had its old, magic charm for the ears of the American people.

The cost of the embargo would have built a fine fleet of line-of-battleships and heavy frigates, and waged a brilliant naval war. But unfortunately Jefferson and his party disliked line-of-battleships, and the declaration of June, 1812, found us with not one two-decked man-of-war afloat, and only half a dozen serviceable frigates. Taking frigates and sloops together, we had in 1812 seventeen national vessels, not one of the first class in power or size, mounting four hundred and forty-two guns, and carrying five thousand men, to match against the thousand ships, the twenty-seven thousand guns and the one hundred and fifty thousand seamen of our great and confident antagonist. America and England in 1812 were the David and Goliath of the ocean. Our little navy did its work valiantly. It won ten out of twelve single-ship actions. The victories of the "Constitution" over the "Guerrière," the "Java," the "Cyane" and the "Levant," of the

"United States" over the "Macedonian," of the "Hornet" over the "Peacock," and of the "Wasp" over the "Frolic" and "Reindeer," the splendid triumphs of Lakes Erie and Champlain, and the gallant defence of the "Essex" are some of the imperishable glories of the nation. But the naval student and historian know what the people do not always remember, that because we had no line-of-battleships, nearly all of our frigates and sloops were finally blockaded by overwhelming squadrons, and that the last frigate which ran the gauntlet, the "President," met with defeat and capture before she could clear the land.

It is as significantly true of the War of 1812, as it is of the War of the Revolution, that it was fought on the sea for the greater part, not by national ships, which were few, but by privateers, which were many. These privateers were usually improvised from merchant vessels; they were always manned by merchant crews. No history of the merchant marine can be complete without at least a brief survey of their exploits.

There were, at least, forty thousand native American merchant seamen at the breaking out of the War of 1812, or enough to man the United States navy eight times over. There was no opportunity for them in the national service, and the independent temperament of most of these Yankee tars would turn, naturally, anyway, to the freer and more gainful, though more perilous, life of privateering. The thoroughgoing Yankee sailor was then, as he is to-day, the *beau idéal* of the ocean rover. He was a consummate master of his calling, a keen lookout, a clever helmsman, bold and active aloft, of iron-like physique, famed the world around for his vigor and endurance. He had his full share of the Yankee characteristic of thriftiness. He could appreciate the profit-sharing plan which made every man and boy of a privateer crew an interested partner in the enterprise. He had a native aptitude for firearms,

large and small, and a wicked predilection for those ugly
tools, the boarding pike and cutlass.

Above all, the Yankee seaman of 1812 was self-reliant.
He learned his trade and lived his life in a world of merciless enemies.   The first thing he realized when, as a boy,
he went to sea, was that if he was to keep out of the
clutches of press-gangs and buccaneers, he must depend
upon himself; that his government could not and perhaps
would not save him.   The British tar had a man-of-war
ever ready to protect him; the Yankee tar probably never
had seen one of the few and rare frigates or sloops that
flew the gridiron ensign.   His own stout heart and steel
nerves and muscles were his only shield and buckler in his
rough knocking about the world.

The net result was a splendid fighting man, often a
little too forceful and aggressive for matter-of-fact naval
discipline, but a perfect privateersman.   Yet real discipline was not lacking in these private armed ships of 1812.
There were instances in which they actually outfought and
took regular British cruisers; and man for man and gun
for gun, they were as superior to British privateers as was
the "Constitution" or the "Wasp" to the stately vessels
that flew the pennant of the king.

These matchless seamen had matchless ships ready to
their hands.   The "right of search" and the practice of
impressment, as enforced by France and England, had set
a tremendous premium upon long legs and lofty canvas.
The result was that the average American merchant ship,
brig, or schooner was fine-lined and tall-sparred beyond all
European precedent.   Our ports were full of these swift
vessels when war was declared.   It was an easy matter to
throw a few more broadside guns aboard, to mount a "long
Tom" eighteen-pounder on a pivot amidships, and to clear
the 'tween decks for hammocks for fifty or a hundred men.
These privateers of 1812 got to sea with amazing rapidity.
Within sixty days after the declaration, one hundred and

fifty of them were harrying British commerce in the North Atlantic.   Meanwhile, only eight warships of the United States had managed to escape from port.

The British blockade of the coast was rigid and unceasing.   It extended from Long Island Sound to the Mississippi.   New England was at first exempted, because of her supposed sympathy with the British cause, but the victories of the "Constitution" and the exploits of the swarm of Northern privateers soon drew a cordon of watchful cruisers across the bay from Halifax to Cape Cod.   The American coasting trade straightway became so hazardous that it was virtually abandoned.   Flour, which sold for $4.50 per barrel in Richmond and $6 in Baltimore, brought $12 in Boston.   Rice, worth $3 a hundred weight in Charleston and Savannah, was worth $12 in Philadelphia.   Coffee doubled in price.   For Hyson tea by the chest $4 a pound was offered.   Salt brought $5 per bushel.   Sugar, which was quoted at $9 a hundred weight in New Orleans in August of 1813, and $21 or $22 in New York, had advanced to $40 in December.   New York's exports fell from $12,250,000 in 1811 to $209,000 in 1814.[1]   The blockade was helped by a last embargo, laid as a distinct war measure on Dec. 17, 1813, and intended especially to prevent disloyal New England shipowners from trading with the country's enemies.

Between the war and the embargo, American ocean-carrying now became almost non-existent.   But our great antagonist was far more vulnerable, and she suffered even worse.   In June, 1813, the British people were paying the famine prices of $58 a barrel for flour, $38 for beef, and $36 for pork, while lumber cost $72 a thousand.   It was this economic distress more than our brilliant victories in a dozen naval duels which brought Great Britain at the last to terms, and this distress was the work less of our national warships than of our priva-

[1] " History of the United States," by Henry Adams, vol. vii.

teers. The regular navy of the United States in the War of 1812 comprised on the ocean only 23 vessels of all classes, mounting 556 guns.[1] These 23 men-of-war captured 254 naval and merchant ships of the enemy. But the Yankee privateers of 1812–15 numbered 517, mounting 2,893 guns. These private-armed ships, nearly all of them merchant ships with merchant crews, took no fewer than 1,300 prizes. The money value of British ships and cargoes captured by our government cruisers in the second War for Independence is estimated at $6,600,000; the money value of ships and cargoes captured by our privateers, at $39,000,000. In this terrible attack upon England's "pocket nerve" our great merchant marine proved six times as potent as our little navy.

The better class of our privateers were very much more successful in their work of commerce destroying than our small regular cruisers of the same tonnage. Nearly all of our navy brigs and schooners that got to sea were pursued and caught by British frigates. Their loss is attributed to an official mania for overloading these smart little craft with heavy batteries. Private enterprise was wiser. The privateers as a rule "ran light." They were thus able to outsail their ponderous foes, and yet, when there was need of fighting, these armed merchant ships rarely failed to whip a Briton of equal power.

The audacity of the Yankee privateersmen was as astonishing as their numbers. The master of a British merchantman, who had been three times captured and as many times recaptured, declared when he reached the shelter of his home port that he had sighted no fewer than ten American privateers in a single voyage. These intrepid adventurers haunted the West Indies. They hung upon the flanks of rich convoys, and cut out the choicest vessels in night and fog, with exasperating defiance of the guardian

[1] "History of American Privateers," by Edgar Stanton Maclay.

line-of-battleships and frigates. But the most dramatic and effective work of the Yankee privateers of 1812–15, was done after the example of Paul Jones and Connyngham, right on the British coast and in the chops of the English Channel. This produced in Britain a comical blending of fury and despondency, which found voice in the memorials of the merchants of Liverpool and other seaport towns. A typical remonstrance is that of the merchants of Glasgow, adopted at a meeting called by public advertisement in September, 1814, under the auspices of the Lord Provost. Scotland's trade had been severely harried, and no less a personage than Sir Walter Scott narrowly escaped being carried off by these indomitable Yankee rovers. The Glasgow meeting unanimously adopted resolutions which read: —

"That the number of privateers with which our channels have been infested, the audacity with which they have approached our coasts, and the success with which their enterprise has been attended, have proved injurious to our commerce, humbling to our pride, and discreditable to the directors of the naval power of the British nation, whose flag, till of late, waved over every sea and triumphed over every rival. That there is reason to believe that in the short space of less than twenty-four months, above eight hundred vessels have been captured by that power whose maritime strength we have hitherto impolitically held in contempt. That at a time when we are at peace with all the world, when the maintenance of our marine costs so large a sum to the country, when the mercantile and shipping interests pay a tax for protection under the form of convoy duty, and when, in the plenitude of our power, we have declared the whole American coast under blockade, it is equally distressing and mortifying that our ships cannot with safety traverse our own channels, that insurance cannot be effected but at an excessive premium, and that a horde of American cruisers should be allowed, unresisted and unmolested, to take, burn, or sink our own vessels in our own inlets, and almost in sight of our own harbors."

What manner of men and of ships these were, that did this bold and telling work, can be gathered from Captain George Coggeshall's story of American privateers, and also from Mr. Maclay's more recent and elaborate history. Captain Coggeshall, like nearly every other officer and man of the thousands who filled the decks and worked the guns of our private cruisers, was a merchant sailor without regular naval training. But every one of these thousands knew that the war was his war; that the nation was fighting at last for the sailor's cause. The privateer was no mere harpy of the deep; it was ready and eager for battle. The famous brig "Chasseur" captured the king's cruiser "St. Lawrence." There were other instances where the royal colors went down before our merchant flag, and there were combats of privateer against privateer almost without number.

These facts are worth remembering, as tokens of the brave and self-reliant spirit that animated the American merchant marine after England and France, by orders and decrees and impressment, had spent long years in an endeavor to crush the enterprise of our merchants and the manhood of their crews. The oppressive policies of the giant powers of Europe and our own embargo may have encouraged sharp practices here and there, and made some American sailors smugglers, and some American shipowners hypocrites. But the merchant marine, as a whole, came out of the long ordeal of 1801–12 sound and honest and brave, to prove its worth in the supreme test of war. Great Britain did not formally renounce impressment in the peace treaty of 1814–15. But the vital truth is, that this injustice was shot to pieces by the broadsides of our few frigates and our many privateers. Never afterward could the "right" to steal sailors from the decks of American ships, and compel them to serve an alien flag, or fight their own flag, be reasserted.

The increase of the American merchant fleet was inevitably much less regular and constant in this turbulent period from 1801 to 1815 than it had been in the period from 1789 to 1800, which has been considered in an earlier chapter. The sharp fluctuations of tonnage faithfully reflect the blows which foreign greed or domestic weakness and folly aimed at the merchant marine. The work of the Barbary pirates is seen to some extent in the shrunken figures of 1802 and 1803; the effect of the Jefferson embargo in 1808. In the year 1811 it was the treacherous seizures of Napoleon which reduced our shipping. In 1812, 1813, and 1814, our ocean-carrying was paralyzed by the British war. Here is the record of our tonnage registered for foreign trade, the value of the trade itself, and the proportions carried in American bottoms from 1801 to 1815, inclusive: —

TONNAGE AND FOREIGN TRADE. 1801–15.

| Year. | Shipping Tons. | Total Foreign Commerce. | Proportion carried in American Ships. | | |
			Imports.	Exports.	Combined Imports and Exports.
1801	630,558	$204,384,024	91.0	87.0	89.0
1802	557,760	148,290,477	88.0	85.0	86.5
1803	585,910	120,466,699	86.0	83.0	84.5
1804	660,514	162,699,074	91.0	86.0	88.5
1805	744,224	216,166,021	93.0	89.0	91.0
1806	798,507	230,946,963	93.0	89.0	91.0
1807	810,163	246,843,150	94.0	90.0	92.0
1808	765,252	79,420,960	93.0	88.0	90.5
1809	906,855	111,603,233	88.0	84.0	86.0
1810	981,019	152,157,970	93.0	90.0	91.5
1811	763,607	114,716,832	90.0	86.0	88.0
1812	758,636	115,557,236	85.0	80.0	82.5
1813	672,700	49,861,017	71.0	65.0	68.0
1814	674,633	19,892,441	58.0	51.0	54.5
1815	854,295	165,599,027	77.0	71.0	74.0

CHAPTER VIII

THE YANKEE WHALEMEN

Bold Pioneers of Cape Cod, Long Island, and Nantucket — Havoc of
the Revolutionary War — The First South-Sea Whalers — A True
Co-operative Industry — Hardships, Perils, and Triumphs of the
Calling — Porter and his Exploits in the Pacific — Rapid Growth
after the War of 1812 — Ventures to Japan and the Arctic —
Three-fourths of the World's Whaleships American — Burke's
Famous Tribute — Strange Fate of the Whaler " Essex " —
Tragedies and Hairbreadth Escapes — Great Profit of Successful
Voyages — Whaling at its Zenith — Ruinous Work of the " Shen-
andoah " — Disaster in the Frozen North — An Almost-Vanished
Industry — Risk and Cost too Heavy, Whales too Few — Whale-
Ship Tonnage for a Hundred Years

MORE than two centuries ago, in the year 1690, when
King Philip's War had left the New England colonists
free and safe to turn their faces to the sea, a group of men
on the sand bluffs of Nantucket was watching a school of
whales playing and sporting just off shore. One of these
men, turning to his comrades and pointing to the ocean,
said, " There is a green pasture where our children's grandchildren will go for bread."

This nameless islander proved a true though unhonored
prophet. Nantucket in the years to come made all the
five great oceans of the globe yield the livelihood denied
by her own narrow, sterile acres. She was not the pioneer
in the bold trade of whaling which has lent so much picturesqueness to the annals of the American merchant
marine. Long Island, Cape Cod, and Plymouth had been
chasing and capturing the monarchs of the deep before
1690. But Nantucket, once embarked in the noble in-

dustry, straightway surpassed them all and dominated the whale fishery as perhaps no community of like size ever dominated so hazardous and important a vocation.

The red aborigines were really the first American whalemen. It astounded the English settlers to observe the audacity with which they attacked the monsters in their fragile canoes. These Indian canoes were the models of the first whaleboats of the white men, and to this day the Yankee whaleboat, the most seaworthy light craft afloat, retains in its clean, sharp, double-ended form the essential canoe characteristics. Whales in the olden time were very much tamer as well as more plentiful than now. They came in great numbers close into the sandy beaches of Cape Cod and Long Island. Captain John Smith in 1614 found whales so thick and so easy of approach that he turned aside from his exploring to take them; and one of the English settlers who came over a few years afterward records in his journal that he saw as the long voyage ended " mighty whales spewing up water like the smoke of a chimney, and making the sea about them white and hoary, as is said in Job, of such incredible bigness that I will never wonder that the body of Jonas could be in the belly of a whale."

It was the New York colonists who took the lead in whale-hunting as a systematic industry. In 1644 the town of Southampton, Long Island, whose waters even in late years have been a favorite playground for marine mammalia, appointed men especially to look for whales cast ashore. From this it was easy to hold boats in readiness to chase and kill whales which came close in, but were not actually stranded. The trade developed in the same way on Cape Cod, which bears so close a physical resemblance to Long Island. There also, as an old chronicler remarks, " Whales formerly for many successive years set in alongshore. There was good whaling in boats. Proper watchmen on shore by signal gave notice when a whale appeared. After some years they [the whales] left this ground and passed further off upon the banks at some distance from the shore. The whalers then used sloops with whaleboats aboard, and this fishery turned to a good account. At present the whales take their course in deep water, where upon a peace our whalers design to follow them. This business is by whaling sloops or schooners with two whaleboats and thirteen men." In 1662 the Cape Cod town of Eastham voted that a part of every whale cast ashore should be appropriated for the support of the ministry.

As whales grew more and more shy and voyages lengthened, these sloops and schooners gave way to brigs and ships, carrying three or four boats and twenty to forty men. But until the Revolution the American whaler was seldom much larger than one hundred tons. In 1690 the people of Nantucket,[1] "finding that the people of Cape Cod had made greater proficiency in the art of whale-catching than themselves," sent thither and engaged one Ichabod Paddock to remove to the island and instruct them in the best ways of killing whales and obtaining the oil. This Cape Cod expert must have had apt pupils, for in 1775 the guns of Lexington found one hundred and fifty Nantucket whalers at sea with an aggregate burden of fifteen thousand tons. The years between 1770 and 1775, says Macy in his history, were exceptionally prosperous for Nantucket. Some of her one hundred and fifty vessels were large brigs. From the very first the whale fishery was pervaded by a spirit adventurous and indomitable. American whalemen pushed farther and farther out into the deep sea, as their gigantic quarry retreated before them. In the early years of the eighteenth century the whale craft of the colonies were cruising within a great triangle formed by the Gulf of St. Lawrence, the Virginia Capes, and the Western or Azores Islands. In 1760 the

[1] "History of the American Whale Fishery," by Alexander Starbuck.

little town of Sag Harbor, Long Island, had three brave sloops searching for whales in icy northern latitudes, and in 1774 bold Captain Uriah Bunker, in the brig " Amazon " of Nantucket, made the first voyage across the equinoctial line to the Brazil Banks and returned to port with a " full ship" on April 19, 1775, just as the redcoats were in full retreat from Concord Bridge.

The Revolutionary War dealt a terrific blow to American whaling. England was intensely jealous of the growth of the colonial industry as a nursery of American sea-power. She saw her chance and made merciless use of it. Her swarming cruisers seized or destroyed American whale vessels wherever they could be found, and forced their hardy and daring crews into the king's service. John Adams, who had been one of our envoys abroad, and was to be an envoy again, wrote on Sept. 13, 1779, from Braintree to the Council of Massachusetts, " Whenever an English man-of-war or privateer has taken an American vessel, they have given to the whalemen among the crew, by order of government, their choice either to go on board a man-of-war and fight against their country, or go into the whale fishery." As a result of this policy, Mr. Adams declared that the British had seventeen vessels in the whale fishery off the mouth of the river Plate, South America, " which all sailed from London in the months of September and October. All the officers and men are Americans." Mr. Adams urged that a frigate or a sloop-of-war be sent out to seize this British whale fleet; that " at least four hundred and fifty of the best kind of seamen would be taken out of the hands of the English, and might be gained into the American service to act against the enemy."

When the war began there were in the whole American whale fleet between three and four hundred vessels of an aggregate of about 33,000 tons, manned by about five thousand seamen. The annual product of this fleet was " probably at least 45,000 barrels of spermaceti oil, and

8,500 barrels of right whale oil, and of bone nearly or quite 75,000 pounds." Not only Nantucket, but Boston, Lynn, Wellfleet, Barnstable, New Bedford, Falmouth, Dartmouth, and Swansea in Massachusetts, Newport, Providence, Warren, and Tiverton in Rhode Island, New London in Connecticut, and Sag Harbor on Long Island had whaleships at sea. At most of these ports the industry was destroyed for the time being by the British cruisers. The solitary island of Nantucket held out the most stoutly, and yet when the war ended in 1783, of the one hundred and fifty Nantucket whale vessels of 1775 one hundred and thirty-four had fallen into the hands of the enemy. The money loss exceeded one million dollars, and, worse still, so many of the young and active men of the island had perished in the war that in eight hundred Nantucket families there were two hundred and two widows and three hundred and forty-two orphan children.

But the brave island rose quickly out of her disasters and her griefs. When news came of the peace of 1783 the "Bedford," just returned to Nantucket from a voyage, was hastily laden with oil and cleared for London. She arrived out safely in February, 1783, and the sensation caused by the appearance of her strange new flag in the Thames is thus described by a London newspaper: —

"The ship Bedford, Captain Mooers, belonging to the Massachusetts [as if the Bostonese were a tribe of red Indians!] arrived in the Downs the third of February, passed Gravesend the fourth, and was reported at the Custom House the sixth instant. She was not allowed regular entry until some consultation had taken place between the commissioners of the customs and the lords of council, on account of the many acts of Parliament yet in force against the rebels in America. She is loaded with 487 butts of whale oil; is American-built; manned wholly by American seamen, wears the rebel colors, and belongs to the Island of Nantucket in Massachusetts. This is the first vessel which displayed the thirteen rebellious stripes of America in any British port. The vessel lies at Horsely down a little below the Tower, and is intended immediately to return to New England."

It is related that one of Captain Mooers's tars, as witty as he was bold, bore a great hump between his shoulders. One day a British sailor, meeting him, clapped his hand on the American's deformed back, and shouted, "Hilloa, Jack, what have you got here?" "Bunker Hill and be —— to you!" replied the Yankee, quickly; "will you mount?"

Other American ships soon followed the "Bedford," — the "Industry," also from Nantucket, and the "Maria," owned by the celebrated Quaker merchant, William Rotch. So it was the adventurous whalemen who first spliced the severed strands of trade between America and England. Nantucket was then one of the most active and interesting communities in the New World. A writer of the time says of the Nantucket youths: —

"At school they learn to read and to write a good hand, until they are twelve years old; they are then in general put apprentices to the cooper's trade, which is the second essential branch of business followed here; at fourteen they are sent to sea, where in their leisure hours their companions teach them the art of navigation, which they have an opportunity of practising on the spot. They learn the great and useful art of working a ship in all the different situations which the sea and wind so often require; and surely there cannot be a better or more useful school of that kind in the world. Then they go gradually through every station of rowers, steersmen, and harpooners. Thus they learn to attack, to pursue, to overtake, to cut, to dress their huge game, and after having performed several such voyages and perfected themselves in this business, they are fit either for the counting-room or chase."

Nantucket boys thus received the same thorough, painstaking preparation for their peculiar branch of the seaman's profession which was being given to their comrades in the trading ships of Salem, Boston, and New York. The fame of this wonderful island of superb whalemen was world-wide. After the Revolution both England and France made strenuous efforts to transplant the Nantucket whaling business to their shores. Massachusetts had offered a bounty to restore this important industry which meant so much to the prosperity and security of state and nation. But England and France with their greater wealth held out very flattering inducements to the people of Nantucket. Indeed, a party from the island, persuaded by generous British bounties, did remove in 1786–87 to the neighborhood of Halifax in Nova Scotia, and there built wharves, warehouses, factories for sperm candles and other accessories of the whaling trade. The new settlement was called Dartmouth, and for a time it was fairly prosperous. But the Nantucketers were not comfortable in their change of residence and change of flag. Some of them returned to their old home ; others, led on by still heavier bounties, emigrated to England and settled in Milford Haven. From this Nantucket colony there sprang in after years England's most skilful and successful whalemen. It is a fine example of the power of heredity which the long supremacy of Nantucket in the whale trade affords. The Enderby Brothers, the famous whaling firm of London, and the only English house which seems to have been able to maintain itself in the hunt for the mighty cachalot, made a practice of engaging expert Nantucket whalemen for each English ship which they sent out.

With the coming of peace and national independence there came a mighty quickening of ambition among the owners and crews of American whaleships. This was especially conspicuous after the favorable national legislation of 1789. In that year an American gentleman, who had been employed by the British East India Company, informed Nantucket whalemen of the presence of sperm whales off Madagascar. Several ships promptly sailed for that distant ground, and their pluck and enterprise were abundantly rewarded. Two years later six whaleships fitted out at Nantucket for the Pacific Ocean. One of them, the " Washington, " Captain George Bunker, was the first to display the stars and stripes in the port of Callao, Peru, which soon became a great resort for Yankee South-Sea whalemen.

These long-voyage whaleships of the eighteenth century were very much inferior to the vessels which came afterward when American merchants and captains had accumulated both wealth and experience. They were short, broad, apple-bowed craft, averaging only about two hundred and fifty tons, slow and unwieldy under the most favorable conditions. But when it is remembered that these early ships went to sea uncoppered and passed nearly all of their voyage in warm latitudes, where weed and barnacles gather quickly on uncovered bottoms, the wonder is that the skippers of these old tubs ever managed to crawl back to Nantucket Island. The " Beaver, " of two hundred and forty tons, one of the six Pacific pioneers of 1791, is a good example of the crudity of the old whalemen. Her whole cost, fitted for the voyage, was $10,212, or less than one-fifth of the cost of a first-class whaleship a half a century later.

There were on board the " Beaver " seventeen men manning three boats with five hands each, and leaving two shipkeepers. The ship carried for her oil four hundred iron-hooped and fourteen hundred wooden-hooped casks (hence the importance of the cooper in Nantucket). For food on the long voyage she had forty barrels of salt meats, three and one-half tons of hard bread, thirty bushels of beans and peas, one thousand pounds of rice, forty gallons of molasses, and twenty-four barrels of flour. Clearly the

American whaleman was no Lucullus. But his plain fare meant good preparation for his hard work, and men as well as owners had thrifty instincts. The "Beaver" was absent seventeen months. In all that time she purchased to eke out her home stores only two hundred pounds of bread, undoubtedly inferior to the Nantucket product.

In after years American whaleships went more liberally provided, but their absences were longer. Three-year Pacific cruises were the rule, and four-year voyages were not infrequent. Ships were larger as well as better built, and coppered. They carried thirty or forty men, and "manned out" four boats, with spare craft for an emergency. Moreover, the custom grew of calling at some of the sunny Pacific islands to overhaul the hull and rigging, vary the monotonous salt diet with tropical fruits and provisions, and give the sea-weary men a run on shore. But this liberty for the crews, as Herman Melville rather sharply hints in his "Typee" and "Omoo," often had demoralizing consequences.

American whaling was one of the oldest and most thoroughgoing of co-operative industries. The wellnigh universal method of engaging officers and men was the "lay" or share, as is now the practice with our deep-sea fishermen.[1] The papers of the Massachusetts Historical Society illustrate this method very well in the accounts of the voyage of the ship "Lion," of Nantucket, in 1807. The vessel secured oil valued at $37,661. Of this, one-eighteenth, or $2,072, went to the captain as his share, in lieu of regular pay; one-twenty-seventh, or $1,381, to the first mate; one-thirty-seventh, or $1,008, to the second mate; one-forty-eighth to each of two leading men of the crew, and one-seventy-fifth to each of the other white able seamen. But the color line was rigidly drawn on board these old Nantucket whalemen almost a century ago. The black men on board received each only from one-eightieth

[1] "History of the American Whale Fishery," Starbuck.

to one-ninetieth, although they were often as brave as their white shipmates, as active and as useful. After the crew was paid and certain fixed charges were disposed of, the balance of the proceeds went to the owners who had equipped and provisioned the ship. In the case of the " Lion " this owners' balance stood at $24,252, — a tidy sum, but only a fraction of what ships earned later in the real golden age of the whaling industry.

On shore as well as on shipboard, the keynote of the trade was co-operation. As Captain Davis says of Nantucket in his vivid and altogether admirable book, " Nimrod of the Sea " : —

" The cooper, while employed in making the casks, took care that they were of sound and seasoned wood, lest they might leak his oil in the long voyage ; the blacksmith forged his choicest iron in the shank of a harpoon, which he knew, perhaps from actual experience, would be put to the severest test in wrenching and twisting, as the whale in which he had a hundredth part interest was secured ; the ropemaker faithfully tested each yarn of the tow-line to make sure that it would carry two hundred pounds strain, for he knew that one weak inch in his work might lose to him his share in the fighting monster. "

Notable for the risk and hardship involved were the so-called " mixed voyages " of half-whalers, half-sealers, to the Falkland Islands, Patagonia, and even southward into the desolate wastes of the frozen Antarctic, for fur seal skins and sea elephant oil as well as whale oil. Much of this perilous work was performed by very small vessels, — sloops and schooners of less than one hundred tons, which were preferred because of their handiness in the ice and among the reefs and islets of far Southern archipelagoes. The length of the voyage out to Cape Horn might well appal a ship's company in one of these little craft, but that was only the prelude to the real undertaking. All that famous explorers now essay for glory and the plaudits of the world, these Yankee sealers attempted out of a hope of gain and sense of duty.   They were the real pioneers of the Antarctic.   An old historian of the American whale and seal fishery tells this suggestive incident.[1]

"A few years since, two Russian discovery ships came in sight of a group of cold, inhospitable islands in the Antarctic Ocean.   The commander imagined himself a discoverer, and doubtless was prepared with drawn sword and the flag of his sovereign flying overhead to take possession in the name of the Czar.   At this time he was becalmed in a dense fog.   Judge of his surprise, when the fog cleared away, to see a little sealing sloop from Connecticut as quietly riding between his ships as if lying in the waters of Long Island Sound!   He learned from the captain that the islands were already well known, and that he had just returned from exploring the shores of a new land to the South ; upon which the Russian gave vent to an expression too hard to be repeated, but sufficiently significant of his opinion of American enterprise.   After the captain of the sloop he named the discovery 'Palmer's Land,' in which the Americans acquiesced, and by this name it appears to be designated on all the recently published Russian and English charts."

An English ship, the " Caribou," sighted under similar conditions Hurd's Island, and regarded it as unknown land. But the schooner " Oxford" of Fairhaven, tender to the " Arab," appeared on the scene, and her captain informed the crestfallen Britons that he himself had discovered the island eighteen months before.

New Bedford was long the chief whaling port in the world, but it was relatively late in entering on the trade which made it famous.   Joseph Russell, who employed several small sloops of fifty tons, was the first New Bedford whaling merchant, in 1755.   His craft cruised in summer down the

[1] "North American Review," 1834.

coast to Hampton Roads. Such little vessels did not "try out" their own oil. There was no room on their narrow decks for the necessary apparatus. The blubber stripped from the whales was cast into the hold, and the oil was not extracted until the vessel returned. Then the reeking whale fat was transferred to the huge kettles of the owners' "try houses." It is plain that those early American whalemen were by no means squeamish.

New Bedford had the advantage of a larger and deeper harbor than Nantucket. As the size and draught of whalers steadily increased, this began to prove an important factor. Moreover, the whole region around New Bedford was full of an active seafaring population, which took instinctively to this always hazardous but often profitable calling. Dartmouth, Mattapoisett, Marion, Falmouth, bred a noble race of whalemen for the New Bedford merchants, and, indeed, fitted out whaleships of their own. The trade has left an ineffaceable impress on all of these communities. The square houses of the successful owners, the fortunate captains, and the thrifty shipwrights still stand thickly in the old towns along the shores of Buzzard's Bay and Vineyard Sound, and here and there the substantial wharves from which the whalers sailed and to which they returned give snug shelter to the smacks of the bay fishermen and the smart yachts of the summer cottagers.

It was not until after the War of 1812 had put an end to the British practice of "impressing" or stealing the crews of American ships and ruining their voyages that there came a very rapid increase in the American whaling fleet. And this war for the time being brought paralysis. Many of our whalers in distant waters, in the South Atlantic, the South Pacific, and the Indian Ocean, fell a prey to British cruisers before they knew that war had been declared. Nantucket, which had forty-six deep-sea whaleships when the war began, had only twenty-three when it ended. But our American fleet was not the only sufferer.

In October, 1812, Captain David Porter, in the thirty-two-gun frigate "Essex," sailed from the Delaware to join the "Constitution" and the "Hornet" in a cruise to the Indian Ocean. The ships were sent away in secret to strike a blow at British commerce far from home. Captain Porter failed to find his consorts at the first rendezvous, Port Praya in the Cape Verdes, and also at Fernando de Noronha and Cape Frio. Thereupon Captain Porter resolved to double the Horn and protect the American and destroy the British whaleships in the South Pacific. When the "Essex," after a terrific passage around the stormy Cape, reached Valparaiso, Porter discovered that the British letters of marque were already seizing American whalers. Porter promptly set himself to recapture the American craft and to sweep the seas of all the whaleships of the enemy. His task was extraordinarily successful. He took his first British prizes and fitted them out to cruise under the stars and stripes. Before March, 1814, when the "Essex" was finally overpowered by the "Phœbe" and the "Cherub" in one of the most glorious of defeats, Captain Porter had caught every British letter of marque or whaler known to be in the South Pacific, and had saved a large part of the American fleet. From the havoc wrought by the "Essex" the British Pacific whale fishery never recovered. The stars and stripes were thenceforth dominant in that trade and that ocean. Admiral Farragut, who sailed in the "Essex" with Porter as midshipman, has left a record [1] that some of the British whalers were captured with small resistance because the greater part of their crews "were Americans who had been pressed into the British service."

Though the Treaty of Ghent in 1814 was silent as to impressment, the wholesale kidnapping of American seamen by British ships-of-war had ceased forever. This was especially important to the whalers cruising far from home in lonely waters where their country's war fleet could give

[1] "Farragut's Journal," edited by Loyall Farragut, his son.

them small protection. By 1820 Nantucket's twenty-three ships of 1815 had increased to seventy-two, of an aggregate of 20,449 tons, and New York, Long Island, New London, Boston, Cape Cod, and New Bedford had all taken hold of the fishery with great vigor and determination. The three decades following 1820 were the golden age of American whalemen. They drew their tribute from all the great oceans of the world. Voyages grew steadily longer, more adventurous, and more profitable. Nowhere could the hunted monsters of the sea find themselves secure from their bold and relentless enemy. In 1818, the Pacific whaler "Globe" of Nantucket, Captain George W. Gardner, steering to the westward of the old track, found in Latitude 5° to 10° south and Longitude 105° to 125° west a new field where whales "seemed to exist in almost countless numbers." Within two years, so keen were our whaling skippers, fifty ships were cruising in this neighborhood, and the famous "Off Shore Ground" of the South Pacific became the scene of some of the richest catches and most exciting adventures recorded in the annals of this mighty fishery.

An American master of a trading ship from China to the Sandwich Islands saw great schools of whales off the coast of Japan, and immediately gave his Nantucket friends this information. The ship "Maro," Captain Joseph Allen, was sent to Japan. In 1821, six or seven other vessels followed, and in 1822 there were thirty American whaleships off that inhospitable coast in those rough and stormy waters. In 1835, the ship "Ganges" of Nantucket, Barzillai T. Folger, master, took the first right whale ever secured on the Kodiak ground, and thus opened the northwest coast fishery. Pushing still further into the frozen north, the ships "Hercules," Captain Ricketson, and "Janus," Captain Turner, both of New Bedford, captured in 1843 the first bowhead whales off the coast of Kamschatka. In 1848 Captain Royce, in the bark "Superior" of Sag

10

Harbor, steered through Bering's Straits and attacked the great bowhead whales of the Arctic. He found them absolutely unused to man and his arts, tame and unsuspecting. In these high latitudes at the whaling season the pursuit could be carried on at any hour of the twenty-four. In fact, Captain Royce struck his first whale at what was nominally midnight, though it was light enough for the harpooner to hurl his deadly barb.

The Arctic fishery appealed most powerfully of all to the imagination of the Yankee whalemen. Within three years after Captain Royce had passed within Bering's icy gates, two hundred and fifty ships had drawn cargoes of oil from Arctic waters. Our supremacy in this boldest of callings in which men anywhere engaged was then unchallenged. In 1849 Charles Enderby,[1] of the most famous of British whaling firms, received a charter for a Southern whale fishery, and to celebrate the occasion a banquet, presided over by the Senior Lord of the Admiralty, was held at the London Tavern, Bishopsgate, London. Mr. Enderby in his speech quoted from the "Whalemen's Shipping List" that in March, 1849, "The United States, whose flag was to be found on every sea, had 596 whaleships of 190,000 tons and manned by 18,000 seamen, while the number of English ships engaged in the whale trade was only fourteen."

In 1842 out of the world's total whaling fleet of 882 sail, 652 were American vessels.[2] New Bedford in that year owned 169 ships and barks and 8 brigs and schooners, with a total tonnage of 56,118; Fairhaven, 43 ships and barks and 1 brig and schooner, of 13,274 tons; Nantucket, 77 ships and barks, and 4 brigs and schooners, of 27,364 tons; New London, 30 ships and barks and 9 brigs and schooners, of 11,447 tons; Sag Harbor, 31 ships and barks, of 10,605 tons, and Salem, 14 ships and barks, of 4,265 tons. In 1846 the American fleet con-

[1] The "Tapu of Banderah," by Louis Becke, pages 255, 256.
[2] "The American Whale Fishery," by Charles M. Scammon.

sisted of 678 ships and barks, 35 brigs, and 22 schooners, of an aggregate tonnage of 233,189 tons, valued at $21,075,000. The total investments requisite to conduct the industry represented many millions more ; and it was calculated that in one way or another seventy thousand persons looked to the American whale fishery for their livelihood.

It was a trade which regularly involved the taking of desperate chances, and it proved to be perfectly adapted to the blended audacity and tenacity of the American temperament. Edmund Burke's famous apostrophe to the Yankee whalemen of his time [1] was even more vividly true of those who came afterward : —

"While we follow them among the tumbling mountains of ice and behold them penetrating into the deepest frozen recesses of Hudson Bay and Davis Strait; while we look for them beneath the Arctic circle, we hear that they have pierced into the opposite region of polar cold, that they are at the antipodes and engaged under the frozen serpent of the South. Falkland Island, which seemed too remote and romantic an object for the grasp of national ambition, is but a stage and resting-place in the progress of their victorious industry.

"Nor is the equinoctial heat more discouraging to them than the accumulated winter of both the poles. We know that while some of them draw the line and strike the harpoon on the coast of Africa, others run the longitude and pursue their gigantic game along the coast of Brazil. No sea but what is vexed by their fisheries, no climate that is not a witness to their toil. Neither the perseverance of Holland, nor the activity of France, nor the dexterous and firm sagacity of English enterprise ever carried this most perilous mode of hardy industry to the extent to which it has been pushed by this recent people, — a people who are still, as it were, in the gristle and not yet hardened into the bone of manhood."

Whaling was the grim trade of stern and iron men. Just as the Spartan mother warned her son to return with

[1] Speech in Parliament on Conciliation with America, March 22, 1775.

his shield or on it, so the merchants of Nantucket, New London, or New Bedford caused their captains to understand that they must return with a full hold or not at all. The success of every voyage was, of course, largely a matter of chance, and beyond all human calculation. No foresight could sometimes fathom the shyness of the whale schools and their eccentricities. A captain who had been out a year or two and still had most of his casks empty felt as might a condemned man riding in a tumbril to the guillotine.

It is related as an example of the mad risks which whalemen would run rather than return without a cargo that fifty or sixty years ago a New London ship and a ship from Sag Harbor, having failed to find whales on the Kodiak ground off the northwest coast, sailed away down the deep Pacific to Australia. The two captains met during a " gam "[1] off Geographe Bay. This was an open roadstead, exposed to the heaviest surges and swept by the fiercest gales. To anchor there would ordinarily have been deemed a deliberate inviting of destruction. But the New London skipper and his Sag Harbor friend agreed that it would be better to drag ashore or sink right there than it would to return and face their owners with empty holds.

So they put down their best ground tackle and all of it they had, and resolved to ride out the gales off that rugged coast, and hunt for whales in the brief intervals of moderate weather. When tempests came the two skippers hooked heavy purchases on to their cables and led them aft and secured them to the mainmast to relieve the awful strain that otherwise might pull the windlass right out of the bows. Thus fighting the full cumulative force of waves rolling in from thousands of miles of open southern ocean, these intrepid men of Long Island Sound vanquished one gale after another until they had filled both ships with the

---

[1] "Gam" is a whaler's term for a visit or conversation.

whales that in those wild waters thought themselves safe from huntsmen. Then the two captains hove their faithful anchors off the bottom and set their course for home. Glad indeed must such men have been to sight the welcome beacon of old Montauk!

It was the invariable practice of American whalemen to attack their prey in light and handy boats driven by four or five oarsmen. The occasions when a whale could be approached and struck from the ship herself were so few as not to be worth considering. These boats were a consummate triumph in themselves. Captain Davis, who had known and used the Yankee whaleboat, pays it this striking tribute in his "Nimrod of the Sea": —

"It is the fruit of a century's experience, and the sharpened sense and ingenuity of an inventive people, urged by the peril of the chase and the value of the prize. For lightness and form; for carrying capacity as compared with its weight and seagoing qualities; for speed and facility of movement at the word of command; for the placing of the men at the best advantage in the exercise of their power by the nicest adaptation of the varying length of the oar to its position in the boat; and lastly for a simplicity of construction which renders repairs practicable on board the ship, the whaleboat is simply as perfect as the combined skill of the million men who have risked life and limb in service could make it. This paragon of a boat is 28 feet long, sharp and clean cut as a dolphin, bow and stern, swelling amidships to six feet, with a bottom round and buoyant. The gunwale amidships rises 22 inches above the keel, rises with an accelerated curve to 37 inches at each end, and this rise of bow and stern, with the clipper-like upper form, gives it a duck-like capacity to top the oncoming waves, so that it will dryly ride where ordinary boats would fill. The gunwale is pierced at proper distances, for thole-pins of wood, and all sound of the working oars is muffled by well-thrummed mats, kept carefully greased, so that we can steal on our prey silent as the cavalry of poor, badgered Lear. The planking is carefully smoothed with sandpaper and painted.

Here we have a boat which two men may lift, and which will make ten miles an hour in dead chase by the oars alone."

The sperm whale,[1] the largest of the toothed cetaceans, was on the whole the most dangerous to attack, and also, because of the fine oil in its head or case, the most valuable to its captors. The sperm whale was found in the Atlantic off the Bahamas, on the so-called " Charleston ground," around the Azores and Cape Verde Islands, and between St. Helena and Africa; in the Pacific off Chile and Peru, around the Sandwich Islands, through the islands of Oceanica, and off the coasts of New Zealand and Japan and the northwest coast of America. While the sperm whale frequented temperate or tropical waters, the right whale, including the bowhead or polar variety, was found far north or far south, — in the Atlantic from Newfoundland to the Bahamas, in Baffin and Hudson Bay, off the coast of Greenland and the northwest coast of America, in the Okhotsk Sea and the Japan Sea, off Patagonia, the Falkland Islands, New Holland, New Zealand, and the Cape of Good Hope.

Sperm whales were not only the largest but the most highly organized species of Cetacea. They were eagerly sought because of the great quantities of oil in the natural fluid state found in their tremendous heads, with the valuable granular substance known as spermaceti. Sperm whales or cachalots have been taken eighty feet long and upward. It was a huge sperm whale which rammed and sank the American whaleship "Essex" in the South Pacific in 1819, — one of the most extraordinary incidents in the history of navigation.

The "Essex" was a stout ship, well provided. She was cruising more than a thousand miles off the coast of South America, and was sailing lazily at about three miles an hour, when an immense sperm whale, thought to have

---

[1] "The American Whale Fishery," Scammon.

been almost ninety feet long, was sighted right ahead. Instead of sinking, as is the habit of these monsters when ships approach them, this whale seems to have become infuriated as by a challenge. The "Essex" had three boats' crews out at the time. They saw the huge whale disappear for a moment, but only to rise suddenly a length away from the ship and then drive headlong at it, striking it just forward of the forechains. "The ship," said First Mate Chase, in his account of the disaster, "brought up as suddenly and violently as if she had struck a rock, and trembled for a few seconds like a leaf." The whale passed under the vessel, scraping her keel as he went, and lay on the surface a moment apparently stunned, then started suddenly off to leeward. Mate Chase set the pumps going, found that the ship was already settling, and was about to get out the boats, — the whale meanwhile lying a quarter of a mile away, thrashing the water and opening and closing his jaws with great fury. Suddenly one of the men shouted: "Here he is. He is making for us again!" The mate turned and saw the giant cachalot coming on like a runaway locomotive, a hundred rods right ahead. "And to me at that moment it appeared with tenfold fury and vengeance in his aspect."

Mr. Chase instantly put the helm hard up, but before the poor "Essex," already sodden with inflowing water, could change her course a single point, the monstrous head of the sea-monarch struck her oak bows and crushed them in as if they were paper. The whale passed under the ship as before and out of sight beneath her. Mate Chase and his men had just time to cut the lashings of a spare boat, throw in a couple of quadrants, navigating books, and compasses, and jump in themselves, when the "Essex" rolled over on her beam ends, full of water. Captain Pollard and the second mate now rowed up with their boats' crews, appalled at the suddenness and completeness of the catastrophe.

By the captain's orders the masts were cut away, and holes were chopped in the deck through which the men secured six hundred pounds of bread and two hundred gallons of water, — a feeble store for such a terrible voyage as lay before them. The "Essex," full of oil or empty barrels, did not actually sink, but she floated with all but her bulwarks submerged, gradually breaking to pieces in the seaway. This position was almost on the equator, just thirteen minutes south of it, and in Longitude 120° west. The Marquesas Islands were the nearest land, but Captain Pollard did not trust their savage reefs and still more savage inhabitants. He decided to reach the South American mainland; and on November 22 he and his crew started in their light, small, but seaworthy boats for the coast of Chile or Peru.

Thus there began one of the most dreadful chapters of human suffering in all the hideous annals of shipwreck. On the night of November 28, Captain Pollard's boat was attacked and nearly capsized by some mysterious savage fish. The scant bread supply was damaged by the breaking seas, and officers and men were scorched by the equatorial sun and consumed by a thirst as fierce as that of the battle-field. On December 20 the boats landed on a small island, and there, without food and shelter, three of the men determined to stay and die if need be, rather than again face the loneliness and tempests of the ocean. On December 27 Captain Pollard and the rest sailed on for the Island of Juan Fernandez, twenty-five hundred miles distant. On January 10 the second mate, worn out by famine and exposure, died. Two days later the first mate's boat disappeared, but the captain's and second mate's boats kept together until January 29, when they also separated in the night and storm. All this time hunger and thirst were doing their sure work, and one by one these brave men were dying deaths of agony. On February 23, Captain Pollard and a solitary survivor of his boat's crew were picked up by

Captain Zimri Coffin of Nantucket. The first mate's boat with three survivors had been rescued a few days earlier by the English brig " Indian. " The three men left on the desolate island were also saved. But the third boat was never heard from. Eight just-alive skeletons were all that remained of the " Essex's " hearty crew of thirty, after those awful weeks of floating in cockleshells on the fiery wastes of the South Pacific.

Another ship destroyed by a whale was the " Ann Alexander," Captain John S. Deblois, in 1850. This disaster also occurred near the " Off Shore Ground," in the South Pacific. Captain Deblois had attacked a fighting whale which smashed two boats in succession. Then the ship herself was steered for the monster, and as she passed, a lance was thrown into his head. The whale became furious and started for the ship to ram her as the cachalot had rammed the " Essex. " But Captain Deblois cleverly hauled his vessel on the wind and dodged his enraged antagonist. Once more the " Ann Alexander " was sent toward the great whale, Captain Deblois himself standing on the knightheads, iron in hand, resolved to finish his dangerous enemy. The whale sank, rose again, rushed for the ship at a fifteen-knot speed, and this time struck her a terrible blow abreast of the foremast. The water rushed in, and the ship began to go down bow first.

Captain Deblois ordered the anchors to be cut away and the heavy cables slipped overboard. One chain, fast around the foremast, could not be cast off in time. Although these expert whalemen instantly cleared away their boats, the vessel seemed to drop beneath them. Captain Deblois, the last man to leave, had to swim for his life; his ship was on her beam ends with her topgallant yards half buried in the ocean. Not a mouthful of provisions had been secured, and the three boats containing eleven men each had only three gallons of water. At daybreak next morning the masts and chain cable were cut away, and the ship once more sat upright, though so far submerged that it was impossible to reach her store of provisions.   All Captain Deblois and his men could find for the long open-boat voyage before them was one jug of vinegar and twenty pounds of bread.   The crew of the " Ann Alexander " seemed doomed to an even more awful fate than that of the crew of the " Essex," but Captain Deblois' boats were providentially sighted and picked up the very next day by Captain Richard C. Gibbs of Nantucket.

Five months after the loss of the " Ann Alexander " the belligerent whale which had destroyed her was killed by the " Rebecca Simms " of New Bedford.   Two of the " Ann Alexander's " harpoons were found in his mighty carcass, and fragments of the ship's timbers were imbedded in his head.   Although these wounds had reduced the whale to poor condition, he yielded his fortunate captors seventy or eighty barrels of oil.

In the same year, 1850, on the other side of South America, a fighting whale attacked the " Pocahontas " and stove in her bow, but the ship managed to get into Rio Janeiro leaking two hundred and fifty strokes an hour.   Of course the destruction of boats was a frequent and familiar occurrence, but an uglier combat has seldom been recorded than that of Captain Pierce of the " Emerald " of New Bedford.   Captain Pierce wrestled with his monster for nine hours.   He lost three boats, five harpoons, and seven bombs, and then when the whale was finally killed, both lines parted, and Captain Pierce's hard-fought-for prize sank and was lost in forty fathoms.

Captain Davis, in his " Nimrod of the Sea," gives this lively account of a battle with another fighting whale off the river Plate.   It was a sperm whale encountered by Captain Huntting : —

" When the monster was struck he did not attempt to escape, but turned at once on the boat with his jaw, cut her in two, and continued thrashing the wreck until it was completely broken up. One of the loose boats picked up the swimmers and took them to the ship; the other two boats went on and each planted two irons in the irate animal. This aroused him, and he turned his full fury on them, crushing in their bottoms with his jaw and not leaving them while a promising mouthful held together. Twelve demoralized men were in the water, anxious observers of his majestic anger. Two men who could not swim had, in their terror, climbed on his back and seated themselves astride forward of the hump as perhaps the safest place from that terrible ivory-mounted war club which he had brandished with such awful effect. At one time another man was clinging to the hump with his hands."

Captain Huntting himself now fired a bomb-lance into the whale, which thereupon "tore right through my boat like a hurricane, scattering all hands right and left." Four boats and their gear had now been demolished, and the men were so "gallied" by their dreadful experience that Captain Huntting gave up the fight and sailed for Buenos Ayres, "as much to allow his men, who were mostly green, to run away as for the purpose of refitting." Most of the greenhorns promptly deserted. A whaleman who had once lost his "nerve" was ever after useless.

But there were many whalemen whose "nerve" was impregnable. One of these was an old skipper whose personal duel with a great angry whale was long a favorite yarn of Yankee forecastles. The whale had smashed the captain's boat and killed two men. Then he attacked the captain himself, literally falling upon him and driving him far down into the water. The whale did this again and again, but the old skipper was fighting mad, too, and would not succumb to his gigantic enemy. The captain repeatedly caught hold of the whale's back and remained there until the terrible flukes swept him off into the ocean. The second mate's boat was watching for a chance to go to the rescue, but the men did not dare to face the whale's

wicked eye, and they backed water nimbly whenever he
started for them.

Meanwhile the captain, to save his strength, was treading
water and feeling around with his sheath-knife for some
vulnerable point in the slippery bulk of his antagonist.
The cooper, left in charge of the ship, tried to run down
and pick up the captain, but could not get the clumsy
wind-jammer near enough.   For three quarters of an hour
this unequal combat lasted.   The old skipper was pounded
and bruised by the blows of the flukes, and almost smothered by constant immersions.   He swam with his arms
only, his legs were paralyzed, and he became unconscious.
But when he opened his eyes again he was in his own
cabin.   His first mate had come up in the nick of time,
pulled him out of the water, and put him aboard the ship.
Then the loyal officer had gone at that whale and after
a desperate battle killed the monster, which, as the mate
dryly said, was " too dangerous a cuss to run at large in
that pasture field."

The ready humor of these Yankee whalemen was one of
their delightful characteristics.   It lightened their toil and
softened their perils.   A fine fellow known as " Jube " was
an officer in a large ship bound out to the South Atlantic.
Before the Desolation Grounds were reached, a school of
sperm whales was sighted, and Jube's boat, hastily fitted,
was sent to the attack.   A whale was struck.   It
" sounded."   The harpoon line was new and " kinky."   As
Jube desperately tried to clear it, he was caught in the
whirling cordage and dragged down like a plummet into
the sea.   Suddenly the harpoon pulled out of the whale,
and as the crew hauled in the line, lamenting their dead
officer, they found Jube twisted in the coils.   He was
apparently dead, but once aboard ship some rough though
skilful treatment revived him.   A chum asked, " Well,
Jube, how did you like it down there?"   " Oh!" the
half-alive man, true to his instinct, answered, " it's a lone-

some road to travel. There are neither milestones nor guideboards that I could see ! "

These hard-worked men on their weary voyages, never entering port for months, fed on monotonous diet and with scant chances for recreation, had need of all their Yankee philosophy. The history of the whale trade is blotted by some awful tragedies, due to the hardship and isolation of the whaleman's life. In January, 1824, the crew of the " Globe " of Nantucket rose in mutiny against their officers, killed them and took the ship into a secluded island to strip and destroy her. But the mutineers quarrelled among themselves, as mutineers have a way of doing, and their ringleader, Samuel B. Comstock, a boat-steerer, was murdered by his second in command, Silas Payne. Six of the crew, who had held aloof from their comrades, managed to seize the ship and escape to Valparaiso, while all but two of the ten mutineers left on the island were massacred by the natives. This worst tragedy which ever stained Nantucket decks had its origin in a friendly wrestling match between Comstock and the third mate, Nathaniel Fisher. Comstock was easily defeated, and swore revenge.

On the day after Christmas, 1857, a mutiny broke out on the ship " Junior " of New Bedford. Cyrus Plummer, the leader, killed the captain and third mate and wounded the first mate. The ship was sailed to Australia, where the desperadoes abandoned her, but eight of them were subsequently captured.

Many American whaleships ended their cruises on the unmarked coral reefs of the mid-Pacific, where their crews suffered terrible deaths at the hands of savages. Other craft foundered in the wintry tempests of Cape Horn. Their trade led them to peculiarly remote and dangerous waters. The whaler " Lawrence," as the records have it, was lost in 1846 off the coast of Japan, only the second mate and seven men surviving. These poor fellows were seized by the Japanese, kept for seventeen months in cages, dungeons, and holds of junks, and passed from port to port until they reached Nagasaki. They were constantly insulted and cruelly beaten, and one man who resented this usage was murdered. At Nagasaki the other seven were forced to go through the ceremony of trampling on the cross, in obedience to an edict proclaimed two centuries before when the Portuguese were expelled from Japan. In this very year, 1846, the squadron of Commodore Biddle lay in the harbor of Yeddo, and our government imagined that it had broken the crust of Japanese conservatism. In the preceding year, the ship "Manhattan" of Sag Harbor, Captain Budd, had visited Yeddo to bring to their homes twenty-two shipwrecked Japanese seamen. Captain Budd was not molested, but was warned that he must never come again. Japan was then a most inhospitable hermit nation, and it is easy to conjecture the fate of the crews of missing American whalers, notably the "Lady Adams" of Nantucket, last spoken off that forbidding coast.

But those whaleships which escaped reef and hurricane were likely to live to a ripe old age. In the first place, they were thoroughly constructed of the best of materials. If an ordinary trading vessel was purchased for the whaling business, it was almost invariably strengthened before being sent to sea. Moreover, after the long voyages there were very complete overhaulings, and whalemen have always insisted that the oil with which a ship's timbers and planking would become saturated by long service acted as a potent preservative against decay. Be that as it may, many whaleships had an extraordinarily long existence. The average life of merchant vessels is only fifteen years, but the ship "Maria," built at Pembroke (now Hanson), Mass., in 1782, for a privateer, and subsequently used as a whaler by the celebrated merchant, William Rotch, performed twenty-seven voyages in seventy years, and was sold at Talcahuano, Chile, in 1863, being then eighty-one years old. The "Maria" was one of the first ships to display the stars and stripes in the Thames after the Revolution. She had taken in all in her many cruises nearly twenty-five thousand barrels of oil.

Another old ship, the "Mayflower," built in Plymouth, Mass., in 1820, was for years a familiar spectacle on the San Francisco water-front, where her crew had deserted her in the rush for the gold fields. This "Mayflower" was of a quaint, high-sterned, drooping-bowed model. Her masts stood plumb or raked forward, and her bowsprit had the ancient "steeve." Confiding strangers were informed that this was actually the ship which brought over the Pilgrims in 1620, and some startling prices were paid for mementoes cut from her honest hull. But this "Mayflower" was dug out of the mud and sent to sea again as a lumber drogher, and thus she rounded out forty years of patient service.

One practical advantage which whaleships had over a freighting vessel was that they always went to sea strong-handed. A ship or bark of three hundred tons would have a captain, four mates, a cooper, a carpenter, four boat-steerers, a cook, a steward, and twenty-two men and boys, — at least thirty-five all told, or about three times the crew of a vessel of similar size engaged in ordinary carrying. This lightened the labors of navigation. So many hands were required to work the boats, but they were all supposed to help about the decks or aloft; and whalers were seldom over-sparred or over-canvased. On the cruising grounds they were kept under easy sail, carrying nothing as a rule above topgallantsails. The nature of their trade prevented whaleships from maintaining that spotlessness of hull and perfect symmetry of rig for which American vessels were distinguished among all seafaring nations.

But in spite of ungainliness and apparent disorder, the

Yankee whalers were a noble school of seamanship which the whole world coveted. Their hard-featured crews were not pretty to look at, nor were the decks, lumbered with try-works, the rusty rigging, or sooty sails. But the smart man-of-war or packet that laughed at the "blubber-hunter" at the same time mentally doffed its cap to him. For every sailor the world over respected the whaleman who took the sea and the weather as they came, had small use for anchors and cables, and much for topsail earrings and reef-points, and waged a war with the elements and his giant foe and prey in which there was never truce or wavering. These ocean-hunters bore warm hearts beneath their rough garb. The deeds of heroism and self-sacrifice performed by Yankee whalemen in the past hundred years are innumerable. There were many who would unhesitatingly have done just as did Captain Isaac Ludlow of the "Monmouth" of Cold Spring, Long Island. He sighted one day the lonely island of Amsterdam in the Indian Ocean, and found on its desolate rocks the starving crew and passengers of the British bark "Meridian," wrecked there a week before. The Long Island skipper not only received and fed the castaways, but gave up his voyage to land them safely in the civilization of Mauritius. "By this act of humanity Captain Ludlow lost a season of whaling where he probably would have taken five or six hundred barrels of oil, but he saved the lives of one hundred and five human beings." [1]

There never was keener rivalry than that among whaling skippers and merchants for the honor of the largest or quickest catch. Careful records have been kept at New Bedford, Nantucket, New London, and the other old whaling towns of the results of successful voyages. Captain Davis, in his "Nimrod of the Sea," says that the largest whale he ever took made 107 barrels of oil. Its length was 79 feet. This was nothing extraordinary.

[1] Mauritius (Isle of France), "Mercantile Gazette."

Much more remarkable was the luck of the "James Arnold" of New Bedford, Captain Sullivan, which took off New Zealand in one "string" eight whales that made over one hundred barrels each; the largest yielded 137 barrels. That was famous fishing, but during the same season and on the same ground Captain Vincent, in the "Oneida" of New Bedford, captured ten sperm whales which made 1,140 barrels. Captain Norton of the "Monka" of New Bedford took on the "Off Shore Ground" a sperm whale which stowed 145 barrels. The well-named "Harvest" of Nantucket in 1853 secured a sperm whale which furnished 156 barrels of oil. In 1862 the "Ocmulgee" of Edgartown took a 130-barrel animal with a jaw 24 feet in length, — almost the length of a whaleboat. Captain Briggs, of the "Wave of New Bedford," as late as 1876 caught a sperm whale which "tried out" 162 barrels.

This was great whaling, but in 1855 the "Adeline" of New Bedford killed a monster in the Okhotsk Sea which produced 250 barrels, and six years afterward the "General Pike," hailing also from the grand old port at the head of Buzzard's Bay, slew a leviathan which stowed down 274 barrels. Each of these made a profit of about $5,000 out of a day's work.

It was this possibility of quick and great gain which drew shrewd merchants and intrepid seamen into the whaling trade, and kept them there even through years of disappointment and disaster. Nowhere except in gold or diamond mining could so much money be so readily made as by fortunate ships like the "Uncas" of Falmouth, Captain Bunker, which arrived in 1831 from a voyage of two years and eight months with 3,468 barrels of sperm oil, valued at $88,000, or the "Loper" of Nantucket, Captain Obed Starbuck, which took a $50,000 catch of 2,280 barrels in fourteen months, or the "Sarah" of Nantucket, Captain Frederick Arthur, which secured in a three years' Pacific

11

cruise 3,497 barrels of sperm oil, valued at $89,000, — the largest sperm oil cargo ever landed at Nantucket from a single voyage. In 1845 the " Lowell," Captain Benjamin, and the "General Williams," Captain Holt, brought into New London from voyages of less than two years about 4,500 barrels of oil and 43,000 pounds of bone, each catch selling for $61,000. It was said that the " Lowell " at one time had sixteen dead whales alongside awaiting their turn for the blubber spades and the kettles.

The arrivals of 1838 at New Bedford included the " William Hamilton," Captain Swain, with 4,181 barrels of sperm oil, valued at $109,000. The " South America " of Providence, Captain Sowle, got in, in 1849, from a two-year voyage with 5,300 barrels of whale and 200 of sperm oil and 50,000 pounds of bone, worth at ruling prices $89,000. It had cost $40,000 to fit out the " South America," so that her owners received in two years the price of the vessel twice over. The " Coral " of New Bedford, Captain Seabury, secured in a three-year voyage 3,350 barrels of sperm oil worth $126,000; the " Favorite " of Fairhaven, Captain Pierce, 4,300 barrels of whale oil, 300 of sperm, and 72,000 pounds of bone, worth $116,000; the " Montreal " of New Bedford, Captain Fish, 3,823 barrels of whale and 195 barrels of sperm oil and 31,700 pounds of bone, worth $136,000; the " Sheffield " of New Bedford, in a four-year voyage, 7,000 barrels of whale oil and 115,000 pounds of bone worth $124,000.

In 1864, when Anglo-Confederate cruisers were afloat to " burn, sink, and destroy " every craft which flew the Yankee ensign, the " Pioneer " of New London, Captain Ebenezer Morgan, defiantly put to sea, and returned in 1865 with 1,391 barrels of whale oil and 22,650 pounds of bone, worth at war prices $150,000, or almost four times the original cost of the brave and fortunate vessel and her outfit. New Londoners insist that this was the best voyage ever made by an American whaler, but still more remarkable was the experience of the "Envoy" of New Bedford. This vessel had returned to port in 1847 and been condemned and sold to be broken up. But the purchaser, Mr. William C. Brownell, fitted the old ship for another voyage and sent her out in command of Captain W. T. Walker, although the underwriters refused insurance. In the Pacific Captain Walker received 1,000 barrels of oil which he had previously purchased from a wrecked vessel. He shipped this from Manila to London, and then in one short cruise in the North Pacific took 2,800 barrels of whale oil and 40,000 pounds of bone, and in a second cruise 2,500 barrels of whale oil and 35,000 pounds of bone. Twenty-five thousand gallons of oil were sold in gold-crazed San Francisco at one dollar a gallon. For the entire 5,800 barrels of oil and 75,000 pounds of bone the "Envoy" received $138,000, or $130,000 more than the ancient tub cost all ready for sea.

But this is only one side of the picture. If these had been typical rather than exceptional voyages, the whole nation would have gone a-whaling. While the gains were sometimes prodigious, the risks were great, and the failure of a voyage meant ruin to the owners unless they were men of large wealth. A mutiny on the "Clifford Wayne" of Fairhaven broke up her cruise and sent her home $10,000 worse off than if she had never sailed. The "Emmeline" of New Bedford went to sea in July, 1841. In July of the next year the captain was killed at his post of duty and the brig returned in September, 1843, with only ten barrels of oil to show for twenty-six months' cruising. Another ill-starred voyage was that of the "Benjamin Rush," Captain Munroe, of Warren, R. I., which sailed in 1852 for the Pacific. The captain and his entire boat's crew perished in a fight with a whale off the coast of Japan, and the "Rush" was brought back to port in 1853 by the cooper with only ninety barrels of oil in her hold. The unfortunate ship had circumnavigated the globe, and in all that time had sighted land but twice, — the Cape Verde Islands outward bound and Trinidad returning.

Out of eighty-one whalers expected to arrive in 1837, fifty-three made profitable voyages, eight made saving ones, eleven lost money, and nine lost much money. Of the sixty-eight whalers of the New Bedford and Fairhaven fleet arriving in 1858, forty-four made voyages that were failures, — the total loss of the two towns reaching at least one million dollars.

But in 1858 there had set in the inevitable shrinkage of the American whaling industry. Between 1858 and 1860, the American shipping registered for the whale fishery fell off from 198,594 to 166,841 tons.[1] This was before the war had begun to turn our whalers over to destruction. The tonnage of the whaling fleet fell from 145,734 in 1861 to 117,714 in 1862, 99,228 in 1863, 95,145 in 1864, and 84,233 in 1865. The peace year of 1866 brought a sharp rebound to 105,170 tons, but this gain was brief and delusive. The next year, 1867, the whale fleet had fallen to 52,384 tons, and while it stood in 1868 at 78,486, the decline since then has been constant to the forlorn 9,534 tons of June 30, 1901.

The deep-sea whalers of both the Atlantic and Pacific suffered severely from the direct attacks of Southern cruisers during the Civil War, and also from the extortionate rates of war insurance. Several of the first twenty victims of Captain Semmes's "Alabama" were whaleships caught between the Azores and the West Indies. In 1864, a swift British East Indiaman, with auxiliary steam-power, the "Sea King," was fitted out expressly to destroy "the American whaling trade in the Japan Sea and the Arctic Ocean, where it had always been a formidable rival to the English."[2] The "Sea King," or "Shenandoah," as she was called when the Confederate flag was hoisted, was

---

[1] Report of the Commissioner of Navigation, 1900.
[2] "History of the Navy," Maclay, vol. ii.

manned by British sailors and armed with British guns.
She received at Melbourne, Australia, coal and stores for a
cruise in the North Pacific. The "Shenandoah" took our
Arctic whale fleet unawares. The captains had not
dreamed that the hatred of an armed foe would add one
more terror to their arduous vocation.

The Yankee whalers, of course, carried no cannon.
They were not prepared for resistance. They were compelled to yield; but there was one stout old mariner,
Captain Thomas G. Young of the bark "Favorite," of
Fairhaven, who would not give up without a fight. He
was a part owner of the bark; his share represented the
hard savings of a lifetime. When the "Shenandoah"
appeared, Captain Young loaded his bomb-guns and firearms, and frightened away the boat which the cruiser sent
to board him. Then the "Shenandoah," ranging alongside, trained her battery on the "Favorite" and prepared
to shell and sink her with all her company. But even now
the gray-haired Yankee skipper would not surrender,
though his officers left him, surreptitiously removing the
caps from bomb-guns and muskets as they went over the
side. A second armed boat from the "Shenandoah" now
approached, and Captain Young was hailed and told that
he would be shot if he did not haul down the Yankee
colors. "Shoot and be ——," Young answered. As the
boat's crew clambered aboard, the old captain snapped his
bomb-gun at them. Of course the capless weapon missed
fire. Young was knocked down, made prisoner, and robbed
of his money, watch, and other valuables.

The English crew of the "Shenandoah" did its cruel
work with thoroughness. Thirty-four captured ships and
barks were burned, and four were bonded. Finally
Captain Waddell discovered that the war had ended and
that he was really playing the part of a pirate. Then he
scuttled away to the shelter of the British flag. It is some
consolation that the ravages of the "Shenandoah" entered

into the "Alabama" claims and figured in the $15,500,000 award of the Geneva arbitration.

For several years after the "Shenandoah's" exploit, American whalemen sailed to the Arctic in considerable numbers. The risks were grave, but there was profit in a favorable season. The autumn of 1871 brought an awful disaster. The ships had met with poor success. The ice was thick and heavy, and in August the fleet was suddenly caught and embayed. A northeaster would have released the vessels, but none came, and the ice closed in more and more relentlessly until on September 12, after several ships had been crushed, it was recognized that the situation of the main body of the fleet was hopeless. Two days later the crews abandoned their vessels, first solemnly hoisting their ensigns Union down. Seven ships fortunately happened to lie below the ice jam, and these bore the twelve hundred castaways out of the icy north and the advancing Arctic winter to the sunny refuge of Honolulu.

New Bedford alone lost a million dollars in this catastrophe. But even now the spirit of our Arctic whalemen was not daunted. In the very next year twenty-seven ships, and in 1873 twenty-nine steered up through Bering Straits. Once more, in 1876, the Arctic whalers were overwhelmed. Twelve out of twenty ships and barks were lost in the ice, with many men, and an investment of $800,000. Steamers or rather sailing vessels, with auxiliary steam-power, now began to be employed in the Arctic fishery. They were handier and safer than were sailcraft, and a small and not increasing fleet of Arctic whalemen still makes its rendezvous at San Francisco.

There has never been any change in the national policy toward our whalemen. Theirs has always been a tariff-protected industry. The catch of American whaleships has been admitted free of duty, while on the product of foreign fisheries a substantial customs tax, frankly protective in its nature, has been imposed. This was, under the

Act of April 27, 1816, twenty-five cents a gallon for sperm
and fifteen cents for whale oil.   In later years this specific
was changed to an ad valorem duty substantially the same.
The decline of the American whale fishery is commonly
attributed to the discovery of petroleum and the extraordinary abundance and cheapness of kerosene oil.   But very
much more important than this factor of competition was
the scarcity of whales and the heavily increased cost of
conducting the industry.   In 1790, a ship with a capacity
of 1,900 barrels of oil could be fitted out for a two years'
sperm whaling voyage in the Pacific for $12,000.   Indeed,
the ship " Beaver, " mentioned earlier in this chapter as one of
the first six Nantucket vessels to clear for the South Sea,
represented an investment of only $10,212.   But in 1858,
a good vessel equipped for a similar voyage, built in the
modern fashion and supplied with a modern equipment,
would involve an expenditure of $65,000.   Meanwhile,
whales had become few and shy and difficult to find, and
the time required for a successful voyage had lengthened
from two to three and even four years.

The value of the oil of the leviathan was not impaired
so much as has been supposed by the rivalry of the cheap
and easy product of the wells of Pennsylvania.   Sperm
oil especially tended to rise in price as the whaling
industry declined.   It brought 84 cents a gallon in
1835, when the trade was highly prosperous.   But the
price had advanced to $1.20 in 1850, $1.41 in 1860, and
$1.45 in 1872.   In 1865, because of the war, it had stood
for a while at $2.25.   But the trouble was that the expense
of securing sperm oil had increased even more heavily than
the price had.   Kerosene would give a good, economical
light, but the sperm oil was distinctly preferable for lubri-
cating and other purposes.   Ordinary whale oil also gained
steadily in value in the years when the whaleships were
disappearing.   It brought 36 cents a gallon in 1835, 49
cents in 1850, 71 cents in 1855, 49 cents in 1860, and 65

cents in 1872. Its war-price, in 1865, was $1.45. Even
more notable is the increase in the price of the bone, that
indispensable product of the right whale or the great bowhead of the polar ocean. Whalebone advanced from 24
cents a pound in 1835 to 34 cents in 1850, 80 cents in
1860, and $1.28 in 1872. For a time, at the end of the
Civil War, in 1865, it stood at $1.71. The value of the
bone has been a chief incentive of the Arctic whalers, and
kept their arduous trade alive when the oil alone would
not have compensated for the risk and suffering.

Another factor in the decrease of the American whale
fishery has been the deterioration of the crews. At first
the men of the whaleships were American born, including
a certain proportion of Indians and coast-bred negroes.
They were of good, stalwart stock, these old crews,—
whether they were all white, or white, red, brown, and
black,— stout, willing, and really homogeneous. But toward
the middle of the nineteenth century, as whales became
more scarce and the profits of the voyages more precarious,
the owners were compelled to fill their forecastles with
the flotsam of the world. Time was when it was easy to
gather at New Bedford or New London a prime crew of
tall and stalwart lads from the fishing towns of the coast
and the farms of interior New England. Maine furnished
a great many fine whalemen, and the trade long had a
powerful fascination for adventurous farmer boys of New
Hampshire, Vermont, and upper New York. Of course,
these fellows were very "green" when they joined their
ship. Most of them did not know a harpoon from a hand-
spike. But they had the redeeming quality of being quick
to learn, and the first year of a three-year voyage would
find them first-class whalers; the second year, first-class
seamen. The thousands of these hardy and fearless young
men whom we had afloat in our unrivalled whale fleet
gave the United States a naval reserve envied of all the
world.

But when the farmer lads came down to the sea no more in adequate numbers, the whaleships were forced to fill up their crews far from home, of very different material. The Portuguese of the Western Islands, the negroes of the Cape Verdes, and even the savages of the Pacific archipelagoes were drawn into our service, until an American whaleship was a kaleidoscope of colors as well as a Babel of tongues. Many successful voyages were made by these polyglot companies. The Portuguese developed a remarkable aptitude, and rose often to officer and sometimes to command ships. They came over with their families and founded the distinctive communities which still remain at a dozen points on our Northern seaboard. Another source of admirable whalemen was the Sandwich Islands. But in general the substitution of aliens and strangers for the Yankee whalers of the old stock meant a decline in efficiency and a further dwindling of the hard-won profits of the trade.

Sometimes it meant even worse than this, as was proved by the tragic experience of the ship "Sharon" of New Bedford. On Sunday, Nov. 6, 1842, while the boats of the ship were chasing whales several miles away, Captain Howes Norris of Martha's Vineyard was treacherously murdered by three Kingsmill Islanders, who, with the captain and a boy, were the only persons left on board. The savages — for such they were — had stolen up behind the captain and cut off his head with one swift blow of that terrible weapon, a cutting spade. When the boats returned they found the ship in the possession of three whooping cannibals. The captain's dismembered body lay on deck; the boy had taken refuge in the rigging. Armed with harpoons, spades, — long-handled articles with a broad blade ground to razor sharpness, — axes, hammers, and belaying pins, the blood-crazed islanders dared the boats to come on. The nerve of officers and men failed them. But the brave young third mate,

Benjamin Clough of Maine, volunteered to board the ship single-handed.

Under cover of night he managed to climb into a cabin window, found the dead captain's cutlasses and muskets, and was loading the firearms when he was discovered by one of the savages. The fellow attacked him, and they had a terrible hand-to-hand struggle, in which Clough received a severe wound, but managed to disable his enemy. A second savage, aroused by the noise of the combat, hurled a cutting spade at Clough, almost severing his arm, while at the same moment Clough shot his new assailant through the heart. The third savage, appalled by the fate of his comrades, leaped overboard, but quickly returned and secreted himself in the forehold. There he was found and seized by the crew, who cautiously boarded the ship when assured by the intrepid third mate that the danger was ended. It is pleasant to know that Clough sailed in the "Sharon" on her next voyage as master, and that he became one of the most successful of New Bedford whaling captains. There were quite enough perils in the whalers' calling without serving as shipmates with barbarians.

The decay of the whaling industry came on as a part of the general decline of the American merchant marine. So closely related were the whaling and the freighting fleet that the shrinkage of one naturally and almost inevitably had its influence upon the other. The discovery of gold in California and the Crimean War were accidental factors which postponed for a little the decrease of our merchant tonnage and raised false anticipations, or the disappearance of our trading ships and whaleships would have been simultaneous. The American whaling fleet has now sunk to insignificant proportions. According to the "Whalemen's Shipping List" of March 5, 1901, it consisted of forty vessels, or only one-fifteenth the number of 1846, with an aggregate tonnage of 8,750, and it was still decreasing, a reduction of 1,726 tons having been recorded since the previous year. New Bedford, with fourteen ships and barks and eight schooners of a total tonnage of 4,250, still bravely held first place in the ancient industry. Provincetown had four schooners of 438 tons; Boston, one bark of 385 tons; and San Francisco, twelve square-riggers and one schooner, of 3,673 tons. The logbook of the one Boston whaler, the " Josephine," showed that the trade still has its traditional perils. In three years of cruising the " Josephine " had secured the moderate catch of two thousand barrels of sperm oil. She had lost her fourth mate in a battle with a fighting whale; had lost the cooper; the shipkeeper and one sailor were obliged to leave, disabled, and a boat-steerer had died of disease. So the scant cargoes of our few surviving whalers are still being purchased at the same high cost.

Nevertheless, the pursuit of the leviathan in deep-sea ships all over the globe was a calling which justified Edmund Burke's memorable eulogy. It was for many years an important source of national wealth, and it bore a part and a strong part in the moulding of the national character. It meant for the men engaged in it long exile from home, arduous labor, habitual self-denial, acute peril, often dreadful suffering. But there are better things for men than mere ease, comfort, and security, and it may well be questioned whether the sons of the old whalemen now earning their livelihood in factories or shops are equal to their fathers in moral and mental stamina, and equal to them as useful citizens of the republic.

Following is a record year by year of the registered and enrolled tonnage of the American whale fishery from 1800 to 1901, inclusive, as presented in the official report of the United States Bureau of Navigation: —

TONNAGE IN WHALE FISHERIES.

Year.	Tonnage.	Year.	Tonnage.	Year.	Tonnage.
1800	3,466	1834	108,424	1868	78,486
1801	3,085	1835	97,649	1869	70,202
1802	3,201	1836	146,254	1870	67,954
1803	12,390	1837	129,137	1871	61,490
1804	12,334	1838	124,860	1872	51,608
1805	6,015	1839	132,285	1873	44,755
1806	10,507	1840	136,927	1874	39,108
1807	9,051	1841	157,405	1875	38,229
1808	4,526	1842	151,990	1876	39,116
1809	3,777	1843	152,517	1877	40,593
1810	3,589	1844	168,614	1878	39,700
1811	5,299	1845	190,903	1879	40,028
1812	2,930	1846	187,420	1880	38,408
1813	2,942	1847	193,859	1881	38,551
1814	562	1848	192,613	1882	32,802
1815	1,230	1849	180,186	1883	32,414
1816	1,168	1850	146,017	1884	27,249
1817	5,224	1851	181,644	1885	25,184
1818	16,750	1852	193,798	1886	23,138
1819	32,386	1853	193,203	1887	26,151
1820	36,445	1854	181,901	1888	24,482
1821	27,995	1855	186,848	1889	21,976
1822	48,583	1856	189,461	1890	18,633
1823	40,503	1857	195,842	1891	17,231
1824	33,346	1858	198,594	1892	17,052
1825	35,379	1859	185,728	1893	16,604
1826	41,984	1860	166,841	1894	16,482
1827	45,992	1861	145,734	1895	15,839
1828	54,801	1862	117,714	1896	15,121
1829	57,284	1863	99,228	1897	12,714
1830	39,705	1864	95,145	1898	11,496
1831	82,797	1865	84,233	1899	11,017
1832	73,246	1866	105,170	1900	9,899
1833	101,636	1867	52,384	1901	9,534

CHAPTER IX

RECIPROCITY ON THE SEA. 1816-30

Merchant Shipping in 1815 a Genuinely National Interest — Misgivings over the First Change of Policy — Protection yielded in Direct Trade with Britain — United States overreached — Plaster of Paris Act — Our Vigorous Retaliation — More Misnamed " Reciprocity " in 1828 — Steamship " Savannah " first to cross the Ocean — Splendid Lines of Yankee Packet Ships — Fight for West India Commerce — The Navy crushes West India Piracy — Tonnage Almost at a Standstill

FROM 1789 to 1815 the American merchant marine, as this narrative shows, had been a carefully fostered and protected interest. It was dear to the whole country. A few Southerners of the eccentric type of Randolph had professed to scoff at it, but they were not really representative. A considerable tonnage was owned at Baltimore, Norfolk, Richmond, Wilmington, Charleston, and Savannah, and the Yankee ship and the Yankee sailor had friends as devoted, if not so numerous, in Virginia and the Carolinas as in New York or New England. The American merchant fleet, after the War of 1812, was more widely distributed geographically than it is now. Dr. Seybert, who wrote in 1818, names as the ports which had the greatest tonnage in proportion to population two of the New England States, two of the Middle States, and two of the South. Boston, as might have been anticipated, led the list with 4.48 tons for every inhabitant. Next came New Hampshire's one seaport, the heroic town of Portsmouth, which manned the "Ranger" and the

"Kearsarge," and long seemed to have the same genius
for trade as for war.   Portsmouth was but little behind
its large neighbor to the southward.   It had 4.15 tons of
shipping for every inhabitant, as against Boston's 4.48.
Next came enterprising Baltimore, with 2.90 tons; New
York, with 2.78 tons; Philadelphia, with 2.23 tons;
Charleston, with 2.14.

All this meant vastly more than mere ownership.
Local patriotism and trade customs of the day combined
to bring these vessels often to their home ports.   There
they were freighted by the merchants who owned them;
thither they returned deep-laden with the odorous spoil of
distant lands.   The black Indiaman, creeping in with the
tide, was an object of keen interest to many more than the
consignees of her cargo and the families of her bronzed
and bearded crew.   The end of a long voyage meant a
thorough overhauling of the good ship or brig.   Once
her hold was clear, she was careened on the beach, or
hauled out on the graving dock for a scrutiny of seams
and planking.   Yards were sent down; topgallantmasts
and topmasts struck; the cumbrous hempen shrouds and
stays stripped off and shrewdly examined.   There was
work for the shipwright, the sparmaker, the rigger, the
sailmaker, the block and pumpmaker, the boatbuilder, —
all the busy trades that clustered about the wharves of an
old-time seaport, and gave it a picturesqueness and a
color that have vanished forever with the stout ships
themselves.

No hands could heal the wounds of a strained and weary
vessel so faithfully as those that had built and fitted her.
It was a work of love; it was a point of honor.   We of
to-day, looking back, can imagine the solicitude with
which the voyages of a ship were followed, when she was
as familiar to hundreds of her townspeople as the walls of
their own homes, and can picture the delight with which
the crowd on the wharf-end hailed a tall vessel from

Archangel, or Mauritius, or Canton, with her canvas festooned by bunt-lines and clew-lines, warping in to her owner's dock. "I made that foretopsail," says one man, proudly. "That mainyard's mine," is another's boast. "Well, my old hawser's stood the strain," smiles another at the tense line, crawling around the capstan to a deep-throated chorus.

Those were the days in which nine-tenths of American commerce was carried in American ships. The law of 1789, which admitted foreign merchandise imported in an American vessel at a rate of duty ten per cent below that exacted from the freight of a foreign vessel, and gave the American vessel an added advantage in the tonnage dues, made it not only profitable but necessary for the merchants of Boston, New York, or Baltimore, to keep their own ships to carry their own trade. It was with grave misgivings that these great ports and the lesser ports alongshore saw a new, so-called reciprocity policy initiated after the treaty of peace with Britain in 1815. Through a commercial convention framed some months after the Treaty of Ghent, the United States and Great Britain bound themselves to impose no discriminating duty on ships or products in the trade between this country and the United Kingdom. But at the same time Great Britain stipulated that she should continue to regulate the trade of her West Indian and Canadian colonies as she might desire, and that American ships should engage in only direct trade with her East Indian possessions.

Genuine reciprocity involves mutual and equal concessions. This was a one-sided arrangement, the unfairness of which became instantly manifest. There was violent opposition in the House of Representatives to the repeal of the discriminating duty on British goods and vessels, but the plea prevailed that the terms of the convention really bound Congress, and the Repeal Bill received a slender majority. Having thus trapped the United States,

Great Britain moved at once to take advantage of her victory. She revived her old colonial policy of exclusion, and shut American ships out of her West India possessions. Our lumber, fish, flour, cattle, and vegetables could be carried thither only in vessels owned by British subjects. This was "reciprocity" with a vengeance. It laid up in idleness an American fleet of 80,000 tons.[1]

Nor was that the end of its disastrous consequences. The repeal of our discriminating duties, in faithful fulfilment of the convention of 1815, opened our ports to British ships from the United Kingdom on even terms with American ships. Straightway British vessels began to bring in great quantities of manufactured goods, — woollens or cottons, or chinaware or hardware, — against which the low tariff offered a scant barrier. Then at Boston or New York a British ship would load with our lumber or flour or provisions, and sail for a British West Indian port, from which our flag was excluded. There the Briton would load with sugar or molasses, and steer for home, or perhaps return to the United States for still another cargo. McMaster says of the actual working of this "reciprocity": —

"The profits of this triangular voyage enabled her [a British vessel] to bring British goods, wares, and merchandise from England to the United States, for much less than the actual cost of transportation on an American vessel, which could not make a similar voyage. An English merchant carrier could even afford to bring goods from Liverpool to New York at an actual loss, inasmuch as he could easily recover on the voyages from New York to the West Indies, and from the West Indies back to Liverpool, on neither of which could American competition affect him. In the hope of doing to American shipping what false invoices and auction sales had already done to American importers, manufacturers, and retailers, the

[1] "History of the American People," by John Bach McMaster, vol. iv.

direct trade between England and America was carried
on by Englishmen so much below the cost of the voyage
that during the summer of 1816, beef and tallow, butter,
hams, and potatoes, were actually brought from Galway
and Newry to New York, where they undersold our home
products. Indeed, companies were formed to continue
their importation. Thus the one trade which, by the
convention, seemed to be on a basis of equality, was conducted in reality in a way wholly favorable to England."

America had held out an olive-branch in March, 1815,
in a general Act offering to withdraw all discriminating
duties in favor of any foreign nation which did the same
thing. That was true reciprocity. But it was not the
reciprocity of the grotesque convention of the following
summer. The British provinces of Nova Scotia and New
Brunswick saw their chance to outwit the Yankees, and
they made prompt use of it. Plaster was then, as now,
a large article of export from the provinces to the United
States. By what is known as the Plaster of Paris Act,
the provincial governments in 1816 laid a prohibitive export
duty of twenty shillings a ton on this material shipped by
an American coasting vessel to any American port east of
Boston. This was too much for the patience of Congress,
which now clearly saw itself deluded. Our lawmakers
retaliated by forbidding foreign craft to bring plaster to
the United States from ports from which American vessels
could not bring it. Moreover, Congress, now in a fighting mood, forbade admission to all British ships from
British ports anywhere from which American vessels were
excluded.

This blow was aimed especially at the British West
Indies. It was the opening gun of a vigorous commer-
cial war of acts and proclamations, which finally brought
Great Britain to listen to reason. But the contest, like
all commercial wars, wrought severe injury to both parties.
In the early part of the struggle, before Congress brought

its heavy batteries to bear, the prostrate condition of our
carrying trade recalled "the days of the long embargo."
"Half the tonnage owned along the seaboard, and engaged
in the coasting and foreign trade," writes McMaster, "was
said to have been laid up.   The number was greatly over-
estimated; yet there was no seaport where many ships
could not be seen dismantled and literally rotting at the
wharves, while American sailors sought occupation abroad,
and American shipwrights went off to New Brunswick to
cut timber and build vessels to carry it to Europe or to
the Indies.   Once more all branches of trade connected
with shipbuilding languished, and thousands of mechanics
were thrown out of employment."

Shipowners who persisted in the West India trade ran
grave risk of seizure and confiscation.   But the colonial
authorities often winked at evasions of the law, which
gave their people cheaper and more abundant necessaries
of life.   Smuggling was frequent, and there was a delightful uncertainty about customs interpretations.   A Senator
from Connecticut, who had been engaged in West India
traffic, told this story illustrating the exigencies of the
trade: He had sent out a quantity of candles, which
were on the forbidden list.   But the people of the colony
happened to be in need of candles, and an ingenious Custom House inspector, rising to the occasion, declared that
they were not candles but herring — and so they were
triumphantly passed!

In March, 1817, half in retaliation, half in conciliation,
Congress passed a law which was modelled substantially
on the Cromwellian Navigation Act of 1660.   It forbade
the importation of goods from any foreign port, except in
American vessels, or vessels of the country from which the
goods came.   But an all-important proviso excepted from
the operation of this Act the vessels of countries that
imposed no such prohibition against American shipping.
This was reciprocity indeed, but the reciprocity of the

steel fist in the glove of velvet. Section 4 of this same
Act absolutely closed the coasting trade of the United
States to foreign vessels. These foreign craft had all
along been barred out, in effect, by heavy tonnage dues.
From the very first our coastwise traffic was a rigidly pro-
tected industry.

Only Great Britain, Sweden, and Algiers had accepted
our reciprocity offer of 1815, covering the direct trade
between those countries and the United States. In 1818,
under the provisions of the Navigation Act of the preceding year, we abandoned our discriminating duties on
the trade with the Netherlands, Prussia, Hamburg, and
Bremen. One by one treaties of reciprocity, now num-
bering thirty or forty, have been negotiated since then
with all the maritime nations, and the policy initiated by
the Act of March 3, 1815, has become complete. This
principle did not win immediate acceptance. Great
Britain, on one pretext or another, still endeavored to
bar Yankee vessels from her West Indian colonies.

Our shipowners, however, sought in other seas for the
trade which the inhospitable British policy denied them.
Shut out of the West Indies, they turned to the East
Indies, where Cleveland, Delano, and their comrades had
shown long before an example of Yankee sagacity and
fortitude. The stars and stripes became a familiar sight
to the junk-sailors of the China Sea, the fishermen of
Formosa, and the Malay coasters of the Philippines.
Yankee keels furrowed thickly the Bay of Bengal. Maine
yards, especially, began to launch large and powerful ships
and barks for this distant commerce. Where the West
India trade had been conducted in light vessels of from
seventy to two hundred tons, the East India trade demanded vessels of from three hundred to seven hundred.
Thus the American merchant marine gathered new dignity, and became undeniably more formidable through the
steady growth of the direct traffic between the far East and

our great seaports.   In May, 1827, the "London Times"
was moved to this significant lament: —

"It is not our habit to sound the tocsin on light occasions, but we conceive it to be impossible to view the
existing state of things in this country without more than
apprehension and alarm.   Twelve years of peace, and
what is the situation of Great Britain?   The shipping
interest, the cradle of our navy, is half ruined.   Our
commercial monopoly exists no longer; and thousands of
our manufacturers are starving, or seeking redemption in
distant lands.   We have closed the Western Indies against
America from feelings of commercial rivalry.   Its active
seamen have already engrossed an important branch of our
carrying trade to the Eastern Indies.   Her starred flag
is now conspicuous on every sea, and will soon defy our
thunder."

Beginning with 1820, there had been a remarkably
steady growth in the American merchant tonnage registered for deep-sea commerce.   This tonnage rose from
583,657 to a high-water mark of 757,998 in 1828.   Our
carrying trade in this era was unvexed by European wars
and home embargoes.   Writes Professor J. R. Soley[1]: "In
every respect we may say that this period represents the
most flourishing condition of shipping in American history.
Although since that time commerce has increased twelve-
fold, and although in the year preceding the Civil War
our registered tonnage was three times as large, yet we
have never since 1830 reached the position in respect to
the carrying trade to and from American ports that was
maintained during this decade, but, on the contrary, have
receded from it further and further."   Throughout this
decade we conveyed on the average about ninety per cent
of our commerce in our own vessels, as compared with
seventy-four per cent in 1815, and seventy per cent in

[1] "The Maritime Industries of America," in "The United States of
America," vol. i.

1816, when our merchant tonnage was nominally larger. Our control of our ocean-carrying in 1820–30 was fully equal to that of the remarkable period from 1800 to 1810. Although we transported much merchandise for foreign nations, the great majority of American ships earned their dividends out of American imports and exports.

Prosperity made our people and our lawmakers over-confident. We were too sure that we could "whip creation" in the economical building and sailing of ships. Many of our merchants ran away with the delusion that if we abandoned the whole system of discriminating duties and tonnage dues, and thereby by our example persuaded all Europe to do the same, we should through our superior skill and experience overwhelm our foreign competitors, and dominate the ocean-carrying of the whole world. Congress, in 1815, fulfilling the commercial convention of July 3, had cancelled the discriminating duties and applied reciprocity in the direct trade between the United States and the United Kingdom. In the severe navigation of the North Atlantic, American ships without protection had held their own. "Why not," it was asked, "go a step further and open the indirect trade on the same terms to the vessels of all foreign nations that will open their indirect trade to us?" Or, as Senator Charles Levi Woodbury, of New Hampshire, eloquently phrased it:

"By this bill [the Reciprocity Act of May 24, 1828] we now hold out the olive-branch to all. If our terms are accepted, we may obtain most of the transportation now enjoyed by foreigners in the eight or ten hundredths of our foreign tonnage; as they are now enabled to compete with us to that extent chiefly by the discrimination they enjoy at home."

It is rather pointed comment on these rainbow-prophecies of the New Hampshire Senator that his home town of Portsmouth, which owned more deep-sea tonnage in proportion to its inhabitants than any other port in the country except Boston, now, after many years of this "reciprocity," possesses not one ship registered for foreign carrying.

Professor Soley well says that this Reciprocity Act of 1828, in its effect upon indirect trade, "has done the United States, especially in South America, a great and lasting injury." There came at once an "enormous reduction in our registered tonnage, while the proportion of our own carrying trade, which we had then maintained for eight years, — namely, ninety per cent, — began almost immediately thereafter to fall, and it has been falling ever since, until it has reached almost the point of extinction." Of course, the misnamed "reciprocity" legislation was not the only cause of this melancholy decline, but that it was a real cause and a great one is a hard fact that admits of no denial. The theory was plausible enough. We were to allow British vessels to bring cargoes from Russia, China, or Brazil into our ports on the same terms as American vessels, and in return our ships were to be allowed to bring Russian, Chinese, or Brazilian freights on the same terms as British ships into Liverpool and London. That what we lost in our own trade we should regain and more than regain in the opened trade of other nations, was the persistent argument and honest belief of the champions of maritime reciprocity. Great Britain, however, did not accept this "olive-branch" of reciprocity in indirect commerce until many years afterward, and she kept her West Indian colonies closed, as far as possible, to American commerce as late as 1849.[1]

On May 29, 1828, Congress had made another especial overture to Great Britain, by authorizing the President to open the direct trade between the British West Indies and the United States to British vessels without discriminating duties, if Great Britain gave like terms to American vessels. The British government professed to consent,

[1] "The Financial History of the United States," by Professor Albert S. Bolles, vol. ii.

and on Oct. 5, 1830, President Jackson issued a formal proclamation opening our West India trade to British shipping. We had not asked for a participation in the trade between the British West Indies and the United Kingdom. This remained a monopoly of the merchants of Hull, London, Bristol, and Liverpool. It was soon discovered that the British concession was apparent and not real. All manner of ingenious discriminations were still imposed in the British West India ports against American vessels or the freights which they carried. It is related as an instance of the insincerity of British "reciprocity" that a firm of American merchants, desiring to test the matter, loaded two brigs, one American, one British provincial, with Maine lumber and sent them out at the same time to the island of Trinidad. One vessel received her cargo in an American port; the other, in New Brunswick, whither the lumber had been rafted. Both cargoes sold for the same price, and "the earnings of each vessel on the principle of reciprocity ought to have been alike;" but "an adjustment of accounts proved that the voyage under the British flag produced $893 more than that conducted under the American."

Such an experience naturally led to the giving of a preference to British vessels in West India trade, and to the swift development of the shipping interests of the Canadian provinces. All this time British West Indiamen, by the terms of our Reciprocity Acts, were receiving the same treatment in our ports as our own vessels. They were free to bring in any cargo from the British islands. There was no discrimination against them whatever.

This period between 1815 and 1830 witnessed the birth of several new and interesting forms of maritime enterprise. Before the War of 1812, a keen Boston merchant, Frederic Tudor, had sent small cargoes of New England ice out to the West Indies. After 1815 Mr. Tudor secured a monopoly of the ice trade for the city of Havana, and later he extended his shipments to Charleston, Savannah, and New Orleans. That was before the day of ammonia ice machines. The crystal blocks of Yankee coldness, though sadly shrunken from the original Wenham size, brought quick sales and high profits in the parching tropics. Mr. Tudor managed, by careful packing, to get a few cargoes of ice out to Calcutta. The wealthy European and Indian merchants bought the whole supply, and a regular trade in Massachusetts ice sprang up which remained active and lucrative for thirty years thereafter. Indeed, the ice ships gave Boston a long mastery of the general Calcutta traffic. The originality and audacity of this ice-export business were vividly American. No man who was not very sure of himself would ever have sent· such a perishable freight out upon a four or five months' voyage, which involved crossing the fiery equator, doubling Da Gama's stormy Cape, and steering through the furnace-heart of the Indian Ocean.

This period, 1815–30, witnessed the first transatlantic passage of a ship equipped with steam-power. The bold pioneer was an American, — the ship "Savannah," William Scarborough, of Georgia, owner, and Moses Rogers, master. Steam had come into use in navigating the rivers and coast waters of the United States after Fulton's successful experiment with his "Clermont" on the Hudson. Steamcraft began to run on the Mississippi in 1812–13. Sidewheelers of crude design conveyed freight and passengers from one seacoast town to another. The "Savannah" was a New-York-built ship, of a little more than three hundred tons, an excellent vessel for the time, designed for the Atlantic packet service. Her engine would now be reckoned a poor and weak one; her paddle-wheels were iron wings, which could be detached and taken on deck in boisterous weather. Like all early ocean-going steamships, the "Savannah" had large sail-power. In fact, she was of the type which later came to be known as an auxiliary steamer, trusting to canvas under ordinary conditions, and resorting to machinery when the wind was light or ahead.

The "Savannah," starting on May 26, 1819, from the Southern port whose name she bears, arrived at Liverpool on June 20. A twenty-five days' passage may seem intolerably long in this era of six-day greyhounds, but the "Savannah's" voyage was considerably shorter than the sail-ship average of 1819, although the weather was unfavorable. Steam was used on eighteen of the twenty-five days. When the "Savannah," with her one chimney smoking furiously, approached the English coast, she was mistaken for a ship on fire. Revenue cutters and men-of-war set out to aid her. Their officers were bewildered by the calmness with which the supposedly distressed vessel received their signals, and the ease with which she slipped away from her rescuers. The "Savannah" did not have a pleasant experience in England. She was viewed with suspicion by the naval authorities and dislike by the merchants. The newspapers suggested that "this steam operation may, in some manner, be connected with the ambitious views of the United States." The adventurous Yankee teakettle was closely watched while she lay in British waters. Mr. Richard Rush was at that time American Minister in London. Volume II. of his "Memoranda of a Residence at the Court of St. James" gives the full log of the "Savannah." In Despatch No. 76, from Minister Rush to the State Department, he reports the arrival of the ship and the stir which she created: —

LONDON, July 3, 1819.

SIR, — On the twentieth of last month arrived at Liverpool from the United States the steamship " Savannah," Captain Rogers, being the first vessel of that description that ever crossed the sea, and having excited equal admiration and astonishment as she entered port under the power of her steam.

She is a fine ship of three hundred and twenty tons burden, and exhibits in her construction, no less than she has done in her navigation across the Atlantic, a signal trophy of American enterprise and skill upon the ocean.

I learn from Captain Rogers, who has come to London and been with me, that she worked with great ease and safety on the voyage, and used her steam full eighteen days.

Her engine acts horizontally and is equal to a seventy-two horse-power. Her wheels, which are of iron, are on the sides, and removable at pleasure. The fuel laid in was fifteen hundred bushels of coal, which got exhausted on her entrance into the Irish Channel.

The captain assures me that the weather in general was extremely unfavorable, or he would have made a much shorter passage; besides that, he was five days detained in the channel for want of coal.

I have the honor to be, etc.,   RICHARD RUSH.

This pioneer steam voyage across the Atlantic, however, was more interesting than important. The "Savannah" proceeded from England to St. Petersburg, and then returned to the United States. She had proved that even the crude marine engines and clumsy sidewheels of 1819 could be employed in deep-sea navigation. But she had not demonstrated that in transoceanic passages steam-power was an adequate substitute for sail-power, for she had crossed under canvas, and could have gone right on as smartly as any merchantman if her machinery had broken down. Not for nineteen years afterward did the idea of employing steamships in the trade between the United States and Great Britain take firm hold of the imagination of shipbuilders and merchants. By that time marine boilers and engines had been developed beyond the stage of mere experiment, and coasting voyages in this country and abroad had established the safety and practicability of full-powered steamers.

Of far more value to the commerce of the United States than this bold passage of the solitary "Savannah" was the

starting in 1816 of the first line of sail packets, the famous
Black Ball line, between New York and Liverpool. In
1822 a second line to Liverpool was founded; in the next
year a third line, to Hull. These packets were the real
predecessors of the present steam lines. They wrought a
revolution in the transatlantic traffic. They had fixed
sailing days. They arrived and departed with great regularity. The packets were larger and better ships than the
ordinary merchant vessels. They must not be confounded
with the clippers. These came many years later, and were
designed, as a rule, for longer routes than that between
Queenstown and Sandy Hook. The packets were built
especially for North Atlantic service. That meant that
they must be very strong of hull, with a moderate height
of spars and breadth of canvas. They were not intended
for extreme speed. They had square sterns and bluff
bows, but their under-water bodies, like those of the
"Constitution" and her sister frigates, were sufficiently
fine-lined to permit of handsome passages in fresh, favorable winds.

The packets carried the higher-cost cargoes, that could
afford to bear the higher freight charges. They conveyed also cabin and steerage passengers. The first-class
accommodations were in a capacious and often elegant
house aft of the mainmast, running thence to the stern.
Here the captain lived with his chief officers. The immigrants were berthed between decks. Ventilation was
almost unthought of in those early years. When a storm
came the steerage people would be driven below, and the
hatches clapped down upon them. Until the gale blew
over, the sufferings of the unfortunates, huddled there in
the 'tween decks, would be almost those of the slavers of
the Middle Passage. Even in the cabin, the quarters
were cramped and choking, as compared with modern
standards. But with all their faults the packets marked
a great improvement over the ordinary freighting craft

which they superseded. They were not only more skilfully designed and built, but more liberally administered.
Practically all of the packets were American. Britain
could not compete with our builders in the style of the
vessel and the luxury of her appointments; nor could
she compete with the seamanship of our commanders.
The captains of the first-class packets were the sea's aris-
tocracy. They won their posts by a process of natural
selection. Their life was one of large dignity, but of even
larger responsibility. They were given generous compensation. The result was that the packet service attracted
the very flower of the young men of the American merchant marine.

Some of these packet lines developed such a reputation
that they remained in existence until the Civil War. A
voyage in a packet's cabin was a memorable experience.
Fore and aft, the ship was governed by regular man-of-
war discipline. Dinner was a stately ceremony. Rigid
etiquette ruled the quarterdeck. The voyage was shorter
and rougher, but otherwise packet life bore a close likeness
to the life of the old East Indiamen, as depicted in innumerable English romances. The rivalry of the various
lines was intense. It finally led to the building of ships
of almost clipper model. But from 1816 to 1830 the
Atlantic packets were comfortable rather than fast. Their
occasional quick passages were due to clever handling and
to a habit of carrying a press of sail, which had early
become a characteristic of Yankee seamen. If one ship,
close-reefed, met another in mid-Atlantic with full topsails
set, and perhaps a maintopgallantsail as rigid as iron in
the gale, there was no need for the audacious craft to
show her colors. Mariners of any race would know her at
once as an American.

But this habit was the courage of cool calculation, not
mere rashness. Our ships carried sail because their captains knew that they had the spars and gear to stand it.

The American packet service was conducted with very few accidents. That was one secret of its long prosperity. Our vessels commanded the best insurance rates. There had as yet come no combination of foreign underwriters against America. A passenger or a merchant instinctively sought the stars and stripes. Not until steam came in with foreign subsidies behind it, was our supremacy on the North Atlantic seriously challenged.

Our struggle with Spain for fair play for American ships in her West India colonies was almost as severe as that with Britain. For a long time American vessels were compelled to pay the exorbitant tonnage duty of $2.50 a ton in Cuba. Meanwhile the tonnage duty in Porto Rico under the same Spanish authority was only $1 a ton. To show still further her animus toward American vessels, Spain admitted English and French craft into Porto Rico at a duty of 62½ cents a ton. An American vessel of one hundred tons paid $167 more in tonnage dues in a Spanish West Indian port than did a Spanish vessel in an American port. This discrimination was so intolerable that Congress retaliated against Spain, and finally forced her to abandon it.

These arbitrary exactions of Britain and Spain upon American ships in West Indian waters were all the more cruel because they fell for the most part upon small vessels and poor men. The character of the West Indian trade was such that many of the craft employed in it were of less than one hundred tons. Indeed, by ingenious regulations, both Britain and Spain had sought to limit American traders to types of vessels that were unseaworthy and ineffective. In the winter months the trade always had been very hard and perilous. Something of its severity may be suggested by the experience of the brig "Polly," one hundred and thirty tons, from Boston for St. Croix, with lumber and provisions. Sailing in December, the "Polly" ran into a violent northeast gale in the Gulf

Stream. She sprang a-leak, capsized, and would have sunk but for her lading of lumber. The masts were cut away, and the brig righted. Her deck was a-wash; the wretched crew clung to the cabin-house and remained there twelve days, wet and hungry, when the cook, an Indian, bethought himself of his native practice of kindling a fire by rubbing two sticks together. The artifice succeeded, even on the water-logged brig, and the men stopped gnawing raw pork to eat some cooked provisions.

Day after day went by, and no rescuing sail was sighted. After eighteen days their fresh water gave out, and they had to catch rain. After forty days their little store of salt meat was exhausted. Two passengers had been lost when the brig capsized. On the fiftieth day the mate, a robust man of thirty-five, died. Two seamen and the cook soon followed. Driven desperate by their awful loneliness, the survivors were eating barnacles from the vessel's side, and a large shark which they had caught in a running bow-line. They managed to fish up out of the wreck a teakettle and one of the captain's pistols, and contrived a rude apparatus for distilling fresh water. It was now the middle of April. The barnacles were gone, but they caught another shark and many fish. The sodden hulk had drifted two thousand miles from December 15 to June 20, one hundred and eighty-seven days, when the survivors were picked up by the "Fame" of Hull, bound home from Rio Janeiro. This is one of the most extraordinary stories of shipwreck on record. But the annals of the West India trade in small and feeble vessels include many disasters almost as astonishing. The Yankee seamen, who year after year faced such perils, were the men whom British and Spanish functionaries mercilessly fleeced, when their arduous voyages had brought them into the sunny ports of the sugar islands.

Our West India traders had enemies crueller than the tempests, greedier than the most avaricious of colonial officers of customs. For two centuries the Caribbean archipelago had been an infamous nest of piracy. England, Spain, and France either could not or would not punish these sea-thieves and destroy their accursed calling. The Spanish flag gave them especially hospitable shelter, and time and time again Spanish colonial authorities were accused of being in league with the pirates and sharers of their blood-bought wealth. Most of the pirates were of the Latin races, but there were among them desperate outlaws of all nations, even sometimes English and Americans. After the War of 1812–15, the pirates of the Spanish Main became particularly bold and numerous. They had been reinforced by many of the so-called privateers fitted out by the Spanish-American republics in their wars for freedom. American commerce with the West Indies suffered so much loss of life and property by the ravages of the pirate craft that the United States government sent one of its most celebrated officers, Captain Oliver Hazard Perry, to the Caribbean in 1819. It was Captain Perry's delicate task to discover which were the real pirates and which the Spanish-American privateers. While engaged in this duty, the hero of Lake Erie died of a sudden fever, contracted in the pestilent reaches of the Orinoco.

In 1821, our government sent out a half-dozen light cruisers to smite the West India pirates, wherever they could be found. One of these cruisers, the "lucky 'Enterprise,'" that had already distinguished herself in three wars, was fortunate enough to pounce upon four piratical craft in the act of plundering some American merchantmen off the west end of Cuba. The "Enterprise" captured three of the pirate vessels and forty of their cutthroat crews, who were sent to Charleston for trial and execution. This warfare with the pirates became such serious business that in 1822 our little cruisers were reinforced by the thirty-eight-gun frigate "Macedonian," the thirty-six-gun "Congress," and several corvettes under the command of Commodore James Biddle. One of our cruisers, the "Shark," Lieut. Matthew Calbraith Perry (who afterward led the memorable expedition to Japan), captured five pirate craft in a single season. Another young officer who figured brilliantly in this service was Midshipman David Glasgow Farragut.

In 1823 Captain David Porter succeeded to the command of the West India squadron, which was strengthened by eight more schooners and five twenty-oared barges for hunting the pirates to their lairs in creeks and inlets. The Spanish colonial governors sharply resented this Yankee interference with the profitable business of their friends, the "brethren of the coast." In Porto Rico a Spanish fort fired on the "Fox" and killed her commander. The Spaniards soon found, however, that the American officers and their government were in grim earnest, and they began to give them a rather grudging co-operation. Between the soldiers on shore and the Yankee tars at sea, piracy was wellnigh smothered by the end of the year 1825. For several years afterward the United States maintained a strong squadron of light, swift cruisers on the West India station. Once in a while a pirate would be run down and captured. Vessels of other navies made desultory efforts to clear the West Indies of the followers of the black flag, but the work of no foreign service was so systematic, persistent, and successful as that of our own.

The final crushing of the West India pirates was of vast benefit to the American merchant fleet, and one of the noblest tasks which the United States navy had ever performed in the cause of civilization and humanity. The deadly climate and the sanguinary encounters with foes that gave no quarter cost the navy a great many valuable lives. It was one more demonstration of the truth of Washington's maxim that "to an active, external commerce, the protection of a naval force is indispensable."

The official record of the tonnage of the American merchant marine engaged in foreign carrying in the fifteen years from 1816 to 1830, inclusive, shows rather violent fluctuations. The sharp fall from 1817 to 1818 is due, in large part, to the striking off the list by customs collectors of a certain number of vessels missing since the war.

TONNAGE AND FOREIGN TRADE. 1816–30.

| Year. | Shipping Tons. | Total Foreign Commerce. | Proportion carried in American Ships. | | |
			Imports.	Exports.	Combined Imports and Exports.
1816	800,760	$229,023,052	73.0	68.0	70.5
1817	804,851	186,921,569	79.0	74.0	76.5
1818	589,954	215,031,133	85.0	80.0	82.5
1819	581,230	157,267,521	77.0	82.0	84.5
1820	583,657	144,141,669	90.0	89.0	89.5
1821	593,825	109,117,157	92.7	84.9	88.7
1822	582,701	141,221,796	92.4	84.1	88.4
1823	600,003	140,807,414	92.1	87.4	89.9
1824	636,807	141,141,277	93.4	88.7	91.2
1825	665,409	180,927,643	95.2	89.2	92.3
1826	696,221	150,984,300	95.0	89.6	92.5
1827	701,517	145,642,885	94.3	87.5	90.9
1828	757,998	145,041,293	91.4	84.5	88.9
1829	592,859	134,523,566	93.0	86.0	89.5
1830	537,563	134,391,691	93.6	86.3 •	89.8

CHAPTER X

A NEW-WORLD VENICE

Salem and her Adventurous Commerce — Always a Shipbuilding and
Shipowning Town — Active in the Revolution — First Voyage to
Cape of Good Hope — On to India and China, Oceanica and the
Philippines — Salem Ships in Africa and South America — No
Ports unvisited, no Seas unexplored — Shipowners and Merchants
Both in One — The Frigate " Essex " — Salem Privateers of 1812
— Hawthorne and the Old Custom House — Trade and Fleet now
but a Memory

SET in the northerly bight of Massachusetts Bay, midway between the sentinel-islands of Boston Harbor and the
granite cliffs of Cape Ann, there is a little, old gray town,
whose annals speak more eloquently than those of any
other port on this continent of the enterprise, the sagacity,
and the triumphs of the golden age of the American merchant marine.

Almost half a century ago, when the United States had
launched in a single twelvemonth (1854) three hundred
and thirty-four ships and barks for foreign voyaging, and
our deep-sea merchant tonnage of two and a half millions
was scattered over all the navigable waters of the globe,
a great London journal,[1] in an ungrudging eulogy of the
merchants and sailors of the republic, said : " We owe a
cordial admiration of the spirit of American commerce in
its adventurous aspects. To watch it is to witness some
of the finest romance of our time." It was in old Salem —
" well named the city of peace from its civilizing com-

[1] The " London Daily News."

merce " — that this spirit found its highest and noblest embodiment, — a spirit which reminded this English writer
of " Venice and the old Hanse towns." And there is
poetic fitness in the comparison. Indeed, in one sense
Salem's career was even more remarkable than that of the
famous old ports of Europe, for the trade which gave her
world-fame and made her merchants princes was the work
of a very small but an exceedingly bold and vigorous
population. Salem never was one of the large cities of
America. She had in 1850 only twenty thousand inhabitants. She has always been overshadowed by her
greater neighbor, Boston, fifteen miles away to the
southwest.

No study of the life and especially of the romance of the
American merchant marine would be complete without a
consideration of the extraordinary part borne in it by this
most characteristic coast town of Puritan New England.
Salem won and held her unique fame because the pioneer
instinct was strong in her people. Her ships sailed where
no other ships dared to go. They anchored where no one
else dreamed of looking for trade. The first American
vessel to the Cape of Good Hope hailed from Salem; the
first to open commerce with Hindostan, Java, Sumatra,
and, through the Dutch, with Japan. If not the earliest,
Salem ships were almost the earliest on the west coast of
Africa, where they were long masters of the situation.
They were first in the Fiji Islands, first in Madagascar,
first in New Holland and New Zealand, and among the first
in South America.

The Puritan colonists of Winthrop and Endicott had
scarcely settled on the peninsula between the North and
South rivers before their minds turned to foreign adventure. As early as 1640 they were engaged in trade with
the sugar islands to the southward. Their first West Indiaman was the one-hundred-and-twenty-ton " Desire," Captain William Pierce, which brought home cotton, tobacco,

and negroes from the Bahamas and salt from Tortugas.[1]
As to the outward cargo, it seems to have been composed
just as were many cargoes which for two centuries followed,
for Winthrop's shrewd comment says of it that "dry fish
and strong liquors are the only commodities for those
ports." In 1664 an historian records of Salem: "In this
town are some very rich merchants." From the West
Indies Salem's trade extended naturally to Europe. In
1640 advices are received that "the 'Desire' of this place
has made a passage to Gravesend, Eng., in twenty-three
days." This would have been a fast voyage for a Yankee
clipper two hundred years afterward. Indeed, it is not
always equalled in these times of steam. It is stated that
the swift "Desire" was built at New England's now-famous
yachting station of Marblehead, — an interesting sugges-
tion for students of heredity.

In 1700 Salem's commerce was thus described: "Dry
merchantable codfish for the markets of Spain, Portugal,
and the Straits. Refuse fish, lumber, horses, and provisions
for the West Indies. Returns made directly to England
are sugar, molasses, cotton wool, logwood, and Brasiletto
wood, for which we depend on the West Indies. Our own
produce, a considerable quantity of whale and fish oil,
whalebone, furs, deer, elk, and bear skins, are annually sent
to England. We have much shipping here and freights
are low." These early ships, of course, were small craft,
very far from elaborate or expensive. West India commerce was carried on in vessels of less than one hundred
tons; European trade, in vessels of from one hundred to
three hundred tons. In 1768 Salem had 7,913 tons of
shipping; in 1771, 9,223 tons. Soon after came the Revolution, and for a while, of course, Salem's merchant tonnage ceased to grow. But the temper of the town was
ardent for the patriot cause, and Salem citizens, headed by
Elias Hasket Derby, the most famous and successful mer-

[1] "Annals of Salem," by Joseph B. Felt.

chant of his time, fitted out one hundred and fifty-eight armed vessels to cruise against the enemy, — a larger number of craft than the regular Continental navy contained from the beginning to the end of the war.

In 1791 Salem's shipping comprised only 9,031 tons, or no greater fleet than the town owned twenty years earlier. But under the favorable legislation of the new Federal government, the golden age of Salem's commerce was dawning. Between 1791 and 1800 the town's merchant tonnage increased to 24,682, and in 1807, when the embargo fell upon and stifled our deep-sea trade, Salem possessed [1] 252 vessels of 43,570 tons, — undoubtedly the greatest fleet owned by a community of like size in America, and probably in all the world.

Before even the merchants of New York, Boston, and Philadelphia, the far-seeing and courageous men of Salem spread their canvas to the first winds of peace. In June, 1784, Elias Hasket Derby sent his bark " Light Horse " to St. Petersburg with sugar, thus opening a lucrative traffic with remote North Europe. Derby followed this with an adventure bolder still. He despatched his ship " Grand Turk," of three hundred tons, Captain Jonathan Ingersoll, on a voyage to the Cape of Good Hope. The "Grand Turk" was a smart ship, a celebrated privateer of the Revolution. New England rum formed part of her outward cargo, as it did of many other vessels " bound foreign " in the eighteenth and nineteenth centuries. By way of variety Captain Ingersoll brought home a freight of West India rum from Grenada where he touched on his return from the Cape. He sent the " Grand Turk " to Salem under another master, and sailed himself in the " Atlantic."

His homeward passage furnished a strange instance of the vicissitudes of the life of those old seamen. One day, far out on the deep, a boat was sighted. Captain Ingersoll promptly stood down toward it and picked up the

[1] From a list of Salem property returned to the General Court.

master and mate of the English schooner "Amity," whose crew had mutinied and set their officers adrift. Soon after reaching Salem, Captain Duncanson of the "Amity" was sitting in Mr. Derby's counting-room and sweeping the harbor with a glass, when far down the bay he saw his own vessel standing in. The mutineers, all unsuspecting, had brought their prize to Salem to sell. A couple of guns were hastily put aboard one of Mr. Derby's brigs, and the great-hearted merchant sailed down the bay, met the "Amity," boarded and captured her, and restored the astonished and grateful English captain to his own quarterdeck.

Though the first Cape of Good Hope voyage brought no profit, it did not daunt Mr. Derby. Those Salem merchants were as persistent as they were audacious. Mr. Derby immediately fitted his "Grand Turk" under Captain Ebenezer West for a still longer voyage to the Isle of France, India, and China. The stars and stripes were almost unknown in those distant seas. An American merchant ship could expect no protection from her own government, and nothing but suspicion and jealousy from the chartered East India monopolies of Europe. Nevertheless, the "Grand Turk" went and returned in safety, bringing back to Salem a genuine East India cargo of teas, silks, and nankeens. In 1789,[1] the year of the adoption of the Federal Constitution and the enactment of the first laws protecting and encouraging American ship-owners, Elias Hasket Derby, Jr., in the ship "Atlantic," was the first captain to display the stars and stripes in Bombay and Calcutta. Another Derby ship, the "Peggy," brought to New England the first cargo of Bombay cotton. Of fifteen American ships at Canton in 1789, five hailed from Salem, and in 1790 there came into port consigned to Mr. Derby 728,000 pounds of China tea.

Those old Salem merchants were shipowners, and some-

[1] "Historical Sketch of Salem," by Osgood and Batchelder.

thing more. They did not, as a rule, carry freight for others. When Mr. Derby or Mr. Gray or Mr. Peabody built a ship he calculated to use it in his own mercantile ventures. He would furnish it with an outward freight, and the sale of this procured a homeward cargo which the merchant would dispose of from his own warehouses. Mr. Derby owned about forty vessels, and the largest of them made forty-five voyages for him to India and China. Most of his enterprises were very successful. In 1799 the ship " Mt. Vernon," sailing to the Mediterranean with sugar, and returning with wines and silks, earned a net profit of $100,000. But the merchant prince to whose long wharf the precious argosy was steering never knew of this stroke of good fortune. For Mr. Derby died on Sept. 8, 1799, before the " Mt. Vernon " arrived, leaving an estate of more than a million dollars, then supposed to be the greatest in America.

The gathering of the outward cargoes for strange ports on the other side of the world called for a rare knowledge of men and affairs and an unerring mercantile judgment. In a previous chapter it has been shown why the important voyage of the earliest of our first-class East Indiamen failed because the cargo of the " Massachusetts " was not wisely selected for Batavia and Canton and was not properly laden. The relatively crude products of the farms, forests, and fisheries of America were not the merchandise which the far East particularly desired. Ships bound out beyond the Cape of Good Hope needed to be freighted, in part at least, with European manufactures. Thus it happened that an essential preliminary to an East India voyage was the procuring of iron, duck, and hemp from Gothenburg, Archangel, or Kronstadt, and miscellaneous wares from England. This work was performed by the smaller ships and brigs, while the greater vessels were reserved for the long voyages to the stormy Cape and up the Indian Ocean. If no outward cargo were available, the ships carried silver bullion with which their return lading could be bought outright. But these early voyages were conducted substantially on the basis of barter. There was a delightful uncertainty in it all which quickened and broadened the imagination. As a loyal Salem writer (the Rev. George Bachelor) says: —

" The foreign commerce which sprang up in the last century in Salem was the cause of a wonderful intellectual and moral stimulus, not yet spent. After a century of comparative quiet, the citizens of this little town were suddenly dispersed to every part of the Oriental world and to every nook of barbarism which had a market and a shore. The borders of the commercial world received sudden enlargement, and the boundaries of the intellectual world underwent a similar expansion. This reward of enterprise might be the discovery of an island in which wild pepper enough to load a ship might be had almost for the asking, or of forests where precious gums had no commercial value, or spice islands, unvisited and unvexed by civilization. Every shipmaster and every mariner returning on a richly loaded ship was the owner of valuable knowledge.

" Rival merchants sometimes drove the work of preparation night and day, when virgin markets had favors to be won, and ships which set out for unknown ports were watched when they slipped their cables and sailed away by night, and dogged for months on the high seas, in the hope of discovering the secret well kept by owner and crew. Every man on board was allowed a certain space for his own little venture. People in other pursuits, not excepting the merchant's minister, intrusted their savings to the supercargo, and watched eagerly the results of their adventure. This great mental activity, the profuse stores of knowledge brought by every ship's crew and distributed together with India shawls, blue china, and unheard-of curiosities from every savage shore, gave the community a rare alertness of intellect."

It was no mere fancy, — this reference to secret voyages and mysterious islands where rich cargoes were all ready for the gathering. A wide-awake Salem captain, Jonathan Carnes, happening to call at the port of Bencoolen in 1793, heard that pepper grew wild on the north coast of Sumatra. He told the story to a Salem merchant, Jonathan Peele, who fitted out the schooner "Rajah" of one hundred and thirty tons, four guns, and ten men, in 1795, and sent her out to the East with Carnes in command. Nobody but owner and captain knew of the "Rajah's" destination, and not a word was heard from the adventurous little vessel for eighteen long months. Then she came triumphantly to port with a cargo of pepper in bulk, the first, it is said, ever imported into this country. From this venture the lucky owner of the "Rajah" reaped a profit of seven hundred per cent. When Carnes prepared for another voyage, rival merchants tracked him to Bencoolen, but the shrewd skipper kept the secret of his pungent monopoly. Though the truth finally transpired, as all such mercantile facts must, Salem still continued to dominate the trade with Sumatra, and to furnish a large part of the pepper of the world.

The Salem ship "Friendship" was engaged in this traffic when she was seized and plundered by the treacherous Malays of Qualla Battoo, a Sumatran coast town, who murdered the first mate and several seamen. But Captain Endicott, who was on shore at the time, escaped to sea, and, summoning the help of several American ships from a near-by port, he managed to recapture his robbed and empty vessel. A year later, the forty-four-gun frigate "Potomac" visited terrible vengeance on the Malay pirates. Qualla Battoo was bombarded and destroyed, and a hundred Malay warriors were killed and two hundred wounded in retaliation for the attack upon the "Friendship." Thus vigorously the United States, in the years when our merchant flag flew on every sea, protected the humblest of its sailor-citizens.

For three quarters of a century the name of Salem was better known than that of either Boston or New York on both coasts of Africa. The old Puritan town entered on a wretched business when in 1789 it sent the schooners "Sally" and "Polly" out to debauch the black tribesmen of Senegal with cargoes of New England rum. Rum, gunpowder, and tobacco were long the staples of this commerce, and the homeward freights were hides, palm oil, gold dust, and gum-copal. Though this west coast of Africa trade still continues, and once in a while there is still heard the familiar joke about the clearance of a ship with "rum and missionaries," it long since ceased to be a monopoly of Salem. The best years of this traffic with the miasmatic shores of the Dark Continent were between 1832 and 1864, when there were 558 arrivals at Salem from the west coast of Africa.

In 1820, reaching out still further, Salem merchants sent vessels up the east coast of Africa to Madagascar, and later to Zanzibar. Years before this they had opened a coffee trade with Mocha and Arabia Felix. The ship "Recovery," Captain Joseph Ropes, left Salem for Mocha in April, 1798. Never before had the stars and stripes been seen in those waters, and Captain Ropes found his ship an object of acute Moslem interest. The dignitaries wished to know where lay the strange country America, and "how many moons the vessel had been coming." In 1801 the "Recovery" brought to Salem the first full cargo of the fragrant berries which give Mocha its wide fame. In 1805 there were landed at Salem two million pounds of Mocha coffee, which seems to have had strong charms for the New England palate. Salem in 1805 had forty-eight vessels "round the Cape;" and from 1801 to 1810 the duties collected on the transactions of Salem merchants amounted to $7,272,000.

In May, 1802, a ship in the Canton trade, the "Minerva," Captain Folger, arrived from Salem's first voyage of circumnavigation. The "Minerva" went out *via* Cape Horn, secured a catch of seals in the South Pacific, proceeded to

China, and came home around the Cape of Good Hope. Another Salem vessel was the first to carry the stars and stripes [1] through the narrow and swirling waterways of the Straits of Magellan. This was the "Endeavor," Captain David Elwell. She made her passage in 1824.

Long before Commodore Perry by a judicious combination of big guns and diplomacy opened Japan to the commerce of the world, Salem mariners were familiar with the coasts of the strange kingdom of the twin isles. The Dutch and Portuguese were very early allowed to trade with Japan, under servile conditions and degrading espionage, — for the Japanese of that time had more than the Chinese contempt for "outside barbarians." The Dutch East India Company, in the last years of the eighteenth and the first of the nineteenth century, chartered American ships to conduct this hazardous business. In 1799,[2] the company engaged the ship "Franklin" of Boston, Captain James Devereux of Salem, to take the annual freights to and from Japan; in 1801 the Dutch employed the Salem ship "Margaret," Captain Samuel Derby. Thus Japan, her people and her trade, came clearly within the horizon of Salem seamen and merchants, and it is not strange to learn that, after Perry and his war squadron had sailed in 1853 to open the way,[3] the first vessel to clear from any port in the United States direct for Japan and a market was the Salem bark "Edward Koppisch," Captain John H. Eggleston. The departure of this Yankee craft on her unique voyage moved an Essex County journal [4] to recall with fine local patriotism the historic names of the Derbys, Grays, Crowninshields, Peabodys, and others, by whom Salem "became more wealthy and distinguished than any

---

[1] "History of the Flag of the United States," by Rear-Admiral George H. Preble.

[2] "Historical Sketch of Salem," by Osgood and Batchelder.

[3] Hunt's "Merchants' Magazine," vol. xxxi.

[4] "Newburyport Herald," 1853.

other port on this continent. In that early time and to
the present it has been peculiar to Salem to trade where
nobody else traded, to seek new and distant peoples, and
to carry on a commerce of her own. We will venture even
now that Salem has commenced the trade with more different peoples in Asia, Africa, South America, and the
islands of the sea, than all other American ports put
together."

This was no reckless boasting. As early as 1796 one of
the Derby ships, the "Astrea," Captain Henry Prince,
had found her way to Manila, in the Philippines. There
Captain Prince secured a cargo consisting of 750,000
pounds of sugar, 63,000 pounds of pepper, and 29,000
pounds of indigo, and with this he arrived at Salem in
May, 1797, paying a duty on his freight of $24,020.
Nathaniel Bowditch, afterwards famous as a mathematician
and navigator, was on board the "Astrea" on this memorable venture, and his journal of the voyage is preserved in
the archives of the East India Marine Society. This voyage was the beginning of a great and profitable commerce.
Salem merchants were quick to discover the fine qualities
of the Manila hemp, unsurpassed for cordage. Between
1797 and 1858 there were eighty-two arrivals at Salem
from Manila, the trade flourishing especially in the decade
between 1829 and 1839. Dewey's shotted guns on that
famous May morning of 1898 stirred echoes which had
first been aroused by the friendly Salem salutes of a century before. Indeed, so great a prominence did the
Philippines hold on the Salem maps, and so familiar was
the whole archipelago to Salem merchants, that the last
fleet of large Salem Indiamen, not long since vanished
from the seas, bore the distinctive Philippine names of
Panay, Sooloo, and Mindoro.

Very interesting and odorous places were those old
Salem warehouses, where under one roof would be gathered
the characteristic products of the four corners of the

world. Hemp from Luzon, pepper from Sumatra, coffee from Arabia, palm oil from the west coast of Africa, cotton from Bombay, duck and iron from the Baltic, tallow from Madagascar, salt from Cadiz, wine from Portugal and the Madeiras, figs, raisins, and almonds from the Mediterranean, teas and silks from China, sugar, rum, and molasses from the West Indies, ivory and gum-copal from Zanzibar, rubber, hides, and wool from South America, whale oil from the Arctic and Antarctic, and sperm from the South Seas. It is probable that no equal population, on a narrow mile of shore anywhere, conducted such a wonderfully varied commerce.

Salem merchant ships were as well known in South America as they were on either coast of the Dark Continent. This southern trade began early. It was not wholly smothered by our ocean war with France in 1798–1800, or by the war with England later. But it reached its largest development after 1812–15. It was another example of the diverse and interesting trade for which Salem merchants had such conspicuous genius. Sugar, of course, was the chief import, but rubber, hides, cocoa, and coffee were purchased in large quantities. Salem had an especially active traffic with Cayenne. For many years she was conspicuous at the rubber port of Para, in Brazil, whence there were 435 arrivals at Salem between 1826 and 1860, twenty of them in the single year 1853. Salem ships went also to Surinam and Maranham, and far down the coast to Buenos Ayres and Montevideo, to Rio Grande do Sul and to Rio Janeiro.

It was in a Rio voyage in 1832 that the Salem brig "Mexican" had an exciting experience with pirates. Our light cruisers had been making it very hot for these ruffians in the Spanish Main, but not all of them had been exterminated. The "Mexican" was unfortunate enough to be caught and boarded by the Spanish pirate "Pinta." Twenty thousand dollars of specie, which the brig carried to purchase a return cargo, were promptly seized, and the unarmed and helpless crew were shut into the cabin. A fire was then kindled on the deck, and the pirates hurried away to chase another merchant craft, leaving the people of the "Mexican" to die a horrible death in their prison-house. But before the flames reached the cabin, the sailors discovered a hatch that had been left open. They climbed out through it, fought the fire, and extinguished it, and headed their empty brig for home. The "Pinta" was captured by a British man-of-war a short time afterward, and the government considerately sent sixteen of the pirates to Salem as prisoners. They were tried in Boston before Justice Story, and five of them were summarily hanged. But one De Soto, the mate of the "Pinta," was pardoned by President Jackson because a few years before — so strangely inconsistent sometimes is poor human nature — as master of the Spanish brig "Leon" he had saved seventy-two persons from the burning ship "Minerva" of Salem, at great risk to his own life. Why a man humane enough to do such a deed as this should straightway turn pirate, is one of life's inexplicable mysteries.

Salem masters were as cautious as they were brave, but even their prudence and skill were not always proof against disaster. One of the most harrowing catastrophes recorded in marine annals was that which overwhelmed the Salem ship "Margaret," Captain William Fairfield. The "Margaret" had left Naples on April 10, 1810, with a crew of fifteen and thirty-one passengers. On Sunday, May 20, when the vessel was approaching the American coast, a sudden squall hurled her a hopeless wreck on her beam ends. All her people managed to climb on to the side or bottom of the water-logged hulk. For some reason the captain left the wreck the next day in a boat with fourteen men, and was picked up within a week by a brig from Boston. But the sufferings of those whom the captain left behind were awful. 'The endless seas swept away their

shelter and provisions, while day after day thirst and
starvation did their cruel work. On June 5, twelve of the
wretched company perished. Two days later five left the
wreck in a small boat, while ten clung to the vessel. For
sixteen days the five persons in the boat had nothing but a
mouthful of brandy to sustain them. Then they caught a
little rain-water, but one died, and then another. When the
three who remained out of thirty-one were picked up at
last by a Gloucester vessel, they had been twenty-three
days in the boat with almost no food and water. The
others had died by slow inches. If the ship had sunk
headlong when she was first overwhelmed, it would have
been a mercy to these victims of thirst and hunger fierce
beyond the power of imagination to conceive.

One notable fact about Salem's world-wide commerce
is that most of it was developed in vessels of small
or moderate size. Even a century ago European merchants
and seamen made their long East India voyages in ships
of a thousand tons, armed and manned as generously as
men-of-war. But Salem built up her vigorous Eastern
commerce in vessels of three hundred tons or under. Even
as late as 1825, the largest ship in Salem's merchant fleet
was the "Nile" of four hundred tons, and in 1828 the
largest was the "Arabella" of four hundred and four.
Later still, when the California trade developed, Salem
owned vessels of larger dimensions. The famous ship
"John Bertram," named after one of the most distinguished
of Salem's shipmasters and merchants, was of eleven hundred tons, and although she went to sea within ninety days
of the laying of her keel, she was afloat more than thirty
years afterward under a foreign flag, — a fine specimen of
the durability as well as the beauty of Yankee merchantmen. It was Captain Bertram who happened to call at
Zanzibar in the "Black Warrior" in 1831, just as the
Sultan's frigate was getting ready to carry gum-copal to
India. Bertram was shrewd enough to see that his own

country offered a better market for this valuable gum, so essential in the manufacture of varnishes. He purchased all there was at hand, contracted for more, and brought into Salem in March, 1832, the first cargo of uncleaned gum-copal ever imported into the United States. Salem thereby became a centre of the gum-copal trade. It was by such bold and original strokes as these that Salem merchant navigators won for their old port its fame and for themselves their generous fortunes.

Salem's instinct for strange, out-of-the-way trades brought her ships to the remote and savage Fiji Islands in the years just before the War of 1812. The bark "Active," Captain William P. Richardson, was the pioneer in this venturesome traffic. She sailed from Salem June 1, 1810, and cleared from Fiji July 26, 1811, for Canton. Thus there was opened a new gateway to Yankee enterprise, and the trade which followed was one of the queerest under the sun. In and around the Fiji Islands there grows abundantly a peculiar sea-slug, known as the bèche-de-mer, highly valued as food in the Orient. The Salem mariners collected quantities of these slugs and dried and prepared them for the market. This process required much time, so that Fijian voyages were always long ones. When a proper cargo was secured the ship would steer for Manila to exchange the bèche-de-mer for the hemp and sugar of Luzon or to Canton for a freight of tea. Two years were required for a round voyage in this traffic. It was so arduous and perilous that Salem found few competitors.

The risks which were involved are well illustrated by a voyage of the brig "Charles Doggett," Captain Batchelder, in 1833. The brig was lying at Kandora, one of the Fiji Islands, while Captain Batchelder's men were curing bèche-de-mer for the East India market. A war party of savages suddenly attacked the busy and unsuspecting crew, killing the mate and five sailors, and dangerously wounding James Magoun of Salem, who had lived among the islands several years. On the voyage to Manila the brig touched at the Pelew Islands, where she was again assailed by natives, and a ship's boy was killed.

This same Salem brig, "Charles Doggett," then commanded by William Driver, had borne a part two years earlier in one of the memorable romances of the sea. She had arrived at Tahiti in time to take back to their lonely rock the homesick Pitcairn Islanders. These people were the descendants of the famous mutineers of the "Bounty." In 1787 the "Bounty," under Captain William Bligh, had been sent out to Tahiti by the British government to procure bread-fruit and other useful tropical plants for cultivation in the British West Indian colony of Jamaica. The soft delights of Tahitian life threw a spell like that of Circe over the "Bounty's" crew. Having once tasted them they were filled with an irresistible yearning to return to this ocean paradise, where it was summer all the year around, where brown maidens smiled and flowers were ever blossoming. Twenty-four days out on the voyage to Jamaica, the greater part of the sailors suddenly rose, seized Captain Bligh and eighteen loyal followers, set them adrift in an open boat, and steered a swift course back to Tahiti.

But a cloud of remorse and fear soon overspread their sunny horizon. Captain Bligh and his men, after an awful voyage in their boat, had reached the island of Timor, thirty-six hundred miles from the spot where they were heartlessly left to perish. The mutineers, in dread of pursuit and punishment for their crime, fled from Tahiti with a number of native women and sought a castle of refuge on Pitcairn Island, a solitary rock in the deep heart of the Pacific, at the southeast edge of the Polynesian archipelago, and far out of the track of ships and trade. Here the mutineers burned the "Bounty," and settled down on this islet of only a little more than one square mile.

They had left Tahiti in 1792. For sixteen long years

14

they were buried in oblivion. In 1808 an American whale-man, Captain Folger, happened to sight Pitcairn Island, and seeing signs of life there, sent a boat ashore. All of the "Bounty's" mutineers save one had died, but several of the women and a numerous progeny were living. In 1831 these forlorn colonists had increased to eighty-seven, and as water and food on their islet were desperately scarce, the British government caused them to be brought to Tahiti.

But in this beautiful and fertile archipelago the Pitcairn Islanders were discontented. They sighed for their barren islet far away. They were perishing from sheer homesickness when the Salem brig touched at Tahiti, and they besought Captain Driver of the "Doggett" to carry them back to Pitcairn. The Salem skipper seems to have had a better heart than head, for he consented to convey sixty-five of the islanders fourteen hundred miles for a lot of old copper, twelve blankets, and one hundred and twenty-nine dollars in missionary drafts. This was certainly not high pay, but Captain Driver carried out his bargain. However, his was mistaken kindness, for in 1856 the "Bounty's" grandchildren, increased to two hundred and two, had to be removed again to Norfolk Island. But some of these tenacious folk returned once more to Pitcairn, and are there now.

Fiji never was so inviting as Tahiti, but Salem was not to be frightened away from the peculiar but lucrative commerce. When Commodore Wilkes sailed on his famous "South-Sea" exploring expedition in 1838 he chose a Salem merchant captain, Benjamin Vandeford, as the best pilot and interpreter among the strange South Pacific archipelagoes. Even as late as 1858 an English work on the Fiji Islands noted the interesting fact that the trade in bêche-de-mer, tortoise-shell, and sandalwood "has been and still is chiefly in the hands of Americans from the port of Salem."

After ventures to the Pacific and Indian Oceans, sailing
up and down the Atlantic may seem very prosaic, but
many a fine Salem mansion was built out of the profits of
commerce with the West Indies and South America. The
West India trade was the oldest of all. Salem ships and
sailors followed this for two full centuries, undaunted by
press-gangs, pestilence, or hurricanes. Of the three the
press-gangs were the greatest evil, and the most persistent,
and oftentimes the greedy European men-of-war, not
content with stealing our sailors, would confiscate our
ships. Thus old records [1] say, under date of 1794, " It is
calculated that the English have condemned four hundred
American vessels in the West Indies of which Salem had a
full proportion. April 25. Captain Ropes comes home
passenger. His vessel after long detention was cleared at
Dominica. All his crew had been forced from him except
the mate and boy. With these he sailed. Soon after the
vessel leaked and foundered. They took to their boat and
were saved."

Under 1796. " December 20. James Barnes, a native of
Salem, and having a family here, had recently escaped from
an English frigate in the West Indies. It was seven
months that he was held in such durance. When impressed he was second mate of the ship ' Astrea ' of New
York. He was forced with the point of the sword into
several battles with the French. Once he swam with a
messmate to an American vessel, whose captain did not
dare to take them on board. They were compelled to
return, and his companion perished by a shark."

Under 1799. " March 5. News that Captain Richard
Wheatland of the ship ' Perseverance ' had fought in the
old Straits of Bahama a French privateer one hour and
twenty minutes ; and that the latter was beaten off with
several men dangerously wounded and four feet of water
in her hold." March 22. " That Captain Barket was

[1] " Annals of Salem," by Joseph B. Felt.

attacked by four French launches and luggers near Bilboa and that he drove them away, killing fifteen and wounding others of their men."

These are examples of the trials which Salem mariners were called on to meet in the old years with such fortitude as was in them. It is very wholesome and refreshing, after a long list of such outrages on our commerce and our flag, to read that we had learned at last that the way to win respect was to compel it, and that "There is a rendezvous here to enlist men for the United States government." No doubt that Salem naval recruiting station was well filled at once by men who knew how to fight for their rights, and had the spirit to undertake it.

Indeed, the merchants of Salem, with a patriotism as keen as their enterprise, had very early given token of their approval of Washington's maxim that "to an active, external commerce the protection of a naval force is indispensable." In October, 1798,[1] when French ravages on our West India trade were very costly and exasperating, a mass meeting in the Salem Court House had resolved unanimously to build a ship-of-war for the United States by private subscription, and to make it a frigate of thirty-two guns. In the following winter the white oak for her frames was hauled into town with great rejoicing, and in April, 1799, the keel was laid at Winter Island of the "Essex," smallest of our frigates and one of the most glorious. The ship was launched in the presence of cheering thousands on Sept. 30, 1799. Two months later the "Essex" sailed to protect our commerce in the Indian Ocean, and was the first United States man-of-war to double the Cape of Good Hope.[2] Later the "Essex" joined in the defence of American trade and the chastisement of the Barbary pirates in the Mediterranean. But the service for which this splendid gift of Salem merchants to their

[1] "Salem Gazette," Oct. 26, 1798.
[2] "History of the Navy," Maclay, vol. i.

country is best remembered is her cruise against the British in the Pacific in the War of 1812, when a boy-midshipman named Farragut trod her decks and the gallant Porter was her commander. A summary of this cruise and of the heroic defence of the "Essex" against overwhelming odds has been given in this work, in the chapter devoted to American whalemen whom Porter had made it his especial duty to protect.

Salem sent forty privateers to sea in the War of 1812. In the longer War of the Revolution, as has already been stated, this Massachusetts town had had one hundred and fifty-eight private armed ships afloat. They captured in all four hundred and forty-five prizes,[1] — "more than half the prizes made by our entire maritime forces in this war." The forty Salem privateers of 1812 included some very powerful and successful vessels. One of them was the famous Derby ship "Grand Turk," which had been built as a privateer in the Revolution, and had won distinction by making, in 1784, the first American voyage to the Cape of Good Hope. The "Grand Turk" was an old ship in 1812, but she seems to have been a remarkably strong, swift, and able vessel. She went to sea carrying eighteen guns and one hundred and fifty officers and sailors, — the battery and complement of a regular sloop-of-war. She cruised in the West Indies, off Brazil, and in the chops of the English Channel. The audacity of these Yankee privateersmen was astounding. The "Grand Turk" took prize after prize for twenty days, almost in sight of the British coast, without meeting a single British warship. But in other voyages the fleet Salem rover was repeatedly chased by angry frigates. She always escaped, however, as the "Constitution" did, through better speed and better seamanship. After the war the "Grand Turk" was sold to a great Salem merchant, William Gray, and she ended her stirring career as a peaceful trader. She had captured in

[1] "A History of American Privateers," Maclay.

the War of 1812 three ships, twelve brigs, seven schooners, and eight sloops of the enemy.

Another Salem merchantman, which won much glory and profit in the second War for Independence, was the fast and beautiful ship " America, " owned by a fine family of seamen and patriots, the celebrated Crowninshields. Like the " Grand Turk," the " America " was a veritable sloop-of-war in force. She carried twenty guns and one hundred and fifty seamen, spread a huge cloud of canvas, and could simply make sport of the heavy British frigates, while no British merchantman, once sighted, was ever able to escape her. The " America " took in all twenty-six prizes, and brought to port property valued at $1,100,000, besides destroying a greater amount at sea. It was just such scourging of British commerce by American merchant sailors in private armed ships, that, added to the victories of our little navy, enabled Adams, Gallatin, and Clay to win an honorable peace at Ghent, though the war on land had brought us little but discomfiture. America was really saved in that struggle, as she had been in the crisis of the Revolution, by the extraordinary vigor and aggressiveness of her merchant shipping transformed into privateers.

Salem took as conspicuous a part in this warlike work as she had in pure mercantile adventure, and after 1813 she was paid the compliment of being rigorously blockaded by the overwhelming British squadrons. But the shrill northwesters sweeping down off the Massachusetts hillsides, and the northeasters roaring in from the Grand Banks, defied all the power of the lookout frigates, and, shrouded in tempest, fog, or darkness, bold Salem privateersmen came and went, until both sides welcomed the joyous news of peace.

When the embargo was proclaimed in 1807, — the first step toward war, — Salem had one hundred and fifty-two vessels engaged in foreign commerce. At the close of the war, in 1815, there were only fifty-seven. But the Salem privateers quickly exchanged their warlike equipment for profitable cargoes, and their crews laid aside rammer and sponge, boarding pike and cutlass. In 1816[1] forty-two vessels sailed from Salem Harbor for the far East, and in 1817 this noble trade employed thirty-two full-rigged ships, two barks, and eighteen brigs. In 1812, the deep-sea Salem fleet numbered one hundred and twenty-six vessels, fifty-eight of them Indiamen. It was of this era that Nathaniel Hawthorne, once surveyor in the Custom House, wrote " when India was a new region and only Salem knew the way thither."

But others found the way. No new trade in Africa and the South Seas could compensate for the noble traffic with the magic Orient. Salem merchants made a stout fight, however. Their commerce slipped away only as it slipped away from all American shipping. In 1821, as has been said, there were one hundred and twenty-six Salem vessels engaged in over-seas trade. In 1833 this number had shrunk to one hundred and eleven. The system of discriminating customs duties and tonnage dues which had served so well in the early years of the republic had meanwhile been chiefly abandoned in a series of so-called reciprocity treaties. It would be interesting to know how far the repeal of ship-protection and the decline of Salem shipping bore the relation of cause and effect; at least, they were undeniably simultaneous. But Salem's maritime habit was too tenacious to yield all at once. The old town held a considerable though a dwindling commerce up to the outbreak of the Civil War. The last entry at Salem from ports in India was that of the bark " Brenda," Captain Bridges, in 1845. The last entry from Havana was in 1854; from Manila, in 1858. The last Salem vessel on the coast of Sumatra, where Salem keenness had been first to find the wild pepper crop, was the ship "Australia," Captain Dudley,

[1] " Historical Sketch of Salem," by Osgood and Batchelder.

owned by Stone, Silsbee, and Pickman.   This was in 1860.
The next year saw the end of the Para rubber trade.   The
last arrival at Salem from Zanzibar was the bark "Glide,"
on May 1, 1870, and this was also the last entry at Salem of
any vessel from beyond the Cape of Good Hope.   The last
arrival from a South American port was the schooner
"Mattie F." on March 21, 1877, and with this Salem's
glorious foreign trade became but a memory.   On June
30, 1900, Salem owned not one vessel of any kind per-
manently registered for deep-sea commerce.[1]

No solitude could be more complete than that of the
shore of Salem's harbor, where her roving fleet once
moored.   Derby Wharf still stands, stretching its decrepit
length seaward as if beseeching old ocean for vanished
trade which never comes.   The other day a dismantled
schooner yacht, at the head of a near-by dock, was the only
craft visible.   But the old town wears its dignity well.
Its historic past, the noble mansions of its merchant princes,
its association with the name of Hawthorne and the stately
old Custom House where he dreamed and wrote, " intended
to accommodate a hoped-for increase in the commercial
prosperity of the place — hopes never to be realized — and
built a world too large for any necessary purpose," — these
things make Salem almost as irresistible an American Mecca
as the other gray town of Plymouth across the bay.

If we look for the secret of the extraordinary fame which
Salem won upon the sea we shall find it not in her harbor,
for it is simply good without being great, nor in her store of
shipbuilding timber, for this was early cut off and suitable
oak had to be brought in from the surrounding country.
Salem was not favored over other American towns in legislation, nor had she originally larger wealth.   It was Salem
men of the old Puritan stock, Americans of the Americans,
who built up that romantic commerce that left no land
unvisited, no sea unexplored.   Merchants in the truest

[1] Report of United States Commissioner of Navigation.

and broadest sense were the sagacious gentlemen who sat in their counting-rooms and planned voyages to the other side of the world, to the colonial dependencies of jealous Europe, or to reef-girdled, savage archipelagoes. Their business required iron will and iron nerve, a noble imagination, belief in themselves, and belief in their fellow-men. Among these Salem merchants were some of the great souls of America, and it is not strange that some of them were called on to fill the high places of the State.

And the merchants had fit mates in their sterling seamen. They would unhesitatingly go wherever they were ordered. They loved their country and they loved their old town. They were men of honor and ambition, and consummate masters of their hazardous trade.   As one [1] says who knew them : —

" In those days crews were made up of Salem boys, every one of whom expected to become an East India merchant.   When a captain was asked at Manila how he contrived to find his way in the teeth of a northeast monsoon by mere dead reckoning, he replied that he had a crew of twelve men, any one of whom could take and work a lunar observation as well, for all practical purposes, as Sir Isaac Newton himself.

" This crew had in Nathaniel Bowditch an uncommon supercargo, but it would be difficult now to find a crew of common sailors who, even under such a teacher, would willingly master the mysteries of tangents and secants, dip and refraction, sines and cosines.

" When in 1816 George Crowninshield coasted the Mediterranean in the ' Cleopatra's Barge,' a magnificent yacht of one hundred and ninety-seven tons, which excited the wonder of even the Genoese, the black cook, who had once sailed with Bowditch, was found to be as competent to keep a ship's reckoning as any of the officers."

The glories of the old ships and the old trade are cherished to-day in the Essex Institute and East India

[1] Rev. George Bachelor.

Museum. They are the pride of the Essex port, and well they may be. The history of Salem and its bold ventures into many seas shows commerce in its noblest aspect, with its sordidness subordinated to its romance, and transfigured by a wisdom like that which guides the councils of a nation, and a courage finer and more enduring than the fierce passion of the battlefield.

CHAPTER XI

THE INCOMING OF STEAM. 1831-45

An Era of Maritime Activity all over the World — Can American
Shipping stand without Protection ? — Splendid Sailing Packets —
Yankee Vessels everywhere "most in Demand" — Great Britain
begins to subsidize Steamships — The State-aided Cunard Line
and Other Enterprises — Competition which our Merchants and
Shipowners cannot meet — Brave Struggle for the Supremacy of
the Ocean — A Yankee Merchantman as Richard H. Dana saw her
in 1836 — Fifteen Years' Growth of Tonnage

THE fifteen years which followed 1830 were a period of
peace for the United States and, in the main, for Europe.
There were no more hostile decrees, no more embargoes.
It was a period of intense commercial activity and expansion all over the world. Increased trade demanded everywhere an increased shipping to transport it. Nearly every
maritime nation in those fifteen years added to its merchant
tonnage. The United States was no exception to the rule.
In 1831 there began a steady growth of American shipping, which continued until it was checked by the severe
mercantile panic of 1837. Shipbuilders and shipowners,
like all other classes of business men, were overwhelmed
by that catastrophe. In a year or two, however, there
set in a revival, which carried our deep-sea fleet in 1840
up to 762,838 tons. In 1845 it reached 904,476. This
was a handsome total, but it was less than the 981,019 of
1810. The growth of our merchant shipping had failed
to keep pace with the growth of population. In 1810 the
United States had owned 13.43 cubic feet of registered
tonnage per capita. In 1845 it owned only 4.54 cubic
feet.

The American Union was no longer a thin fringe of commonwealths along the edge of the sea. Brave and determined men had turned westward to the wilderness as well as eastward to the ocean. The problem of internal development vied with the problem of external commerce, and divided the energies of the people and their government. The shipping interest was no longer the overshadowing interest, the object of deep and incessant concern, that it had been in the administration of Washington, Adams, or Jefferson.

In 1831–45 the United States had every apparent reason to be satisfied with its maritime position. Its ships rode on all seas in ever-increasing numbers. It is true that foreign vessels began to be more frequent and familiar in American ports. In 1830 only 78,947 tons of British shipping had entered the United States. In the ten years previous British entries had averaged only 76,518 tons. But in the first year of the new reciprocity British arrivals increased to 143,806 tons, and in the subsequent ten years the annual average was 212,661 tons. "In this decade [1831–40] while our own tonnage gained but 40 per cent in all the ports of the world, British tonnage increased nearly 400 per cent in American ports alone."[1]

The fact that in 1840 the proportion of American imports and exports carried in American ships had fallen to 82.9 as compared with the 86.5 of 1831, was not regarded as a sinister omen when viewed side by side with the fact that our total registered tonnage had increased in this decade from 538,136 to 762,838. "What if foreign ships were carrying more of American trade?" was asked by maritime optimists. "Is there not more American trade for both American and foreign ships to carry than there was ten years ago? And are not American vessels finding it possible and profitable to carry more of the trade of other nations?"

[1] "American Marine," by Captain William W. Bates.

This appeared in 1840 to be a conclusive reply to the shipowners, who still mourned the loss of most of the encouragement afforded by the discriminating duties and tonnage dues of 1789. It really seemed as if the American merchant marine, after forty years of generous national protection, had by 1831 outlived the need of it; that it was so deeply rooted, so strong, and so prosperous that it could defy competition, just as the greatest steel mills of the United States are now probably able to do, after forty years of equally effective tariff-fostering. American ships in 1831-40 were the cheapest as well as the best in existence. No other nation possessed such vast supplies of wood, which was then the one shipbuilding material. The United States had a host of the best mechanics. For many years higher wages and steadier employment had been drawing to New England, New York, Philadelphia, and Baltimore the most skilful shipwrights of Great Britain and North Europe. The art was the proud inheritance of many generations. All alongshore there were families that had never done anything year after year but to build ships or to sail them. The business held the confidence of investors and commanded always an abundance of capital. Most of the yards were constantly active. They were thus able to keep their workmen together, and to procure on favorable terms a regular supply of the best materials.

American shipbuilding and shipowning presented in 1840 as sound, efficient, and well organized an example of human industry as the world had ever known. If, as was universally assumed, wood was to remain the shipbuilding material and sails the motive-power, the United States seemed inevitably destined to crowd Great Britain into second place, and to become the absolute mistress of the seas. Says the British historian, Grantham: —

"Previous to the development of steamships, the preponderance of shipping was falling rapidly into the hands of American shipowners. Thirty years ago one of the great objects of interest at the docks in Liverpool was the American sailing packet, and it was considered that a stranger had missed one of the lions of the port who had not visited these celebrated ships. The same prestige was felt everywhere: on the Atlantic and Pacific oceans, in India, China, and in all the best trades American ships were most in demand."

It was American enterprise, in the "Savannah" of 1819, which had made the first steam transatlantic passage. But nothing came of the venture of this pioneer. The "Savannah" sailed, or sailed and steamed, as far as St. Petersburg, and returned in safety. None of the sterling merchants who made our packet lines so brilliantly successful read the significance of this memorable voyage. The "Savannah" herself never again crossed the ocean with her seventy-two horse-power and her flopping side-wheels. Our shipwrights went on building larger and faster packets, but they were sail-ships only. Perhaps the builders ought not to be blamed for their apparent shortsightedness. For these packets were noble vessels, and their exploits aroused the pride and affection of their owners and the country. The swiftest of our ocean grey-hounds of to-day awakens no such enthusiasm as the "North America " or the "Columbus " or the "England," of the famous Black Ball line, did by their sail-passages of eighteen or twenty days from the Hudson to the Mersey, or the "Independence " in her record-breaking run of fourteen days, six hours. Something of the safety, regularity, and general efficiency of these old packets can be gathered from the tribute of the "New York Herald " to a Black Ball liner, as the fine old veteran was about to leave the "roaring forties " for the humdrum service of the coasting trade. This ship had passed twenty-nine years in battling with the Atlantic tempests between New York and Liverpool. She had made 116 round passages without losing a seaman, a sail, or a spar. She had brought 30,000 passengers to this country from Europe, and had witnessed 1,500 births and 200 marriages.

In the golden days of the packet service there were sailing out of New York, besides the Black Ball line, the Swallowtail line, so called because of the shape of its private signal, of Grinnell, Minturn & Co., the Dramatic line of E. K. Collins (composed of the Roscius, Sheridan, Siddons, Garrick, etc.), the Red Star line, the Williams and Guion line, and half-a-dozen others. There were two or three lines to London, and two or three to Havre. Philadelphia had a Liverpool line; so had Boston. But New York controlled most of the packet service, just as it now holds the greater part of the transatlantic steam service. Most of the high-class packets were built at famous old yards along the East River; a few came from New England. Careful laws governed the passenger trade of the packet fleets. Each ship was allowed to take so many in the cabin and so many in the steerage, and no more. The packets carried the higher-cost freight, and their charges were above those of ordinary merchantmen. But they earned this money by the swiftness and regularity of their voyages.

Many of the old packets bore names which testified to the pride of their owners in their noble ships. Marine nomenclature was not then a mere matter of John Jones and Peter Q. Robinson. There were the "Star of the West," the "Queen of the West," the "Montezuma," the "Harvest Queen," the "Universe," the "Marmion," the "Admiral," the "Victory," the "Shenandoah," and the "Constellation." Their captains were the picked men of their profession. Some of them were very Chesterfields of courtesy. Others were more celebrated for keen Yankee wit. One of this latter class was Captain Larrabee, of the "Sir Robert Peel." It is related of him that he was once accosted by a cockney passenger with the remark, "Well, Captain, that flag [pointing to the stars and stripes at the mizzen peak] has not braved for a thousand years the battle and the breeze." "No," Larrabee instantly responded, "but it has licked one that has!"

Against these magnificent square-riggers, sailed with such vigor and exactness, Europe could not compete. So long as the transatlantic service was a question of sheer seamanship, America held the undisputed mastery. This Western Ocean, with its vast range of heaving waters, its fierce gales and its bitter cold, has always been the most important field of maritime adventure. Supremacy there has ever been the coveted prize of seafaring nations. Year after year, in the era of wood and canvas, the advantages of the United States were overwhelming. Our superior ships actually cost less to build than did the ships of Britain, and scarcely more than the cheap soft-wood craft of Northern Europe. The price of a 500-ton sailing vessel, fully equipped, was $37,500 in this country and about $43,000 in England.

A London shipbuilder and owner, engaged in trade with all parts of the world and familiar with the merchant marine of all nations, asserted that the cost of a year's voyage of a 500-ton American vessel was £2,191; of a 500-ton English vessel, £2,623. Wages were undeniably higher in the American than in the British service, though the difference may not have been so wide sixty years ago as it is now. But American vessels habitually carried fewer men in their crews, and abler officers worked these crews under a more rigid discipline. These American ships, because of better design and bolder navigation, could make four voyages while British or Dutch ships were making three. Such was the fame of Yankee models, not for speed only, but for strength and durability, that between 1815 and 1840, 340,000 tons of shipping built in the United States were sold to foreigners. This was highly creditable to our shipyards, but there was another side to these foreign purchases. The excellent American-built ships, in the service of foreign merchants whose wage scale was lower than our own, competed directly with American-owned ships in our carrying trade, and in the carrying trade of other nations.

In 1840 Great Britain was still a stiffly protectionist country, as she had been for two or three centuries. Many years of almost prohibitive tariffs had developed British manufacturing to a high efficiency. This was especially true of British workshops in iron and steel. Fortunately for Great Britain her coal and her ores were as cheap and as abundant as the oak and hard pine of America. Hulls of ships were not built of iron in 1840, but the nation which had the cheapest metal and the most numerous workshops had an important advantage in the production of steam boilers and marine machinery. There were long-headed men in the British government who saw even before 1840 that the salvation of the maritime prestige of the United Kingdom lay in the prompt utilization of steam power on the North Atlantic. At first an experimental steam packet service was started to the Isle of Man. Then a longer service was established across the North Sea to Rotterdam and Hamburg; then a longer service still, to Gibraltar.

Every one of these early steam lines was a state-aided enterprise. Not one of them would have come into being without the fostering care of the royal government. British economic policy at that time was frankly protectionist. No good Briton protested when in 1834 the subsidy to the Rotterdam and Hamburg steam packets was set at $85,000 a year, or of the Gibraltar packets at $150,000. These government subventions were exceedingly important. They encouraged British shipyards to turn their attention to steam machinery, and gave them experience in such work. When it was recognized that the European packet service was entirely successful, the government proceeded to a still greater step.

15

In October, 1838, the Admiralty asked for proposals for a steam service to America. In this year two British steamships, the "Sirius" and "Great Western," had made successful voyages to New York. The "Sirius" of 700 tons was built at the enterprising port of Bristol; the "Great Western," at London. Both were wooden-hulled, side-wheeled, with a sea speed of about 10 miles an hour. These ships came over in $17\frac{1}{2}$ and 15 days, and returned in 17 and 14. Twenty days eastward and 21 to 26 days westward was then the best average of the American sailing packets. The British government realized at once that with proper protection and encouragement to British shipowners, the redoubtable Yankees would be surely vanquished.

In 1839 the government awarded an Atlantic mail contract calling for a subsidy of $425,000 a year to Samuel Cunard and his associates. This was the genesis of the world-famed Cunard Company. From its very first hour it was a protected enterprise. It began in 1840 with four wooden, side-wheel steamers of moderate size and power, — the "Acadia," "Britannia," "Columbia," and "Caledonia." "It is beyond question," declares Professor James Russell Soley, in his review of "The Maritime Industries of America," "that the sum paid to the Cunard Company in its early days, amounting to about 25 per cent per annum on the cost of the running plant, and subsequently increased to $550,000, to $750,000, and to $850,000, was clearly a subsidy; that it was given with the plain intention of establishing firmly in English hands the transatlantic traffic, and that it accomplished the desired result." The Cunard steamers sailed at first from Liverpool to Halifax and Boston, with an occasional visit to Quebec. Later the route to New York was made the main line, the subsidy was increased, and more power and speed were given to the steamers.

Gradually the Cunard vessels, though once in a while

beaten by the Yankee sail packets, laid hold of the choicest of the passenger and freight trade. Even now, however, the spirit of our shipowners was undaunted. The merchants of Boston and New York showed a splendid tenacity. Without national protection, at least equal to that enjoyed by Mr. Cunard, they could not build costly steamers. But they improved the construction and speed of their sailing ships, and in 1844, four years after the Cunard steam service began, a famous merchant, Enoch Train, established an entirely new line of packets from Boston to Liverpool. The fleet consisted of four ships, the "Dorchester" of 500 tons, the "Cairo" of 600, the "Governor Davis" of 800, and the "St. Petersburg" of 800, — "all first class, Medford-built, copper-fastened, coppered, and fast." These vessels were about half the size of the Cunarders. They were compelled to accept lower rates for freight and passengers. But the Train line lived for a dozen or more years, and the New York packet lines ran successfully down to the outbreak of the Civil War.

There was nothing extraordinary about the first Cunard liners. They were fairly good wooden steamships, — that is all. The "Britannia," one of the earliest, was built on the Clyde,[1] and was 207 feet long, 34 feet wide, and 22 feet deep, with a horse-power of 403, a tonnage of 1,155, and a speed of $8\frac{1}{2}$ miles an hour. She burned about 450 tons of coal in an Atlantic passage. In 1844 the "Cambria" and "Hibernia" of 500 horse-power and 1,422 tons were added to the Cunard fleet. These vessels had the modest speed of $9\frac{1}{2}$ miles an hour. In 1848 the "America," "Niagara," "Europe," and "Canada" were brought out, with a horse-power of 680, a tonnage of 1,820, and a speed of $10\frac{1}{4}$ miles. In strong and favorable winds the American packets could run for a day at a time at a rate of 12 or 13 miles an hour, and in mid-ocean the Cunard steamers were repeatedly passed by these powerful sailing

[1] "History of Merchant Shipping," Lindsay.

ships. But the difficulty was that the winds were not always strong and favorable. Often they were light and fickle; often, dead ahead. Then the steadily turning side-wheels of the "Britannia," the "Canada," and the rest gave them the victory. It was very much like the traditional race of the hare and the tortoise.

American merchants finally recognized that their splendid packets never could prevail against their British steam competitors, aided as these were by an annual subsidy, which represented about twenty-five per cent on the investment. The merchants of Boston made a brave trial. One of their number, Mr. Robert Bennett Forbes, caused auxiliary steam-power to be fitted into the packet ship "Massachusetts," for use in light or contrary weather. The "Massachusetts" did save time in her passages over the sailing ships, but she was smaller than the Cunard steamers, and her engine and screw propeller were not sufficient to give her equal sea speed.

The screw, as a means of propulsion, was long looked upon askance by marine architects. As far back as 1836, Ericsson, the great Swede, to whom America owes gratitude imperishable, made a successful trial of a boat equipped with a propeller on the Thames. The conservative Admiralty gave the unknown foreigner no encouragement, but Ericsson was fortunate enough to attract the attention of an American naval officer of a bold turn of mind and a genius for practical mechanics, Commodore Robert F. Stockton. The commodore authorized Ericsson to build a small screw steamer. The vessel was constructed in 1838 by Laird, of Birkenhead, and brought to the United States. Ericsson came also, and thus, among the freer opportunities of the New World, entered upon his career of distinguished achievement. The screw propeller was adopted by the United States navy in a successful sloop-of-war, the "Princeton," and it also came into use in some steamers of the coastwise service. Side-wheels, however, remained the favorite of all but the most progressive designers and builders on both sides of the ocean. The Great Western Company launched a fine screw steamer, the "Great Britain," in 1843, for the transatlantic route. The Cunard line clung stubbornly to its side-wheelers, and it was employing some of them as late as 1870. The belief was that a given horse-power would drive a side-wheel steamer faster than a screw-ship, and that especially in strong adverse winds and rough seas the side-wheel type was the more effective. It required many years to overthrow this delusion.

Though Great Britain, thanks to her early policy of subsidy-protection, was the first to apply steam successfully to ocean commerce, long before Mr. Cunard secured his Liverpool-Boston contract steam vessels were plying in freight and passenger traffic on the rivers and lakes and along the seacoast of the United States. Fulton's "Clermont" of 1807 was the pioneer of a great fleet of side-wheelers on the Hudson River and Long Island Sound. The success of these craft led naturally to the use of larger and more powerful steamers, all at first of side-wheel design, in the service between the chief cities of the Atlantic seaboard. Steam began to appear in the coastwise trade about 1830. Its advantages were so manifest that within a dozen years afterward nearly all the Southern ports were connected with New York by steam lines, and the Eastern ports in the same way with Boston.[1] In 1841 the first seagoing propeller was built, — the "Clarion" of two hundred and fifty tons, driven by an Ericsson screw, and designed for the route between New York and Havana. In 1842 six propellers for the coasting trade, also equipped with Ericsson screws, were built at Philadelphia.

More than sixty years before the "Retvizan" was

---

[1] "American Navigation," by Henry Hall.

launched from the Cramp yard on the Delaware, the first war steamer was built in America for the Russian government. It was the "Kamschatka" constructed at New York in 1838. This interesting vessel is described as a "sharp and fast frigate." She was 227 feet long, 45 feet wide, and 24 feet deep, and her registered tonnage was 2,282. The "Kamschatka" was, therefore, considerably larger than the early Cunarders.

It was the superior strength and speed of the large coastwise steamships of America which before and after 1840 drew to our shipyards the eager attention of foreign governments. The early Savannah, New Orleans, and Havana steam packets were quite as good in every way as the first vessels built on the Clyde for the Cunard Company. Private enterprise had created in both America and Britain the mechanical facilities for constructing the hulls and machinery of seagoing steamships. In 1840, so far as skill in this form of construction was concerned, the two countries were practically equal. After 1845, when the Washington government gave a real though temporary protection to its steamship interests, as is shown in a succeeding chapter, the American ocean-going steamers proved to be distinctly superior in their performances to their British rivals. It is important to remember this fact, because it has been too often asserted that the change from sails to steam found America unprepared and incapable of meeting British competition. Britain had more workshops, it is true. Her machinery-making industry, after many years of rigid protectionism, had become very firmly established. But there were no British workshops that were better than those at Boston, New York, Philadelphia, or Pittsburg. If our government had grasped the situation and acted as promptly, as boldly and generously as the British government acted, we should have beaten our kinsmen at building steamships, as we beat them at building sail-ships. American mechanics had just as much native aptitude for the one as for the other.

Great Britain did not stop with the Cunard line. Another liberal subsidy was offered for a steamship line to the far East. This resulted in the establishment of the Peninsular Company, afterward the Peninsular & Oriental, now a glory and bulwark of the British Empire. The growth of this huge, State-aided corporation began to affect directly and indirectly the high-class business of the splendid Yankee East Indiamen, which, as Grantham has said, "in all the best trades" "were most in demand." In 1840 British steamships invaded another field where American sail-ships had long been pre-eminent. The manner in which this was brought about forms a truly illuminating episode.

The American Consul at Guayaquil was William Wheelwright, of Newburyport, a shrewd, energetic, far-seeing New Englander. Mr. Wheelwright recognized the great commercial possibilities of a steam line up and down the west coast of South America. He came home full of his idea, and broached it to a number of merchants of his acquaintance. They acknowledged the attractiveness of Mr. Wheelwright's proposal, but one and all of them declared that the idea never could be carried into practice without a subsidy like that which the British government was paying to Mr. Cunard. Congress at that time would grant no subsidy. Rebuffed by his own government, Mr. Wheelwright went abroad, and laid his plan before the merchants of Liverpool and London. He met everywhere with a cordial reception, secured an ample subsidy from the government, built a fleet of ships in England after the American model, and started the Pacific Steam Navigation Company, now one of the most powerful steamship corporations in the world. If the authorities at Washington had been as willing to listen to Mr. Wheelwright as were the authorities at London, that great line of steamers would have been built in this country, officered and manned by our own seamen, and controlled by our own merchants. In that case American and not British influence would to-day be dominant along the west coast of South America, in whose development the Pacific Steam Navigation Company has been for sixty years a most important factor.

This period brought on the North Atlantic the earliest steamship tragedy, to warn America and Europe that not even the new power had vanquished all the old terrors of the sea. A fine British steamer, the "President," launched in 1839 for the British & American Steam Navigation line, sailed from New York on her homeward voyage in the spring of 1841, but never reached her destination, nor was so much as a splinter of her wreckage ever seen. The "President" carried down into the depths a large and distinguished company. Her commander was Captain Richard Roberts, who had brought the "Sirius" over on her pioneer voyage in 1838. A stone, bearing the name of Captain Roberts, in a little churchyard near Queenstown, commemorates "the first officer under whose command a steam vessel ever crossed the Atlantic Ocean." This honor is Captain Roberts's own so far as his country's service is concerned, but ahead of him by nineteen years was an American, Captain Moses Rogers, of the "Savannah."

In 1840, and even in 1845, the steamships afloat upon all oceans were still only a petty squadron as compared with the vast fleets of sailing ships. It was the square-rigger, the ship, bark, or brig, that was still the world's real sea-carrier. To this period belongs the swift growth of East India commerce. The Western World, in its peace and new prosperity, developed a large demand for the strange wares of the Orient. Discriminating duties protected American ships in the traffic between our ports and the East until 1834. By that time our merchants had secured a hold upon this romantic and profitable trade that could not easily be shaken. The great houses of Boston and New York that brought teas, silks, and spices from China and India owned their own ships and supplied them with both outward and homeward cargoes. These American firms began to establish branches in Hong Kong, or Canton, or Calcutta. In 1840, twenty-one Calcutta cargoes were brought to the United States, amounting in quantity to seventeen thousand tons, and in value to $1,250,000. This trade had doubled since the first years of the century, and it was destined to a further and much greater increase.

Another long-distance commerce, in which the stars and stripes were conspicuous, was that with the west coast of North America, where the brave "Columbia" had been the Yankee pioneer. This great region was still a no-man's land. Ventures thither were full of hazard. The furs of wild animals and the hides of cattle were the chief articles of export, and they were secured by barter with the Indians and Mexicans. Nobody dreamed as late as 1845 of the golden possibilities of California. The best picture of this west coast trade as it existed in the decade from 1830 to 1840 — indeed, the most vivid and entrancing portrayal of sea life in our language — is to be found in Richard H. Dana's "Two Years before the Mast." Mr. Dana, a youth from Harvard, overworn by hard study, went out around Cape Horn in 1834-35 in the brig "Pilgrim," of Boston, and returned in the following year in the ship "Alert." His experience was the typical experience of the American sailor of that period. The brig was a small craft, but indispensable in certain kinds of commerce. She was slow, crowded, uncomfortable. The darker chapters of Dana's sea life came first. They made him appreciate all the more deeply his good fortune, when he was transferred to the broad decks and clean forecastle of the "Alert," that came very much more nearly than the old brig to the typical American merchantman. Dana has written in enthusiastic words his admiration for the "Alert," which began the moment he first saw the "tall gallant ship, with royals and skysails set, bending over before the strong afternoon breeze," as she came in around the point at San Diego. And how smartly she was brought to her anchorage!

"Her light sails were taken in as she passed the low, sandy tongue of land, and clewing up her head sails she rounded handsomely to under her mizzentopsail, and let go her anchor at about a cable's length from the shore. In a few minutes the topsail yards were manned, and all three of the topsails furled at once. From the foretopgallant yard the men slid down the stay to furl the jib, and from the mizzentopgallant yard, by the stay, into the maintop, and thence to the yard; and the men on the topsail yards came down the lifts to the yardarms of the courses. The sails were furled with great care, the bunts triced up by jiggers, and the jibs stowed in cloth. The royal yards were then struck, tackles got upon the yardarms and the stay, the long-boat hoisted out, a large anchor carried astern, and the ship moored. This was the 'Alert.'"

Even to the veriest land-lubber, Mr. Dana's nautical words convey a distinct idea of zeal and precision. "She looked as well on board as she did from without. Her decks were wide and roomy, flush fore and aft, and as white as flax, which, her crew told us, was from constant use of holystones. There was no foolish gilding and gingerbread work, to take the eye of landsmen and passengers, but everything was 'shipshape.' There was no rust, no dirt, no rigging hanging slack, no fag-ends of ropes and 'Irish pendants' aloft, and the yards were squared to a 't' by lifts and braces."

Young Dana managed to be transferred from the cramped little "Pilgrim" to this noble ship. His book has this clear-cut description[1] of his first day's work and of the "Alert's" routine: —

"After all hands were called at daybreak, three minutes and a half were allowed for the men to dress and come on deck, and if any were longer than that, they were sure to be overhauled by the mate, who was always on deck, and making himself heard all over the ship. The head-pump was then rigged, and the decks washed down by the second and third mates; the chief mate walking the quarterdeck, and keeping a general supervision, but not deigning to touch a bucket or a brush. Inside and out, fore and aft, upper deck and between-decks, steerage and forecastle, rail, bulwarks, and water-ways, were washed, scrubbed, and scraped with brooms and canvas, and the decks were wet and sanded all over, and then holystoned. . . . There were five boats belonging to the ship, — launch, pinnace, jolly-boat, larboard quarter-boat and gig, — each of which had a coxswain, who had charge of it, and was answerable for the order and cleanness of it. The rest of the cleaning was divided among the crew: one having the brass and composition work about the capstan, another the bell, which was of brass, and kept as bright as a gilt button, a third, the harness-cask, another, the man-rope stanchions; others, the steps of the forecastle and hatchways, which were hauled up and holystoned. Each of these jobs must be finished before breakfast; and in the mean time the rest of the crew filled the scuttled-butt, and the cook scraped his kids (wooden tubs out of which sailors eat), and polished the hoops, and placed them before the galley to await inspection. When the decks were dry, the lord paramount made his appearance on the quarterdeck, and took a few turns, eight bells were struck, and all hands went to breakfast."

[1] "Two Years before the Mast," by Richard H. Dana, chap. xxiii. pp. 208-210.

This is Mr. Dana's description of the manner in which the "Alert" was got under way: —

"We paid out on the chain by which we swung, hove in on the other, catted the anchor, and hove short on the first. This work was done in shorter time than was usual on board the brig; for though everything was more than twice as large and heavy, the cat-block being as much as a man could lift, and the chain as large as three of the 'Pilgrim's,' yet there was a plenty of room to move about in, more discipline and system, more men and more good-will. Each seemed ambitious to do his best. Officers and men knew their duty, and all went well. As soon as she was hove short, the mate, on the forecastle, gave the order to loose the sails; and in an instant all sprung into the rigging, up the shrouds and out on the yards, scrambling by one another, — the first up, the best fellow, — cast off the yardarm gaskets and bunt gaskets, and one man remained on each yard, holding the bunt jigger with a turn round the tye, all ready to let go, while the rest laid down to man the sheets and halyards. The mate then hailed the yards, — 'All ready forward?' — 'All ready the cross-jack yards?' etc., etc.; and 'Aye, aye, sir!' being returned from each, the word was given to let go; and, in the twinkling of an eye, the ship, which had shown nothing but her bare yards, was covered with her loose canvas, from the royal-mast-heads to the decks. All then came down, except one man in each top, to overhaul the rigging, and the topsails were hoisted and sheeted home, the three yards going to the mast-head at once, the larboard watch hoisting the fore, the starboard watch the main, and five light hands (of whom I was one), picked from the two watches, the mizzen. The yards were then trimmed, the anchor weighed, the cat-block hooked on, the fall stretched out, manned by 'all hands and the cook,' and the anchor brought to the head with 'cheerly, men!' in full chorus. The ship being now under way, the light sails were set, one after another, and she was under full sail before she had passed the sandy point."

The "Alert" was no exceptional Yankee merchantman. She was indeed superior to the tub of a "Pilgrim," which had no right on the west coast, and should never have gone "off soundings." But the "Alert," after all, was only a "hide-drogher," and an object of the lofty disdain of the immaculate Atlantic packets and stately East Indiamen. Her smart seamanship was a common characteristic of all the deep-sea vessels of the American merchant marine.

The period of fifteen years from 1831 to 1845 closed with bright skies and clear seas for the American ship, but with one ugly cloud far down toward the Eastern horizon. This was the subsidized British steamship service, destined in the succeeding decade to spread to every ocean, and to absorb much of the fine and profitable traffic that had been almost a monopoly of American sea-carriers. But the decline in our tonnage was not to become manifest at once. It was even to be delayed by fortuitous and temporary causes. That decline, however, was inevitable from the shifting conditions of the ocean trade. The change from sails to steam was less important and less harmful to our established maritime interests than the change from wood to iron. This was something which came in the next period to be considered, that from 1846 to 1860. The distinguishing characteristic of the period from 1831 to 1845 was the introduction of the wooden steamship, protected and fostered by British subsidies, in the navigation of the North Atlantic, where the sailing ships of the United States had long been pre-eminent. The following table presents the statistical record of our tonnage in the deep-sea trade, and our foreign commerce for the fifteen years which this present chapter has discussed, from 1831 to 1845, inclusive: —

TONNAGE AND FOREIGN TRADE. 1831–1845.

Year.	Shipping Tons.	Total Foreign Commerce.	Proportion carried in American Ships.		
			Imports.	Exports.	Combined Imports and Exports.
1831	538,136	$168,180,831	91.0	80.6	86.5
1832	614,121	176,642,365	89.4	75.8	83.1
1833	648,869	188,576,675	90.7	75.5	83.8
1834	749,378	210,869,915	89.0	74.4	83.0
1835	788,173	251,980,097	90.2	77.3	84.5
1836	753,094	300,917,858	90.3	75.4	84.3
1837	683,205	241,915,930	86.5	77.6	82.6
1838	702,962	200,948,858	90.6	82.8	84.2
1839	702,400	268,748,629	88.7	78.3	84.3
1840	762,838	221,927,638	86.6	79.9	82.9
1841	788,398	234,775,015	88.4	77.8	83.3
1842	823,746	195,953,066	88.5	76.3	82.3
1843 [1]	856,930	125,259,153	77.1	77.0	77.1
1844	900,471	208,350,438	86.7	70.5	78.6
1845	904,476	219,224,433	87.3	75.8	81.7

[1] Nine months.

CHAPTER XII

MAIL SHIPS AND CLIPPERS. 1846–60

American Merchant Marine at the Height of its Strength and Glory
— Mail Subsidies granted by the United States — Quick Success
of the New Departure — A Steam Line to Havre and Bremen —
Pacific Mail Company — Collins Line to Liverpool and its Superb
Fleet — Cunarders eclipsed in Size, Comfort, and Speed by the
New Americans — Evolution of the Yankee Clippers — Ocean-
Racing around Cape Horn — Britain's Safe Repeal of her Navi-
gation Laws — Few Vessels purchased from America — Famous
American Shipbuilders: William H. Webb, Donald McKay — The
"Great Republic" — Captain Samuels and the "Dreadnought" —
American Ships and Seamen Everywhere Superior — The Fateful
Year 1855 — Loss of the "Arctic" and "Pacific"— Rise of Southern
Opposition to the Ocean Mail Law — Collins Subsidy reduced
in 1856 — Renewed Southern Attack upon Northern Steamship
Interests — Overthrow of the Subsidy System in 1858, and
Destruction of American Steam Lines to Europe — Great Britain
Now Supreme on the North Atlantic — British Subsidies More
Persistent and More Liberal — American Shipbuilding on the
Wane before the Civil War — High-Water Mark of Merchant
Tonnage

THE years that lie between 1846 and 1860 are the most
interesting and important in the history of the United
States merchant service. They saw the deep-sea tonnage
of the republic mount to its highest figure, and they saw
the beginning of the melancholy decline. This fifteen-
year period is memorable for the appearance of splendid
though short-lived American lines of transatlantic steamships, and for the exploits of the superb Yankee clippers
in which the sailing ship of commerce came to its apothe-
osis. The period opened with the promise of renewed and

absolute American mastery of ocean-carrying. It closed beneath the shadows of actual or impending defeat. It is a hasty and superficial judgment, which dates the shrinkage of the American merchant marine from the Civil War of 1861–65. The war was one of the powerful contributive causes. But the decline in shipbuilding and shipowning had set in several years before the first shots were fired from the batteries of Charleston, against the merchant steamer "Star of the West" hastening to the relief of Sumter. The decay of our sea trade would have gone on if the war had never been fought, though it might not have begun at all if the war had never been contemplated.

England's bold stroke for maritime supremacy in the state-aided Cunard line of steamships, and the other subsidized lines that followed it, had not been ignored by the vigilant lawmakers in Washington. It should be remembered to the lasting credit of the South, that her statesmen took the lead in the national movement to protect our merchant shipping from this new and strange foreign menace. As early as 1841, the year after the first Cunarders sailed from Liverpool for Halifax and Boston, Senator Thomas Butler King, of Georgia, began a very able and persistent advocacy of national encouragement for the building and maintenance of American ocean steamships.[1] Mr. King, who had an earnest lieutenant in Senator Thomas J. Rusk, of Texas, urged that the sum of one million dollars be appropriated annually for the carriage of the foreign mails. This proposition at the time came to nothing, but the deepening inroads of the subsidized British steamships on our unprotected sail-packet trade induced Congress, in 1845, to pass an Act authorizing the Postmaster-General to make contracts with the owners of American vessels, steamships preferred, for the regular transportation of the United States mails.

This Act of 1845 is all-significant as the beginning of

[1] "American Navigation," by Henry Hall.

American steamship service in the foreign trade. Not until national protection was offered in the form of generous subsidies, could our enterprising merchants and sailors see their way clear to enter the rivalry with the state-aided steam fleets of Europe. The mail subsidy legislation of 1845 was a wise step and indispensable, but it was too long delayed. Congress should have acted five years before, when the first Cunarder, floated and maintained by a liberal subsidy from Parliament, came across the ocean, beating the time of our celebrated packet ships. Individual resource could never compete with the great treasury of the British Empire. In advocating his ocean mail legislation, Senator Thomas Butler King, of Georgia, had said: —

"It is sufficient to show that they (British statesmen) are resolved, as far as practicable, to monopolize the intercourse between these two important points. This movement shows clearly that the time has arrived when we must decide whether we will yield this essential branch of navigation, and this indirect means of extending our naval armaments to our great commercial rival, or whether we shall promptly extend to our enterprising merchants the necessary means to enable them to bring American energy, enterprise, and skill into successful competition with British sagacity and capital. Of all the lines of sailing packets which cross the Atlantic, not one is owned in Europe, and it is not to be doubted that American merchants, properly encouraged, will assuredly excel in them (steamship lines) as they have done in sailing vessels; and when we reflect that this may be accomplished to the mutual advantage and advancement of our commercial and military marine, it would seem that no statesman ought to hesitate for a moment to give his support to a measure which is demanded alike by prudence and the necessities of our position."

These words of the Southern statesman and patriot

16

show something of the motives which guided Congress in enacting the ocean mail law of 1845, and a supplementary law of 1847, authorizing contracts for the construction of four large war steamers, the "Susquehanna," "Powhatan," "Saranac," and "San Jacinto," and also for five merchant steamers to carry the mails to Havana and the Isthmus of Panama, and three steamers to carry the mails to Europe. This early legislation recognized just as frankly as the Act of 1891, under which the "St. Louis" and "St. Paul" were launched to figure brilliantly as merchant cruisers in the Spanish War, the intimate relation between the fighting navy and the merchant service. The early mail steamers were built exactly as were the later ones, under the supervision of the Navy Department, but they were the property of the contracting companies. President Polk, in the annual message to Congress in which he recounted the steps that had been taken in pursuance of the ocean mail legislation of the previous session, said:

"The enlightened policy by which a rapid communication with the various distant parts of the world is established, by means of American-built steamers, would find an ample reward in the increase of our commerce, and in making our country and its resources more favorably known abroad; but the national advantage is still greater — of having our naval officers made familiar with steam navigation, and of having the privilege of taking the ships already equipped for immediate service at a moment's notice, and will be cheaply purchased by the compensation to be paid for the transportation of the mail, over and above the postage received. A just national pride, no less than our commercial interests, would seem to favor the policy of augmenting the number of this description of vessels."

President Polk was a Democrat and a Southern man. These words of his are convincing proof that when the national policy of state aid by subsidy to American shipping was adopted, it was not regarded as either a sectional or a party question. A united country upheld it.

The first transatlantic mail contract under the new legislation was made with the Ocean Steamship Company for a service from New York to Havre and Bremen. The company was to receive $200,000 a year for twenty trips, — about half the sum originally given to the Cunard line by the British government. In fulfilment of this contract, two large steamers, the "Washington" and "Hermann," were built at New York for Edward Mills by Westervelt & Mackay. They resembled our beautiful sailing packets, but were much larger. The "Washington" was of 1,640, the "Hermann" of 1,734 tons. Both were side-wheel steamers, bark-rigged, with lofty spars and a great spread of canvas, which was used when the wind was fresh and fair. They were strong ships with exceptionally heavy frames and fastenings, and they crossed from New York to Bremen in from twelve to seventeen days, and returned in from thirteen to nineteen, — a time decidedly better than the average of the sailing packets.

In 1850 two larger and more powerful ships were constructed for the Havre-Bremen line, the "Franklin" and the "Humboldt." They were of 2,184 tons, and they made the passage to Cowes, Isle of Wight, in twelve days or a little more. This enterprise was respectable and adequate, but never brilliant. The vessels, taking them all in all, were just about as good as the Cunard ships, no swifter, but statelier and more capacious.

Of far more enduring importance to the United States were the other contracts entered into at about the same time for mail service to the West Indies, the Isthmus of Panama, and up the Pacific coast to Oregon. The West India contract called for a small expenditure, but the benefits were large and permanent. Never since then have the American people been without steam communication with the Antilles. When the Civil War broke out, some of the largest and fastest of the merchant steamers hastily purchased by the national government and converted into men-of-war, were ships of the West India mail service.

The Pacific route, which was started in 1848, was a very much more ambitious undertaking. The Mexican War had given us control of a vast, unknown country south of Oregon. American pioneers were pouring in there. California was a part of the national domain. The route to San Francisco and San Diego by sea, four or five months in sailing vessels around Cape Horn, was almost as formidable as the perilous journey across the trackless American desert and through the hunting-grounds of the most warlike savage tribesmen in the world. It was recognized in Washington that steam communication was quite as essential as forts and warships to bind California and Oregon to the Union. Contracts were accordingly made with George Law and his associates, for the conveyance of the United States mails from New York to Aspinwall (now Colon) on the Isthmus of Panama, and with C. H. Aspinwall for the conveyance of the mails in the Pacific from Panama north to San Francisco and Astoria.

The first steamship of the Pacific Mail service, the "California," sailed from New York by way of Cape Horn in October, 1848. When the "California" on her way north in the Pacific touched at the Isthmus, she was besieged by a great crowd of excited Argonauts, demanding quick passage to the newly discovered gold fields on the Sacramento. This steamship service to the treasure-coast had been started at just the fateful moment. An enormous passenger and freight traffic immediately began to fill the Law and Aspinwall steamers to their utmost capacity. The new line had procured excellent vessels of what seemed to be prodigious size for such a distant adventure. The "California," built by William H. Webb, was 200 feet long, 33 feet wide, and 22 feet deep, with a tonnage of 1,058. The "Panama" and "Oregon," which followed her to the Pacific, were of almost the same dimensions. They were wooden steamers with side-wheels, after the almost unvarying practice of the time, and they carried generous spars and canvas.

The rush of gold-seekers overwhelmed these thousand-ton ships. Larger vessels were straightway constructed, and both the Atlantic and Pacific services entered upon a period of almost wild prosperity. The "Georgia," 255 feet long, 49 feet wide, and 25 feet deep, of 2,727 tons, the "Illinois," 267 feet long, 40 feet wide, and 31 feet deep, of 2,123 tons, and the "Ohio," 248 feet long, 45 feet wide, and 24 feet deep, of 2,432 tons, were built for Mr. Law's line from New York to Colon, and American capital and engineering skill spanned the Isthmus with a railway, over which passengers and freight were quickly forwarded to the Pacific port of Panama, where Mr. Aspinwall's ships lay, northward-bound for Monterey, San Diego, and San Francisco.

In ten years [1] twenty-nine fine steamers, of 38,000 tons register, had been built for the two branches of the California trade, and the Pacific Mail Company, formed by the union of the Law and Aspinwall interests, became what it has been ever since, the greatest of American steamship corporations. In those ten years it is estimated that the Pacific Mail had carried 175,000 passengers to California, and brought back $200,000,000 of gold.

The Japan and China Transpacific line, which is now the most important part of the Pacific Mail traffic, was not established until after the Civil War, in January, 1867. From the very beginning the Pacific Mail has been a subsidized concern, but as compared with British standards this subvention has always been moderate in amount.

[1] "American Navigation," by Henry Hall.

Indeed, it is asserted[1] that "The contract awarded to it was so insufficient that it is notorious that the line would have failed and been abandoned, but for the opportune discovery of the gold-fields of California, and the immense emigration which ensued just as it commenced its operations." The steamers from New York to Colon received in mail subsidy,[2] in 1852, $276,000, and in 1855, $290,000 — never more than the latter figure in any year down to 1860. The Pacific steamers from Panama to Astoria received $308,000 in 1850, $346,000 in 1855, and about the same sum down to 1860. These two services together did not draw as much support from the United States Treasury as the Cunard line drew from the Treasury of Great Britain. Both concerns were "protected industries," but the British protection was very much earlier, more generous, and more persistent.

Though the United States came tardily into the practice of steamship subvention, which Britain in 1840 had so boldly initiated, our country speedily seemed to make up for lost time and lost ground. The first American transatlantic steam line, from New York to Havre and Bremen, proved so successful that the government was encouraged to take another step ahead. In November, 1847, a contract had been concluded, under the ocean mail legislation of March, 1847, with Edward K. Collins and his associates for a new line of steamers sailing twice a month during eight months and once a month during four months of the year from New York to Liverpool. The mail subsidy offered was $385,000 a year, a smaller sum than that with which the Cunard line had started with its slow steamers ten years before, and a very much smaller sum than it was now receiving. This contract marked the birth of the celebrated Collins line, whose brilliant career, lit with many

[1] "Memorial of New York Chamber of Commerce," 1864.

[2] "Trade and Transportation," by William Eleroy Curtis, State Department, 1889.

triumphs, darkened with two terrible disasters and, finally shrouded in bitter failure and disappointment, is one of the memorable passages in our maritime history.

Mr. Edward K. Collins was a conspicuous New York merchant, the head of the famous Dramatic line of sailing packets, a gentleman of devoted patriotism and the highest ability and character. He knew perfectly the sea and its affairs. He had a remarkable power of convincing and directing other men, and a genius for the shaping of great enterprises. Intellectually he stood head and shoulders above Mr. Cunard. As between the two chiefs of the two national steamship enterprises which were to vie with each other on the important route between New York and Liverpool the advantage seemed to be overwhelmingly with the experienced, ardent, and ambitious American. Mr. Collins at the outset did exactly as Mr. Cunard had done. He fulfilled the letter of his contract, and more. The Cunard ships were then of an average size of about 1,500 tons. The United States government stipulated that the new American ships should be of at least 2,000 tons. With the most admirable motives, Mr. Collins went far beyond this. He caused to be constructed in the best yards of New York City such steamers as the world had never seen. Two of them, the "Arctic" of 2,856 tons, and "Atlantic" of 2,845 tons, were built by William H. Brown, under the supervision of George Steers, the famous naval architect who designed the schooner yacht "America." Two other ships, the "Baltic" of 2,723 tons, and "Pacific" of 2,707 tons, were built by Brown and Bell. The machinery for the vessels was furnished by the Novelty and Allaire Works of New York.

In model these great steamships resembled the beautiful American sailing packets, but they had characteristics of their own which stamp to this day the best steam vessels of the American merchant service and, indeed, of all the world. Mr. Collins for one thing abandoned the clipper or overhanging stem of the ordinary sail craft as unnecessary for a steamer. He gave his ships no bowsprits, but a straight stem, a long, wedge-like bow, and a long, easy run curving to a graceful stern like that of a modern Atlantic greyhound. The Collins ships were relatively high out of water, and, therefore, dry and comfortable, as compared with vessels of scanty freeboard. Here again is a quality that distinguishes the steam vessels of the present American merchant fleet. The "Arctic" and her sisters had full, large steam-power, but they carried three masts and spread a generous amount of square canvas for use in favoring winds or in case of the disabling of their machinery.

For the construction of the mighty hulls of these Yankee leviathans the best shipwrights were summoned from all alongshore, and the master-builders sought the toughest and finest of materials. The "Arctic," the "Baltic," the "Pacific," and the "Atlantic" marked the culmination of the wonderful skill that for thirty years had wrought our strong and handsome packet ships. The "Arctic" and "Atlantic," whose graceful proportions were shaped by the genius of George Steers, were 277 feet long on the keel, and 282 on the main deck, with a depth below the spar deck of 32 feet, and a width of 45 feet. There were four complete decks in all. The frames of the ships were of white oak and live oak, and the stout bottoms were filled in solidly with oak timbers to the turn of the bilge. The huge oak keelsons were especially heavy under the boilers and engines. The planking was hard pine, metal-fastened below the water line by copper bolts and above by galvanized iron. In all points this wood construction was more massive than that of a line-of-battleship. Indeed, the "Arctic" and her sisters were built as are our subsidized merchant cruisers of to-day, for war as well as commerce. To give increased strength and rigidity to the wooden hulls, the frames were strapped with iron, crossing amidships like a lattice-work. Altogether the Collins liners were probably the strongest wooden steamships ever constructed.

They were all driven, as were the Cunarders, by side-wheels and the side-lever engines, which were then the favorite type for ocean service. These engines developed about 800 horse-power, a pigmy figure compared with the 20,000 of the "St. Louis" and "St. Paul." What now seems the absurdly low steam pressure of 16.9 pounds a square inch produced 15.8 revolutions a minute, and gave the great ships an average speed of 316 miles a day. The coal consumption at this rate was about 83 tons in twenty-four hours. One important peculiarity of the Collins liners was that their speed steadily improved. From the very first, however, they were swifter than their Cunard competitors, and the swiftest large seagoing ships afloat.

The machinery of the "Arctic" and the other great vessels was as admirable as the hulls that bore it. Their engines were supported by solid cast-iron beams and wrought-iron columns and braces, and were splendid examples of the marine engineering of the period. Chief Engineers Sewell and Faron of the United States Navy had a great deal to do with the designs and specifications. Every step was taken with the utmost care and thoroughness. The finest men-of-war were never the objects of keener national solicitude.

When the four new ships were ready for sea, it was found that the expenditures upon them had far exceeded the calculations. They had cost about $675,000 each, as compared with the $575,000 of the "Asia" and "Africa" of the Cunard line, which were built to compete with the new Americans. The "Asia" and "Africa" were good ships, but in neither speed nor comfort were they equal to the stately Collins liners. Lindsay, the British marine historian, who had examined the "Arctic," testifies that "her equipment was complete and of the highest order,"

while her cabin accommodation surpassed that of any merchant vessel Great Britain then possessed." She could
carry 250 passengers and 2,000 tons of cargo.

The entrance of the four magnificent American steamers
into the Liverpool trade that had been for ten years a British
monopoly, was felt to be a momentous event on both sides
of the ocean. The Collins liners were commanded by the
best and most experienced officers who could be chosen
from the long-established lines of American packet ships.
The "Atlantic"[1] sailed from New York for Liverpool on
the initial voyage of the Collins line on April 27, 1850.
The "Pacific" followed in the early summer, the "Baltic"
in November, and the "Arctic" in December. For several
years the four great vessels made their voyages with
extraordinary regularity and freedom from serious accident.
The Cunard steamers, smaller and less powerful, had been
crossing from New York to Liverpool in from 10 days, 6
hours, to 14 days, 3 hours, averaging the year through
$11\frac{1}{2}$ days. From Liverpool to New York their voyages
ranged between 10 days, 2 hours, and 15 days, 20 hours,
averaging 12 days, 9 hours. The American steamers[2]
beat the Cunard time by about a day, making their eastward runs in from 9 days, 17 hours, to 12 days, 9 hours,
averaging throughout the year 10 days, 21 hours, and
making their westward runs in from 9 days, 13 hours, to
13 days, 17 hours, averaging 11 days, 3 hours. Travellers
were almost as eager then to sail by the fastest and most
luxurious ships as they are now. The American liners,
with their high speed and their liberal management,
quickly won the best trade away from the Cunarders.
Between January[3] and November of 1852, the Collins line
conveyed 4,306 passengers; the Cunard line, 2,969. Even
when Cunard put greater nominal horse-power into his

[1] Memorial of Chamber of Commerce to Congress, January, 1864.
[2] "Shipbuilding Industry of the United States," by Henry Hall.
[3] "New York Herald," January 1, 1853.

ships, as he did with the " Asia," which had a horse-power of 816, as compared with the 800 of the " Pacific " and " Atlantic," the Americans kept constantly ahead. Lindsay attributes their superiority in speed to the American methods of management, to their "effective boilers and ability in their preparation."

The original subsidy offered to the Collins line was $19,250 for twenty round trips, or $385,000 a year. But in recognition of the fact that the four new ships were very much larger, swifter, more expensive in every way, and more valuable to the nation than the exact terms of the contract required, the government in 1852 increased the subsidy to $858,000 a year, exactly as the original Cunard subsidy of $425,000 had been increased by the British government for similar reasons. The Cunard line was now receiving $856,871 a year for ships that were much less costly than the Collins steamers, smaller, weaker, less adapted to war purposes, and incapable of rendering a first-class service. The " Pacific " in May, 1851, crossed from New York to Liverpool in 9 days, 20 hours, and 16 minutes ; the " Arctic," in July, 1852, in 9 days, 17 hours, and 12 minutes. It was represented to Congress in behalf of the Collins line that "to effect a saving of a day and a half in the run between New York and Liverpool costs the company nearly a million dollars annually." The Cunard vessels sailed oftener, it is true, and there were more of them. But, as was pointed out by the friends of our merchant marine in Washington, the four Collins steamers were equal in tonnage and power to the Cunard seven, and, multiplying the tonnage of the two fleets and the number of voyages, the Cunard subsidy amounted to $5.75 for every ton that crossed the ocean, and the Collins subsidy to $4.82.

Without entering into fine calculations, the general truth is undeniable that a superior steam Atlantic service was worth as much to the United States as an inferior steam service was worth to Great Britain. The Collins line had broken a rather arrogant monopoly, and introduced a wholesome element of competition. Lindsay, the historian of British shipping, says that, " Before the Collins line was established, the Cunard steamers were receiving £7 10s. sterling per ton, freight, which was so much a monopoly rate that in two years after the Collins line had commenced, the rate of freight fell to £4 sterling per ton." Moreover, in the words of a memorial of the New York merchants, the Collins steamers rendered [1] "a great and inestimable service " "in compelling an increase in size, accommodations, and speed of the British line. Thus, in 1847, the average passages of the Cunard steamers to and from Boston were 15 days and 7 hours, which was in 1859 reduced to 13 days, 23 hours, a gain of 1 day, 8 hours. The same year the average of New York passages of the Cunard line was 10 days, 16 hours. On this line the British owners had put their fastest boats. Throughout the period of the competition of the Collins with the Cunard line, all the honor was to the former. Its steamers beat their rivals nearly a day and a half on the average voyages. In nothing was American pride more interested and gratified than in this signal triumph of national industry and enterprise."

The new policy of subsidy protection to ocean steamships had been wonderfully successful in the United States, though Congress lagged ten years behind Parliament in adopting it. In 1847, before the effect of these mail contracts began to be perceptible, and, indeed, before most of them had been made, the United States possessed only 5,631 tons of steamships registered for deep-sea carrying. These were chiefly steamers which touched at Havana or some other West Indian port in the course of a coastwise voyage to Florida or the Gulf of Mexico. But with the

[1] Memorial signed by A. A. Low, Thomas Tileston, and other eminent New York merchants.

starting of the subsidized Havre-Bremen service our registered steam tonnage rose in 1848 to 16,068 tons, and from
that year to 1855 the increase was large and constant.
In 1849 our deep-sea steam fleet amounted to 20,870 tons;
in 1850, to 44,942; in 1851, to 62,390; in 1852, to 79,704;
in 1853, to 90,520; in 1854, to 95,036; in 1855, to 115,045.
Although Great Britain was originally a full decade ahead
of us in the subsidy fostering of her steamship interests,
we had gained so swiftly after 1848 that in 1851 our steam
fleet and Britain's were practically equal. Our deep-sea
steam tonnage in that year was 62,390 tons, as compared
with her 65,921. The American steamships, as a rule,
were newer and swifter than the British ships, and better
adapted to modern commercial requirements. As Dr.
David A. Wells says of this period in "Our Merchant
Marine": —

"During the single year 1849–50 we increased our ocean
steam tonnage one hundred and thirteen per cent, and the
seagoing qualities and performances of our vessels were
so admirable that the Cunard Company, which had then
been in operation ten years, was obliged to bring out new
ships to compete with them. The prospect, therefore, at
one time was that the United States, although late in
the start in this new department of foreign shipping,
would soon equal, if not overtake, her great commercial
competitor."

This was the gratifying outlook of the first years of the
eventful decade that preceded the Civil War. Nor was
it in steamships only that this was in America a period of
extraordinary maritime development. The appearance of
steamers on the North Atlantic and on the Isthmian route
to California gave new wings to the ambition of the builders and owners of the wonderful American sailing ships.
They began at once to improve the size and speed of their
vessels. The celebrated Yankee clippers were the result
of this intensified rivalry of steam and canvas. The first

of them [1] is believed to have been the " Rainbow " of seven
hundred and fifty tons, built about the year 1843, after the
Cunarders had been for three years steaming to and fro
over the Atlantic. The "Helena," the "Howquah," the
"Sea Witch," and others followed. Some of these clippers
were employed in the New York packet lines. One of
them, the "New World," launched for Grinnell, Minturn
& Co., by Donald McKay in 1846, was a one-thousand-
four-hundred-ton vessel, the largest sailing merchantman
then afloat in our service. But more of the clipper ships
were engaged in the long-voyage trade to China and India,
and especially in the booming trade to California.

That began soon after the discovery of gold in 1849.
From all parts of the world, from New England and Old
England, from New York and the Great Lakes, from the
Delaware and the sandy coast of the Carolinas, from the
Mississippi, from the Canadian provinces, from Hawaii,
South America, and Australia, eager keels came crowding
into the Golden Gate. There was the slow, costly, and
perilous route overland, and the swift and costly route *via*
the Pacific Mail steamers and the Isthmus of Panama.
But the steamers could not take more than a fraction of
the passengers and freight that sought them, and the breaking bulk at Colon and the relading at the other end of the
Isthmian railway necessarily made the service expensive
and the charges high. Moreover, nearly all of the Argonauts, after the first rush, had the foresight to carry out
large stores of tools, materials, and food, and these could be
more economically conveyed in sailing vessels. Thus,
though the trails across the Rocky Mountains and the plains
were speedily improved, and the government gave all the
protection in its power to the emigrants, the sea route *via*
Cape Horn remained the cheapest and easiest for bulky
freight, and safer and more comfortable than the overland
route for passengers.

[1] "Notes on Ships of the Past," by Robert Bennett Forbes.

All of the adventurers were, of course, in a consuming fever of eagerness to get early on the ground. Ship-speed rose at once to an unheard-of premium. The fastest vessels commanded the highest figures and were the first to complete their lading and to sail away. The new clipper model, which was just coming into vogue for the China, India, and European service, was seized upon and adapted to the new emergency. Every shipyard on the coast that had the requisite skill and capital turned to clipper-building for California. The magnificent fleet of white-winged racers which we produced in the years from 1850 onward had no equal before and has had no superior since in speed, power, and beauty. The "Sovereign of the Seas," built at East Boston by the celebrated Donald McKay [1] and sailed by his almost equally celebrated brother Lauchlan, left New York for San Francisco in August, 1851. Off Valparaiso, in the South Pacific, the great ship was almost totally dismasted, carrying away everything on the fore and main above the lower mastheads. In fourteen days Captain Lauchlan had put his broken-winged vessel under a wonderful jury rig, and with this he reached San Francisco in 102 days from New York,— "said to be the best passage ever made for the season." The quickness with which the captain retrieved his disaster is a fine example of the resourcefulness of the kingly shipmasters in this golden age of the sailing merchant marine.

From San Francisco the "Sovereign of the Seas" crossed to Honolulu, and there loaded for New York. The passage to Sandy Hook was made in the unprecedented time of 82 days. In 22 days, so the story goes, the great clipper made 5,301 nautical miles, or one-fourth of the distance around the globe. From noon to noon on one day the record was 362 miles, or 15 miles an hour — and that at a time when the fastest ocean steamship was capable of no more than thirteen or fourteen. Another famous

[1] "Notes on Ships of the Past," by Robert Bennett Forbes.

McKay clipper, the "Flying Cloud," made 374 miles one day in a ninety-day run to San Francisco. Most of the Atlantic steam liners were then rolling off about 300 miles, — oftener less than more. The "Comet"[1] is credited with a voyage of 83 days from the Golden Gate to Sandy Hook, "averaging 210 miles a day" in all winds and weathers. The "Palestine"[2] of the Morgan line to London landed her passengers at Portsmouth in 14 days from New York, squarely beating the Cunard steamer that sailed at the same time. Indeed, in anything like a fair, strong breeze these long, finely modelled clipper ships could overtake a lumbering steamship, pass her, and run her hull down in a few hours. The famous "Sovereign of the Seas," in a two-weeks' voyage from New York to Liverpool in June, 1852, made in one day 340 miles, while the Cunarder Canada was making 200.

The redoubtable Captain "Bob" Waterman in the "Natchez" once came from the Canton River to New York in 76 days,[3] — about half the time ordinarily consumed by the heavier sail-ships of to-day. Out of six such voyages of Captain Waterman's, the longest is said to have been 98 days. The extreme clipper "Flying Fish" made three voyages to San Francisco averaging 101 days, and seven voyages averaging 106. A one-hundred-and-twenty-day passage was considered excellent. Between 1851 and 1853 the "Ino" came home from Singapore to New York in 86 days; the "Pilot," from Manila to Salem in 96 days; the "Shooting Star," from Canton to New York in 86 days; the "Atalanta," from Canton to New York in 84 days.

These clipper ships were wonderfully beautiful. Not one of them now remains afloat in ocean service. A few may be tumbling up and down the Pacific coast under stump topgallantmasts, freighting coal and lumber, and

1 Report of Lieutenant M. F. Maury to Secretary of Navy, May 10, 1853.

2 G. W. Sheldon, in "Harper's Monthly," January, 1884.

8 "Notes on Ships of the Past," by Robert Bennett Forbes.

unrecognizable as the splendid racers of half a century ago. But the real clipper ship of those years of glory has utterly departed. The so-called clipper of to-day is a full-bodied, bluff-bowed craft, as unlike its predecessor as a bulldog is unlike a greyhound. When speed is needed now, it is sought in a steamship. Carrying capacity, not swiftness, is the prime consideration in the modern sailing ship of wood or steel. The present model is called a "medium clipper," and it is some satisfaction to know that in the long-voyage traffic around Cape Horn or the Cape of Good Hope, the Yankee vessels, though no longer the record-breakers of the glorious decade from 1850 to 1860, usually manage to keep ahead of their European competitors.

Such ships as the " Surprise," the " Sierra Nevada," the " Westward Ho," the " Phantom," the " Sea Serpent," the "Sweepstakes," and the " Young America " were at once the admiration and the despair of Europe. They were built, most of them, for the trade to California, in which only American vessels could sail from an American port. A voyage from Boston or New York to San Francisco was technically a coastwise voyage, though it involved fifteen thousand miles of deep-water sailing. As such, our navigation laws rigidly reserved it to ships launched in the United States and owned and officered by American citizens. The building of the California clippers, therefore, was a protected industry, but the vessels constructed primarily for this business left it from time to time for voyages to Europe or to Asia if favorable rates offered. Thus the California gold discovery came in most opportunely to give American wooden shipbuilding a longer lease of life against the subsidized steam lines and the multiplying iron shipyards of Great Britain. Nor was this the only favorable circumstance. When the California " boom " began to dwindle, the outbreak of the Crimean War in 1854 brought a feverish demand for our fast-sail-

17

ing ships as transports. Neither France nor England could procure an adequate supply fleet out of her own mercantile marine. Both governments chartered all the suitable tonnage which they possessed, and then paid fabulous sums for the services of American clippers. The British and French ships that were withdrawn from commerce made room for many other American vessels all over the world. The natural result was that American ship-yards produced in 1855 more tonnage than they had built before or have built since. In that memorable year,[1] the zenith year of Yankee ship-building, our country launched 381 ships and barks and 126 brigs for deep-sea trade.

Maritime reciprocity had advanced again in 1849. Up to that year British trade with British possessions in the East or West Indies could be carried in only British ships. The products of America, Africa, and Asia could not be imported into the United Kingdom from any foreign country. Certain goods of European origin could be brought to the United Kingdom in only British vessels, or vessels of the country where the goods were produced. Foreign vessels could not engage in the English, Scotch, or Irish coasting trade, and could not be given free registry if they were purchased by British shipowners. All these time-honored restrictions were swept away by the revision of the British navigation laws in 1849. Of the changes only one drew reciprocal action from America. That was the amendment which opened the "indirect" British and colonial trade to the merchant carriers of other nations. This action was interpreted by our government as a tardy acceptance of our reciprocity "olive branch" of 1828, and on Oct. 15, 1849, Secretary Meredith, of the Treasury Department, issued this circular of instructions to customs officers: —

"First, in consequence of the alterations of the British navigation laws, British vessels from British or other foreign

[1] Report of United States Commissioner of Navigation, 1900.

ports will (under our existing laws) after the 1st of January next, be allowed to enter our ports with cargoes of the growth, manufacture, or production of any part of the world.

" Second, such vessels and their cargoes will be admitted from and after the date before mentioned on the same terms as to duties, imposts, and charges as vessels of the United States and their cargoes."

This circular for the first time made maritime reciprocity complete between the United States and its chief competitor. It stripped our sailing ships and unsubsidized steamships of the last vestiges of government protection. But it was a step taken on our part in entire good faith, although we might justifiably have resented Britain's long delay in accepting the full measure of our proffered reciprocity. She had waited until the situation had changed to her advantage. As Professor Soley says, in his careful review of this question, " the fact was that such were the approaching conditions of competition between America and England that the United States could not carry on the race upon anything like a footing of equality; while the inability to impose restrictions upon English trade between its own ports and those of other foreign countries placed it at a disadvantage in the only field where competition was possible."

Even in 1849, however, British merchants were not really allowed to buy American ships, for the great British marine insurance monopoly of Lloyd's promptly stepped to the defence of British shipyards, and condemned the locust treenails of our high-class vessels, thus forcing every British merchant who bought an American ship to refasten her before she could secure proper insurance. This Lloyd's discrimination virtually nullified the Act of Parliament, as can readily be seen by the official records of American tonnage sold on foreign account. This was only 13,468 tons in 1850, 15,247 in 1851, 17,921 in 1852, and 10,035 in 1853, — an average of only 14,167 tons per annum in the four years succeeding the passage of the British "free ship" act, as compared with an average of 13,244 tons in the four years from 1846 to 1849, inclusive, and of 15,452 tons in the four years from 1826 to 1829. It is obvious, therefore, that the rise of British merchant tonnage, in the early fifties, was due to something else than "free ship" legislation or the purchase of a few vessels from the United States. These figures of American ships "sold foreign" represent, by the way, the acquisition not of Britain only but of all other nations.

In 1854, with Lloyd's gracious permission, British merchants did purchase a considerable number of American wooden vessels. Our sales to all foreign nations, Britain included, in that year rose to 60,033 tons, as compared with only 10,035 tons in the year preceding. In 1855, our sales to foreigners were 65,887 tons; in 1856, 42,168 tons; in 1857, 52,649 tons. A large proportion of these vessels, though not all, undoubtedly went into the British service. Some of them were our famous clippers which British yards could not create at any price. Donald McKay built[1] on English account the "Lightning" that made a passage from Melbourne to Liverpool in sixty-three days, and the "James Baines" of two thousand tons that is said to have run from Boston to Liverpool in twelve days, six hours. But all these American-built vessels together formed only an insignificant fraction of the British fleet. The great British purchases of American tonnage came several years later, during our Civil War, when Anglo-Confederate cruisers compelled American merchants to choose between laying their ships up in port to rot away, or selling them at a half or quarter of their cost to foreigners. But this was in the nature of a forced or bankrupt sale, not of an ordinary mercantile transaction. In the one year, 1864, beneath this extraordinary pressure, more American

[1] "Notes on Ships of the Past," by Robert Bennett Forbes.

ships were disposed of to foreign owners than had been sold in all the years between 1854 and 1860.

One notable event of the decade between 1851 and 1860 was the rise of New York as a shipbuilding centre. Earlier in the century, Boston and the East had had the lion's share of sail-construction. But the New York merchants who owned and managed the successful packet lines preferred to have their fine ships built under their own eyes as far as possible. Straightway a long range of yards grew up along the East River, and these were supplemented, when the ocean mail contracts were let to New York bidders, by several iron-working plants for the production of marine machinery. Not only the Collins and Pacific Mail liners, but the majority of the coastwise steamships were built at New York, and many high-class sailing vessels. For several years before the Civil War ten thousand workmen [1] were called to their labors every morning in New York Harbor by the clang of the shipyard bells. William H. Webb and one or two other master-builders employed each more than a thousand of the most intelligent and skilful mechanics whom the country had ever known, and the row of shipyards on the East River side of New York City had at the same time twenty or thirty great vessels on the stocks awaiting completion.

Mr. Webb built both sailing ships and steamers, of high quality and large size. He launched in all one hundred and fifty vessels.[2] On one memorable occasion three slipped into the water together from his yard. He was an owner as well as a builder, possessing an interest in forty or fifty ships of his construction. Much of his handiwork was remarkably durable. One of his vessels remained in active service for almost half a century. Mr. Webb's fame was world-wide. The largest contracts which he ever undertook were for several immense

[1] " American Navigation," by Henry Hall.
[2] " American Marine," by Captain William W. Bates.

steam ships-of-war, designed for the service of European governments.

In Boston the most celebrated builder was Donald McKay, the head of a noble family of shipbuilders and seamen whom Edward Everett has eulogized as "the sea kings of the United States." The McKays won their great renown in the building of wooden clippers, first at Newburyport and afterward at East Boston. It was in their honor that Longfellow wrote his "Building of the Ship;" and a Massachusetts statesman, Senator George F. Hoar, has paid to them this memorable tribute:—

"I can remember very well the time when the names of the great shipbuilders, Donald and Lauchlan McKay and their brothers, were famous all around the world. They were building or commanding the marvellous clipper ships for which the shipyards of New England were unrivalled. It was a contest which enlisted the feeling and the pride of the whole people of the country. There was no boy's play of yacht-racing in those days. The strife was between nations, and the prize was the commerce of the world.

"It was the time when California, Australia, and Oregon were first opening to trade. The merchant who could get the fastest ship had the market for the fruits of the Mediterranean, for the rugs of Smyrna, for the silks of India, and the teas of China, and supplied the new States of which the Anglo-Saxon race was then laying the foundations. It was the ships of this McKay family, of Donald and Lauchlan and their kindred, that carried off the prize in every contest. When John Bull came floating into San Francisco, or Sydney, or Melbourne, he used to find Uncle Sam sitting carelessly, with his legs dangling over the wharf, smoking his pipe, with his cargo sold and his pockets full of money. The flag of the United States was a flower that adorned every port and blossomed on every soil the world over."

Donald McKay first attracted attention by the speed and beauty of the ships which he built for Enoch Train's Boston and Liverpool packet line, that doughty sail-antagonist of the early Cunarders. These pioneer McKay models were the "Washington Irving," the "Daniel Webster," the "Staffordshire," the "Anglo Saxon," the "Ocean Monarch," and the "Star of Empire,"— good, large, aspiring names, all of them. But it was the California gold rush that gave Mr. McKay his real opportunity. He saw that there was a chance for such ships as the world had never beheld, and he launched in quick succession the great clippers "Staghound" of 1,550 tons, "Flying Fish" of 1,600 tons, "Bald Eagle" of 1,600 tons, "Flying Cloud" of 1,700 tons, "Westward Ho" of 1,700 tons, "Empress of the Sea" of 2,250 tons, and "Sovereign of the Seas" of 2,400 tons. In size fifty years ago all of these magnificent fabrics were colossal, for in 1850 a ship of even one thousand tons was a wonder. Their swiftness and symmetry, however, were even more extraordinary than their huge dimensions. They were built for the California trade, but they found their way all over the world, and they aroused more astonishment than would a 30-knot 25,000-ton steamship if she should to-morrow come tearing up New York Bay.

The McKay masterpiece was a giant four-master, the "Great Republic," which bore the same relation to the sailing vessels of her day that the "Great Eastern" did to steamers. The "Great Republic" was launched on Sept. 4, 1853, at East Boston. She was 325 feet long, 53 feet wide, with four decks and a tonnage of 4,555. Her rig was that of the great steel deep-sea four-masters of to-day,— three square-rigged masts and a spankermast. Her mainyard was one hundred and twenty feet in length, or twice the size of that of the average large merchantman. But the ocean never saw the "Great Republic" in her full splendor. She was partly burned while lying at

New York ready for her first voyage to San Francisco. In the process of repairing the upper deck was not replaced. Yet even thus unceremoniously razeed, the " Great Republic" was the marvel of seafaring men everywhere. She was one of the Yankee clippers chartered by the French government for the transport service during the Crimean War, and it is said that " no steamer could catch her when she had a whole-sail, leading wind."

What the " Great Republic " was to Yankee clippers, the "Dreadnought" was to the Yankee packet ships. For a dozen years the " Dreadnought " was the champion of the Atlantic Ocean, and her proud skipper, Captain Samuels, was a popular hero, the ideal of the Yankee tar. Samuels was worthy of his ship. He had run away from home, a boy of eleven, and learned his first lessons of sailoring on the Hudson River and Long Island Sound. He was "shanghaied," or, in land-lubber language, kidnapped, from a revenue brig into a Baltimore ship bound for Liverpool. This was his launching into deep water. He was chased bv West Indian pirates, served in the Texan navy, sailed in a haunted ship around the world, fell overboard, fought cannibals, became second and chief officer in the British marine, but quit it because of its lax discipline, and at twenty-one stood on a Yankee quarter-deck as master. He outsailed a British man-of-war fleet in the Mediterranean, declined the post of admiral in the Turkish Navy, rescued a Christian lady from a Turkish harem, and battled with Mediterranean banditti. Samuels, in brief, was a real flesh-and-blood example of the sailor of romance. He was so successful as a master that Governor E. D. Morgan, Francis B. Cutting, David Ogden, and other New York merchants subscribed to give him the best packet ship that could be built of wood and metal. Her keel was laid in June, 1853, at Newburyport, on the Merrimac, one of the chief of New England shipping towns. Samuels himself superintended her construction. She was not an extreme clipper, but a large and powerful example of the semi-clipper type, with lofty masts, long yards, and great pyramids of canvas.   On her first homeward voyage,[1] from Liverpool to New York, the "Dreadnought" reached Sandy Hook just as the Cunard steamship "Canada," that had started one day ahead of her, reached Boston.   In 1859 the "Dreadnought" ran from New York to Liverpool, 3,000 miles, in 13 days and 8 hours.   In 1860 she made her most famous voyage, — the quickest transatlantic passage which a sailing ship has ever recorded.   On this occasion the "Dreadnought" ran to Queenstown in 9 days and 17 hours, — an exploit superior to the average steam passage of the time, and better indeed than that of many years afterward.

In his lively autobiography,[2] Captain Samuels pays a heartfelt tribute to the noble old ship which he so long commanded.   "She was never passed in anything over a four-knot breeze," he says.   "She possessed the merit of being able to bear driving as long as her sails and spars would stand.   By the sailors she was nicknamed ' The Wild Boat of the Atlantic,' while others called her ' The Flying Dutchman.'   Twice she carried the latest news to Europe, slipping in between steamers.   The Collins, Cunard, and Inman lines were the only ones (to Britain) at that time. There are merchants still doing business in New York who shipped goods by us which we guaranteed to deliver within a certain time or forfeit freight charges.   For this guarantee we commanded freight rates midway between those of the steamers and those of the sailing packets."

Captain Samuels explains the remarkable success of his ship as due to her iron discipline, and to the " forcing " of the vessel under all the canvas she could carry by night as well as by day.   The marvellous achievements of our packet and clipper ships were only in part, and perhaps in lesser part, the work of their builders.   Large honor was always due

---

[1] "Notes on Ships of the Past," by Robert Bennett Forbes.
[2] "From the Forecastle to the Cabin," by S. Samuels.

to the incomparable seamen who held them rushing on their courses through all the great seas of the world. It was a common practice for foreigners, who bought our vessels, to clip their broad and lofty wings, because they were unable or afraid to spread such pinnacles of canvas. Yet American officers knew how to control these tall ships so that they not only made quicker voyages, but met with fewer accidents and delivered their cargoes in better condition than the stump-sparred craft of Europe.

"Cracking on" sail and "carrying hard" were an exact science with these Yankee commanders, and the very reverse of the sheer recklessness which these things often appeared to astonished foreigners. A British or Dutch or French vessel, snugged down to reefed topsails and holding bare steerage-way in the South Pacific or Indian Ocean, would see a cloud of snow-white cotton canvas burst out of the gloom and vanish like a ghost to leeward, — a Yankee clipper under royals. Then there would be loud objurgations of Yankee foolhardiness, but when the British, Dutch, or French skipper crawled into Valparaiso or Calcutta, he would find the mighty Yankee all loaded and cleared for home, immaculate alow and aloft, without a scratch on her graceful hull, or so much as a rope-yarn awry in her rigging.

Take, for example, the log of the medium clipper "Florence," 1,000 tons, on a voyage from New York to Java Head. On July 1 she made 260 miles, and "passed two barks under reefed courses and closereefed topsails standing the same way, — we with royals and topgallant studdingsails." In the tenth week out the "Florence" averaged 251 miles a day for seven days, and "passed a ship under topsails, we having our royals set." On another voyage the "Florence" arrived at Penang in eighty-one days, and in all these eleven and one-half weeks "the topsail halliards were started only to take in a single reef for a few hours." In a voyage from Shanghai to England, the

"Florence" on January 11, 1859, seventeen days out, exchanged signals with the English ship "John Masterman," that had sailed thirteen days before her.

This carrying of canvas hard and long, with a keen seaman's eye to strength of spar and gear, did quite as much as Yankee modelling to give our ships everywhere their pre-eminence. The superiority of their officers and crews was ungrudgingly acknowledged by their competitors. As far back as 1838, a Parliamentary report had urged the temperate habits of the men of American ships as worthy of British emulation. It was declared by the Parliamentary Committee that "the happiest effects have resulted from the experiments tried in the American navy and merchant-service to do without spirituous liquors as an habitual article of daily use, there being at present more than one-thousand sail of American vessels traversing all the seas of the world in every climate, without the use of spirits by their officers and crews, and being, in consequence of this change, in so much greater a state of efficiency and safety than other vessels not adopting this regulation, that the public insurance companies in America make a return of five per cent of the premium of insurance on vessels completing their voyages without the use of spirits."

Lindsay, the historian of the British marine, who had been a sailor as well as shipowner, says in his authoritative work : —

"During the first half of this century the masters of American vessels were, as a rule, greatly superior to those who held similar positions in English ships, arising in some measure from the limited education of the latter, which was not sufficient to qualify them for the higher grades of the merchant service. American shipowners required of their masters not merely a knowledge of navigation and seamanship but of commercial pursuits, the nature of exchange, the art of correspondence, and a sufficient knowledge of business to qualify them to represent the interests of their employers to advantage with merchants abroad. On all such matters the commanders of English ships, with the exception of the East India Company, were at this period greatly inferior to the commanders of the United States vessels."

A Committee of the House of Commons in 1836 had spoken of the "vast superiority in officers, crews, and equipment, and the consequent superior success and growth, of American shipping." The British Consul for Maine and New Hampshire, in a report[1] to the Foreign Office in 1847 said: "Education is much prized by the citizens; many vessels, therefore, are commanded by gentlemen with a college education and by those educated in high schools who on leaving these institutions enter a merchant's counting-room for a limited time before they go to sea for practical seamanship, etc., or are intrusted by their parents, guardians, or friends with the command of vessels."

Lindsay gives his own personal testimony, further, to the high quality of American masters: —

"Captains of the larger class of packets or merchant ships, therefore, could not only afford to live as gentlemen, but if men of good character and fair manners (which they generally were) they were received into the best mercantile circles on shore. They were also allowed, besides their fixed salary, a percentage (usually $2\frac{1}{2}$ per cent) on all freights, and by various other privileges (particularly in relation to passengers) they were thus enabled to save money and to become in time merchants and shipowners on their own account, — a custom which prevailed to a large extent in the New England States."

The British Consul at Philadelphia is quoted by Lindsay as reporting of the American marine : —

"A lad intended for the higher grades of the merchant

[1] Report of Mr. Joseph T. Sherwood. Parliamentary Paper on Commercial Marine of Great Britain, 1848.

service in this country, after having been at school some years and acquired (in addition to the ordinary branches of school learning) a competent knowledge of mathematics, navigation, ship's husbandry, and perhaps French, is generally apprenticed to some respectable merchant in whose counting-house he remains two or three years, or at least until he becomes familiar with exchanges and such other commercial matters as may qualify him to represent his principal in foreign countries. He is then sent to sea, generally in the capacity of second mate, from which he gradually rises to that of captain.

"Nor were the interests of the common seamen overlooked. Boys of all classes, when fit, had the privilege of entering the higher free schools, in which they could be educated for almost every profession. An ignorant native American seaman was therefore scarcely to be found; they all, with few exceptions, knew· how to read, write, and cipher. Although in all nations a mariner is considered a citizen of the world, whose home is on the sea, and as such can enforce compensation for his labor in the courts of any country, his contract being recognized by general jurisprudence, the cases of dispute between native-born Americans and their captains have ever been less frequent both in this country and abroad than between British masters and seamen, owing in a great measure to the superior education and more rigorous discipline on board American vessels."

Such was the acknowledged superiority of the American merchant officers at the time when Great Britain began to overwhelm our sailing fleet by her huge mail subsidies which were in large part virtually bonuses upon steamship and iron shipbuilding. If we had met subsidy by subsidy, and adhered to this protectionism as tenaciously as Britain did, and if we had offered the same encouragement to iron shipyards that we gave to cotton mills and the iron industry in general by high duties after 1860, our splendid officers and seamen would have won the fight for us, in spite of the temporary havoc wrought among our sailing vessels by the Civil War.

The fateful year 1855 marks the turning-point in the fortunes of the American merchant marine. The year before and the year after it were clouded by two terrible disasters to the greatest of American maritime enterprises. On Sept. 27, 1854, the "Arctic," finest and swiftest of the four original Collins liners, was run into in a dense fog off Cape Race by the French steamer "Vesta." Captain Luce at first felt no concern for his own noble vessel, but gave his thought to succoring the wounded stranger which had vanished in the mist. Soon, however, it was discovered that the great "Arctic" herself had received a mortal injury. The ship was headed under full steam for Newfoundland, sixty miles distant. This race for life was all in vain. In four hours the inrush of waters through the gashed side had drowned the furnaces. The sea was rough; the wind, strong. Although the officers and the real sailor of the crew worked bravely, the boats could not be properly lowered and sent away, and one or two that were launched were seized by rough cowards of coalheavers and firemen. The "Arctic" foundered with 212 of her passengers and 110 of her crew. The "Vesta," which had struck this fatal blow to the most splendid of Atlantic steamships, lost thirteen of her own people, but managed to crawl into St. John's.

In January, 1856, the "Arctic's" sister ship, "Pacific," left Liverpool for New York with 45 passengers and a crew of 141, and never reached her destination. Her exact fate was never known, but it was believed that she struck an iceberg, for, like the "Arctic," the "Pacific" was an extraordinarily strong ship, proof against all the accustomed perils of the sea, save only collision. Ocean steamships were not then built with transverse bulkheads and water-tight compartments. If they struck hard ice or were cut into by another ship, they would fill from bow to stern and inevitably founder.

The loss within two years of two of its four ships was a crushing misfortune to the Collins Company, although in neither case could the corporation be held culpable. Both the " Arctic " and the " Pacific " were destroyed by what seemed to be unpreventable causes. Their commanders, Luce and Eldridge, were two of the most capable and experienced seamen on the North Atlantic, and never until the sinking of the " Arctic " had the Collins line suffered any serious accident. Indeed, so superb was the reputation of the service that not even those two catastrophes shook the public confidence or broke the courage of Mr. Collins, although the loss of the " Arctic " meant to him a double affliction, for his wife and children had perished with his beloved ship. A fifth steamer, the " Adriatic," larger, swifter, and more luxurious, was built for Mr. Collins by George Steers at New York and launched on April 7, 1855. This new queen of the seas was 345 feet long, 50 feet wide, and 33 feet deep, — a bark-rigged side-wheeler of beautiful proportions. Her tonnage was 4,144; her cost, $1,100,000. This noblest of Atlantic wooden steamships had not been afloat a month when a bill " abolishing the present ocean steam service " was introduced, in May, 1855, in Congress, and there began the political war upon our ocean mail fleet which was destined to end in its destruction.

All sections and all parties had united in offering subsidy protection to American steamship lines in 1845 and 1847. The policy was initiated by Southern Democratic leaders in Congress, and first enforced by a Southern Democratic President, the North and East, of course, eagerly consenting. Senator Webster, of Massachusetts, or Seward, of New York, had been no more strenuous in advocacy of national encouragement to steamship enterprise than Bayard, of Delaware, or Badger, of North Carolina, or Bell, of Tennessee. The two ablest champions of the whole system of ocean mail legislation were Senators King, of Georgia, and Rusk, of Texas. Senator Bayard, in debating the subsidy to the Collins line, had said: "I am willing to trust American skill and industry in competition with any people on the globe, when they stand nation to nation, without government interference. But if the treasury of a foreign nation is poured into the lap of individuals for the purpose of destroying the interests of my country, or for building up a commercial marine at the expense of the commerce and prosperity of the United States, I, for one, will count no cost in countervailing such governmental action on the part of Great Britain or any foreign power." Senator Cass, of Michigan, speaking for the West, on the Collins subsidy, had in 1852 eloquently urged: "Well, sir, it is a question of protection — of high and important and holy protection — in the best sense of the term; the protection of our country, of our expatriated seamen, of our commerce, of our interests, of our honor, of our soil, of all that gives dignity and character to nations; protection against defeat, disgrace, and dishonor."

Senator Jones, of Tennessee, had said, "I should regard it as a national misfortune if the enterprise should fail," and "I am willing to vote large and liberal allowance." Senator Shields, of Illinois, had declared that it was "impossible for American private enterprise to succeed against private British enterprise, backed by the money and energy of the British government."

This was the spirit and these the arguments with which our ocean mail policy of fifty years ago was undertaken. Begun in 1847, it had by 1855 completely vindicated itself by its results. Our ocean steam fleet had grown from a tonnage of 5,631 in the former to one of 115,045 in the latter year. Starting far behind, we were now abreast of England, and ship for ship our steam vessels were very much superior. Captain McKennon of the British navy, after voyages of observation in both the Cunard and

Collins liners, declared that "there are no ocean steamers in England comparable with the 'Baltic.'"

By 1856 we had lost two great steamships and some lesser ones, it is true, but so had our competitor. The hazards of the sea made this inevitable. The "Arctic" and "Pacific" were no more mourned in America than the "President" and "City of Glasgow" in Great Britain, and no United States steamship enterprise had had such a melancholy record of wreck and death as the Royal Mail Steam Packet line to the West Indies. An observer who looks only to the actual achievements of our steam marine, and weighs the $1,886,766 which it was receiving in subsidies in 1856 against its military and commercial value to the republic, finds absolutely incomprehensible the bitter tone of hostility toward the steamship interests that sprang up in 1853–1854 among some of the lawmakers in Washington. The increase of the mail pay to the Collins line in 1852, when it was recognized that the great and costly new ships could not be run at a profit for $19,250 a voyage, or $385,000 for twenty round passages, aroused some resentment in the interior of the country where the sea and its business were little understood. Nevertheless, the enlarged subsidy of $858,000 for twenty-six voyages was granted, with the very general and hearty sanction of North, South, East, and West. One of the many petitions for this increased payment came from the shipowners and merchants of Charleston, S. C., who asked for it "not as residents of Charleston, but as patriotic citizens of the United States."[1]

It was the grave misfortune of the American steam marine at this critical period to be drawn into the maëlstrom of sectional strife. The slavery controversy in the early fifties was becoming more and more the overmastering element in national politics. It so happened that the merchant shipping of the United States, and especially the

[1] Thirty-Second Congress, first session, March 15, 1852.

18

steam shipping, was owned chiefly in New England and New York, where the antislavery agitation was most vehement. Moreover, the subsidized mail steamers all sailed from Northern ports, except a line from Charleston to the West Indies. It was a plausible argument that the entire country was contributing to the support of an interest by which only the northern seacoast directly profited. Besides, — though this consideration did not come to count for much until secession was actively contemplated, — these great, swift, strong mail steamers would be a formidable addition to the sea-power of the North, if the unhappy quarrel between the States should ever drift on to the arbitrament of war.

Gradually, therefore, the ocean mail system became more and more an issue of sectional politics, as the tariff system had become a few years earlier. The South never completely deserted the cause of the American steamship. Senator Rusk, of Texas, and a few other Southern statesmen remained its eager and consistent advocates. But in both Senate and House the alignment on the Ocean Mail appropriations as they came up year by year grew more and more sinister, and the friendly majorities steadily narrowed. The subsidy system was in danger. Our shipowners saw it. The mere threat of adverse legislation checked at once the swift, steady growth of our steam tonnage. American steamships registered for deep-sea trade fell off from 115,045 tons in 1855 to 89,715 tons in 1856, to 86,873 tons in 1857 and to 78,027 tons in 1858. The spectacle of an almost solid South backed by much of the agricultural West assailing the mail subventions was an alarming omen, indeed, in those years when Southern influence was supreme in Washington.

In 1856, under this hostile pressure from the South and the interior, Congress reduced the Collins mail pay by the withdrawal of the $473,000 which had been added in 1852 to the original subsidy of $385,000. Of course, the loss of the "Arctic" and "Pacific" had crippled the mail service temporarily, for no other ships equally fast and powerful could be found anywhere for charter, and the great "Adriatic" was not yet ready for sea. This was not the fault of Mr. Collins; it was his misfortune. To punish him for it by the cancellation of the greater part of his subsidy seems to have been a strange refinement of cruelty. It was not that way that Great Britain had rewarded her ambitious shipowners and produced her ever-growing steam marine. Mr. Collins, with his two ships and one or two hired vessels, made an heroic struggle to fulfil the rigid terms of his contract, but the effort was too much for his resources. His company had taken all its earnings year after year and applied them to the improvement of its ships and the quickening of the service. It had looked to the future for its profitable returns, and the action of Congress destroyed all its calculations.

The Collins Company has been accused, perhaps not unjustly, of extravagance. It must certainly plead guilty to the charge of building larger and more powerful steamers than Congress had stipulated for, though Congress had set the size of the ships five hundred tons above the Cunard average. The Collins Company had equipped these steamers with expensive machinery which gave them the then unheard-of sea speed of thirteen or fourteen miles an hour. It had furnished the ships luxuriously; one of the counts in the anti-subsidy indictment was that there were mirrors — actually mirrors — in the cabins! It had steadily reduced the time of the Atlantic voyages, though that involved an increased coal bill of more than a hundred thousand dollars a year. All this was extravagance surely, from one standpoint, and there may have been equal openhandedness in other details of administration. Certain it is that the great New York business men who rallied around Mr. Collins in his patriotic effort to keep his country's flag afloat on the chief route of Atlantic commerce won no personal profit from their undertaking.[1] The Collins line never declared a cent of dividend. It might have survived the loss of its two ships, just as contemporary British companies survived even worse disasters, but it could not and did not survive the loss of its ships and the greater part of its subsidy at the same time.

In the Congressional session of 1858 a proposition was brought forward to change the whole basis of the ocean mail system, and to substitute for fixed amounts of money, payable for a term of years, the sea and inland postage on the letters actually carried by a line of steamships. This measure provoked a long senatorial debate in which the whole question of government aid to steamship enterprise was threshed out by very able and earnest men on both sides.

The Senators of the great Northern and Eastern commercial States were generally in favor of a liberal policy of continued subventions. Most though not all of the Senators of the South and Southwest were opposed to it. A little group of Southern Senators who were destined soon to become very famous led the political battle against the historic principle of national protection and encouragement to our maritime interests. They were Jefferson Davis, a senator from Mississippi, R. M. T. Hunter, a senator from Virginia, S. R. Mallory, a senator from Florida, Robert Toombs, a senator from Georgia, J. M. Mason, a senator from Virginia, and Judah P. Benjamin, a senator from Louisiana. Mr. Davis declared, in the course of the debate on June 9, 1858, "I see no reason why, if we can get our mails carried in British vessels across the Atlantic, we should establish a line of American vessels merely that we may compete with them in a race across the Atlantic." On the same day Mr. Toombs said, "I would as soon have my letters carried in British as in American bottoms, and

[1] Senator William H. Seward of New York in the United States Senate, June 9, 1858.

I would prefer that they should carry them if they did it cheaper."

These were astonishing sentiments to be heard in a chamber which ten years before had rung with the declarations of senators, Southern and Northern alike, that no sacrifice could be too great to protect the American ship and the American sailor from the aggressive designs of our commercial rival and ancient enemy. Great Britain at this time was paying the Cunard line about $900,000 a year. The new legislation gave the Collins line $346,000, and restricted our other transatlantic lines to the sea and inland postage. The bill was passed in the face of the protests of Senator Seward, of New York, and other representatives of the commercial and shipowning North, and of the warning of Senator Bayard, of Delaware, that Congress was deliberately destroying the American steam marine and throwing the whole Atlantic postal service into the hands of the British government.

This startling reversal of a great national policy that had been entered upon with such high, patriotic motives by a united country eleven years before was part of the heavy price which the United States has had to pay for the national crime of negro slavery. But for the rise of the embittering controversy between the States, which smothered for a time the old sense of nationality, the protection to American steamship lines which President Polk and a Democratic Congress initiated would not have been abandoned in the very crisis of the struggle between America and Britain. Within three years the Southern men who were chiefly instrumental in bringing about the downfall of the American merchant marine had left the Senate Chamber forever and had sworn a new allegiance and were living beneath a new flag. Mr. Davis became the President of the Southern Confederacy; Mr. Hunter, the Secretary of State; Mr. Mallory, the Secretary of the Navy; Mr. Mason, the Confederate Commissioner to England with Mr. Slidell; Mr. Benjamin, the Attorney-General; and Mr. Toombs, a member of the Southern Congress and subsequently Secretary of State.

These men had dealt their country a terrible blow, but it is only just to their memories to acquit them of consciously hostile motives. The slavery quarrel in 1858 had hopelessly estranged North and South. Neither section was in a mood to deal fairly with the interests of the other. For the time being the old, broad, national patriotism was dead. Mr. Davis, Mr. Toombs, Mr. Hunter, and the others, as their speeches indicate, saw in the subsidy protection of American steamships only the aggrandizement of the Northern States, where the antislavery sentiment was strongest, at the expense of the agricultural South. They did not see the far-reaching national significance of the contest between America and Britain for the mastery of the ocean. The slavery feud, obscuring all else, narrowed their vision, but they can honestly be acquitted of deliberate wrong.

The actual results of the policy of 1858 were quite as immediate and deadly, however, as if this stroke at our steam fleet had been intentional. The Collins line was at once abandoned. Its steamships were seized by the mortgagees and sold. The noble, new "Adriatic," which had made her first voyage only the year before, was purchased by one of the subsidized British steamship corporations for the Galway line. The stars and stripes came down from her peak; the red ensign of Britain went up, — a vivid sign of our national defeat and humiliation. The steamships of the pioneer line to Bremen were withdrawn and dismantled. The line to Havre, which had two new vessels on its hands, ran a little longer, but soon disappeared. Commodore Vanderbilt, the ablest steamship manager of his time, undertook the Bremen service with three of his unemployed steamers, and thoroughly tested the new law which gave him the "sea and inland postage."

He, too, quit the field, finding it impossible to compete with the cheap labor and the cheap and abundant capital of Europe, fortified by heavy government subsidies. Thus the flag of the United States absolutely vanished from the steam routes of the North Atlantic. At the end of 1861, the only American-built steamship in the regular ocean service was the former Collins liner "Adriatic," which, under British colors, held for several years the trans-atlantic record with a passage of 5 days, 19 hours, from Galway to St. John's. This magnificent steamer, alienated from the country that had refused to protect her, and receiving the subsidy and flying the flag of our persistent and victorious rival, was an eloquent object lesson of the causes that had wrought the ruin of the American merchant marine.

Our West India and Pacific Mail lines were injured by the change of national policy, but they were not destroyed. Unlike the transatlantic lines, they were not paralleled by heavily subsidized foreign competitors. The rivalry which they met was indirect and, therefore, much less severe and exhausting. Moreover, both the West India and Pacific Mail services were in a sense coastwise, and thus protected in another way than by their mail subventions. Only American steamers could carry passengers and freight between our Atlantic and Pacific coasts *via* the Isthmus. These fortunate conditions saved the West Indian and Pacific Mail steamers when the American lines to Europe succumbed.

In the years when the United States withdrew its protection from Atlantic steamship enterprise and left it to perish, the nations of Europe, our competitors, were steadily increasing their ship-subventions, and extending their steam lines from one ocean to another. Great Britain in the year 1850-51 granted $3,699,853 [1] to her ocean

---

[1] Report of British Post Office in Annual Report of United States Commissioner of Navigation for 1900.

steamships. In 1860-61 she was expending $4,537,223. France, in 1858, following the British example of marine protectionism, offered $620,000 a year for twenty-six voyages between Havre and New York, or about $24,000 a voyage; $940,000 a year for a steam service to Brazil, and $1,300,000 for a line to the West Indies and Mexico. Germany at about the same time had begun to subsidize the North German Lloyd for an American service.

The reason why Great Britain succeeded and the United States failed in that contest of subsidy protection half a century ago is that Great Britain persisted and the United States did not. Take, for instance, the British treatment of the Royal Mail line to the West Indies and compare it with our treatment of the Collins line, and there is no need to look further for an explanation why ever since 1858 the British flag has been dominant on the North Atlantic. The Collins line, as has been shown, was splendidly successful in the ships which it produced and the service which it rendered, until the loss of the "Arctic" and "Pacific" and the simultaneous reduction of its subsidy dealt it a mortal blow. Now mark the contrast:[1] In March, 1841, the Board of Admiralty awarded a subsidy of $1,200,000 to a company of British merchants for a steamship line to the West Indies and the Gulf of Mexico. The moderate speed of eight knots an hour was required of these vessels, and their course lay through a region where the skies and the sea are kindly and no fog or ice disturbs the mariner. Nevertheless, this British company lost seven ships in the first ten years of its career. The "Isis" went down off Bermuda in 1842; the "Solway" sank in 1843 off Corunna with sixty of her company; the "Tweed" dragged seventy-two more to death in 1847 on the reefs of Yucatan; the "Forth" crashed on the same reefs two years afterward; the "Medina" was also

[1] Lindsay's "Merchant Shipping," vol. iv.

wrecked; the " Actæon " went to her doom in 1850 off
Carthagena; the " Amazon," a new ship on her first voyage, the largest of the fleet, was burned off the Scilly Isles
in 1852, one hundred of her people perishing. No
American steamship line ever matched this record of disaster, but the Royal Mail West India Company was not cried
down by Lords or Commons, or abandoned by the government. On the contrary, when its first year's operations
showed a deficit of nearly $400,000, the Admiralty re-
duced the required service one-half, but left the subsidy at
the original generous figure of $1,200,000, so that a net
profit was guaranteed. Lindsay says of this West India
enterprise that, " The contract for the conveyance of the
mails was never exposed to public competition," and he
adds that the company never carried out its time schedule.
Nevertheless, when the contract was renewed in 1850 the
British government actually increased the subsidy from
$1,200,000 to $1,350,000, asking in return a new service
to Brazil and an improved speed in new ships of from
eight to ten knots an hour. Just then the Collins line
was putting its thirteen and fourteen knot steamers on the
route to Liverpool.

Great Britain stood loyally by her shipowners, and with
constant and unceasing subsidy protection tided them over
their years of trial and misfortune. We deserted our shipowners in their time of need, leaving them to fight single-
handed the hazards of the sea, the vicissitudes of the
unfamiliar trade of steam navigation, and the treasuries of
foreign governments. Who can wonder that they were
beaten in this unequal contest, and driven from the
sea?

The American people are not less tenacious than the
British people, or less enterprising, or less patriotic. But
for the brief and melancholy stifling of the passion of
nationality in the sectional quarrel that produced the Civil
War, our splendid steamship lines never would have been

abandoned. The merchant marine in that critical period of transition from sail to steam was as truly and directly the victim of the feud between the States as was that fair region of Virginia meadow, hill, and forest between the Potomac and Richmond, the scene of the death-grapple of the two mighty armies from 1861 to 1865.

The whole question of the survival of our steam fleet in the deep-sea trade between 1846 and 1860 was a question of national protection or the lack of it. One of the greatest New York merchants and shipowners of his time, A. A. Low, Esq., father of Mayor Seth Low, has left [1] this authoritative statement of the cause that ruined the American merchant marine, and of the remedy that would have saved it: —

"My own belief is that the policy of England in subsidizing lines of steamers to the various ports of the world, has given her a prestige which is almost insuperable. . . . My own impression is that large subsidies should be given as an inducement and that these subsidies, while they would cost the government something in the beginning, would cost the government nothing in the end.

"I only know the English have always, in peace and war, manifested a determination to hold the supremacy on the ocean, and the supremacy which they acquired by arms in war they have in peace acquired by subsidies. They have deliberately and intentionally driven the Americans from the ocean by paying subsidies which they knew our Congress would not pay. I believe it has been the deliberate purpose on the part of England to maintain her supremacy upon the ocean by paying larger subsidies than any other nation, as long as subsidies were necessary to preserve their control.

"I believe that when the Collins line was running, the subsidy to the Cunard line was renewed for the express

[1] Testimony before a special committee of Congress.

purpose to enable it to run off the Collins line.   It was renewed several years before the expiration of the subsidy
granted, so that the Cunard line might enter upon contracts
for new ships, and a committee of the English Parliament,
similar to this committee, was employed to make the most
minute investigation into the matter.   It was after the
most careful inquiry by that committee that the contract
with the Cunard was renewed for the express purpose of
enabling that line to run the American steamers from
the ocean; and they have driven us from the ocean by that
policy just as effectually as they ever did drive an enemy
from the ocean by their guns."

The record of American tonnage registered for foreign
trade, in the period from 1846 to 1860, inclusive, is a
record of swift expansion under the influence of the California trade and the Crimean War up to 1855, when these
chance impulses lost their force.   For several years
afterward, when the ocean mail subsidies were being reduced or withdrawn, our tonnage was practically at a
standstill.   Indeed, looking beneath the surface to the
record of shipbuilding, the truth was even worse, for the
583,450 tons launched in 1855 had fallen off to 156,602
in 1859 and to 214,797 in 1860,—the swiftest and most
alarming shrinkage in our maritime history.   The 381
ships and barks built for foreign commerce in 1855 had
fallen to a pitiable 89 in 1859 and to 110 in 1860.   These
figures do not appear in the following table, but they are
essential to an understanding of the real truth, not
adequately declared by the record of the total tonnage,
that the years from 1855 onward were years of unmistakable decline.'   Moreover, another indication of the shrinkage of our sea-power which does appear is the alarming
decline of the proportion of our commerce carried in
American ships from 81.7 in 1846 to 66.5 in 1860:

TONNAGE AND FOREIGN TRADE. 1846-60.

Year.	Shipping Tons.	Total Foreign Commerce.	Proportion carried in **American Ships.**		
			Imports.	Exports.	Combined Imports and Exports.
1846	943,307	$227,497,313	87.1	76.1	81.7
1847	1,047,454	279,165,947	77.2	65.3	81.1
1848	1,168,707	286,829,159	82.9	71.1	77.4
1849	1,258,756	281,557,371	81.4	68.0	75.2
1850	1,439,694	317,885,252	77.8	65.5	72.5
1851	1,544,663	399,686,688	75.6	69.8	72.7
1852	1,705,650	374,424,629	74.5	66.5	70.5
1853	1,910,471	467,266,547	71.5	67.1	69.5
1854	2,151,918	534,847,588	71.4	69.3	70.5
1855	2,348,358	476,718,211	77.3	73.8	75.6
1856	2,302,190	591,651,733	78.1	70.9	75.2
1857	2,268,196	642,252,102	71.8	60.2	70.5
1858	2,301,148	535,349,928	72.0	75.0	73.7
1859	2,321,674	624,235,392	63.7	69.9	66.9
1860	2,379,396	687,192,176	63.0	69.7	66.5

CHAPTER XIII

THE DEEP-SEA FISHERIES

An Historic Industry of America — Marblehead and Gloucester Pioneers — British Jealousy of New England — After the Revolutionary War — National Bounties for the Fishermen — Rapid Growth of the Yankee Fleet — Splendid Service in the War of 1812 — British Persecution renewed — Toilers of the Sea undaunted — A New England Monopoly — Unfailing Nursery of Seamanship — Perils and Profits of the Calling — Canadian Hostility Persistent — Withdrawal of the Bounties and Decline of the Deep-Sea Industry — Gloucester's Success and its Secret — Canadian Bounty-Fed Competition and "Free Fish" — Our Fishing Fleet now a Small but a Superb One — Still a Source of Naval Strength — The Tonnage Record

EVEN more ancient than the whale fishery, and as famous a source of wealth and naval strength, is the deep-sea fishery for cod, halibut, and mackerel, as it has been pursued for three centuries off the northeast coast of America. This, too, has always been a notably bold and manly calling. The fishing craft of the United States have been regularly licensed by the government, and recognized as an integral part of the American merchant marine. For many years the Yankee fishermen on the offshore banks were the most numerous, as they always have been the most persistent, audacious, and successful, of the nations. Even now, though our fleet has dwindled in size, it is incomparably the first in quality. Its vessels are the most skilfully constructed, the swiftest and the most seaworthy, and its equipment for fishing is the most ingenious and complete.

This prestige is ours by goodly right of heritage. The first white settlers on our northern shores were fishermen.

Before the Pilgrims came to Plymouth, the Dutch to New Amsterdam, or the Quakers to Philadelphia, the catchers of the cod had established stations along the coast of Maine, as well as farther north in Nova Scotia and Newfoundland. These stations lacked the permanence of an industry that roots down into the soil, but they bore their part and a great part toward convincing Europe that there were other and surer riches in the New World than phantasmic El Dorados and fountains of perpetual youth. The thrifty Puritans of Salem and Boston and Hollanders of New York took cod and mackerel very seriously into their calculations. Dried fish and rough lumber formed the basis of their earliest over-seas trade with the mother-continent and the European colonies in the West Indies.

Six years before the founding of Plymouth, the redoubtable John Smith, in 1614, set up a fishing station at Pemaquid, Maine, where his men caught and cured twelve hundred quintals of fish that sold in Spain for five dollars a quintal. The " Trial, " pioneer of a long line of Boston-built merchantmen, voyaged to Bilboa and Malaga soon after 1633 with a cargo of fish, which was profitably exchanged for a lading of wine, oil, iron, and wool. It was their harvest of the sea, not the first fruits of their thin and grudging acres, which won for the early colonists their few luxuries and the indispensable materials of their tools and clothing. How closely the prosperity and perhaps the very life of the American settlements hung upon the fisheries was realized by the New England law-givers, who, in 1652, provided for " the appointment of sworn fish-viewers at every fishing place within the jurisdiction, who were required to reject all unmerchantable, all sun-burnt, salt-burnt, and dry fish that hath first been pickled, to be paid one-half by the dealer, the other half by the receiver. "

This jealous care for the quality of the product was due to a knowledge that the foundations of the colonies really rested on the decks of the fishing smacks. These craft, of ketch and sloop rig chiefly, soon swarmed all alongshore, to the dismay of the Indians. Many and bloody were the encounters in which, in King Philip's War and afterward, the vengeful red men sought to surprise and overwhelm the winged canoes of the pale-faces. These early fishermen met other perils than those of the sea, — other perils than those of lurking savages. The growth of their industry drew the hostile attention of French and Spanish cruisers, and even of the pirates of the Spanish Main. But the courage of men who were ready to fight old Ocean for their finny prizes, could not be daunted by mortal foemen, be they red or white. The fishing industry of the northeast prospered. At the opening of the eighteenth century, and perhaps before, the northern colonies were sending their fisher craft beyond Cape Sable to the off-shore banks.

The rock-girdled Massachusetts town of Marblehead, with its deep, snug harbor opening on the free sea, was the leader in this enterprise. In 1741, out of the four hundred Massachusetts fishing vessels, Marblehead owned almost one-half. Gloucester, a dozen miles away to the northeast, nestling in the granite cliffs of Cape Ann, is now the most famous fishing port in America and perhaps in all the world. But a century ago Marblehead was her superior. It was Gloucester, however, which sent the first "scooner" to the Grand Bank of Newfoundland. The schooner rig, by its simplicity and handiness, soon became the fisher rig, *par excellence*. The clumsy ketch and sloop vanished before Captain Andrew Robinson's invention. Robinson, by the way, a Gloucester man himself, was a celebrated fisherman. It is said of him that he was so ardent on the banks, when the fish were keen and numerous, that " he would not leave his place on deck even to eat, but when he was hungry he had a ship biscuit brought him, which he contrived to eat by working it round in his mouth with his teeth and lips, while his hands were attending to the hook and line." Old Captain

Robinson, father of the schooner, was an embodiment of
the shrewd, indomitable spirit which years afterward made
Gloucester pre-eminent, and has now gained for her almost
a monopoly in the most arduous and perilous calling known
to civilized man.

For this is unquestionably what the North American
deep-sea fishery is, as the hardy sons of New England have
pursued it for almost three centuries. Many, many years
ago, the annual losses began to be appalling. French and
English, under the patronage of their governments, had
followed the Grand Bank fishery in cautiously navigated
vessels of considerable size. The poverty of New England
forbade such large investments. Of the seventy or eighty
Cape Ann schooners that sailed to the Grand Bank for
cod in the half dozen years before the Revolution, few
were of above fifty tons, and the average cost of the craft,
with outfit complete, is said to have been about a thousand
dollars. Such puny vessels were ill-fit to meet the furious
tempests and giant waves of the North Atlantic. Disaster
was frequent and inevitable. Gloucester records relate
that " In March, 1766, 19 vessels sailed for the Grand
Bank, and while on the passage thither were met by a
violent storm which wrecked and scattered the fleet and
sent many to the bottom. Two were cast away at Nova
Scotia; seven foundered at sea with all on board; and
several others were so much disabled that they were obliged
to return."

Even heavier than the storm of the elements fell the
storm of war. The Revolution swept utterly away the
Gloucester fisheries. Bereft of their livelihood, Gloucester
tars turned eagerly to the perilous work of privateering
and to the scarcely less perilous service of the little Continental navy. The victory of Yorktown found three hundred
Gloucester sailors dead or missing, — one-third of all the
able-bodied men of the heroic town. Marblehead when
the war closed had 166 of her sons in British prisons,

while 122 more were absent with their fate unknown. Of the 1,069 women in Marblehead, 378 were widows, and of the 2,242 children, 672 were fatherless. The "ratable polls" of Marblehead had decreased from 1,202 before the war to 544, and the tonnage "owned, employed, and manned" by Marblehead from 12,313 to 1,509.[1]

Nor was it strange that the deep-sea fishermen of New England threw themselves with such ardor into our fight for independence. They knew that it meant life or death for their calling and for them. Their hard-won success had aroused the bitter jealousy of the less bold or persistent fishermen of Britain. One of the specific causes of the Revolution was Lord North's attempt in 1775 to reduce the Northern colonies to terms by closing the foreign market for their fish, and destroying the deep-sea fisheries altogether. Lord North sought to forbid exports to France, Holland, Spain, Madeira, and South America, and to prevent colonial craft from resorting to the Bank of Newfoundland. "In the list of parliamentary acts which did so much to bring on the Revolution," says McMaster,[2] "there is none so infamous as" this. The British Tories believed that this stroke at the fisheries would starve New England into submission. The bill passed by a great majority, although twenty-one of the House of Lords remonstrated against it, declaring that "the attempt to coerce by famine the whole body of the inhabitants of great and populous provinces is without example in the history of this or perhaps of any civilized nation."

The next year, when our American Commissioners in Paris were invoking French aid in our battle for freedom, the most difficult objection which they had to overcome was that the extinguishment of the fisheries would be fatal to New England. Even Vergennes, Minister of Foreign Affairs, says McMaster shared this belief, and he could

[1] "The History and Traditions of Marblehead," by Samuel Roads, Jr.
[2] "A History of the American People," by John Bach McMaster, vol. iv.

scarcely be convinced that the American colonies could live without access to the Bank of Newfoundland, and a foreign outlet for their salted quintals.   Here is picturesque historic testimony to the vast importance of the Yankee fishing fleet of a century and a quarter ago, as the Old World regarded it.   The same estimate was loyally held here at home.   John Adams and his colleagues faithfully reflected the sentiment of the American people, if not of the feeble Congress, when they insisted at Paris that the retention of equal rights in the northeastern fisheries was an indispensable condition of peace.

The Treaty of 1783 guaranteed to our fisher-citizens substantially all the rights and privileges which they had enjoyed as subjects of the British king.   They were allowed to take fish of every kind on the Grand Bank and all other banks of Newfoundland, in the Gulf of St. Lawrence, and in all other places whither they had been accustomed to resort before the Revolution.   Our vessels were furthermore permitted to take fish on all parts of the coast of Newfoundland that were open to British fishermen, and on all the other coasts and in all the harbors, bays, and creeks of British North America.   But they could dry and cure their fish only on the unsettled shores of Nova Scotia, the Magdalen Islands, and Labrador.

All this was generous enough.   Great Britain frankly recognized the inherent right of American fishermen to share the fishery privileges of the Canadian provinces which these stout Yankees under Phipps and Pepperell, both New England fishing merchants, had helped the Crown to wrest from the French.   The treaty of peace was all that our deep-sea fishing interests could desire, but it did not restore to them the anticipated prosperity. McMaster testifies that from the signing of the treaty in 1783 to the adoption of the Constitution " the fish industry was prostrate."   " It did, indeed," he says, " give employment to 540 ships and 3,300 seamen.   But the business had steadily declined until, in 1789, the average yearly earnings of each vessel were $273, and the average yearly expenses $416."

The fishing industry, in other words, shared the paralysis that bound all our maritime industries until Congress, by special legislation, came to their relief. This volume has already told how in 1789 the first law of the first Congress under the Constitution was a law for the protection and encouragement, not of American manufactures only, but also of American shipbuilding and shipowning for the foreign trade. The same protection was now thrown around the fisheries in a form that was even more direct and more significant.

It is a striking historical fact that this step for the protection and encouragement of our deep-sea fishing fleet was taken largely because of the direct appeal and on the personal initiative of Thomas Jefferson, the great founder of the Democratic (then the Republican) party. Jefferson had suggested the payment of bounties from the Federal treasury as the surest and most effective means of reviving our moribund fisheries. This is the method which was actually applied. In 1792 Congress passed an important law, providing that there should be paid annually to the owners of vessels employed in the cod fisheries for four months in the year a bounty of $1.50 a ton for every ton of burden over twenty and under thirty, and $2.50 for every ton above thirty.[1] The practical result of this, of course, would be to encourage the building of larger, more seaworthy, and more expensive vessels. It was stipulated that three-eighths of the bounty should go to the owners of the vessels and five-eighths to the crews.

The American fishing fleet responded as quickly and handsomely to these government bounties or subsidies as the American cargo-carrying fleet had done to the protec-

[1] Hon. Zeno Scudder of Massachusetts, in House of Representatives, Aug. 12, 1852.

tion of the discriminating customs duties and tonnage dues. In 1805-1807, there were 57,465 tons of shipping and 8,000 men employed in the American fisheries, and their exports in 1805 amounted to more than $2,000,000. In 1807 the bounty act of 1792 was repealed, and at the same time the duty was removed from foreign salt, as if that were an equivalent. "Free salt" speedily proved to be no offset to the loss of the bounty. The fleet and the fishermen decreased so alarmingly that in 1813 Congress re-enacted the bounty law, greatly increasing the allowances to $2.40 a ton to vessels over twenty and under thirty tons, and $4 a ton to vessels above thirty tons. In 1819 Congress amended the bounty act and made it still more liberal, granting $3.50 a ton to all vessels between five and thirty tons, for four months of sea service, and $3.50 a ton to vessels above thirty tons for three and one-half months of sea service, if the crews consisted of ten or more men. This bounty law remained in force for many years thereafter, — a period which was the genuine golden age of the American deep-sea fisheries.

The War of 1812 dealt the American fishing fleet almost as severe a blow as the Revolution. The 'longshore boats were not always interfered with by British blockaders, but the "bankers" abandoned their trips and were dismantled and laid up in snug ports beyond the reach of "cutting out" expeditions, while the best men of the idle crews swarmed eagerly on board our frigates, sloops, and privateers. There were in 1812 enough American deep-sea fishermen in the New England States to man our entire navy twice over. Fishermen, young, hardy, and impetuous, made up a large part of the splendid ship's company of "Old Ironsides" on each of her victorious cruises. But the fisherfolk took even more naturally to the private armed ships than they did to the men-of-war. Every fishing town on the north coast — Salem, Marblehead, Gloucester, Newburyport, Portsmouth, Portland — was a nest of privateering, and right smartly did these audacious fellows spoil their proud and wealthy foe. When Great Britain retired from the war, in the memorable words of the "London Times," "with the stripes still bleeding upon our backs," it was with a vengeful spirit toward the Yankee fishermen.

This spirit found expression in the stubborn insistence of the British Peace Commissioners at Ghent that the fishery privileges on the Nova Scotia and Newfoundland coasts, which the Americans enjoyed under the treaty of 1783, should be surrendered. It was the British contention that the treaty had been abrogated by the war. So fierce was the dispute and so hopeless seemed a settlement that when the peace treaty was framed it was found to say not one word about the fisheries; it was as silent as it was with regard to the burning question of impressment on which in large part the war had been fought. But the sturdy fishermen had no thought of yielding their prerogatives. They set sail in 1815 for the Banks as usual, in spite of the threat of the Collector at Halifax that he would drive all the Yankees out of the waters where fish could be found. A British sloop-of-war attempted to make the threat effective. She boarded American fishermen far at sea, warned them not to come within sixty miles of the Nova Scotia coast, and virtually broke up their summer season. The reckless work of the captain of the man-of-war was disavowed by the British government, and Lord Bathurst declared that in 1815 the American fishing craft should not be interfered with, but that after that year they would be denied the privilege of fishing within three miles of the Canadian shore and of drying or curing their fish on either the settled or unsettled coast-line. John Quincy Adams had not long before become American Minister at London. A Massachusetts man from a seaport town, he understood the fisheries and their importance as a basis of trade and nursery of sea-power. Mr. Adams vigorously combated the British purpose to such effect that Great Britain consented to make the fisheries the object of a new and special negotiation. This resulted in the celebrated Convention of 1818, the basis of three-quarters of a century of constant wrangling, and time and time again almost the cause of war.

Great Britain secured substantially what she desired in this negotiation. Her purpose was to curb and punish the men who had helped to strike her such a terrible blow at sea. The privilege of landing to dry and cure fish, which American fishermen, under the Treaty of 1783, had enjoyed on the unsettled coasts of the Canadian provinces, was reduced by the Convention of 1818 to the southern coasts of Newfoundland and the coast of Labrador. The privilege of fishing within three miles of the shore was similarly restricted to the southwestern and western coast of Newfoundland within certain limits and the coast of Labrador northward and eastward from Mt. Joly. The United States renounced forever its former rights to take fish within a marine league of the remaining portions of the British shore-line. American fishing vessels might enter the bays and harbors of the prohibited territory to seek shelter, repair damages, and obtain wood and water, but for no other purposes.

This Convention of 1818, in which Great Britain gained so much and we retained so little, was for the time being a sharp disappointment to our fishermen. For a year or two the enrolled tonnage of the fishing fleet fell away. It had been 65,045 tons in 1819.[1] In 1820 it was 60,843; in 1821, 51,352. But the new and liberal plan of government bounties soon made its influence felt. It had been further guarded by the requirement that three-fourths of every fishing crew must be American citizens. Encouraged by national protection to go afloat, our fishermen were not long in discovering that Britain's victory in the Convention of 1818, while a severe blow, was by no means

[1] Report of the U. S. Commissioner of Navigation, 1900.

fatal to the ancient industry. In 1822 the enrolled tonnage in the fisheries once more began to grow, and with some fluctuations it continued to increase for thirty or forty years thereafter.

Great Britain's chagrin that she had once more failed to destroy the Yankee fisheries was manifested in some very ugly work. Our fishing vessels were harassed whenever they entered provincial harbors. They were confiscated for small technical violations of law. They were even seized by British cruisers while out of sight of land. On some occasions, as the affidavits of the fishermen stated, the men were driven out of their captured vessels, without a dollar and without food, the prize officers refusing them a single biscuit. This was the experience of the crew of a Portland schooner that was seized fifteen miles at sea. Such conduct inevitably bred a spirit of retaliation. In September, 1824, two American schooners, the " Reindeer " and the " Ruby," were seized by the British war sloop " Dotterel " at Grand Manan. The next day, as the vessels in charge of prize crews were on their way to St. Andrew's for condemnation, they were attacked by two hundred armed men in two schooners and a boat, led by a Captain Howard of the Eastport militia. The British bluejackets and marines prudently surrendered, and the " Reindeer " and the " Ruby " were borne back in triumph to American waters. This affair was the text of voluminous protests from the British government, but it does not appear that the doughty Eastport militia captain ever lost his epaulets.

Most of the seized vessels, however, were not so fortunate. When the King's broad arrow had once marked their masts, they never saw again their native harbors. It meant a cruel loss to many poor and hard-worked men. The northeastern fishery has always been conducted, as a rule, on a co-operative or profit-sharing basis. The owners, who were generally far from rich themselves, provided the vessel and her outfit, and took as compensation a certain portion of the catch. Captain and crew shared the remainder. If the voyage was profitable, the good fortune was enjoyed by all concerned. But if the trip was broken up by storm or seizure, the fishermen had nothing to show for a hard season's work but calloused hands and threadbare clothing. Their income was a narrow one at best. It averaged for a long time at Gloucester only $17 or $18 a month, bounty included. Out of this the family of the fisherman had to be housed and fed while he was absent. Thus iron industry had to be matched with iron economy in the gray old villages of the New England coast.

The deep-sea fishery in the form which it finally assumed was a New England monopoly pure and simple. Dr. Adam Seybert, in his admirable "Statistical Annals" (1818), declares: "Our fishermen have been almost exclusively confined to the New England States; of these Massachusetts had the greatest share. . . . In the cod fishery no vessel (except $48\frac{44}{95}$ tons returned for New Jersey in 1803 and $66\frac{26}{95}$ tons for Virginia in 1796) was owned south of New York."

McMaster, in his vivid picture of the great westward drift of emigration in the early years of the nineteenth century, pays an eloquent tribute [1] to the constancy and hardihood of these New England fishermen. The farmer deserted his acres, the tradesman his shop, but "no whaler left his vessel. No seaman deserted his mess. No fisherman of Marblehead or Gloucester exchanged the dangers of a life on the ocean for the privations of a life in the West. Their fathers and their uncles had been fishermen before them, and their sons were to follow in their steps. Long before a lad could nib a quill or make a pothook or read half the precepts his primer contained, he knew the name of every brace and stay, every sail and part of a

[1] "A History of the People of the U. S.," by John Bach McMaster, vol. ii.

Grand Banker and a Chebacco, all the nautical terms, what line and hook should be used for catching halibut and what for mackerel and cod. . . .

" Till he was nine a lad did little more than watch the men, pitch pennies in the road, listen to sea stories, and hurry at the cry of 'rock him,' 'squael him,' to help his playmates pelt with stones some unoffending boy from a neighboring village. By the time he had seen his tenth birthday, he was old enough not to be seasick, not to cry during a storm at sea and to be of some use about a ship; and went on his first trip to the Banks. The skipper and the crew called him 'cut-tail,' for he received no money save for the fish he caught, and each one he caught was marked by snipping a piece from the tail. After an apprenticeship of three or four years the 'cut-tail' became a 'header,' stood upon the same footing as the 'sharesman' and learned all the duties which a 'splitter' and a 'salter' must perform. A crew numbered eight; four were 'sharesmen' and four were apprentices : went twice a year to the Banks and stayed each time from three to five months. Men who had passed through such a training were under no temptation to travel westward. They took no interest; they bore no part in the great exodus. They still continued to make their trips and bring home their 'fares,' while hosts of New Englanders poured into New York, opening the valleys, founding cities, and turning struggling hamlets into villages of no mean kind."

The resourcefulness of this shrewd, tough New England race, that had been first in 1775 to challenge British tyranny, made short work of the hedge-fences of the vexatious Convention of 1818. When the fishermen of Maine and Massachusetts were shut out of the three-mile limit along the coast of the Canadian provinces, they found new and rich banks far at sea. In 1821 three venturesome Gloucestermen sailed to George's, where Davy Jones was supposed to lie in wait for any rash vessel that dared to anchor in the tideway. Tradition had it that the green seas would soon be roaring through the hawseholes, and the poor craft would " ride under " and go down like a stone. Two of the Gloucester skippers threw spare hands aboard the third schooner, which dropped her best bower with plenty of scope. Nothing terrible happened, save that when they " checked " the cable on the windlass the vessel seemed to slide through the water at a three-knot gait, and her consorts drifted away in the current. This Gloucester pioneer on George's did not stay to fish; he hove up his anchor with an hour and a half of hard work, and sailed for home to tell his story. A few years afterward George's was crowded with Gloucester vessels that did not hesitate to anchor while they plied their lines for halibut or cod. But they hastened to get under way at the first sign of a breeze of wind, to escape dragging to their doom beneath a heavy sea or in the death-shock of collision.

George's, like the Grand Bank, lies too far away for the extension-paw of the British lion. The Yankee fishermen learned to deepen their water and to range over a greater area of the Grand Bank than the original forty fathoms. They even sailed to remote and stormy Labrador, where the Convention of 1818 expressly made the fishery legitimate. Soon after the War of 1812, a company was organized at Gloucester to build a dozen large craft for the Labrador and Bank industry. Some of these vessels were of eighty tons, with the square topsail rig of trading schooners. They were sturdy vessels, with bluff, almost square bows, straight sides, round, or "kettle" bottoms, square sterns, and tall quarterdecks. Newburyport, Provincetown, and Portsmouth also sent their craft to Labrador. In 1820, Captain Robinson of the British navy reported that he found on the Labrador coast an American fishing fleet of 530 sail, manned by 5,830 sailors.

The enrolled vessels of the United States engaged in the fisheries, not including licensed craft of less than twenty tons, increased under the bounty system from 60,843 tons in 1820 to 94,014 tons in 1830. In the next year the fishery tonnage rose for the first time above 100,000, — to 103,450. Here was a thriving industry. No one port and no few ports monopolized the traffic. Wherever, alongshore, there was wharf-room for a fifty-ton schooner and sunny fields broad enough for the wooden flakes or frames to dry her finny freight, vessels could be fitted out for the banks, and a regular fishing station established. The requisite investment was not a large one. In the smaller communities the vessels were held by many owners. Here and there a merchant, more thrifty or more fortunate than his fellows, might own three or four schooners, or a dozen, or a score. Scarcely an inlet in the hundreds of miles of coast between the St. Croix River and Hell Gate was without at least one fishing vessel. The business was widely distributed. It employed on sea and on shore thousands of men who could never have wrung a livelihood from the sterile Northern soil. Many of these men were fishermen during a part of the year and farmers during the remainder, and their best efforts at this double calling barely managed to keep the wolf from the door of their weather-beaten homes.

The deep-sea fishermen of the years before the Civil War were nearly all native Americans, although there was a steady inflow of people of the same hardy original stock from the British provinces. The fishermen were following an hereditary trade of which they were intensely proud. There was keen rivalry, but a rough-and-ready comradeship among the fleets of Maine, of the north shore of Massachusetts, of Cape Cod, and of Long Island Sound. Their numbers, their daring, and the steady though never large profit of the trade, which was such a noble school of seamanship and great reserve of naval strength, were the admiration and the envy of Europe.

To the people of our own interior States the Yankee fisherman was a picturesque and heroic figure. Year after year the bounty was ungrudgingly voted in Congress. Dr. Seybert, the open-eyed annalist, who had himself been a Middle-State member of the House of Representatives, voiced the affection which the whole country felt for its toilers of the sea in his chapter on the fisheries: "Every person on board our fishing vessels has an interest in common with his associates; their reward depends upon their industry and enterprise. Much caution is observed in the selection of the crews of our fishing vessels; it often happens that every individual is connected by blood and the strongest ties of friendship; our fishermen are remarkable for their sobriety and good conduct, and they rank with the most skilful navigators."

The unity of interest among the company of a fishing vessel was always one large factor of success. Summer sojourners on the rugged coast of New England often wonder nowadays when they find in some secluded cove or creek a crumbling wharf or fallen warehouse, the tokens of a vanished commerce. These memorials of the deep-sea fishery are everywhere. Half a century or more ago each one was the centre of the life of a thriving neighborhood. Along the wharf, now gaunt and tottering, lay a newly fitted schooner with her crew aboard, taking in salt or the last barrels of provisions, while the whole little town hung over the rail, bidding farewell to father, husband, or son, — for it was literally true, as Dr. Seybert says, that these old-time crews were often all "connected by blood and the strongest ties of friendship." When at last everything is below hatches, and the schooner, with a kind west wind filling her canvas, is outward bound toward the dim horizon, the women and children on the shore know that three long months must pass before her sails will lift into sight again, and more, if her destination is far Labrador. The happiness, the prosperity, even the very existence of the little village about the silent pier, hang upon the voyage of that one vessel and her few consorts gone before.

Only those who have lived through such years can know the tense eagerness with which every word from the fleet is awaited.

At the end of three months or four, the schooner, deep-laden, rust-covered, sea-weary, comes in, in the autumn sunshine or on the midnight tide. No great victory of arms ever won such rejoicing. But there is work to be done and small chance for words. The half-salted fish must be hurried ashore for a careful curing on the ranges of flakes about the warehouse. In such labor the home-people can lend a hand, and this is the festival which crowns the harvest of the deep.

Sometimes, indeed often, the looked-for sail never came. Old ocean keeps its secrets well; the fate of hundreds of New England fisher craft remains to this day an impenetrable mystery. These old tragedies explain why the wharves have crumbled in so many Eastern towns, and why once-crowded little ports are silent and sailless.

In spite of all the perils and hardships, the fishery industry alongshore bred a fine type of manhood in the days of its best prosperity. It was quickening to nerve and brain. Competition was intense. After the fish were caught and cured, there was the eager search for markets. It was a point of pride with New England to eat much of her own salt fish. Dr. Edward Everett Hale, in his reminiscences of " A New England Boyhood, " quotes Dr. Palfrey's statement that the most ceremonious Boston feast was never set out without the salt codfish at one end of the table, — " abundance, variety, pomp of other things, but that unfailingly. It was a sort of New England point of honor; and luxurious livers pleased themselves, over their nuts and wine, with the thought that, while suiting their palates, they had been doing their part in a wide combination to maintain the fisheries and create a naval strength. " Patriotic New England, however, could consume only a small fraction of her enormous catch. Shipment by sea was fortunately easy. Some of the surplus went over the Atlantic to the Catholic countries of South Europe; some to our own Southern States; some to the West Indies and South America. The salted fish of New England was in demand by Southern and West Indian planters as a cheap food for their negro slaves. Our deep-sea fisheries really received a serious blow from emancipation.

The freighting of the fish formed in itself an important business. Sometimes the fishing craft themselves, if they were of large tonnage, bore their catch to the Southern markets after it had been cured. Sometimes fishing merchants owned their own trading vessels, and transshipped their cargoes from their own wharves and warehouses. Every fishing town of importance was familiar with foreign trade. Cadiz, Bilboa, Leghorn, Havana, Ponce, Surinam, Paramaribo, — these were ports for which the smart brigs and topsail schooners, with fish below decks and lumber above, were ever clearing. Trader and fishing craft lay side by side at the home wharves, and the merchant Jack's yarns of the fair sugar islands of the Spanish Main were matched by the fisher Jack's stories of the swarming halibut and cod of the Newfoundland banks and the tall icebergs of Labrador. It was easy to slip from one deck to another. Sooner or later most of the smart young fellows who had served their fishing apprenticeship would be sure to "ship foreign," and come home a year or two later as fine square-rig deep-water sailors as there were afloat. Indeed, it was from the fishing fleet that the best crews of the merchant fleet were regularly recruited. As an observer in the Boston Custom House wrote:

"Were it not for the fisheries, in less than ten years we should not have American seamen enough to navigate our ships as masters and mates, and even now Cape Cod furnishes a large, a very large, proportion of the active, intelligent shipmasters and mates out of this port, and very many out of New York."

Judged by modern standards, the earnings of the deep-sea fishermen in the golden era of the industry were pitiably small. An authority [1] on the fisheries estimated that the annual average income of the men of the cod-fishing fleet during the ten years ending with June, 1851, was only $63. To this the government bounty added $14 for each man, making in all $77 as the compensation for at least four months of the severest and most hazardous of callings. Yet until the Civil War drew the loyal fishermen into the Federal navy by the thousands, there was never any lack of crews. The danger and the suffering only seemed, so far at least as the young men were concerned, to give new zest to the vocation.

In the last decade before the war there came a gradual change in the Grand Bank cod fishery, which increased at once its perils and its profits. Hitherto the hand-line fishing had been carried on from the decks of the schooners. Certain alert Marblehead mariners, it is said, discovered that if they took with them the light, seaworthy boats called dories, long used for fishing alongshore, and plied their lines from these boats, instead of from the vessels, they could secure quicker and larger fares. The new idea won instant acceptance. The "Barnstable Patriot" of May 10, 1859, says : —

"It is becoming a custom quite general among the Grand Bank cod fishermen to take dories with them upon the fishing ground, and fish in them at a short distance from their vessels. Codfish will often take a hook from a dory while they will not notice a hook from the vessel anchored within a rod from the boat. . . . The motion of the boat, giving a quicker movement to the hook, renders it more attractive to the fish than that from the vessel. It is a great change in the habit of a fish thus to desert the vessel for the dory."

[1] Hon. Zeno Scudder of Massachusetts, in House of Representatives, August 12, 1852.

In 1858 the schooner "American Eagle" on Banquereau, equipped with dories, had stowed 900 quintals of good cod into her hold, while another vessel near by, hand-line fishing, had only 160. It was supposed that a dory fisherman year in and year out would average at least one-third more fish than the hand-liners. Hand-lining even now has not been wholly abandoned. It is followed especially by old-fashioned fishermen from the coast of Maine. The larger catches of the dory method were purchased at a very high price. In spite of the utmost vigilance, the little boats would often capsize in a seaway, or go adrift in squall or fog, drowning their crews or leaving them to a less merciful death by thirst or starvation. The fishermen always have been singularly reckless and improvident. With the fate of lost shipmates before their eyes, they habitually launch their dories with little drinking water and no food, and they scorn every effort of humane owners or captains to compel them to guard against emergencies.

The use of trawls has also intensified the danger and the labor of the fisheries. A trawl is a long, stout line, anchored on or near the bottom and buoyed, with smaller lines bearing the baited hooks attached to it at intervals. The idea is said to have been brought from Scotland about the year 1843, and applied to halibut-fishing in Massachusetts Bay by a Cape Cod fisherman. It is a highly effective method, but the trawls must be set and hauled from boats, and the task is difficult and perilous in the extreme in the heavy seas and high winds of the north Atlantic. "Gone adrift," or "gone overboard," while at work on the trawls in a jumping and yawing dory is the epitaph of unnumbered New England fishermen.

The third modern process of the northeast fisheries is the use of the great purse seine. This is an immense portable net, many fathoms long, which can be circled about a school of fish and drawn in upon tons of frantic captives. It has long been the favorite device of the mackerel-catchers. It is set not from dories, but from a noble, great long-boat of whaler model, of which large mackerel seiners carry always one and sometimes two. The sight of a smart crew tackling a school of sportive mackerel, with their swift boat and their immense net, is an exciting spectacle surpassed only by a harpoon attack on the great sperm whale of the Southern Ocean.

Hand-lining for mackerel is not even now obsolete, but its best days have departed. One hears no more of such luck as that of the "Bloomer" of Hingham,[1] with a crew of ten men, which caught one day, between ten o'clock and two, 5,700 mackerel. In the old time a "high-line" fisherman has caught from ten to fifteen barrels in a day, each barrel holding 150 to 200 fish. The graceful, "gamey" mackerel is the aristocrat of the Northern seas. The sober cod is plebeian, but useful and reliable. The huge halibut, the "American turbot," and the third important product of the deep-sea fisheries, has shrunk sorrowfully in numbers since the "Baltic" of Gloucester took two hundred and forty, a full fare, hand-lining on George's in a single day. No longer are halibut seen "thick as a school of porpoises."

Great Britain watched with jealous eye all through the years the steady growth of the American deep-sea fisheries. Her resentment was twofold, — first, that her great maritime rival was finding in the fisheries an inexhaustible reserve of the bravest and hardiest seamen in the world; and, second, that though their homes were far from most of the fishing banks, the Yankees were much more skilful and successful in their pursuit of the industry than Britain's own provincial subjects, who had all the advantage of nearness of position. From 1815 to 1854 those Yankee fishermen who were unlucky enough to fall in with British cruisers, or to be caught by British officials at anchor in Canadian ports, received such inhospitable treatment as

[1] "Barnstable Patriot," May 28, 1861.

would scarcely be suffered outside of Fiji or Patagonia. To facilitate the British policy of seizure, fine, or confiscation, the ingenious " headland theory " was promulgated.

The Convention of 1818 forbade our vessels to take fish within three miles of the provincial coast, save on certain parts of the shore of Newfoundland, and at the Magdalen Islands and Labrador. The new British contention was that this three-mile line did not follow the indentations of the coast, but that wide bays were included in the forbidden area. Thus it happened that many an American schooner far at sea, and perhaps out of sight of land altogether, would be pounced upon by a British warship, carried to the nearest provincial port and condemned on a charge of fishing in British waters, because she was within an imaginary line drawn from one invisible headland to another. This " headland " theory was susceptible of grave abuse at the hands of tyrannical or unprincipled officials. A vessel ten miles or more at sea is so far out that ordinary range-marks count for little, and her exact position can be fixed only with much difficulty. If a British captain and his officers swore that the hapless Yankee prize was seized at a certain point, it was a brave provincial judge who would reject their word. Time and time again our schooners were condemned on the most one-sided of evidence.

So flagrant did these outrages become that in 1852 the fishermen of Massachusetts sent an urgent memorial to Congress that an armed force of the United States be assigned to their protection. The " Boston Journal " exhorted the government to remember that " two thousand vessels and thirty thousand men and boys are now exposed to the cannon of a British fleet and the cruelties and horrors of British prisons." In response to these appeals, one of the most distinguished officers of our navy, Commodore Matthew Calbraith Perry, soon to sail on his memorable expedition to Japan, was ordered to cruise

upon the fishing grounds with the powerful steam frigate
"Mississippi," "for the purpose of protecting the rights
of American fishermen under the Convention of 1818."
In the summer of 1853 Commodore W. B. Shubrick
gathered a squadron at Portsmouth, N. H., and went to
sea to protect the northeastern fisheries with the "Princeton," "Fulton," "Decatur," "Cyane," "Albany," and
"Columbia." This service was tactfully performed. There
were no conflicts with the British cruisers, and the tension
was relieved somewhat by the fishery sections of the
Reciprocity Treaty of 1854.

This arrangement was a broad one, covering the general
commercial relations of the United States and Canada.[1]
As to the fisheries, it guaranteed to our vessels all the
rights and privileges of the Convention of 1818, and granted
to them, besides, the privilege of taking fish, except salmon,
shad, and shellfish, within the three-mile limit along the
shores of New Brunswick, Nova Scotia, and Prince Edward
Island, and of drying nets and curing fish on all these
coasts. Similar privileges were given to British fishermen
on the coasts of the United States as far south as the
thirty-sixth degree of latitude. This was a nominal concession. The real gift to Canada was the admission of
her fish into our ports free of duty.

At first this privilege of "free fish" was of small advantage to our provincial neighbors. Their fishing industry
was not so boldly directed or so well developed as that of
the United States. But, unfortunately for our fishermen,
a clamor arose in Congress for the repeal of the long-
tried and successful bounty system. The slavery quarrel
was rending the country asunder. Sectional hatred was
strong in Washington. The same motives which in-
fluenced the Southern leaders to strike at the sea-power of
the North by cancelling the mail subsidies to American
steamships were fatal to fishery protection and encourage-

[1] Theodore S. Woolsey.

ment.   In 1858, the system of fishing bounties was
repealed, and the Yankee fleet was left for the first time
in forty-four years without any national assistance.

The fisheries did not immediately shrink.   In fact, our
enrolled tonnage (of vessels over 20 tons) increased for a
few years, reaching the maximum (193,459) in 1862.[1]   But
it is very generally agreed alongshore, among the older
fishermen who remember those days, that the withdrawal of
the bounties was the first step in the process which has now
reduced our deep-sea fishing fleet to one-fourth of the tonnage of forty years ago.   These old men insist that, like a
wounded bull, the industry drove on for a time with the
sheer force of its own momentum, before it fell to the
fatal blow.

The first sinister tokens were the shrinkage of the
fishery in the smaller towns.   Maine and Cape Cod
began to lose their vessels and their seamen.   The large
merchants of Gloucester, Provincetown, and Portland en-
dured the loss of the bounties better than the small owners
of the outports.   The bounty system had been denounced
for fostering monopoly; as a matter of fact, it had set a
premium on individual thrift and local enterprise.

But there were undoubtedly other factors in the gradual
concentration of the deep-sea fishery at a few large ports.
Gloucester's supremacy was honestly earned.   In the first
place, the Cape Ann harbor is deep, safe, and accessible
from the open sea.   Then the town is near, but not too
near, to the great fresh-fish market of Boston.   Finally,
the men of Gloucester are extraordinarily bold and thrifty,
and have a marvellous aptitude for all branches of the fishing trade.   They deserve to-day the eulogy of Richard H.
Dana as truly as when he uttered it: —

"There is not a rich, idle man, apparently, in the town of
Gloucester.[2]   The business of Gloucester cannot be carried

---

[1] Report of the United States Commissioner of Navigation, 1900.
[2] Richard H. Dana, before the Halifax Commission, 1877.

on, as mercantile business often is, by men who invest their capital in the business and leave it in the hands of other people to manage. It cannot be carried on, as much of the mercantile business of the world is carried on, in a leisurely way, by those who have arrived at something like wealth, who visit their counting-rooms at ten o'clock in the morning and stay a few hours, then go away to the club, return to their counting-rooms for a short time, and then drive out in the enticing drives in the vicinity, and their day's work is over. . . . No, the Gloucester tradesmen are hardworking men, and they gain their wealth and prosperity on the terms of being hardworking men. The Gloucester merchants, if you see fit to call them so — they are not particular about their title, but are content to be 'fish-dealers,' — are men who go to their counting-rooms early and stay late."

This habit of going early and staying late, carried into all departments of the business, has now made Gloucester so far the first of American fishing ports that there can scarcely be said to be a second. Her vessels range all along the coast. They bring the first of the Southern mackerel into New York. They supply a large part of the fresh cod, haddock, and halibut of Boston. They dominate the Newfoundland Banks,; they carry the flag to Greenland and to Iceland. But Gloucester pays every year a dear price for her supremacy. It is grimly true that "the history of the Gloucester fisheries has been written in tears.[1] No other industry by sea or land sustains such a drain upon its resources and employés. Other callings may shorten life, but none show such constant and whole-sale destruction. The men who go out upon the Banks take their lives in their hands as surely as he who goes in-to battle; nay, the proportion of fatal casualties upon the battlefield is much smaller than in this perilous calling."

[1] "Fishermen's Memorial and Record Book," Procter Brothers, Gloucester.

Between 1830 and 1873, Gloucester, by authentic records, lost 281 vessels and 1,252 men in her maritime ventures. One awful gale, that of Feb. 24, 1862, cost her fifteen schooners, with 120 men. The dead left 70 widows and 140 children. Altogether, Gloucester's wreck roll for that black year 1862, in the Newfoundland, George's, and shore fisheries, was 19 vessels and 162 lives. In 1871 the losses were 19 vessels and 140 lives. In a gale of Sunday, Aug. 24, 1873, Gloucester lost nine vessels and 128 of her brave men. As might be conjectured, the greater part of these casualties have occurred on the dreaded George's, where indomitable Gloucester plies her calling throughout the entire year. It was not always thus. In the early days the fishing season was the fair Northern summer and that only. As a New England orator familiar with the fisheries, in a plea for the retention of the bounties, said : [1] —

"Long since, I can remember, but few vessels started out until March or April, and then, pursuing their labors until November, they were stripped and laid up until March came round again. But with the increased expense of living, an increased amount of effort was demanded by the fishermen ; and in my particular neighborhood large numbers of vessels, returning from their summer cruises, are hauled upon the graving dock, thoroughly examined about the hull, fitted with new sails, strong and reliable ground tackle, and running rigging, and start out in December for George's Bank to fish for cod or halibut. This is to the fisherman a dire necessity, and the peril of such a voyage would appall the oldest and bravest navigator. Scarcely a season passes without the loss of several vessels and whole crews, and the wear and tear of hulls and spars and sails and rigging of vessels in these trips is ruinous to the owners. Still they cannot refuse to fit the

---

[1] Hon. Timothy Davis of Massachusetts, National House of Representatives, Feb. 10, 1857.

vessels. The fishermen need the money and must go on their voyages; and the owners are forced to keep them supplied with vessels and stores, or they will seek other employment."

The Civil War brought disturbance to the fisheries, but no very severe loss of property, though once or twice Confederate cruisers dashed along the Northern coast, burning and sinking. The war was most heavily felt in the diversion of the fishermen to their country's service. A part of the splendid crew of the victorious " Kearsarge," which sailed from the old fishing town of Portsmouth, N. H., came from the New England schooners. Toward the close of the war, when the government was paying high bounties for every sailor whom it could find, the fisher craft coming in from Newfoundland or George's would be deserted by their men the moment they arrived. There was nothing to do, then, but to dismantle the schooners and lay them up until peace. Between 1862 and 1866 the enrolled tonnage in the fisheries shrank from 193,459 to 89,386, — an appalling loss which never was recovered.

On March 17, 1866, the reciprocity treaty which gave the Canadians free admission for their fish in return for fishing privileges in provincial waters was terminated by the United States government, chiefly because of Canada's ostentatious sympathy with the Confederate cause. Another period of harassment and exasperation followed, for our fishermen were now held down to the rigorous British interpretation of the hostile terms of the Convention of 1818. In 1871 the treaty of Washington, for the adjustment of the Alabama claims and other open disputes between the United States and Great Britain, revived substantially the fishery conditions of the reciprocity treaty of 1854. That is, our vessels were allowed to take and cure fish in the coast waters of Canada, and the Canadians were given a free market for their ocean-fishery products in this country. This seemed to our fishermen a sufficiently hard bargain, and they were astonished when the Halifax Commission, convoked in 1877 under the provisions of the treaty, awarded Canada the sum of $5,500,000, as added compensation for the fishery privileges of her coasts. The United States promptly paid the money, but the Yankee fishermen have always believed that they were wronged by this tribunal. The arbiter was the Belgian Minister at Washington. It was insisted alongshore that he ought not to have been chosen for this delicate task, because of Belgium's peculiar relations to the British government.

Canada took her $5,500,000 of American money and made it the basis of a generous bounty system for the encouragement of her deep-sea fisheries. At once this Canadian interest began to grow and prosper as never before. Nova Scotia, New Brunswick, and Prince Edward Island built a fine fleet of large schooners after the American model, fitted them in the American way, followed the American fishing methods, and having the double advantage of their cheaper labor and their government bounty, pushed their fish free of duty into our home market to the serious injury of the New England fleet.

It was contended by the New England fishermen that the $5,500,000 of the Halifax award was greater than the total value of the fish that could possibly be taken in Canadian waters. And the event proved that we could not really command the privileges for which we paid so dear. The fishermen of Newfoundland, a turbulent race, regarded their shore herring fishery as their own prerogative, of which they ought not to be deprived by the British government. Twenty-two Gloucester vessels [1] reached Fortune Bay in December, 1877, prepared to seine herring after the American fashion, as they were plainly authorized to do under the terms of the treaty of Washington. But the rough-and-ready Newfoundlanders knew little and

[1] "Fishermen's Own Book," Procter Brothers, Gloucester.

cared less for the obligations of diplomacy. They saw
slipping through their fingers the trade of catching herring
for the American vessels, which had been the main reliance
of their bleak and lonely coast. A mob of natives in their
wrath surrounded the Yankee schooners, seized and tore
their huge seines and threatened them with destruction
unless they left the bay. One skipper, the celebrated
Solomon Jacobs, of the schooner "Moses Adams," armed
his crew with revolvers, withstood the infuriated New-
foundlanders, and secured a partial catch, but the fleet, as
a whole, was compelled to clear with empty holds and
return to Gloucester. This was the "Fortune Bay affair"
of Jan. 6, 1878. There were similar attacks at Aspey and
Conception Bays. Four years later the British government paid the sum of £15,000 as compensation for the
broken voyages of the Gloucester men.

The fishery sections of the treaty of Washington were
to remain in force for at least ten years. After that they
could be terminated by either party to the agreement.
Due notice was given by the United States in 1884, and
on July 1, 1885, the arrangement lapsed, and the northeastern fisheries in their international aspect were once
more upon the basis of the ancient Convention of 1818.
There immediately set in a revival of what a Canadian
Cabinet Minister too frankly called the policy of "harassing the Yankees." Several American fishing vessels were
seized and confiscated on a charge of fishing within the
three-mile limit. Others were refused provisions and
roughly ordered out of port. The anger which these outrages produced spread far beyond the borders of New
England, and caused emphatic protests to be made to the
British government. Secretary Bayard, in 1888, negotiated
a new treaty along the general lines of the treaty of
Washington. But the New England fishing merchants
and their men rose in vigorous remonstrance against it.
They declared that they did not care for the privilege of

fishing within the Canadian three-mile limit; that they did desire an opportunity to visit Canadian ports, to transship their catch and buy bait and provisions, and that they demanded these things not as privileges, but as rights under the ordinary commercial usages of civilized lands. They did not wish to pay for them by opening our market free of duty to the bounty-fed Canadian fishermen. That would be an extravagant price, and intolerable.

The arguments of New England prevailed, and the Bayard treaty was rejected by the Senate. Canada offered to sell to our fishing vessels, for a certain sum, the privilege of entering her harbors to procure bait and land their catch for shipment home. A few of these licenses were purchased, but they became significantly fewer every year. The fishermen discovered that Canadian hospitality was by no means essential to their trade as it is now conducted. Interference with our vessels of late years has become unusual, because they seldom resort to Canadian waters unless driven in by actual stress of weather. Newfoundland has adopted a kindly policy toward the New England craft, and the provincial people generally acknowledge that the old idea of "harassing the Yankees" was a grievous blunder.

The deep-sea fishing fleet no longer grows. Its tonnage has scarcely changed for four years. It was 43,996 in 1898; 42,901 in 1899; 43,694 in 1900; and 44,074 in 1901. As the older vessels fall out, they are replaced by new craft of greater capacity, speed, and power. Except in the menhaden or "porgy" fishery, steam is little used. The typical Yankee fisherman is still, as a hundred years ago, a sailing vessel; still of the neat and handy schooner rig. In size, model, and seaworthiness, however, there has been a revolution. Instead of the old fifty-ton craft, the first-class vessels are now of from eighty tons to one hundred and twenty. The bluff bows, square sterns, and clumsy quarter-decks have disappeared. The modern schooner is a flush-decked vessel, or almost that, for there is a slight break forward of the cabin-house. There is a fine Yankee sheer to her low rail. The clipper bow lifts to the surges like the breast of a bird, and the after-body narrows to a clean, easy run, and a stern graceful and overhanging. The new fisherman, in other words, embodies the best characteristics of the modern seagoing schooner yacht, and a yacht, indeed, it very closely resembles.

For this transformation New England owes a debt of gratitude to the late Edward Burgess, yacht designer, and Captain J. W. Collins, long of the United States Fish Commission. The fishing schooners of twenty years ago were beautiful vessels, but they possessed some grave faults. They were, as a rule, too wide of beam and shoal of draught. They rode hard at anchor in a seaway. They were liable to be capsized in a sudden squall under a press of canvas. When the Fish Commission constructed a schooner for its service, it endeavored to produce a craft which should be a model for the fishing fleet. The " Grampus " combined moderate width with increased depth. She carried her ballast low down, gaining thereby stability and power to work to windward. The new vessel was so manifestly superior to the broad, flat schooner of the old type that she served as an illuminating object lesson. Her example was enforced by Mr. Burgess, who applied in a modified form to new fishing craft the wholesome principles of design that had won success in the sloop yacht " Puritan " and schooner " Sachem. " The " Burgess fisherman " beat everything afloat. Soon the yards of Essex, Maine, and Cape Cod learned to imitate his models. Now all the newer vessels of the fleet have the fair, deep underbody, the long, narrowing stern and the lifting bow, which make the deep-sea craft not only swifter but easier at their anchors and surer to ride out any gale that blows. There has been an undeniable diminution in the loss of life and property since the new model came into general use.

The Yankee fishermen are now, in one sense, Yankees no longer. Very many of the crews of Gloucester, Provincetown, and Portland are of alien birth. Some are Scandinavians, some Portuguese, some British provincials of Scotch, Irish, or French lineage. But they are good men, brave and true; they need to be to stand alongside the Yankee of the old stock on the deck of his own vessel. Some of the foreign-born fishermen are birds of passage, — here to-day, there to-morrow. The greater number of them, however, have their homes and their interests in this country, and are whole-heartedly loyal to the flag that flies overhead and the land of their adoption. The deep-sea fisheries are still a nursery of seamanship, a reserve of naval strength, as was demonstrated in our hundred days' war with Spain, when Gloucester, although most of her crews had already sailed before war was declared, furnished to the navy many more recruits of a desirable class than any other community of like size in the nation.

At the Gloucester recruiting station, in the early summer of 1898, 76½ per cent of the men examined were accepted. At Boston the per cent accepted was 14½; at New York, only 6. This means that in physique and intelligence the fishermen of New England are very much superior to the merchant sailors of the great seaports. So valuable a national resource as the deep-sea fisheries cannot be suffered to decline.

There is a small but a good fleet of sailing vessels and a few steamers engaged in the fisheries of the Pacific coast. Now and then a schooner has gone out from New England to enter this Pacific industry, which is still a pigmy, however, as compared with the deep-sea fisheries of the North Atlantic. Sixty-one vessels of 6,900 tons are enumerated by the Fish Commission in its Bulletin No. 20 as belonging to Washington and California. Some of these craft fish for cod on the Alaska banks; others take halibut. They hail from San Francisco and the enterprising ports of

Puget Sound, and are certain to increase in number with the steady growth of the Pacific slope in wealth and population. These vessels and their crews are forced to contend often with heavy seas and fierce weather, and the calling is almost as valuable as the Atlantic fishery in training a race of mariners fit for any arduous service and quick to respond to the nation's need.

Following is the official record of the tonnage of the seagoing vessels of the American fishing fleet, exclusive of mere boats and such craft, from the beginning of the national government: —

TONNAGE OF DEEP-SEA FISHERIES, 1789-1901.

Year.	Tonnage.	Year.	Tonnage.	Year.	Tonnage.
1789	9,062	1817	53,990	1845	91,240
1790	28,348	1818	58,552	1846	108,979
1791	32,542	1819	65,045	1847	101,629
1792	32,062	1820	60,843	1848	126,210
1793	28,974	1821	51,352	1849	116,824
1794	17,498	1822	58,405	1850	143,758
1795	24,887	1823	67,041	1851	138,015
1796	28,509	1824	68,239	1852	175,205
1797	33,406	1825	70,626	1853	159,840
1798	35,477	1826	63,535	1854	137,235
1799	23,933	1827	73,709	1855	124,553
1800	22,307	1828	74,765	1856	125,703
1801	31,280	1829	97,889	1857	132,901
1802	32,988	1830	94,014	1858	140,490
1803	43,416	1831	103,450	1859	147,647
1804	43,088	1832	99,153	1860	153,619
1805	48,479	1833	107,295	1861	182,106
1806	50,353	1834	113,555	1862	193,459
1807	60,690	1835	136,817	1863	157,579
1808	43,598	1836	104,838	1864	148,244
1809	26,110	1837	121,866	1865	100,436
1810	26,251	1838	120,623	1866	89,386
1811	34,361	1839	101,151	1867	68,207
1812	21,822	1840	96,196	1868	74,763
1813	11,255	1841	71,877	1869	55,165
1814	8,863	1842	66,039	1870	82,612
1815	26,510	1843	66,677	1871	82,902
1816	37,879	1844	94,350	1872	87,403

Year.	Tonnage.	Year.	Tonnage.	Year.	Tonnage.
1873	99,532	1883	84,322	1893	62,737
1874	68,490	1884	72,609	1894	63,493
1875	68,703	1885	73,975	1895	60,838
1876	77,314	1886	73,445	1896	60,107
1877	79,678	1887	73,237	1897	58,103
1878	74,560	1888	69,146	1898	43,996
1879	66,543	1889	67,669	1899	42,901
1880	64,935	1890	61,507	1900	43,694
1881	66,365	1891	61,912	1901	44,074
1882	67,015	1892	61,819		

CHAPTER XIV

WAR AND ITS RUIN. 1861–75

American Marine Declining and Steam Lines lost before War came
— Our Vulnerable Sailing Ships — The Anglo-Confederate Cruisers
— British Ships, British Seamen, and British Guns with Southern
Officers — The " Florida " and " Alabama " — Burning Yankee
Clippers in Mid-Atlantic — Harrying our Commerce in Eastern
Seas — The " Alabama's " End off Cherbourg — Destroyer of
Merchantmen sunk by Yankee Merchant Tars — American
against British Gunnery and Seamanship — Cost of Anglo-
Confederate Depredations — Three Quarters of a Million Tons of
Shipping disappears — The Merchant Service in the Civil War —
An Indispensable Reserve for the United States — Peace brings
no Revival — Mail Lines to Brazil and China — Rise of "Free
Ship" Idea — The Case for and against It — Our One Trans-
atlantic Line — Why There Were No Others — A Fast-Shrinking
Fleet

THE next fifteen-year period to be considered in the
history of the American merchant service — that between
1861 and 1875 — was an era of stunning disaster and swift
and humiliating decline.   The Civil War in this country and
the growth of iron steamship-building abroad are the chief
causes which wiped off the register almost one-half of the
American ocean fleet, and reduced by more than one-half the
American share of our own import and export carrying.
In 1861 the deep-sea shipping of the United States
amounted to 2,496,894 tons; in 1875, to only 1,515,598
tons.   The percentage of our foreign commerce carried in
American ships was in 1861 65.2, and in 1875 only 26.2.

It has already been shown that this deplorable shrinkage had set in long before the firing on Sumter, though

it was due to influences not wholly disassociated from the war.   The old sentiment of vigorous nationality, which led Washington, Jefferson, and Madison to join with the North in framing laws for the protection and encouragement of the American merchant marine, and later moved other Southern men to vote generous subsidies to American mail steamships, had been weakened by the slavery controversy and sectional attack.   The withdrawal of these subsidies by Congress in 1858, under Southern leadership, was not a war measure; it was not an act of conscious disloyalty.   It was the natural and perhaps inevitable result of sectional strife, enfeebling the old sense of national patriotism.   But it began to close American shipyards and to drive the stars and stripes from the great highways of commerce several years before the stars and bars had been hoisted above the first Anglo-Confederate cruiser.

This stripping away of protection from American steam-ship lines in 1858 had struck our merchant marine at just the point where it was most vulnerable.   It did not immediately affect the building of wooden sailing ships, though for the half-decade before the war this industry had steadily declined.   We launched only one-fourth as many ships and barks in 1859 as in 1855.   The withdrawal of the subsidies fell as a crushing blow upon the few American marine engine and boiler works, upon the young, ambitious, and skilful firms that had launched some noble wooden ocean steamships and were now experimenting with iron hulls, upon the progressive American merchants and ship-owners who saw that the ships of iron and steam were the sea carriers of the future, and were ready to create a net-work of American mail lines if their government would give to them such recognition as should fairly offset the subsidies enjoyed by their European competitors.

These men saw their hopes ruined by national legisla-tion, against which the Senators and Representatives of the shipowning North had protested and voted all in vain.

When the war actually began, in April, 1861, of all our proud steam fleet only one poor and struggling line was left in the transatlantic trade, and that was very soon abandoned. There is no popular error more prevalent than the idea that the Civil War destroyed the American merchant marine, but there is no delusion more inexcusable. The war did not destroy our merchant marine; it found it already shrinking, and hastened its disappearance.

In the spring of 1861, the United States had a total tonnage registered for foreign trade of 2,496,894. Some of these vessels were laid up in port awaiting remunerative freights; others were receiving or discharging cargoes. But the greater part of this immense fleet was scattered all over the seven seas. Nearly all of these Yankee merchantmen were owned in the North, and were, therefore, the lawful prey of Confederate cruisers and privateers. Nearly all of them were sailing ships. All were unarmed and defenceless, for merchantmen no longer carried the six-pounders, nines, or twelves that had frowned from the ports of important trading craft in the first years of the nineteenth century. The South, in 1861, owned relatively few ocean-going ships or steamers, and these were immediately shut up in their home ports by the iron blockade of the overwhelming Federal navy. The Southern government sought to strike back not at the Northern warships, with whose swarming numbers it could not cope, but at the helpless and unsuspecting Northern ships of commerce. As a war measure this was wholly justifiable, and from the Southern standpoint it was a wise expedient, though nobody regrets more bitterly now than Southern men themselves the terrible after-effects of this blow at American prestige upon the ocean.

At first a few privateers were fitted out from the Southern coast at points which the Federal blockade had not yet gripped with its bristling steel, but these enterprises were short-lived and inglorious. Then the "Sumter" and a few other hastily armed merchant steamers were sent to sea. They were more successful. They easily made several captures in the North Atlantic, and aroused intense alarm among Northern shipowners, underwriters, and merchants. Moreover, they awakened the Richmond government to a fuller sense of the potency of this mode of ocean warfare.

It was the good fortune of the Confederacy to be represented in Great Britain by a naval agent or commissioner of remarkable persistence, resource, and audacity, Captain James D. Bulloch. This gentleman, a Southern uncle of President Theodore Roosevelt, was intrusted with large funds and extraordinary power to expend them for the best interests of the Confederate cause. He recognized very early that sail craft and converted merchant steamers were not fit instruments to chase and seize the peerless Yankee clipper ships. He secretly procured the building in British yards of two vessels modelled after the latest type of British steam sloops-of-war. Indeed, both the "Florida," when she ran the blockade of Mobile, and the "Alabama," in her fight with the "Hatteras," passed themselves off as cruisers of Her Majesty's navy. They were, of course, inferior in all points save speed to our larger men-of-war, but they were very formidable vessels for the peculiar service for which they were designed. They were the first steam commerce-destroyers. The "Alabama" and "Florida" were graceful, fine-lined corvettes, bark-rigged with a full spread of canvas. They were capable of cruising under sail alone, and could, therefore, keep the sea for long periods without re-coaling. Their steam machinery was supposed to be sufficient to enable them to overtake the fastest of our clipper merchantmen, and to escape from our heavy warships.

It was an obvious breach of neutrality to build these ships in Britain for use against a friendly power, and Captain Bulloch cleverly managed to encourage the fiction that they were intended for the service of some continental power at peace with all the world. In all this the Confederate agent was met more than halfway by the British government. The first of the Anglo-Confederate cruisers was the "Florida," built at Liverpool on British man-of-war designs. It was pretended that she was the property of Italy, but though the Italian Consul at Liverpool officially denied this, and the American Minister, Charles Francis Adams, protested that she was really a Confederate vessel and gave formal evidence to support his charge, the "Florida" was not interfered with. She was allowed to sail from Liverpool in March, 1862, for the British colony of Bahama, where she received her battery of British naval guns, and filled her magazines with British ammunition.

Under cover of the British flag, the "Florida" ran into Mobile, outwitting the Union cruisers, which took her for a British corvette inspecting the blockade. At Mobile the "Florida" completed her outfit and shipped a crew, and then, escaping to sea on a dark and stormy night, began in January, 1863, her destructive work on the North Atlantic. At Nassau, in the Bahamas, the British authorities, in defiance of the obligations of neutrality, allowed the "Florida" to take aboard a three months' supply of coal. Thus provided, the "Florida" hovered like a hawk on the trade routes between Boston, New York, and Brazil, seizing fourteen prizes, and converting one of them into an armed tender, which wrought havoc among the fishermen and coasters of New England. One of the captured vessels was used to seize the revenue cutter "Caleb Cushing" at Portland, but the "Florida's" bold fellows had now reached the end of their rope. They were chased to sea and taken after they had fired their prize.

The "Florida" refitted in France and sailed in 1864 on a second cruise of depredation. But American ships were now few and far between on the deep sea, and the "Florida's" hunt for the gleaming skysails of Yankee clippers was not especially successful. In October, 1864, the "Florida" was caught at Bahia, Brazil, by the United States cruiser "Wachusett," a sister ship of the "Kearsarge," which had destroyed the "Florida's" younger sister, "Alabama," in the English Channel four months before. A battle between the "Wachusett" and the "Florida" could have had only the same ending, so the Confederate captain hung to his anchors until, in the early morning of October 7, the Yankee corvette surprised and seized her enemy, and bore her away in triumph toward the United States. This act of the "Wachusett" was a clear violation of international law. It was an affront to Brazilian neutrality, and it was disavowed by our government. But Captain Collins of the "Wachusett" could plead much provocation in the easy disregard of neutral obligations by England and France, and the destruction of the "Florida" — for soon after she reached our coast she foundered — brought no grief to the American shipowners and seamen who had been her victims.

Very much more successful than the "Florida," though her career filled a shorter period, was the celebrated "Alabama," whose name was made historic by the Geneva arbitration. She, too, was built under the superintendence of Captain Bulloch at Liverpool, and, in spite of the remonstrances of Minister Adams, was allowed, on July 29, 1862, to go to sea, ostensibly for a trial trip. But from this trial the "Alabama" never returned. Instead, she steamed to the Azores and was there transferred to Captain Raphael Semmes, a Confederate officer formerly of the United States navy, who had won some distinction in commerce-destroying on board the Confederate cruiser "Sumter." Captain Semmes promptly mounted the powerful naval battery which had been sent out from England and shipped a crew composed mostly of British sailors, half of them[1] veteran English man-o'-war's men, who were glad of this chance to strike a blow at their

[1] "Two Years on the 'Alabama,'" by Arthur Sinclair, Lieutenant C. S. N.

country's great maritime rival and at a flag they did not love.

The "Alabama's" first victims were a number of unsuspecting Yankee whalers, which were burned at sea. This policy of immediate destruction, generally by fire, was the plan which Captain Semmes habitually followed, and he constituted himself prize court as well as captor. The Confederacy had no ports open into which his prizes could be sent for formal condemnation. The "Alabama" was wonderfully fortunate, or, rather, she was wonderfully well handled by an accomplished sailor and devoted partisan. Crossing the Atlantic, the "Alabama" took twenty prizes on the way. Semmes re-coaled in the West Indies with fuel sent out for him from England. Then he steamed into the path of the Pacific Mail treasure ships, returning from the Isthmus of Panama with the United States mails and California bullion. The first vessel which came along, however, was not a northbound treasure ship, but the "Ariel," outward bound from New York for Colon with five hundred passengers. There was nothing to do but to bond the great liner for ransom and permit her to go on her way. Semmes now dashed into the Gulf of Mexico to attack a fleet of Federal transports supposed to be proceeding from New Orleans to Galveston. He did not find the transports, but he did meet and destroy a light cruiser, the "Hatteras," transformed from a Delaware River passenger boat. This was the "Alabama's" only encounter with a ship-of-war until she met the "Kearsarge."

Semmes's thorough knowledge of the sea and his genius as an officer were apparent in his next move, which recalls the brilliant dash of Porter of the "Essex" in 1813 against the British whale fleet in the Pacific Ocean. The "Alabama" steamed southward from the West Indies, and took up a station near the equator, where the tracks of East India and Pacific commerce converge. Here and off the coast of Brazil Semmes captured in quick succession

eighteen prizes, nearly all of them large, costly, and beautiful sailing ships, the pride of Northern merchants and the
glory of the nation. However Captain Semmes himself
may have regarded it, it was a melancholy task for his young
officers, with the help of an English steamer and an eager
and vindictive English crew, to "burn, sink, and destroy"
these noble fabrics, which, in the years before the slavery
feud had rent the country asunder, the South had cherished
almost as dearly as the North.

Most of the great, deep-water clippers led the "Alabama"
a merry race. They could not fight her; they knew it; they
could only run. The war had made them wary, and as
soon as the rig and other characteristics of Captain
Semmes's ship were spread abroad after her first startling
exploits, it was usually "a stern chase and a long one" for
the "Alabama." The watchful masters of the New York
and New England merchantmen would put on their seven-
league boots at the first glimpse of a black, bark-rigged
steamer, British-built, with long lower-masts and lofty
royals. If it had been a mere matter of seamanship, the
"Alabama" would have fared ill, for the average Yankee
India or California trader was more than a match for the
lean Liverpool model. The narratives of the "Alabama's"
officers are full of expressions, half of pride, half of anger,
at the difficulty of getting alongside a Northern ship so
long as it was a question of canvas. But the "Alabama"
would connect her propeller and turn on her steam, and
sails and engines together were too much for the broad
wings of the brave clipper.

Even then it often required persistent shelling to bring-
to these proud Yankee sea lords who had been wont to sail
the ocean freely, asking no man's leave. The "Alabama"
would have been outrun by some of her prizes but for her
long-range artillery, and one great ship which she chased
toward sundown did manage to escape in the gathering
night. Captain Semmes treated his prisoners with no

unnecessary harshness. They were transferred as soon as possible to neutral vessels. He would sometimes endeavor to persuade the sailors of captured craft to enlist in his own service, and it is an interesting fact that the real American seamen would always refuse. His only recruits came from the foreigners, who were not so numerous then as now in Yankee forecastles.

Before Captain Semmes left England he had planned a careful itinerary, and he followed this with unwavering exactness. There were in 1862–64 no transoceanic telegraph cables. The presence of the "Alabama" in the few ports where she touched could be reported only by the slow and uncertain mails. Semmes timed his stay in the West Indies so that when the Yankee cruisers were close after him, he was speeding away to a new field on the equator. When he had lingered there as long as he thought was safe, he steered down the South Atlantic for Cape Town, where he and his ship were received with delight by the British colonial government and populace.

Of all the fleet of frigates, sloops, and gunboats which had been hurried out of the Northern naval stations or drawn from the blockade to chase the "Alabama," only one had accurately followed her track. This was the powerful side-wheel merchant steamer "Vanderbilt," one of the fine vessels with which, after the mail subsidies were withdrawn, New York's famous steamship manager had unsuccessfully sought to maintain an American line to Europe. When the war broke out, Mr. Vanderbilt gave this splendid steamer to the government. Like the Collins liners, she was swifter than any of our regular men-of-war, and though she burned eighty tons of coal a day, — then a prodigious consumption, — she could carry a vast store of fuel in her huge wooden hull and steam at a high speed for a long distance. This formidable "merchant cruiser" — a fine prototype of the "St. Louis" and "St. Paul" — actually reached the Cape of Good Hope before the

"Alabama," and missed her by the barest chance. If fortune had been a little kindlier, the Anglo-Confederate never would have gained the Eastern seas, and Captain Baldwin in the "Vanderbilt," not Captain Winslow in the "Kearsarge," would have become her conqueror.

Our British kinsmen promptly informed Captain Semmes that the "Vanderbilt" was in search of him, and gave him all the details of her power and armament. Semmes and his officers were brave men. It is an unjust charge that they were afraid of meeting armed ships in battle. Their vessel was built for a peculiar service, and she could be far more valuable to the Confederacy if she were held steadily to her appointed work than if she were exposed to the hazards of an ocean duel with the United States sloops-of-war, most of which were superior in weight of metal and strength of hull, and all superior in discipline and fighting efficiency. Semmes and his lieutenants were as wise as they were brave when they took leave of Cape Town and stood up through the Indian Ocean to those crowded gateways of the Far East, where the great routes of commerce wind through the reefs and headlands of the Malay archipelago.

Here and near China the "Alabama" cruised for six months, making prizes of several large and important East Indiamen. She eluded the sloop-of-war "Wyoming," our lonely cruiser on the East India station, which was endeavoring to protect American commerce over too many degrees of longitude and latitude. For the time being the stars and stripes vanished from the Eastern seas. Our ships could procure no cargoes. They were forced to pay enormous insurance rates. Some of them cleared in ballast; others were laid up in the nearest port, — the "Alabama" found a whole fleet of Yankee clippers chafing at anchor at Singapore. Many of these vessels were sold to foreigners at one-half or one-third their cost. Hoisting the British or another neutral flag, they were able to put to sea again. But not even the neutral ensign was always respected. On the day before Christmas, 1863, the "Alabama" met in the Straits of Malacca an American-built bark under British colors, — the "Martaban" of Maulmain, formerly the "Texan Star." Captain Semmes promptly declared fraudulent this transfer from one flag to another, and the "Martaban" was seized and burned with her cargo.

When the Indian seas seemed to be swept clear of Yankee merchantmen, the "Alabama" steered again for Cape Town and England. In the Atlantic on her way home, she met and destroyed a few vessels. June 11, 1864, she entered the English Channel, and, turning aside, ran into the French port of Cherbourg. Though Captain Semmes and his officers did not know it, their cruising was forever ended, their work was done.

Three days after their arrival a United States sloop-of-war, the "Kearsarge," Captain John A. Winslow, steamed into Cherbourg Harbor, sent a boat ashore with a message to the Consul, and then, without anchoring, moved slowly out to a position off the breakwater. The "Alabama" and her people saw that there was an unsleeping bulldog whose grip would never be relaxed. Captain Semmes was not afraid of an encounter. He signified through the United States Consul his willingness to fight the "Kearsarge," and began his preparations for the battle, while the "Kearsarge" grimly waited on the edge of the neutral water just beyond the port.

Never were foemen more closely matched than the "Kearsarge" and the "Alabama." They were built at almost the same time, and they might almost have been wrought from the same moulds, so alike were they in size and tonnage. Their rig was the same, — that of a bark, — though the "Kearsarge" then had pole topmasts and carried nothing above topsails. Both ships were of wood. Both, following the new naval practice, sat rather low upon the water. Both carried a few heavy guns instead of the many light guns of the old sailing frigates. The "Kearsarge" and "Alabama" represented with great precision the latest American and the latest British ideal of a steam sloop-of-war. Their combat was in effect a test of the gunnery and seamanship of the American and British navies half a century after the exploits of the "Constitution."

This famous battle is all the more worthy of a large place in a history of the American merchant marine because on the American side it was fought almost entirely by merchant seamen. When the "Kearsarge" sailed in February, 1862, from the navy yard at Portsmouth, N. H., where she was launched, the war had already absorbed practically all of our seasoned man-o'-war's men. The crew of the "Kearsarge" was therefore made up for the most part of men who had never burned powder, — sailors from the deep-sea or coasting fleet, fishermen from the bank schooners, and active and willing young landsmen. Untrained though they were in naval work, their personal quality was incomparable. The "Kearsarge" was built in a region which had been famous for two centuries for the skill of its shipwrights and the hardihood of its seamen, and many of the company of the beautiful new sloop-of-war came from Portsmouth and its neighborhood, — from the river towns and farms of the Piscataqua and Merrimac, and the rugged coast between Cape Ann and Portland. These recruits were sprung from the same granite stock as the men who had sailed out of Portsmouth with Paul Jones in the "Ranger" eighty-five years before, or had fought on the "Constitution," the "Enterprise," and the "Wasp" in our second War for Independence. The "Kearsarge" and her crew were going, exactly as the older ships had gone, to meet the veteran man-o'-war's men of Britain.

Two years of constant drill and cruising in unfriendly European waters had brought the merchant sailors of the

"Kearsarge" to a fine state of discipline before they caught the "Alabama" at her Cherbourg anchorage. They were sure of themselves, sure of their ship, sure of their officers. These officers, by the way, save only Captain Winslow, Lieutenant-Commander Thornton, the chief engineer, and a few others, were themselves volunteers from the merchant service. The captain and lieutenants of the "Alabama" were Southern men who had resigned from the United States navy, so that the advantage in professional experience was clearly on the side of the Anglo-Confederate. There was scarcely one Southern white man among the "Alabama's" sailors. They were nearly all Britons, with a few from North Europe. The leading men of the "Alabama's" gun-crews, it is said,[1] were drawn from the British gunnery ship "Excellent." The "Alabama's" company numbered 149, all told; the "Kearsarge's," 163, all but eleven of whom were native Americans.[2]

On a beautiful Sunday morning, June 19, 1864, the "Alabama" steamed out of Cherbourg toward the "Kearsarge," which lay awaiting her. It was 10.20 o'clock. Divine service was about to be held on the American cruiser. Captain Winslow laid aside his prayer-book, seized his trumpet, and cleared ship for action. Half an hour later the "Alabama" fired a first ineffective broadside. The grim Yankee did not respond. Again and again the English gunners thundered at their silent enemy. Then Captain Winslow, having closed in to the desired range, discharged his two great eleven-inch pivots, his two thirty-two-pounders, and the little thirty-pounder rifle on the forecastle, — five guns against the "Alabama's" seven. In sheer weight of broadside the "Kearsarge" had a slight advantage. She threw at one fire 366 pounds of projectiles to the "Alabama's" 328. But the forward pivot gun on the "Alabama," a fine Blakely one-hundred-

---

[1] Statement of Hon. Gideon Welles, Secretary of the Navy.
[2] Statement of Surgeon John M Browne.

pounder rifle, ought to have been superior in accuracy and penetration to the Yankee smooth bores. There can be little doubt that with a change of gun crews the result of this famous ocean duel would have been different.

As it was, the two eleven-inch pivot guns of the "Kearsarge," handled with consummate coolness and skill, steadily tore the "Alabama" to pieces. Captain Semmes's British seamen lost their "nerve" under this awful hammering. Their fire became furiously rapid. They planted a shell in the sternpost of the "Kearsarge," but it did not explode; and if it had done so and spoiled the Yankee rudder, it would have been too late, for this was a battle of straight shooting, not of manœuvring. On the other hand, those terrible Yankee projectiles were searching the "Alabama" through and through. Captain Winslow had told his gunners to use their light thirty-two-pounders to sweep the enemy's decks, and to aim their huge eleven-inch shells at the water-line or below it. The order was perfectly obeyed. Soon the sea was rushing into the British vessel through many gaping wounds. The "Kearsarge" wore a belt of anchor chains roughly fastened to her side, but she did not require this protection, for it was struck only twice, and then far above the water-line and above the boilers.

One shell, entering the "Alabama's" after pivot port, cut down half of the gun's crew. Another shell exploded in the engine-room. The inrush of the sea now drowned the furnaces. Captain Semmes caused sail to be set in a desperate effort to escape from the awful Yankee fire and to reach the three-mile limit. But the "Kearsarge" steamed relentlessly to a position between the stricken ship and the shore, while her guns boomed with the cool deliberation of target practice, and shell after shell burst in the "Alabama's" shattered and blazing 'tween-decks. At last the Confederate flag is hauled down, Captain Semmes gives the order, "every man for himself," and the survivors leap overboard, just as the "Alabama" plunges stern-foremost into the sea, whither she had sent the charred hulks of so many gallant merchantmen.

Captain Semmes himself and many of his people were rescued by the British yacht "Deerhound," but they could have safely given themselves up to the "Kearsarge." The "Alabama" was not a "pirate" nor yet a "privateer," but a regular cruiser of the Confederacy, and the wild threats of "hanging" Semmes and his officers were merely the results of his peculiarly exasperating work. Until the slavery quarrel estranged North and South, the splendid American merchant fleet had been the very apple of the eye of the nation. The rage of the North at the men who had so fearfully injured it was natural and human, but the cooler judgment of after years has acquitted Captain Semmes and his comrades of all blame for doing what seemed to be their duty to the Confederate government.

As to Great Britain's part in the burning and sinking of the Yankee clippers, American resentment has been very much deeper and more enduring. And yet that bright June morning off Cherbourg brought its own heavy punishment, for the battle of the "Kearsarge" and the "Alabama" was to all intents and purposes as clearly a battle of an American and a British man-of-war as were the sloop and frigate duels of our struggle for "Free Trade and Sailors' Rights" fifty years earlier. To the student of maritime affairs it is very interesting, — the close, significant resemblance between this combat of the steam cruisers of 1864 and the combats of the sail cruisers of 1812–15. The "Kearsarge" and "Alabama" were even more nearly matched than the "Constitution" and "Guerrière," or the "United States" and "Macedonian." In all these conflicts the advantage in gun power was with the American ship, though only slightly so in the action off Cherbourg. But in all these conflicts the damage wrought by the American victor was out of all proportion to this preponderance.

The " Guerrière," the " Macedonian, " and the "Alabama "
were all torn to pieces, while the Yankee ships were so
little hurt that they could have immediately met and
overwhelmed a new antagonist. The bulwarks and rigging of the " Kearsarge " were cut here and there, and she
had one man mortally and two severely wounded. The
"Alabama " lost twenty-two killed or drowned and twenty
wounded. The disparity of loss in this, probably, the
last action that will ever be fought between an American
and a British ship, was greater even than the astonishing
difference in the War of 1812. It strikingly recalls the
record of the sea victory of Santiago.

There was little or no manœuvring in the combat off
Cherbourg, for the ships steamed in concentric circles
broadside to broadside.   Even here, however, the traditional Yankee superiority in seamanship became manifest
when the sinking " Alabama " turned shoreward for a refuge
in neutral waters, and found her vigilant foe squarely
across her path. As to the Yankee superiority in gunnery,
it was more conspicuous off Cherbourg than it had ever
been before. Captain Winslow and Lieutenant-Commander Thornton passed the word forward that "every
shot must tell. "   Just as in 1812, the American gunners
waited until they had a sure range, and then aimed and
fired, and loaded and aimed and fired again, as steadily as
the Bunker Hill riflemen of Prescott, Stark, and Putnam.
The " Alabama's " men, like the Spaniards at Santiago,
fired with a frantic haste in significant contrast with the
Yankee coolness. Altogether, the "Alabama " discharged
in the one hour of the combat 370 shot and shell, of which
only 28 even touched the hull or rigging of her enemy.
The " Kearsarge " discharged only 173 missiles, but it is
said that "nearly all" of these crashed into the battery or
the hull of the " Alabama." Her spars and top-hamper
were very little hurt. The ship herself, however, was a
splintered, blood-stained sieve when she went down.

This battle of the "Kearsarge" and the "Alabama" must always be a theme of keen interest and pride to the thoughtful American, not only because of the brilliance of our triumph, but because of the vivid light which it throws upon the character of the merchant sailors by whom, chiefly, it was won. Very few of either the officers or the crew of the "Kearsarge" were professional man-o'-war's men. Few of them before this memorable action had ever heard a shot fired in anger. Yet the conduct of the "Kearsarge" manifested a perfect discipline and efficiency which, in the belief of Europe, can be gained only by long and incessant training. That battle proved even more conspicuously than the earlier victories of the "Constitution" and her sister frigates the value of a great and prosperous merchant shipping as a national naval reserve. It was real Homeric justice that the "Alabama" should be sent to the bottom of the English Channel almost within sight of the jealous coast that had launched her, by the steady skill and daring of men of the service on whose unarmed vessels she had preyed.

There is another significant aspect of this combat, and that is the test which it enforced of the seamen of the two divided branches of our English-speaking race. Sailors of the two nations that had for fifty years been strenuous rivals in peace met there for the first time in this half-century in battle. The earlier tests of 1812–15 had resulted to the unquestioned advantage of the Americans, — not in mere courage, indeed, for braver men than our British kin there never can be, and here the antagonists were equal, but in those moral qualities which are the natural result of the freer life of the New World and of the good Yankee habits of self-control and self-reliance. Just as the "Constitution" was sailed and fought with a superior intelligence and precision that were the logical fruits of the town meeting and the free school, so the "Kearsarge" shot straight that June morning off Cherbourg because the "men behind the guns" had been taught to think as well as to act.

In the height of the action a shell from the " Alabama " struck the waterways of the " Kearsarge " near the forward pivot, and bounded, spent, on deck right among the gun crew.   One of the loaders, a stalwart young fisherman from Cape Ann, caught up the frightful missile and threw it into the sea.   When his officer praised his bravery, the man quietly replied, " Oh, that was nothing.   Those blanked fools forgot to take the patch off the fuse ! "

This episode illuminates the whole contrast between the " Alabama " and the " Kearsarge."   It was not strange that the crew that grew flurried and fired away shells sealed from exploding was quickly whipped by a crew that could coolly note this fact in an instant of apparent awful danger.

The fifty years from 1814 to 1864 had brought no weakening of the manhood of the American sailor.   The test of fair and equal battle is, after all, the crucial test, and the merchant seamen of the " Kearsarge " showed themselves to be even more intrepid, skilful, and resourceful than that other crew of merchant sailors with which Hull in " Old Ironsides " had crushed the boastful veteran " Guerrière."   This splendid battle of American tars of our own time, men whom we have seen and known and talked with, is a conclusive demonstration, if such a thing were needed, that the shrinkage of our merchant shipping, which began before the war and became so swift and appalling afterward, was not due to any deterioration in the personal or professional fibre of the officers and men of the American fleet.

No other Anglo-Confederate commerce destroyers equalled the " Alabama," for none had so fair a chance or so able a commander.   The work of the " Shenandoah " among the Yankee whalers of the North Pacific is described in the chapter devoted to the whaling industry.   Another British-built vessel, the " Georgia," cruised for some time with indifferent success in the Atlantic in 1863–64 and was finally captured without a fight by the United States cruiser

" Niagara." The British Admiralty sold its despatch boat " Victor " to Confederate agents, and an official in the royal dockyard at Sheerness shipped a crew. But this vessel under the name of " Rappahannock " never got further than Calais, for France would not allow her to proceed.

Altogether the Confederate cruisers destroyed 110,000 tons of American shipping. But this represents only a fraction of the real havoc wrought among our maritime interests by the war. We lost, of course, the carrying trade of Southern ports and Southern products, and at the same time Northern ocean commerce was reduced by the war-blight on the industries that had furnished our exports. All this was natural and inevitable. But when in 1862 the capture and burning of an American ship and her cargo began to be reported almost every week, the merchants of our own and other countries took fright and would not send their goods in American vessels if a foreign and neutral vessel could possibly be chartered. Our own ocean carriers, thus shunned at home and abroad, were kept in port by other causes than mere fear of capture. They could procure no freights, or if by favor or by accident they did get cargoes, the cost of war insurance made their voyages unremunerative.

All around the world our splendid American ships and barks that had long been the aristocrats of the ocean, commanding the choicest freights and the highest prices, now suddenly became outcasts, reduced to hunting for trade in ballast or accepting cheap or offensive cargoes that nobody else would take.

As the war dragged on, and the destruction of American ships spread from the Atlantic up the Indian Ocean to the Eastern seas, the lethargy of despair settled down upon American shipowners. Many a noble A 1 vessel in perfect condition was hastily sold to neutral merchants, usually British, at a mere fraction of her value. In 1860 only 17,418 tons of American shipping had been sold abroad, —

about the average of several years preceding. In 1861 the foreign acquisitions were only 26,649 tons. But in 1862, under the pressure of the war panic, 117,756 tons of American shipping were bought at bankrupt prices by British and other shrewd foreigners, eager to take advantage of the misfortune which they had helped to bring about. In 1863 there were "sold foreign" 222,199 tons; in 1864, 300,865; in 1865, 133,832. Altogether in the four years of the war we lost to alien flags 751,595 tons of shipping, or nearly one-third of our entire fleet registered for deep-sea carrying.

In 1861 this fleet consisted of 2,496,894 tons; in 1866, of only 1,387,756 tons. For three-quarters of this loss of more than a million tons the Anglo-Confederate cruisers were directly and indirectly responsible. There is a popular impression that Great Britain paid full indemnity in the $15,500,000 judgment of the Geneva Court of Arbitration for her part in this destruction of our commerce. Perhaps our merchants might have won adequate compensation if the court had granted what were known as the indirect claims, but the arbiters decided that these claims could not be considered. The award probably covered the actual value of the ships and cargoes captured by the "Alabama" and her consorts. But it did not make good the vastly larger sums of money lost by those American shipowners who were forced by the depredations of the cruisers to pay excessive insurance premiums, or accept unremunerative freight rates, or lay their ships up in idleness or sell them at one-half or one-third of their cost to foreigners. It did not make good what American shipowners suffered by the diversion of their accustomed trade to European carriers. Fifteen and one half millions of dollars is a very large amount of money, but, after all, ten times that sum could not compensate the country for the disappearance of almost one out of three of the deep-sea ships of American register.

Without its great merchant marine of 1861, the United

States could never have drawn the relentless cordon of the blockade about the Southern coasts, which in the end smothered and starved the Confederacy. More than half of the ships, four-fifths of the officers, and five-sixths of the men who performed this vital work came directly from the merchant service. When the Civil War began, the United States navy contained only thirty steam ships of war, with about twice as many obsolete sailing vessels. There were 1,450 officers and 7,600 seamen. Before the war ended, this force had been expanded to 600 steamers, 9,000 officers, and 51,000 seamen.

The 7,500 volunteer officers who joined the navy between 1861 and 1865 were a superb body of men, intelligent, zealous, skilful, and brave. Most of them were captains, mates, or engineers of the merchant marine. They were thorough masters of their calling, and with a few months of instruction in gunnery, signalling, and the navy routine in general, they became so efficient that on many of our vessels in 1863–64 they were performing all the duties of watch and division officers, and in not a few cases had risen to actual command. They were followed into the navy by 40,000 merchant sailors.

Although the government began immediately to build many new ships-of-war in the spring of 1861, it could not await the slow processes of construction. The arduous work of cruise and blockade required something more powerful than ninety-day gunboats. So the Navy Department. purchased scores of iron and wooden merchant steamers of the coastwise and West India service, armed them, and converted them into excellent "merchant cruisers." Until the end of the war it was these merchant ships that made up the bulk of our blockading squadrons. Some of them, notably the " Vanderbilt," already mentioned, the " Santiago de Cuba," the " Rhode Island," and the " Connecticut," proved to be among the most valuable ships of our entire fleet, because of their excellent speed and "coal endurance." Until a fast special class of light steamers was built in 1863–64, the large converted merchantmen were almost the only vessels on our navy list that could overtake the flying British blockade runners. Without their help an adequate blockade never could have been maintained by the regular navy sloops and frigates,—fine ships of their type, but heavy, slow, and encumbered with worse than useless top-hamper.

The War Department, as well as the Navy Department, drew deeply upon the great resources of the merchant marine. The transports which conveyed General Burnside's expedition to the North Carolina Sounds and General Butler's to New Orleans were bought or chartered merchant vessels. This mobility by sea which enabled us to send great bodies of troops to any point along the beleaguered coast of the Confederacy, or to shift the base of army operations suddenly from Washington to Hampton Roads, would have been impossible had not the North possessed a large fleet of commercial ships and a skilful and hardy seafaring population.

Never in the history of maritime warfare has a great fighting fleet been created so swiftly and made so terrible an instrument of defence or offence. The six hundred war steamers of the United States at the end of the War of the Rebellion included some weakly armed, "improvised" craft, but many more thoroughly modern, serviceable vessels. The American monitors were then incomparable armor-clads. In the last year of the war, anticipating serious trouble with Great Britain over the Anglo-Confederate depredations on our merchant ships, the Navy Department built several very large, long, and powerful "commerce-destroyers" of which the famous "Wampanoag" was a fine example. This great vessel steamed for twenty-four hours at an average speed of seventeen knots. The best speed of the British transatlantic liners of that time was about fourteen knots, and the engineer board that conducted the tests of the " Wampanoag " reported that " the maximum performance can be easily maintained during a passage across the Atlantic or for any required service." It is one of the great unwritten facts of history that it was the warlike potentialities of the " Wampanoag " and her sisters, rather than any abstract love of peace, which persuaded the British government to submit the Alabama claims to arbitration. There was then in the British navy no vessel capable of a speed of more than fourteen knots. The " Wampanoag " and the other ships of this redoubtable class could have taken awful revenge for the " Alabama " if they had ever been loosed upon the mission for which they were designed. But fortunately this was not necessary.

The wonderful performance of the " Wampanoag " and our other large war steamers of the period between 1865 and 1870 is a conclusive demonstration that there was no lack of engineering skill and experience in this country that could have turned to the creation of a great steam merchant fleet if there had been proper inducements. The war had called into existence many marine engine works and had increased the business of the shipyards, for the government wisely built a part of its new steam fleet, including nearly all the armor-clads, by private contract. Several of the later gunboats were constructed with iron hulls. The close of the war found American steamship building a very much better-equipped and more confident industry than it had been in 1861. The yards had gained experience in four years of hard work for the government. They had acquired the essential machinery, and had developed an adequate force of skilled workmen.

Why, then, did not American merchant shipping increase and prosper, as all our other great industries did, with the return of peace ? The answer is complex ; the causes were many. In the first place, as has been shown in a previous chapter, the withdrawal of the mail subsidies at the dictation of the South in 1856 and 1858 had destroyed every line of American steamships to foreign ports except the short-distance service to the West Indies, and the Pacific Mail service *via* the Isthmus, which was really included in the coasting trade. The four years of the war had strengthened the already formidable grip of subsidized foreign steamship concerns upon the best routes of Atlantic carrying. There was not one American steamship regularly employed in 1865 between our ports and Europe, Africa, or Asia. But this foreign preoccupation of ocean-carrying was not the whole secret of the paralysis that rested on American ship-building. There were other important factors.

The high tariff and internal revenue taxation, especially the latter, required by the war, bore heavily upon the ship-yards. American builders did not use foreign materials to any great extent and did not care to ; but the internal revenue burden upon domestic iron, steel, copper, and lead and also upon spars, sails, paints, and cordage, was a severe handicap. Moreover, there was a special internal revenue tax of two per cent on the hulls of vessels, and of three (later of five) per cent on marine engines, which was not repealed until 1868.

A third factor adverse to shipbuilding and shipowning was the tremendous development of manufacturing and of Western trade and industry that came close upon the heels of peace. In 1870 there began the marvellous era of American railroad expansion. This new form of enterprise, right in our own country and beneath the protection of our flag, began to absorb more and more the energy and the capital of even the seaboard States. Many a New York or Boston fortune won out of the sea went into the prairies, and greater wealth than packet lines or India voyages had ever accumulated began to roll up out of our own magic West.

The percentage of American imports and exports carried in American ships had fallen during the Civil War from

65.2 in 1861 to 27.7 in 1865. Peace brought an immediate but an ominously small recovery. The American percentage of our ocean-carrying was 32.2 in 1866 and 35.6 in 1870. Five years after Appomattox we had so far failed to regain our old prestige upon the sea that we were carrying only half as much of our own commerce as we had conveyed in our own ships before the war, and we had lost even more heavily in our participation in the general ocean freight business of the world. After 1870 there set in another decline, which brought the American percentage of our deep-sea carrying down, in 1875, to 26.2, a share actually smaller than that of the last year of the war. Every token showed that the American merchant marine was in a desperate condition.

Soon after the end of the war, this fainting industry drew the attention of Congress, and the decline of American shipbuilding and shipowning in the foreign trade was made the subject of a careful official investigation. Representative Lynch of Maine, Chairman of the Committee on Commerce, made an elaborate report to the National House in February, 1870, urging, as a result of the long inquiry, that shipbuilding material and ship supplies be admitted free of duty, and that a subsidy or bounty be granted to American steam and sailing ships engaged in foreign commerce. This report led to much acrimonious discussion in the press and to some debate in Washington. But the main thought and energy of Congress were now absorbed in domestic problems, and the sea and its affairs had lost their old importance.

Congress neglected to do anything for the merchant marine at this time for the same reasons that it neglected to do anything for the navy. Both our mercantile and our war fleet were steadily decaying, and a strange quietude seized the once-busy shipyards of New England, New York, and the Delaware River. The war had left the great West dominant in Congress, and the West seemed to know little of and to care less for the American ship and the American sailor. But it is significant that the thorough investigation of the Lynch committee, four or five years after the war, into the actual conditions of American shipbuilding and shipowning resulted in the same judgment which the commercial States had expressed in Congress before the war, when the mail subsidies were withdrawn, that against intense European competition the American merchant marine could not hope to prosper without national protection and encouragement.

Something of this kind had been attempted in a slight and partial way. An act of May 28, 1864, authorized the Post-Office Department to contribute $150,000 a year toward a monthly mail service to Brazil, the remainder of the subsidy being paid by the Brazilian government, which had no ships of its own. This international plan gave us a good American line of steamers to St. Thomas and Rio Janeiro. California's desire for steam communication with China and Japan was recognized in an Act of Congress of Feb. 16, 1865, which created the Asiatic service of the Pacific Mail Company, now the most important line of this greatest of American steamship corporations. The new line began its work in 1867 with a subsidy of $500,000 a year for carrying the United States mails. Unfortunately, instead of procuring good iron steamers, which American yards had already proved that they could build, the Pacific Mail put on this long route from San Francisco to the Orient four wooden side-wheel steamers, large and luxurious, but obsolete in design and costly in operation. This was a grave error of judgment, which is scarcely mitigated by the fact that side-wheelers were still in vogue in the service of the British lines on the more boisterous Atlantic. The Pacific Mail management should have looked further ahead into the future.

Soon after the Civil War a new maritime policy, known as the " free ship " idea, began to find advocates among our public men, and to a lesser degree among our merchants. Ever since 1789 the privilege of American registry had been restricted to ships that were American-built. For seventy years the entire merchant fleet of the United States, save a few vessels captured in war or wrecked and repaired on our coasts, had been of home construction. All of the triumphs of the golden age of our sea-carrying had been won in ships wrought out on our own soil from our own materials by the peerless Yankee mechanics. The splendid packets and clippers and the swift and powerful mail steamers of 1847–58 were of distinctively American design. All the improvements in the model, rig, and equipment of our merchant shipping had originated in our own yards or among our seamen. In all this technical progress America had led the world, and through all these years shipbuilding had been the industry that most aroused the national pride of the American people. A strong patriotic interest, therefore, was bitterly opposed to any amendment or repeal of our historic national policy, especially as " free ships " would prove to be of great, immediate benefit to the shipbuilders and shipowners of Britain who had struck a foul blow at our maritime prosperity in the Civil War.

On the other hand, the champions of " free ships " urged that Congress ought frankly to meet the changed conditions of ocean trade by a change of national legislation ; that wood had ceased to be and iron had become the chief shipbuilding material ; that iron was far more costly in this country than it was in Great Britain, and that the status of the two shipbuilding nations was completely reversed ; that it was Britain, not America, that now had the advantage. The " free ship " partisans urged that we ought to meet this hard, undeniable fact by admitting cheap British iron ships to American registry, just as Great Britain had admitted our cheap wooden ships.

This was the " free ship " argument. Unfortunately it was not altogether honest, and perhaps that is one reason why it never became convincing.   The persons who were exhorting the United States to follow the British example did not tell the whole truth about the situation.   Wood was always more abundant and wooden ships were cheaper in the United States than in Great Britain, but all through the years when the commerce of the world was carried exclusively in wooden ships the British government would not permit its merchants freely to purchase our excellent American-built vessels.   That privilege was not opened until 1849, when iron shipbuilding had become so firmly established on the Thames, the Mersey, and the Clyde that all could see that this was destined to be the British ship-building of the future.   Moreover, the arbitrary action of Lloyd's in compelling American ships to be re-treenailed with English oak completely nullified until 1854 the " free ship" Act of Parliament.   By 1854 iron shipbuilding had become so powerfully intrenched that Britain felt that she had nothing to fear from American competition.   Not until 1862–65, when British-built cruisers had destroyed our ocean-carrying, did any considerable number of American vessels pass over to the British flag, and then they were caught up at panic prices.   The large growth of the British mercantile marine was in iron ships, of steam or sail, not in wooden ships bought from us or built after our models. Indeed, one ingenuous argument for a " free ship" policy in Britain when it finally prevailed was that few British merchants would buy American wooden ships, but that if the United States could be persuaded to reciprocate by opening its registry to British ships, the iron shipyards of the United Kingdom would soon be building all the new tonnage of America.

Yet if the "free ship" idea had been presented in a different way, with less rancor against American maritime interests, it might at one time have been applied to the real advantage of the United States.   From 1865 to 1875 the argument for the repeal, or at least the modification, of the stringent American registry laws rested on a basis of expediency which has now disappeared. In that period our iron and steel production was still small as compared with Great Britain's,[1] and it was absorbed in railroad building and other forms of home development. The price of iron and steel until toward the end of this period was abnormally high, not because of the tariff, or only partly because of that, but because of the general post-bellum inflation of values. If iron plates, beams, and angles for at least shipbuilding for the foreign trade had been placed on the free list, as the Lynch committee recommended, and as was actually done twenty years afterward, there would have been some equity in permitting American merchants for a few years to buy new iron foreign-built steamships for deep-sea service.

But this, after all, is mere conjecture. Certain it is that most of the ship merchants themselves who would have profited by a "free ship" policy, if there were any benefit in it, were overwhelmingly opposed to such legislation. The shipbuilders, of course, objected to it, but the idea never won much favor among the men who owned ships and sailed them. Looking back over the years, it may be all for the best that the United States did not change its historic policy, and grant American registers to the iron tonnage of the Clyde and the Tyne. For it is an eloquent fact that every maritime Power of the Continent of Europe that adopted the "free ship" idea, when Great Britain's mastery of iron shipbuilding seemed to be absolute, has found the policy inadequate and disappointing. Every one of these Powers, including even Norway, has been compelled to supplement "free ships" with some form of subsidy or bounty to protect and encourage native shipbuilding or navigation. There is no reason to believe that the experience of the United States with "free ships"

[1] In the year 1870 Great Britain produced 5,962,000 tons of pig iron; the United States, 1,865,000 tons.

would have been different from that of France, which saw its merchant marine actually shrink away until the present subsidy system was adopted, or of Germany, which grants subventions to new lines of steamships on condition that the vessels shall be built in German yards. Every one of the many millions of francs or marks paid in subsidy by Continental governments to their home ship owners or builders is a confession that the " free ship " policy has been insufficient if not entirely ineffective. The shrewd Yankee instinct of self-reliance is seldom at fault.

It cannot be said of the American shipowners of this period that they leaned too heavily upon their government. It was only after their own brave individual efforts had failed that they invoked national aid. Soon after the close of the Civil War, some merchants of Boston, experienced and wealthy men, organized the American Steamship Company and attempted without a subsidy to compete with the heavily subsidized Cunarders. They launched two screw steamers, the " Ontario " and " Erie," built at Newburyport. Though the two ships were of wood, they were fine strong vessels. The " Ontario," which arrived at Liverpool in August, 1867, on her pioneer voyage from Boston, made the passage in the excellent time, for a new steamer, of twelve days. She was 350 feet long, 44 feet wide, and 29 feet deep, with a tonnage of 3,000, — a large ship for her day. The massive wooden hull was divided into five water-tight compartments ; the engine-room bulk-heads were of iron. Atlantic liners of all nations still relied much on canvas, and the beautiful " Ontario " was full ship-rigged. The " Ontario " aroused much admiration in Liverpool because of her symmetrical hull and powerful machinery, but she made only a few voyages in the Liverpool service, and her sister, the " Erie," did not get to sea at all. The company which owned them became embarrassed. These handsome steamers were withdrawn and sold by auction in 1869 for about one-half of their original cost of $1,500,000.

Undoubtedly these Boston merchants erred, as did the Pacific Mail Company at the same time, in constructing such great vessels of wood instead of iron. But this technical mistake did not break down the Boston enterprise. If the wooden steamers from the Merrimac had been replaced by iron steamers from the Clyde, it would still have been found that private American capital, unaided, could not compete with the Cunard Company, firmly established in the trade and fostered by an annual subsidy of several hundred thousand dollars. Indeed, the Cunard liners could have carried passengers and freight at cost, and defied American rivals, whether they were wood or iron, Massachusetts or Scotch built, for the mail subsidy was in itself equivalent to a handsome dividend on the entire Cunard investment. So well was this lesson learned that since 1868 not one American steamer has sailed regularly out of Boston in the transatlantic trade, and in 1898 no less than 98 per cent of the entire foreign commerce of what was long the boldest and most patriotic of American ports was monopolized by foreigners.

Another American transatlantic line [1] started from New York in 1866 with side-wheel wooden steamers and lasted a little longer. It made twelve voyages in 1866, fourteen in 1867, eight in 1868, and seven in 1869. In this last year the service was extended from England to Copenhagen in Denmark and Stettin in Prussia. But the enterprise failed because, as the owners explained, " A combination was formed by the English and German steamship lines to put on a steamer for New York at the same port and on the same day that the vessels of this line were to sail, and to take freight and passengers to New York at reduced rates. The result of this combination was death to the line." Here was another painful example of the difficulty of breaking again into the transatlantic steam trade when it had once become a monopoly of foreign corporations, upheld,

---

[1] Report of Joseph Nimmo, Jr., to the Treasury Department, 1870.

some of them, by the treasuries of European governments. A third American line of wooden steamers began to run from Baltimore to Liverpool in 1866, but it was always a feeble enterprise and it was abandoned in 1870.

A fourth American experiment in transatlantic navigation was somewhat more fortunate. In 1872–73 the American Steamship Company of Philadelphia built four excellent iron steamers in the celebrated Cramp shipyard on the Delaware and put them on the route to Liverpool. These vessels, the " Pennsylvania," " Indiana," " Ohio," and " Illinois," were well adapted for the service, admirable seaboats, swift for their time and luxurious in their appointments. It was on one of the ships of this line that ex-President Grant, with characteristic patriotism, sailed on the first stage of his memorable journey around the world. For a quarter of a century these four substantial American iron steamers swung to and fro between the United States and Europe, bearing the stars and stripes almost alone in the whole steam fleet engaged in transatlantic navigation. It is said of this one American company that it not only never lost a ship, but never lost a passenger or so much as a mail bag, — a record of safety and regularity unique in the annals of the North Atlantic trade.

This lone American line never had a subsidy, but it did have the powerful support of the great Pennsylvania Railroad. Even then, however, the line could scarcely have existed if there had been a competing subsidized British service out of Philadelphia, as there was out of New York and Boston. It is understood that the Pennsylvania Railroad did not find the venture lucrative. It continued to operate the four steamers, but it built no others. Finally the four ships passed into the hands of the International Navigation Company, controlling the Inman line from New York to Liverpool and the Red Star line to Antwerp. The " Pennsylvania " and her sisters ran for a while longer in the Atlantic service, but have now been

transferred to the Pacific coast. No merchant steamers
ever built have met more satisfactorily the perils of the sea
and the demands of commerce. When they were launched
they were regarded as veritable giants. The " Pennsylvania " was 340 feet long, 43 feet wide, and 24 feet deep, with a
tonnage of 3,200. She and all her sisters were at first full
brig-rigged, and they will be remembered by many Atlantic
travellers as among the most graceful and sturdy ships that
ever flew the starred flag on the Western Ocean.

The period of 1861–75 closed even more darkly for the
American merchant marine than it had opened. The war
had swept off one-third of our deep-sea tonnage, but even
after the war our fleet had gone on declining. We were
carrying in 1875 only 26.2 per cent of our own commerce,
or less than half of the proportion of 1861. Everywhere
American wooden sailing ships were being supplanted by
foreign iron steamers. This process had been hastened by
the refusal in 1870 of the powerful British insurance monopoly of Lloyd's to class and register " foreign," meaning
especially American, vessels for more than one year at a
time. In 1869, 91 ships and barks for deep-sea carrying
had been launched in America. In 1870 the number had
shrunk to 73; in 1871, to 40; in 1872, to 15. There was
no excuse for this discrimination save the same hostile
commercial spirit that a few years before had sent out the
" Alabama," for these American ships and barks were
built of the choicest of materials by thoroughly trained
mechanics and sailed with admirable skill. They were,
perhaps, less economical carriers than iron ships, but that
they were unsafe or unseaworthy could not be pretended.

Another influence, though this time a normal and una-
voidable one, adverse to the American merchant marine,
was the opening of the Suez Canal in 1870. This shorten-
ing of the voyages between the Atlantic and the far East
naturally benefited steamers at the expense of sailing
vessels. Around the nucleus of the subsidized Peninsular

& Oriental Company there had grown up a great British steam fleet running to India and China, and these craft now cut more severely than ever into one of the few profitable trades that were left to the great Yankee square-riggers.

Meanwhile we had acquired only three important new routes of navigation, — one line of American steamships from Philadelphia to Liverpool, one line from New York to Brazil, one line from San Francisco across the Pacific to the Orient. The Philadelphia enterprise owed its life to the patronage of the Pennsylvania Railroad; the Brazil and China lines were the direct result of special government subventions. The Pacific Mail Company was replacing its wooden steamers by new American-built iron ships, two of which, the "City of Peking" and "City of Tokio," were five-thousand-ton vessels, more than four hundred feet long, the greatest merchantmen thus far constructed on this Continent. They were launched by John Roach from his well-equipped yard at Chester on the Delaware, where he constructed the Brazil liners and many excellent iron coastwise steamships. Mr. Roach had now become the foremost shipbuilder in America. Save only the Roach establishment, the Cramp yard further up the river, the Harlan & Hollingsworth yard in Wilmington, and a few smaller concerns, American iron shipbuilding was now moribund, and the New England yards were not producing enough wooden vessels for deep-sea service to replace the ships and barks that were being lost, worn out, or sold to foreigners. Here is the official record, for the fifteen years, of the steady decline of our merchant tonnage and our deep-sea carrying: —

TONNAGE AND FOREIGN TRADE. 1861–75.

| Year. | Shipping Tons. | Total Foreign Commerce. | Proportion carried in American Ships. | | Combined Imports and Exports. |
			Imports.	Exports.	
1861	2,496,894	$508,864,375	60.0	72.1	65.2
1862	2,173,537	380,027,178	44.8	54.5	50.0
1863	1,926,886	447,300,262	43.3	40.0	41.4
1864	1,486,749	475,285,271	24.6	30.0	27.5
1865	1,518,350	404,774,883	29.9	26.1	27.7
1866	1,387,756	783,671,588	25.1	37.7	32.2
1867	1,515,648	690,267,237	28.0	39.1	33.9
1868	1,494,389	639,389,339	33.0	36.6	35.1
1869	1,496,220	703,624,076	31.3	34.9	33.1
1870	1,448,846	828,730,176	33.1	37.7	35.6
1871	1,363,652	963,043,862	31.0	32.6	31.8
1872	1,359,040	1,070,772,663	26.8	29.8	29.1
1873	1,378,533	1,164,616,132	27.0	25.7	26.4
1874	1,389,815	1,153,689,382	30.2	24.6	27.2
1875	1,515,598	1,046,448,147	29.2	23.7	26.2

23

CHAPTER XV

OUR COASTWISE CARRIERS

Always Protected, Always Prosperous — The Larger Half of the
Merchant Marine — Coasters of the Colonies — The Yankee
Schooner — Protective Act of 1789 — American Coast Trade closed
to Foreigners — Magical Increase of the 'Longshore Fleet — The
"Clermont" and her Successors — Evolution of the Many-
Masted Schooner — Long-Voyage Coasting — Need of Strong
Ships and Hardy Seamen — From Four Masts to Five, Six, and
Seven — Noble Steamers of the Coast Trade — Protective Law
extended to Hawaii and Porto Rico — The River Fleet — Our
Coastwise Shipping all American — Its Remarkably Steady
Progress

WHEN we speak of the American merchant marine in
the years of its glory, we think of Archangel and Bordeaux and Smyrna and Mauritius and Canton and Madras,
and of the long, long roads leading thither across the deep
sea, — of Western Ocean packets close reefed among the icebergs, great clippers slipping down the trade winds, whalemen striking their giant quarry a thousand leagues from
land. The thought is of remoteness, of almost illimitable
distances, of perils braved in alien climes beneath strange
constellations. It is ever true of humankind that it is the
thing far off that enchains its imagination. Our own horizon, once known, becomes prosaic; the fancy loves to turn
to the wonderful things that may lie beyond.

Thus it has come to pass that the larger half of the
American merchant fleet, the more distinctively national
and the more prosperous, has almost no annals of its
own. It has gone straight on through the years, performing its appointed work, increasing its tonnage, an-

ticipating every improvement of navigation or demand of trade, until it is now many times the largest and most efficient fleet of domestic carriers in the world. This development of the American coastwise shipping, like the evolution of American railroading, is one of the industrial marvels of the crowded century just closed. It has lacked, however, the dramatic elements that challenge popular attention, and from its meagre records relatively little can be gathered and utilized by the historian.

The American coastwise traffic is as old as the beginnings of white colonization on this Continent. The settlers of Jamestown, hemmed in by the Indians and the wilderness, found their only safety in their shallops sailing on river or sea. The Pilgrims of Plymouth brought a ship-carpenter over shortly after they themselves came, and he built two small vessels for trading with the fishing stations on the coast of Maine. In those early years when an important ship like the "Mayflower" was of only one hundred and eighty tons' burden, the colony craft were necessarily small almost to insignificance. Many of them at first were really undecked boats instead of vessels proper. The maritime records of Boston note the clearance in 1661 from that port for a five-hundred-mile voyage to Virginia of a "ketch" of only sixteen tons, that could have been little more than a covered long-boat. Among those old, venturesome traders the ketch and the sloop predominated. The sloop was the familiar one-masted rig, carrying sometimes on the larger craft a square topsail. The ketch was the two-master of the young colonies, but very different from the two-masted rig to which subsequent generations were accustomed.

A ketch of the seventeenth and eighteenth centuries, as has been described in the chapter on "Old Rigs and Models," had one square-rigged mast set well back from the bow toward amidships, and a smaller mast, sometimes square-rigged also and sometimes fore-and-aft-rigged, near the stern. This was an arrangement which the colonists brought from their native Europe. It may have served the purpose in the winds and waters of the Old World, but it proved to be poorly adapted to the American seaboard. The ketch required elaborate gear to work its square-sails, and there was scant room to handle this quickly on the narrow deck of a small vessel. A ketch would heave-to handsomely under its after canvas, but it would not sail well close-hauled on the wind, and that was a grievous fault in a light craft caught off the North Atlantic coast in a furious winter northwester.

The schooner, whose origin is described in the earlier chapter referred to, came into vogue in the first half of the eighteenth century. For more than a hundred and fifty years it has been the characteristic vessel of the American coasting trade. In the schooner the square-rigged mast of the European ketch disappeared. Foremast and mainmast bore fore-and-aft sails, simple in design, hoisted from the deck, and easily lowered, reefed, or furled. Before a fair breeze the foresail could be boomed out on one side, and the mainsail on the other, — wing-and-wing, so called. With a free wind and the booms above the rail, every yard of canvas could be made to draw. Close-hauled, the schooner could outpoint any square-rigged craft, and for quickness and sureness in stays was incomparable. A final advantage, of large weight with provincial merchants, was that the schooner-rig cost less money than the square-rig, and could be worked by fewer men.

The first guns of the Revolution found the schooner intrenched in maritime favor all along the shore from the Penobscot to the Carolinas. It was supplanting not only the ketch but the brig for coastwise voyages. The dried fish and lumber of New England were carried to market in New York, Philadelphia, Norfolk, Charleston, and Savannah by schooner-rigged craft, of a hundred tons or less, which brought back to Eastern ports Southern produce, tobacco, and naval stores. Baltimore began the building of schooners of superior beauty and speed, and fore-and-aft craft were employed in the off-shore trade to the West Indies and South America. Later still Yankee schooners made long voyages of adventure to the other side of the world, and the rig was quickly adopted and utilized on the northern and western shore of Europe. It is in the coast trade of the United States, however, that the sailing schooner has been pre-eminent. It is as conspicuous there as the prairie schooner in the great tide of Western overland migration.

Until the railroads drew their ribbons of iron through the cities of the Atlantic States, almost all of the bulky freight that represented the interstate commerce of the time passed to and fro in the indispensable carriers of the coast fleet. Passengers could travel from New York and Boston to Philadelphia, Washington, and the South in stage-coaches and chaises. Merchandise, save only that of a very compact and valuable kind, could not stand the expense of the land journey. Indeed, the coasting-packets took not only freight, but many passengers. Especial vessels ran regularly between the same ports. Their days of arrival and departure were not as hard-fixed as the laws of the Medes and the Persians. The uncertainties of wind and weather would not permit that. These packets did, however, manage to create an organized business, and to carry it on with success until they were gradually crowded out by the swifter, more capacious, and more reliable steamers to which calm and storm were almost the same. Even now, in the early years of the twentieth century, sail packets ply from the shore villages of "Down East" to Boston and New York, with all the constancy if not the imposing presence of steam "liners."

The coasting trade of the Atlantic seaboard was smothered by the Revolutionary War. The peace of 1783 brought a disappointingly slow revival. Many of the best coasters had been captured by British blockaders or destroyed by hostile forays on the snug harbors where they lay. Merchants could find small encouragement, in the distressed condition of the country and the squally foreign outlook, to build new craft, even if they had the means to do it. Coastwise as well as deep-sea shipping languished, until the memorable year 1789 brought the birth of the present Federal government, whose first formal legislation threw national protection about the whole American merchant marine. The Acts of Congress of July, 1789, which gave such a mighty impetus to the ocean-carrying trade of the new republic, have been recited in an earlier chapter on "The First Swift Growth." American ships in foreign commerce were thereby given the encouragement of customs duties and tonnage dues which discriminated heavily against the ships of Europe. The smaller, humbler, but not less useful, coastwise craft were not forgotten.

An Act of Congress of July 20, 1789, imposed tonnage duties of six cents a ton on American-built ships owned by American citizens, and of fifty cents a ton on ships built and owned abroad. As to the coasting trade, it was provided that American vessels should pay the tonnage tax only once a year, while foreign vessels should pay it whenever they entered an American seaport. Thus, although foreign vessels were not in set terms excluded from the American coasting trade, they were made subject to a discriminating tonnage tax that was virtually prohibitive. A British brig of one hundred tons' burden, for example, sailing from New York for Norfolk, would have to pay a tonnage duty of fifty dollars on arrival at her destination. An American schooner of one hundred tons on a similar voyage would pay only six dollars. But if the British vessel reloaded and cleared for Philadelphia, she would have to pay another tax of fifty dollars after she had sailed up the Delaware, while the American vessel on the same voyage would pay not one cent. Fifty dollars would sweep away a very large share of the profit of such a venture in a craft of only one hundred tons, and it was unquestionably the purpose of the Act of 1789 to bar alien carriers out of our domestic navigation.

From 1789 onward the coasting trade of the United States has been monopolized by American shipowners and seamen. An Act of Congress of April 5, 1808, supplementing the Embargo Act, absolutely forbade foreign vessels to enter this trade, of which they could have been able, anyway, to avail themselves only on rare occasions. In 1809 this prohibition was modified, but the Act of March 1, 1817 (known as the American Navigation Act), renewed this absolute prohibition, and this has remained to the present day the rigidly enforced maritime policy of the American republic.

Section 4 of this Act of 1817 declared that "no goods, wares, or merchandise shall be imported under penalty of forfeiture thereof from one port of the United States to another port of the United States in a vessel belonging wholly or in part to a subject of any foreign Power."

When the protection of heavily discriminating tonnage duties was applied to our domestic shipping by Act of Congress in 1789, the coastwise fleet was almost insignificant. It comprised only 68,607 tons all told, or only a little more than one half of the tonnage of the small fleet then registered for overseas commerce. The effect of the new national protective policy was almost as wonderful on the home fleet as on the other. By 1794 the tonnage of enrolled vessels (not including licensed craft under twenty tons) had risen to 145,601 tons, or more than doubled. By 1800 the coastwise tonnage had grown to 245,295. In 1807, when the embargo was proclaimed, this domestic tonnage stood at 318,190; in 1812, when our second war with England began, at 443,181.

This war brought a temporary paralysis to the coasting trade except to the northward of Cape Cod, where British cruisers winked at the traffic for a time because of the supposed disloyalty of New England. When hostilities ceased and the iron blockade was relaxed, coasting revived with more than its old activity. In 1818 our domestic fleet reached, for the first time, a tonnage of more than half a million. It stood at 503,140 in that year, while the deep-sea fleet contained a tonnage of 589,954. Never before had the two divisions of the American merchant marine come so near together. By 1826 the coastwise fleet had far exceeded the six-hundred-thousand-ton mark. Then after 1828 there set. in a decline in sympathy with the shrinkage of our deep-sea shipping. But in 1838 the coast fleet had reached a tonnage of a round million, far surpassing the deep-sea fleet, and steamers of the side-wheel type were beginning to run beween the principal cities of the seaboard.

Robert Fulton had made his first trip from New York to Albany on Aug. 7, 1807, in his "Clermont," the first successful steam vessel in the world. That was a most important day for the American coastwise service. The "Clermont" was a domestic craft, pure and simple. She never visited any foreign port, but continued to ply, throughout her life, as a Hudson River packet. This pioneer of the world's vast steam fleet was a vessel of rather ambitious size, in an era when few of the sailing ships of deep-sea commerce were much more than one hundred feet long. The "Clermont" had a length of 133 feet, a breadth of 18, and a depth of $7\frac{1}{2}$. Her engine, which had a 24-inch cylinder and a piston stroke of four feet, came from the works of Boulton & Watt, in England. There was a low-pressure boiler 20 feet long, made of copper for safety, and the crude side-wheels were 15 feet in diameter, with four-foot buckets and a dip of two feet. The "Clermont," like her immediate successors, was masted and rigged, and could spread canvas to a favoring breeze. After her first summer the "Clermont" was enlarged and improved, and she was soon joined by other steam vessels built for the Fulton & Livingston line, which had secured the exclusive privilege of navigating the waters of New York State by steam, — a reward that was no more than just to the brave inventor and his loyal and generous patron.

After the "Clermont," the most celebrated of the early steam craft was the "Chancellor Livingston," built in 1816, of oak, cedar, and locust, by the accomplished naval architect, Henry Eckford. It is significant that this time it was not necessary to send overseas for the steam machinery. The "Chancellor Livingston's" boiler and engine were both constructed in New York by James P. Allaire. The engine had a 44-inch cylinder with a five-foot stroke, developing a horse-power of 65. The hull of this really notable vessel was 157 feet long, 33 feet wide, and 10 feet deep, and her tonnage was 496, at a time when there were few merchantmen of more than 300. For several years the "Chancellor Livingston" ran on the Hudson from New York to Albany. Then, in 1826, she was given a new engine of 120 horse-power and new boilers, and transferred to a longer and more exposed route, on Long Island Sound and Narragansett Bay, from New York to Providence. In 1832 this fine old steamer was transferred again to a still rougher and more perilous service, the stormy "outside route" along the rugged northern shore, from Boston to Portland.

The "Chancellor Livingston" in her final form was essentially a seagoing steamship, with the wide guards of the river-boats, but a strong and fairly deep oak hull, three smokestacks, and the spars and sails of a three-masted schooner. Her long career shows how steam navigation was rapidly extending from point to point on the American seaboard. A steam line had been started

from Boston to the Kennebec River in 1823. Good,
strong side-wheelers of an ocean model were soon running
in the passenger and cargo traffic between New York and
the chief seaports of the Southern States. Eventually this
steam service was extended as far as New Orleans. In
1823, when the steam merchant fleet of the United States
was first enumerated, it had a total tonnage of 24,879.
From 1825 onward, it grew very rapidly as steam craft
made their way up and down the coast, and began to appear
upon the Great Lakes and western rivers. In 1833 the
domestic steam tonnage had advanced to 101,306, and by
1840 it had almost doubled, reaching 198,184. At that
time the American steamships registered for foreign commerce had a tonnage of only 4,155, — presumably coastwise
liners that occasionally visited West Indian ports.

The speed of these early coastwise steamers was like
that of the fabled tortoise. Thus the "Clermont" on
her first trip to Albany made only five miles an hour; and
great was the wonder and rejoicing when, in 1817, the
"Chancellor Livingston" ran from Albany to New York
in eighteen hours, — a distance now covered regularly
in ten. The first iron seagoing steamer of the United
States — the "Bangor," built in 1844, at Wilmington,
Del., by the still active house of Harlan & Hollingsworth
— is said to have attained a speed of fifteen miles an
hour on her trial trip, but that was far above her regular achievement on the route from Bangor to Boston.
The average speed of commercial steamers previous to
the Civil War was not more than ten miles an hour.
That was, of course, exceeded by the "floating palaces"
that conveyed the large and constant traffic of the Hudson
River and Long Island Sound. On the other hand,
the ordinary steam craft in the 'longshore trade could
not keep up with a smart sailing vessel in a fresh, fair
breeze. As late as 1860 the sail tonnage outnumbered the
steam tonnage of the coast fleet by more than two to one.

The American seaman clung lovingly to his schooner, brig, or bark, and met every advance of the iconoclastic steam engineer by some ingenious improvement of rig or model. The bark of the deep sea was made more adaptable to the coastwise service by the substitution of a fore-and-aft mainmast, and thus became transformed into the distinctively Yankee barkentine, — almost as good as a bark off the wind, and better on any other point of sailing. The full brig underwent a similar metamorphosis, and with a schooner mainmast became the familiar hermaphrodite brig or brigantine. As for the schooner itself, its evolution from 1815 onward to the present time is an astonishing proof of Yankee maritime resourcefulness.

The schooner of the first years of the nineteenth century — the most frequent rig in American waters — ranged in size from twenty to two hundred tons. A one-hundred-and-fifty-ton schooner was reckoned a large one. So skilled and far-seeing a merchant navigator as Captain Richard Cleveland had insisted, in 1806, as told in a previous chapter, that his schooner " Aspasia," of one hundred and seventy tons, was "unwieldy, unsafe, and uncomfortable," and altogether too large for ordinary use. Most of the schooners of above fifty tons — even the small coasters of Maine — then carried a square foretopsail and perhaps a topgallantsail, and were technically topsail schooners. They set their square canvas with a fair breeze, and could furl it and depend on their large fore-and-aft sails alone, when working to windward.

The cotton, sugar, and hard lumber of the South were brought North in sail craft of this kind, and their return voyages bore to Wilmington, Charleston, Savannah, St. Augustine, Pensacola, or New Orleans Northern manufactures, ice or coal. The coal trade from Pennsylvania to New England employed a vast fleet of schooners, brigs, and barks, and as the years went on it was discovered that the thorough-going schooner was altogether best adapted to the service.   By 1860 two-masted fore-and-aft schooners had been built up to 250 or 300 tons.   This proved to be almost the maximum size of which that rig was capable.   Indeed, 300-ton two-masted schooners began to earn alongshore the sinister nickname of "man-killers," — so heavy were their gaffs, booms, anchors, and gear in general.   That was long before the era of steam-hoisting apparatus.   The foresail and mainsail of a 300-ton schooner, especially the latter, were stiff and ponderous fabrics for a small crew to handle, and many a craft of this type, under-manned and overmasted, ran away with her poor "rattled" company in a gale of wind.   Yet the steady increase in the volume of the coasting trade demanded larger and larger vessels, and shrewd owners and skippers saw that a new rig or model must be developed to meet the modern need.

The three-masted schooner was not unknown on either side of the Atlantic in even the first decades of the nineteenth century, but the type was unusual, and the few craft that had been constructed were of the topsail-schooner class.   Three-masted schooners of about one hundred and fifty tons were built in eastern Maine as early as 1835 and 1840.   Commodore Robert B. Forbes, in his "Notes on Ships of the Past," states that the first three-master launched in the Penobscot Valley was the "Aurora," of Ellsworth, built in 1831.   She was of 147 tons' register.   The "Fame," of Ellsworth, built in 1833, of 130 tons, was another three-masted craft, and so was the "Savage," of 179 tons, built in Eden in the same year for Boston owners.   It was many years, however, before the third mast came into general use in the American coastwise fleet.   It was of no especial advantage in vessels of less than 250 tons, but when vessels grew to 300 or 400 tons it became indispensable.   The two-masted schooner reached its climax in the "Oliver Ames," of 456 tons, a sturdy New England collier.   After 1870 three masts became the favorite rig for sailing coasters of 300 tons and upward. The three-master had her necessary canvas subdivided into more sails, which were consequently smaller, lighter, and easier to handle. Her spars were not so heavy as those of a two-master of the same tonnage.

The three-masted schooner, as it was evolved in the American coasting trade from 1870 onward, was a brilliant example of Yankee genius for shaping the means to the end. The character of the coastwise service was such that a fore-and-aft rig was preferable, although barks were often employed on long coast voyages like those from Baltimore or Charleston to New England, and brigs, or rather brigantines, have not yet disappeared. The schooner was much the better vessel for beating up and down a body of water like Long Island Sound, or into or out of bays or harbors. Moreover, the schooner was economical because she cost less for sailmakers', riggers', and ship-chandlers' bills, and could be worked by fewer seamen. In the seventies and eighties the three-masted schooner, with no square canvas except perhaps a brailing foresail, cast her long and graceful shadow upon every mile of open ocean and every port and inlet between Passamaquoddy and the Rio Grande. It was found that an increase in size and thus of carrying capacity in the three-masted schooner involved no corresponding increase in the cost of building or of maintenance. The larger the vessel, the smaller was the price per ton for which she could afford to carry a cargo. Freight rates on coal, ice, lumber, and other merchandise that sought sea transportation fell lower and lower with the enlarged tonnage of the coastwise carriers. Three-masted schooners grew to 500, to 600 and even to 700 tons, culminating in the "Bradford C. French," of 968 tons, a veritable giant of the tri-pyramid fleet.

These three-masters, like the two-masters before them, were built of wood in the shipyards of Maine, Massachusetts, Connecticut, New York, New Jersey, Pennsylvania, or Virginia. Their frames were, as a rule, of oak, and their planking and ceiling of hard Southern pine. If they were well constructed and well cared for, and "salted," such vessels were very durable. Many of them are still in active service after twenty-five or thirty years. They were handsome models, most of them, with good wholesome beam, a smart Yankee sheer, well-proportioned spars, long, square mastheads, and neatly cut canvas that could not be wholly spoiled by the grime of many cargoes.

There was a minimum of work and danger aloft on these really admirable vessels. The foresail, mainsail, and spanker, the largest and heaviest sails, lowered on the booms, and could quickly and safely be reefed or furled there. The gaff topsails, or main and mizzen topmast staysails if they were carried, were hauled down and snugly stowed against the mastheads. This handling of the light canvas on the dizzy footing of the crosstrees did involve much exposure and peril in a heavy sea and wind, but the topsails were generally got out of the way, and the vessel brought down to lower sail only before the weather became severe. At the same time the outer head sails would be furled on the jib-boom, and the good Yankee schooner was now in fine trim to meet the storm king. Her gear could be handled surely and smartly from the solid deck.

It must not be thought that, though the coasting trade lacked something of the romance of voyages to strange lands and distant seas, it bred a race of weaklings. On the contrary, this great American coast trade, especially in winter, is crowded with perils and hardships that test the utmost fibre of manly fortitude. Though the shoreline of the United States from Hatteras northward is generously lighted and buoyed, it is feared by mariners the world over. In the north of Europe, with a climate corresponding to our own, navigation is almost entirely suspended in the inclement season of the year, and this was once done on our own seaboard. Now the heaviest and most important coast traffic goes steadily on beneath the frozen gales of February as well as in the zephyrs of July. The older and feebler craft may be laid up in port from December to March, but most of the coast vessels, steam or sail, know no rest save that required to make good the wear and tear of an arduous service.

The United States has a coast-line of 5,000 miles on the two great oceans and the Gulf of Mexico. The American coast trade east or west is a trade of magnificent distances. From Boston to New York by sea — one of the shortest of coastwise routes — is 300 miles, or a little less than the voyage from Hull to Hamburg. From Boston to Philadelphia is 477 miles, or rather more than the distance from Plymouth in Old England to Bordeaux. It is 515 miles from Boston to Newport News, while it is 530 from Plymouth across the Bay of Biscay to Corunna in Spain. A Yankee coaster sailing from New York covers 629 miles before she passes in over the bar of Charleston, while the deep-sea or "foreign" voyage of a British freighter from Sunderland to Copenhagen is only 586 miles. From Portland to Savannah the most direct sea route is 971 miles, while from Plymouth to Lisbon is only 755 miles. A four or five masted schooner with coal from Philadelphia for Key West traverses 1,093 miles, while a British "tramp" would steam but 1,053 miles from Shields to Riga on the Baltic. From Portland to Key West the distance is 1,400 miles, or more than the 1,383 from London to Kronstadt in Russia. A Morgan or Cromwell liner from New York to New Orleans rolls off 1,740 miles, and could have gone from Glasgow to Algiers. The longest voyage in all our Atlantic coast trade is from Calais, Maine, to Point Isabel, Texas, — 2,597 miles. It is 2,219 miles from London to Genoa, and 2,455 from Cardiff to Greece. Moreover, there are the four and five month coastwise voyages of Yankee clippers around Cape Horn, — 13,610 miles from

New York to San Francisco and 15,000 from Boston to Puget Sound. This noble traffic employs a large fleet of wood and steel sailing ships and barks, from 1,400 to 3,500 tons, —noble vessels, swift and strong, that splendidly maintain the traditions of Yankee square-rig seamanship.

The modern coasting vessel of the United States is not a scow or a hulk ill rigged, ill manned, shaky, and leaky, crawling from port to port when the wind serves and the sea is quiet. It is a thorough seagoing schooner, of two masts, three, four, five, six, and soon to be seven, able to look a gale right in the eye and to take whatever comes without flinching. American coasters of all types and sizes are loftily sparred beyond the cautious European practice, and, as a rule, are very deeply laden. Yet their models are so wholesome, and they are so resolutely handled by their few but good officers and men, that their work is done with no very high rate of disaster. Collision and stranding are the two causes that account for most of the catastrophes, and some loss of this kind is inevitable in crowded waters or on courses that lie near the land.

This coasting service demands a versatile order of seamanship. A great stately collier, coming out of Hampton Roads for New England, steers from Cape Charles to Montauk across the open sea, cutting the perilous "steamer lanes " of the European liners. From Montauk up through narrow Vineyard Sound and over the treacherous shoals south of Cape Cod, the great vessel is in constant danger of taking ground through baffling winds or labyrinthian currents. Fog or snow shut out landmarks and seamarks, and the coasting captain has literally to feel his way by a faculty half instinct, half experience.

The long, fierce northwesters of winter, following on the heels of icy northeast gales, and blowing day after day with tigerish fury, are another terrible foe of the coast fleet of the Atlantic. It often happens that sailing vessels caught in these blizzards are driven, broken-winged, with crews frozen and exhausted, as far down as Bermuda, seven hundred miles, or even St. Thomas, fourteen hundred miles, from New York, and there have to be thoroughly refitted with sails and gear before they can reach their destination.

A square-rigger inward bound from India or China, after many weeks of speeding in the trade winds over warm and kindly seas, approaches the American coast in winter very much as a captive prepares to run the cruel line of an Indian gauntlet. Light spars are sent down, the newest and strongest sails bent, and all the gear critically examined. As the ship nears the latitude of Bermuda, officers and men nerve themselves for the real battle of the voyage. Sometimes it happens that when they have fought their way up to the very mouth of the harbor, and the Scotland Lightship or Minot's is close aboard, and a stout tug ahead with a towline, the northwester bursts upon them with almost the weight of a cyclone, the cable snaps like thread, and the tall ship goes whirling seaward to struggle on to the coast again perhaps two weeks hence, an ice-clad ghost, with all hands congealed, and starving cases for the marine hospital.

Yet this conflict with cold and tempest which strangers find so terrible is the familiar atmosphere in which the North Atlantic coast trade is conducted. The larger part of this traffic is from Hampton Roads northward, and therefore in weather that is very rigorous during half the year. It is a fine school of seamanlike skill and endurance; and though an increasing proportion of this traffic is carried by steamers, it has produced of late years the most remarkable sailing vessels in the world.

When the three-masted schooner reached six or seven hundred tons, it became in turn as heavy and unmanageable as the two-master at three or four hundred. The masts, gaffs, and booms of a seven or eight hundred tonner

24

were gigantic. These schooners were now equipped with steam-engines to hoist sails and anchors, which saved much labor and enabled a first-class three-master to go to sea with no more than four or five men in her forecastle. In the early eighties, far-seeing builders and owners began to experiment with schooners of four masts. The "Francis C. Yarnall" of 495 tons was launched at Wilmington, in 1881. She was none too large for a three-master, but the "Elliott B. Church," built at Taunton in 1882, was of 1,000 tons and genuine four-mast proportions. The first four-masters were looked at askance by old "shell-back" mariners. Some of them did come to grief because their hulls had been given added length without the added stiffening of frame which that length made necessary. However, the builders quickly learned the value of iron straps and braces and heavy keelsons, and the great wooden schooners of four masts and of 800 to 1,500 tons proved to be fit for any work and any weather. The splendid four-master "Haroldine," of 1,361 tons, built at Weymouth in 1884, carried the flag to China and Australia, and filled distant ports with wonder at this latest and strangest of Yankee maritime notions.

From the four-master to the five-master was not a difficult step. Indeed, such a rig was already in use on the Great Lakes when the first of ocean five-masted schooners, the "Governor Ames," named after the Chief Executive of Massachusetts, was launched at Waldoboro. On her first voyage the "Governor Ames" was dismasted off Cape Cod because of a defect in her rigging, but her owners, nothing daunted, gave her five new spars at Boston, and sent her out lumber laden to South America. Subsequently this great schooner of 1,778 tons went around Cape Horn to San Francisco, and was successfully employed in Pacific commerce. Then she returned to the work for which she was designed, — the trade between the Southern coal ports and New England.

For eight or nine years the "Governor Ames" was the only five-masted fore-and-aft vessel afloat. Four masts seemed to Yankee builders to be sufficient for a safe and handy division of a great schooner's spars and canvas, even when the size of the vessel was carried up far above the 1,778 tons of the "Governor Ames" to the 2,014 of the "Frank A. Palmer." In 1898 Maine yards launched the five-masters "John B. Prescott" and "Nathaniel T. Palmer," of 2,454 and 2,440 tons. In 1900 there came, also from Maine yards, the first of the six-masted schooners, the "Eleanor A. Percy," of Bath, 3,401 tons gross, and the "George W. Wells," of Boston, 2,970 tons. By a strange twist of fate these two gigantic schooners, the only six-masted sailing ships afloat, crashed together in collision off Cape Cod one summer night in 1901. Fortunately, the "Wells," whose side was terribly gashed in the encounter, was "light," having just discharged her huge coal cargo of almost 5,000 tons, and the deeply laden "Percy" escaped with the loss of her headgear.

These long, powerful schooners, with their range of masts a hundred and seventy feet tall and the vast sweep of their fore-and-aft canvas, are capable of genuine steamer speed in strong, fair winds. Thus the "Wells" on her maiden voyage, with coal from Philadelphia to Havana, made the run of more than a thousand miles from the Delaware Breakwater to the Morro in six days. Returning, the "Wells" loaded an immense cargo of railroad ties at Brunswick, Georgia, and four days after sailing she stood in by Sandy Hook.

The greatest schooner of all, and one of the most extraordinary vessels ever planned, is a seven-master of steel, constructed in the winter of 1901–1902 by the Fore River Ship & Engine Company on the Quincy shore of Boston Harbor, from designs by B. B. Crowninshield for Captain J. G. Crowley, a celebrated owner and manager in the coastwise service. This Fore River yard is in many ways the most interesting in America. Its great workshops stand in what a year and a half ago was an open field on the edge of the old town of Quincy. The new yard is the swift outgrowth of a modest concern that used to build steam yachts a couple of miles up the Fore River, and built them so well that it secured Navy Department contracts for the torpedo-boat destroyers "Lawrence" and "Macdonough," and the cruiser "Des Moines." The cruiser, of 3,200 tons, compelled a removal further down the river to deep water and a wide bay, and there, when the "Des Moines" was nearing completion, were laid the ponderous keels of two first-class 15,000-ton battleships, — "Rhode Island" and "New Jersey." For the company which had shown itself faithful in a few small things was now intrusted with great responsibilities. Here alongside the battleships, and stretching almost as far as they, the huge and yet graceful hull of the world's first seven-masted schooner and second largest sailing vessel was constructed.

Twenty-one years before, the famous Cramp yard at Philadelphia had launched an iron coasting schooner of three masts and 365 tons, the "Josephine." But the cost of this craft so far exceeded the price of wooden vessels of the same tonnage that oak and hard pine continued for two decades thereafter to be preferred for the sailing coaster-trade to steel and iron.

It is the perfect modern equipment of the Fore River Ship & Engine Company which has made it possible to produce an economical cargo-carrier of entire steel construction. This new yard possesses a mechanical plant of the highest order. It is said to be the only shipyard in the country which does all of its own heavy forging, and its machine shops are capable of fabricating the engines of either a steam-cutter or a ship-of-the-line. Its bending rolls, its travelling cranes, and other labor-saving appliances, and its electrical plant for the development and transmission of power, are a revelation to foreign visitors of the intensified competition that must be expected now that the mechanical genius of America has turned resolutely to the building of modern steel ships.

This steel schooner, which is undoubtedly the forerunner of a new fleet of sail-freighters under the American flag, is 368 feet long on the water-line, 50 feet wide and 34 feet deep, with a draught, fully laden, of 26 feet, and a gross tonnage of 5,200. It is expected that the steel schooner will carry 7,000 or 8,000 tons of coal, as compared with the 5,000 of the six-masted wooden schooners "Wells" and "Percy." But though she will convey two or three thousand more tons of cargo, she will require only two more men than the six-masters, or sixteen in all. A square-rigged ship 368 feet long would have a crew of forty. The seven lower masts of the giant schooner and the bowsprit are steel tubes; the masts are 135 feet long, and the wooden topmasts, 60 feet. These seven spars will carry the enormous area of 43,000 square feet of canvas. Like steel steamers, the steel schooner has a double bottom, so that there is practically one hull within another, — a valuable expedient that has saved the life of many a noble ship. This double steel bottom can receive 1,200 tons of water ballast that is readily pumped out when it is no longer needed. As the great schooners in the coal trade usually carry a cargo only one way, this water ballast that costs nothing to procure is an important consideration.

The steam tonnage of the United States coasting fleet now exceeds the sailing tonnage by about twenty per cent.[1] This enumeration includes, however, not only tugs, excursion steamers, and other harbor craft, but the steam freighters of the Great Lakes which heavily predominate in that fresh-water navigation. On the seaboard, the sailing vessels are still in the majority, and it

[1] Steam tonnage, 2,462,084; sail, 2,070,411. **Report of United States Commissioner of Navigation for 1901.**

will be long before they disappear or before their tonnage
seriously diminishes.   The experiment of towing barges
up and down the coast, after the Great Lakes example,
has not proved altogether successful.   A few years ago it
seemed probable that barges towed in a line of three or
four by a powerful ocean tugboat would put an end to
schooner-building, but they have not done so.   The large
four, five, and six masters have managed to hold their
own, and something more.   Meanwhile the dismantled
ships and barks of deep-sea commerce have been slipping rapidly to their last rest in the graveyard of the
ocean, whither an appalling number have plunged with
all on board.   The new barge of heavy wood or steel,
especially designed and built for the service, is the only
vessel with no motive-power of its own that ought to be
exposed to the winter gales and seas of the North Atlantic
—and even then it is and always will be an extra-hazard-
ous undertaking.

With very few exceptions the steamers of the Atlantic
and Pacific coast run in regular lines, and the majority of
them carry passengers as well as cargo, though the freight
steamers of an economical type are undoubtedly increasing.   There are not many coastwise steamers of the "tramp"
class that go here, there, and everywhere as the demands of
trade may call them.   Nearly all of this general business
is done by sailing vessels.   The distinctive cargo steamships of the coast are engaged, as a rule, in the coal and
lumber traffic, and are often owned by the companies which
furnish their freights.   The Standard Oil corporation has
its own fleet of tank steamers and barges to deliver its product to its chief coastwise markets, just as it has its own
fleet of steamers and sailing vessels for its European and
Asiatic export trade.   Other steamers and barges are owned
by the railroad or coal-mining corporations of New York,
New Jersey, Pennsylvania, Maryland, and Virginia.   Yet
the great bulk of the American coastwise tonnage is con-

trolled by individuals or corporations that are distinctly
shipowners and give their chief thought to their ships,
not employing them as a mere adjunct to other business.

The most valuable section of the steam coastwise fleet is
composed of the combination cargo and passenger liners,
running between Boston, New York, and Philadelphia,
or out of these great ports to the southward, and on the
Pacific, from San Francisco to Puget Sound and Alaska.
The ships of this dignified service are nearly all screw-
propellers, and nearly all of iron or steel. They are almost
as characteristically American as the fine great schooners.
These coastwise lines are arranged in natural groups.
One connects Boston with Portland, the Kennebec and
Bath, the Penobscot and Bangor, and Eastport and St.
John. The next connects Portland and Boston with
New York, and Boston with Philadelphia, Baltimore,
Norfolk, Charleston, Savannah, and Jacksonville. The
celebrated passenger and freight steamboats of Long
Island Sound form a luxurious group by themselves,
quite distinct from anything else upon the surface of
the waters.

New York is the chief centre of the network of steam
coastwise communication. It has admirable lines to all
the Atlantic coast ports southward, and also to New
Orleans and Galveston. Philadelphia and Baltimore in
their turn are knit to the South by regular lines of
steamers. On the Pacific San Francisco has the same
kind of steam service north and south with ships of the
same excellent quality, many of them built in the new
steel shipyards that have sprung up on the Western seaboard under the influence of a generous policy of naval
construction. The great schooner is also conspicuous in
our Pacific commerce. It is usually a wooden vessel, and
it sometimes differs from the Atlantic fleet in possessing
auxiliary steam-power, of great value in Pacific calms or
for entering or leaving harbor.

The Union Iron Works at San Francisco, which launched the "Olympia" and "Oregon," is one of the great shipyards of the United States, and the national government has recognized the maritime possibilities of Puget Sound by establishing a naval station and dry dock at Bremerton in Washington. The trade and shipping of the Puget Sound ports have received a powerful impetus from the Alaska and Yukon gold discoveries. Most of the passenger and freight trade that has been developed is American coastwise traffic, and is thus reserved by Federal statute to American ships and American seamen.

An Act of Congress providing a government for the territory of Hawaii, which went into effect on June 14, 1900, admitted Hawaiian vessels to American registry, and restricted to American vessels the trade between the islands and the United States. The Act of Congress providing a civil government for Porto Rico, which went into effect on May 1, 1900, accomplished the same results. This inclusion of Hawaii and Porto Rico in the great coasting trade of the United States has benefited American shipping, without injury, but with actual gain to insular commerce. The Commissioner of Navigation declared in his report for 1900 that "the new steamships already ordered for the Hawaiian trade will more than offset the foreign tonnage which has been withdrawn," and as to Porto Rico, "the restriction of this trade to American vessels has caused no inconvenience, but, on the contrary, has led to a marked improvement in the transportation facilities of the island by steamships."

The American-Hawaiian Steamship Company, when the annexation of Hawaii was seen to be inevitable, established an important steam service in new American-built vessels from New York to San Francisco and Honolulu. Its first steamers, the "Californian," "Hawaiian," "Oregonian," and "American," were fine, powerful vessels of 5,600 tons, and the "Arizonian" and "Alaskan" of 8,500 tons, among the largest ships in the Pacific Ocean, have since been added to the service. American steam lines carrying passengers and cargo were promptly organized between Porto Rico and New York and Boston. Two of the steel steamships especially constructed for this trade were the "Ponce" and "San Juan," of 3,500 tons. American sailing vessels also bear their share in the carrying of Hawaiian and Porto Rican commerce.

The coasting laws of the United States apply inevitably not only to the Great Lakes, whose immense merchant shipping is considered in a separate chapter, but to the steam and barge traffic of the inland rivers. No foreign vessel is permitted to trade above New Orleans, and the Mississippi, the Ohio, the Missouri, and their tributaries bear a tonnage which, like the coast fleet, is all American. This water commerce has, on the whole, held its own against even the vast, spreading network of the railways. Three hundred and eleven vessels of 22,888 tons are noted by the Bureau of Navigation as having been built in 1901 on the Mississippi and its connecting rivers, and this is by no means a full record, for certain mastless craft are not included. The steam fleet employed on the western rivers on June 30, 1901, consisted of 927 vessels of 164,548 tons. On that same date there were in service on the Atlantic coast 2,328 steamers of 879,338 tons; on the Pacific coast (excepting Hawaii), 493 steamers of 176,744 tons; on the Great Lakes, 1,768 steamers of 1,231,879 tons. The total enrolled or coastwise tonnage, steam and sail, on the Atlantic coast was 16,744 vessels of 2,849,342 tons; on the Pacific coast (excepting Hawaii), 2,387 vessels of 676,682 tons; on the Great Lakes, 3,253 vessels of 1,706,294 tons; on the Western rivers, 1,584 vessels of 249,454 tons.

The old "Clermont" and "Chancellor Livingston" have now grown in the steam coast fleet to steel monsters of several thousand tons. The Fall River liner "Priscilla," queen of Long Island Sound, has a length of over 400 feet and a gross tonnage of 5,290. The service between Boston and Portland, all "outside," in deep water and along a shore rockbound and peculiarly dangerous, where the "Chancellor Livingston," of 496 tons, used to run, is now performed in part by the majestic steel-built "Governor Dingley," of 3,836 tons and a speed of 16 knots, — a noble steamer worthy to bear the name of one of the strongest and wisest champions of American shipping. The new Morgan liners, "El Cid," "El Norte," "El Rio," and "El Sud," built for the Southern Pacific service from New York to New Orleans, to replace the four merchant cruisers of the Spanish War, are of 4,600 tons and a speed of $15\frac{1}{2}$ knots. The "Kansas City" of the New York-Savannah line is of 3,600 tons and 16 knots.

If none of our American coastwise steamships, save the Long Island Sound and Hudson River boats, are of the very highest speed — of 18 knots and over — very few of the modern liners fall below 12 knots, a rate which is still far ahead of the attainment of the great majority of the world's steam merchantmen. Moreover, in the quality of their construction, their durability, their safety, and their efficiency and economy of operation, the ocean-going coast steamships of the United States are of an admirable class, far superior to the coasting fleet of any other nation. They bear in their solid and yet symmetrical appearance the unmistakable impress of their nationality. They are, as a rule, not so long and narrow-waisted as European steamships. They have the wholesome beam on which American naval architects have always insisted. Their boilers and engines are designed to give them a moderate speed, with reserve power enough to maintain a steady pace in all winds or weathers. The coast railroads convey the mails, and such greyhounds as those of the transatlantic fleet are not necessary in the coastwise service, nor would they be profitable. However, the average speed of the coast ships exceeds that of all but the great mail liners especially subsidized by government.

Our vast American coastwise shipping, steam and sail, represents the outcome of more than a century of strenuous competition of American shipowners and builders among themselves, without foreign interference. National protection in this case has been actually prohibitive. The opening of this domestic traffic to alien ships has never been seriously considered. American shipping interests have held this coasting trade as an unshaken monopoly. It is a most significant fact that as between the coast fleet of the United States which has never felt foreign competition, and the deep-sea fleet which has to meet such competition everywhere, the former is not only the more prosperous, but the more modern and progressive.

The deep-sea tonnage of the United States has been subject to sharp fluctuations, but the coastwise tonnage has increased with extraordinary steadiness from the year 1789 to 1901. This coastwise trade is a perfectly normal industry, representing an enormous volume of business carried on with great energy and prudence, and returning a good but not an excessive rate of profit. As it stands to-day, there is no safer or more inviting investment than this immense modern fleet of steam and sailing vessels in the coastwise service of the Atlantic and Pacific oceans and the Gulf of Mexico. It is a splendid vindication of the firm and sagacious statesmanship which has reserved this distinctively American trade for our own flag and our own sailor-citizens.

Following is the statistical record, from the Bureau of Navigation, of the growth of the enrolled tonnage of the United States engaged in coastwise commerce from 1789 to the present: —

TONNAGE OF COASTWISE SHIPPING. 1789-1901.

Year.	Tonnage.	Year.	Tonnage.	Year.	Tonnage.
1789	68,607	1827	732,938	1865	3,353,657
1790	103,775	1828	787,226	1866	2,689,152
1791	106,494	1829	490,468	1867	2,627,151
1792	120,957	1830	496,640	1868	2,658,404
1793	114,853	1831	516,086	1869	2,470,928
1794	145,601	1832	624,159	1870	2,595,328
1795	164,796	1833	717,423	1871	2,722,372
1796	195,424	1834	755,463	1872	2,883,906
1797	214,077	1835	769,795	1873	3,116,373
1798	227,344	1836	846,116	1874	3,243,656
1799	220,904	1837	927,250	1875	3,169,687
1800	245,295	1838	1,008,146	1876	2,547,490
1801	246,255	1839	1,120,311	1877	2,488,189
1802	260,543	1840	1,144,664	1878	2,444,801
1803	268,676	1841	1,076,036	1879	2,545,059
1804	286,840	1842	1,018,253	1880	2,584,418
1805	301,366	1843	1,048,209	1881	2,590,836
1806	309,977	1844	1,078,868	1882	2,740,206
1807	318,190	1845	1,190,898	1883	2,774,248
1808	387,684	1846	1,289,871	1884	2,813,919
1809	371,501	1847	1,452,623	1885	2,822,598
1810	371,114	1848	1,620,988	1886	2,865,317
1811	386,259	1849	1,731,411	1887	2,935,527
1812	443,181	1850	1,755,797	1888	3,096,212
1813	433,405	1851	1,854,318	1889	3,133,812
1814	425,714	1852	2,008,022	1890	3,330,377
1815	435,067	1853	2,082,782	1891	3,529,315
1816	479,979	1854	2,273,900	1892	3,617,700
1817	481,458	1855	2,491,108	1893	3,770,096
1818	503,140	1856	2,211,935	1894	3,611,723
1819	523,556	1857	2,300,399	1895	3,644,276
1820	539,080	1858	2,361,596	1896	3,702,393
1821	559,436	1859	2,439,320	1897	3,808,433
1822	573,080	1860	2,599,319	1898	3,873,594
1823	566,409	1861	2,657,293	1899	3,878,397
1824	589,223	1862	2,578,546	1900	4,195,875
1825	587,273	1863	2,918,614	1901	4,488,421
1826	666,420	1864	3,204,227		

CHAPTER XVI.

NEARING LOW-WATER MARK. 1876-90.

Gloomy Outlook of the Centennial Year in Deep-Sea Shipping —
The Great California Grain Trade — American Sailing Ships Swiftest, Safest, and Most Efficient — Lloyd's Discrimination drives
them from the Ocean — Building at a Standstill — The Brazil
Mail Line — High-Class American Iron Steamers — Why our
Steam Tonnage did not Increase — Four-Fifths of Our Mail Pay
given to Foreigners — Sharp Contrast between Britain's Policy
and Our Own — Beginning of Steel Navy a Bright Omen for Merchant Marine — Steadily Dwindling Tonnage.

STILL another period of unbroken, melancholy decline in
the deep-sea shipping of the United States followed 1875.
The centennial year 1876, with all its rejoicing over a
century of national independence, found nearly three-
fourths of our commerce dependent upon foreign, chiefly
British, carriers for the means of reaching its destined port.
The proportion of American imports and exports conveyed
in American vessels in 1876 was only 27.7 per cent, a share
as feeble as that of the worst years of the Civil War.
In the fifteen years from 1876 to 1890, inclusive, this
American proportion fell to only 12.8 per cent, and one-
third of the 1,553,705 tons of American shipping registered
for foreign commerce disappeared. In 1890 our merchant
tonnage, steam and sail together, had shrunk to 928,062,
or a total actually less than the 981,019 of 1810.

These fifteen years are a period of unredeemed gloom
in our country's maritime history. Until 1883 the war
navy of the United States was as neglected as the merchant navy. There was no lack of commerce for our ships

to carry, for the aggregate imports and exports increased between 1876 and 1890 from $1,001,125,861 to $1,647,-139,093, a gain of about 60 per cent. The only beneficial shipping legislation of this entire period was an unimportant Act of June 16, 1884, permitting supplies for merchant vessels to be withdrawn free of duty from bonded warehouses, and a more important section of the McKinley tariff law of Oct. 6, 1890, allowing the free importation of plates, beams, angles, etc., for iron and steel vessels for the foreign trade. Thus, since 1890, American shipbuilding for deep-sea commerce has had the advantage of all the virtue which there may be in " free materials." Neither of these measures has had any appreciable effect in checking the decline of American deep-sea tonnage.

Only two thoroughly American lines of deep-sea steamers came into existence in all these fifteen years. One was the " Red D " line from New York to Venezuela. It was the outgrowth of a line of sailing packets. At first German steamers were employed; then three excellent iron steamers of moderate speed and tonnage were built in the United States. Through close management and the happy fact that it did not have too much direct foreign competition, the "Red D" service has lived and prospered. Since 1893, when the United States & Brazil Mail Company succumbed, the " Red D " has been the only regular American steam line running to South America beyond the Isthmus of Panama.

Another American company, the Ward line, began in 1877, with American-built iron steamships, a service to Cuba that was subsequently extended to Mexico. The Ward line absorbed the Alexandre line, an older American enterprise, so that there was not so much an addition to, as a change of name in, the American steam service to the West Indies. The Ward steamers carried both passengers and cargo, and as the foreign ships in the West India trade were chiefly of an inferior type, freight "tramps," pure and simple, the American company managed to secure a moderately profitable business.

Although the building and use of steamships increased steadily on both sides of the ocean, the sailing ship *par excellence*, the great square-rigger, did not disappear, nor has it yet disappeared, from the longer routes of commerce. The development of the Pacific coast of the United States, after the completion of the first transcontinental railroad, opened a new traffic for the noble, white-winged three-masters. The grain of the Pacific slope could not bear the railway charge to the East, but it could bear the ocean rate around Cape Horn. To San Francisco and Portland now flocked the largest and best sailing vessels of all the maritime nations of the world. Grain was a treacherous cargo, liable to shift to one side, if loaded in bulk, and always imposing a severe strain on the hull that conveyed it. Only the strongest and most powerful ships and the boldest and most experienced seamen were fit for the fourteen-thousand-mile voyage around the stormy Cape.

It was a contest of truly Olympian dignity, — of the best ships of many flags with each other and with the elements. Out through the Golden Gate there rode every year in the later seventies and the eighties, southward bound, the long, lean iron models of Liverpool and Glasgow, the broader-waisted, wooden New Englanders, with their fine Yankee sheer and tall, gleaming skysails, the sturdy, careful Norwegian and German ships, often launched on the Penobscot or Kennebec, and here and there a graceful Frenchman or Italian. The British were the most numerous, because the total tonnage of their merchant marine was by far the greatest. Next came the Americans. The other flags looked small by comparison. In this splendid grain trade there sailed from San Francisco for Europe in 1881–85, 761 British iron ships and 418 American wooden ships. The Americans were the largest vessels. Their average registered tonnage was 1,634, and of the fourteen ships above

2,000 tons that sailed in 1880–81, twelve flew the stars and stripes. The average tonnage of the British iron ships was 1,356.

The wooden yards of Maine had seen their opportunity and built in quick succession many great ships and barks of from 1,400 to 2,400 tons, very strongly constructed on models happily combining carrying capacity with speed, loftily sparred, and clothed with the symmetrical, snow-white canvas for which Yankee sailmakers were famous the world around. These new vessels were not strictly clippers, though they were often called so. They were really medium clippers; that is, they were less racer-like and more capacious than the celebrated greyhounds of the decade before the Civil War. They could not compete with steam; their owners knew it. But they were launched in confident hope that they were adapted for the grain trade and for some other forms of long-voyage, bulky carrying, and that they could find a profitable occupation during their lifetime of fifteen or twenty years. They were just as fine ships in their way as the extreme clippers, and in all but speed they were more efficient. They were framed with oak, and ceiled and planked with the hard pine of the South. They were generously supplied with all the new, approved devices in rig and equipment.

The double topsail, that labor-saving and life-saving invention of Captain Howes of Massachusetts, had come into general use long before this period. Now the same principle of division, with one yard fixed and one hoisting above it, was applied to the topgallantsails of many of our largest American ships, lessening still further the work and the risk of deep-sea crews, and leaving these new leviathans with no large and heavy sails above the courses. Thus great vessels of sixteen hundred tons and upward could be handled with half as many men as had crowded the fore-castles of the Yankee clippers of twenty years before. Reefing topsails, the most difficult and dangerous of the seaman's duties aloft, because it is generally performed in rough seas and boisterous weather, was now reduced to a minimum. The sailors of all nations owe an everlasting debt of gratitude to the memory of the Yankee master who found a way to bring the vast thrashing area of the most valuable sail of a square-rigger within reasonable human control.

It was very soon found that the blue pennant of victory in this grand ocean-racing from San Francisco down the Pacific and up the Atlantic to the English Channel streamed from the dizzy main trucks of the American merchantmen. Not only did they make the fastest passages, but they met with the fewest accidents and delivered their cargoes of grain in the best condition. For a brief time it looked as if the departed glory of the clipper era might be revived by these modern medium clippers from Bath and Waldoboro and Camden and Thomaston. That, however, was not to be.

Captain William W. Bates, once United States Commissioner of Navigation, was a close observer of the California grain trade from 1882 to 1886. The striking results of his study of the relative performances of American and European vessels in this noblest branch of sail-borne commerce are presented in his admirable work,[1] the "American Marine." Captain Bates found that in this period of several years the American ships, nearly all of them of wood, made their passage around the Horn to Europe in time averaging five days less than that of British iron vessels, that the American ships met with far fewer disasters, and that they landed their grain in better order. These are the gratifying facts that stand out from an elaborate statistical record, too long and complex to be quoted here. It may be added that the few American iron ships seem to have made a slightly better showing than the American wooden ships,

---

[1] Published by Houghton, Mifflin & Company, Boston, 1893.

though the small number of the iron craft precluded a fair comparison.

The powerful British protective agency of Lloyd's, which had already interposed to save the British ship from the competition of our safer and more effective carriers, now stepped to the front again with a discriminating insurance rate against American grain vessels. Captain Bates explains at length how it was done. Most of the marine insurance houses in California were British concerns. Most of the grain cargoes were consigned to British merchants. It was an easy thing, therefore, as Captain Bates shows, for Lloyd's to enforce against American ships seeking charters any rates it saw fit to demand. Soon our American ships found that instead of commanding higher freights, as they used to do and should now have done, on the basis of their safer and superior performance, they were compelled by Lloyd's hostile ruling to accept freights below those of the meanest of their foreign competitors.

These American ships were the most expensively manned. Their officers and sailors, who received the highest wages, were undoubtedly the most skilful and reliable mariners that steered out of the Golden Gate. They should have won the best returns for their employers. But the British insurance monopoly drove these brave and capable American seamen ashore or into the coasting traffic. In the period from 1881 to 1885 an average fleet of one hundred American ships had sailed from San Francisco in the grain trade to Europe. In the year 1889 only thirty American ships sailed in this trade, as compared with 167 British. These American ships, because of Lloyd's discrimination, received 15 per cent lower freight rates than foreign ships, although the American vessels made their passages to their destination in Europe in an average of 113 days, as compared with the 131 of their favored British rivals.

Of course this warfare on American shipowning produced an immediate effect upon American shipbuilding. In 1881 the yards of this country had launched twenty-nine ships and barks for deep-sea carrying, the largest and most important of them for this California grain trade. In 1882 our yards launched thirty-one ships and barks; in 1883, thirty-three. But in 1884 our new ships and barks fell off to twenty-four; in 1885, to eleven; in 1886, to eight; in, 1887 to seven; in 1888, to four; in 1889, to one.

Driven out of the California grain trade, the great American square-riggers of wood and iron took refuge in the coastwise trade between the Atlantic and Pacific ports, which is reserved by an old law to American vessels. There was a steady business in transporting assorted cargoes or coal out to the Pacific coast. Once in a while these vessels on their return would accept a grain cargo at reduced rates to Europe, because a profitable freight from New York to San Francisco was guaranteed. Other square-riggers were laden by the Standard Oil Company with kerosene in cases for the East Indies, where hemp or sugar or China goods could be procured for a homeward voyage to the United States. American ships and barks, which used to have a share of the best carrying trade of Europe, now vanished from the North Sea, the Bay of Biscay, and the Mediterranean. They would probably have been unable to compete in any event with steamers, but their disappearance was forced many years before its time by Lloyd's discrimination.

Meanwhile, the steam iron marine of the United States was only a little less fortunate. There was still only one American line in the transatlantic service, — a small fleet of four iron ships, supported by the Pennsylvania Railroad, and sailing out of Philadelphia for Liverpool. This fleet did not increase. When, in the course of time, the railroad required more vessels, it hired British steamers, more cheaply built and more cheaply manned. But the four American liners remained in the service, winning a high reputation for the safety and regularity of their voyages.

As has been said, all four vessels are still afloat in the Pacific trade, having outlasted nearly all of their low-cost foreign competitors.

The American line to Brazil, for which John Roach had built several excellent 3,500-ton iron steamers, did not survive the expiration of its moderate special subsidy of $150,000 in 1876. This was scant pay for a long-distance mail service, well performed at rates far below those given to the State-aided steamships of Great Britain and France. The "City of New York," the "City of Para," and the "City of Rio de Janeiro" were transferred to the Pacific Mail Company, and the American mail service to Brazil was left to foreign "tramps," slow and haphazard. In 1883 New York merchants, exasperated by the lack of communication with the greatest country of South America, organized a new Brazil line on their own account, and built three iron steamers, the "Finance," "Advance," and "Reliance," of from 2,500 to 3,000 tons, designed for carrying mails, cargoes, and passengers. These steamers touched at several Brazilian ports on their way to and from Rio Janeiro and earned a small mail subsidy from the Brazilian government without which the line could not have lived a year. Even as it was, the enterprise lost $277,000 in the first four years of its operation.[1] When its chief competitor, the Royal Mail West Indies Company, of England, had come out of its first year with a deficit, the British government reduced the required service one-half and permitted the annual subsidy of $1,200,000 to continue. And later, when the service was extended, the subsidy had been increased to $1,350,000. The mail pay which the United States gave to this American line to Brazil from 1883 onward averaged only a few thousand dollars a year, or actually less than it cost the company for the cartage of the mail-bags between post-office and shipboard.

The "Advance" and her sisters were very much superior

[1] Hon. William P. Frye, in the United States Senate, July 3, 1890.

to the ordinary "tramps," as mail and passenger steamers must be, and they were, therefore, very much more expensive. After a gallant struggle the second American line to Brazil succumbed in 1893, and since then it has been quicker and easier for an American merchant doing business in the South to send his letters out *via* England and her generously subsidized mail lines, or to go that way himself if he wishes to interview his correspondents in Rio or Buenos Ayres.

It is impossible for an American citizen to read unmoved the story of the dealings of his government with its small and shrinking fleet of deep-sea steamships in the years onward from 1876 to 1890. In 1876 there were 188 steamships of 198,227 tons registered for foreign commerce; in 1890 there were 233 of 197,630 tons. During this period our deep-sea steam fleet had fallen in 1880 to 132 vessels of 146,604 tons, and it had only slowly and painfully recovered. Very few of these steamers in either 1876 or 1890 were cargo carriers, pure and simple. They were most of them combination ships; that is, they conveyed both freight and passengers. They were adapted to the carriage of the mails, for they were swifter vessels than the average. Nearly all of them were of iron; wood had been almost abandoned for ocean-going steam hulls in American shipyards. Steel was gradually coming into use.

American steamers for the foreign trade were built side by side with American steamers for the coastwise trade, and as the latter class was the more numerous, it naturally affected the characteristics of the former. The steamer which the coastwise trade required was a combination vessel, a passenger and freight ship in one, of from 1,200 to 3,000 tons register, fore-and-aft-rigged, and fitted with moderately powerful engines that could drive the stout iron hull from ten to fourteen knots in ordinary weather. These American steamers of the coastwise or deep-sea fleet were usually broader than foreign steamers of like tonnage, less lean and pinched of waist, but they had the traditional long wedge-like American bow and easy entrance, a smart sheer, and a light and graceful run. They had, as a rule, more freeboard; that is, they stood higher out of water. The passengers on these ships were usually carried on the upper deck of the iron hull, and in the wood or iron cabin-house above it, leaving the lower decks for cargo. This arrangement was eminently sensible, for it gave the passengers a maximum of the light and air so indispensable to comfort on an ocean voyage, especially in Southern latitudes. These steamers were as distinctively American as the packet ships and clippers of an earlier generation. There were no grey-hounds among them, for the traffic would not support high speed without government subventions. On the other hand, they were swifter than all but the largest and best of foreign mail ships, and there was a fine sturdiness and dignity about these American steamers that made the onlooker proud of them, while he wondered why they were so few.

It must not be thought that because the deep-sea steamers of the United States followed closely the coastwise model, they suffered thereby in strength or seaworthiness. There is no more arduous all-the-year-round service in the world than that of the steam lines between New England, New York, and the Southern ports, with their wintry battles with icy northwest and northeast gales, and the constant rounding of dreaded Hatteras.

A steamship southward bound has passed the severest of its perils when it has reached Charleston or Savannah. The voyage to New Orleans or Galveston is longer than one down through the West Indies, and no stancher ship would be required for the route to Rio Janeiro. The coastwise steamships of iron and steel always have been first-class vessels, and the general approximation of our deep-sea steamships to the coastwise type is a distinct advantage. For this has made it easy to transfer Florida liners, for example, to the West Indies and back to the coast, as the exigencies of trade required. When the Brazil line was abandoned in 1893, the "Finance" and "Advance" were utilized in what was virtually the coastwise trade from New York to Colon, in the California traffic *via* the Isthmus of Panama. From this coastwise commerce foreign vessels are debarred, and the fact that American ships could be employed in this protected trade, while foreign ships could not be, is almost the only national encouragement which has been enjoyed by American deepsea steamships in general since the Civil War.

It is an advantage which has just saved three or four American steam lines from extinction, and that is all. From 1876 to 1890 absolutely nothing else was done to protect American steamship owners in the foreign trade by the national government. The Pacific Mail subvention, like the Brazil subvention, was not renewed when the contract expired. Both of these subsidies were examples of unwise special legislation. Just as our tariff policy is justifiable only as it covers many industries, so a policy of marine protectionism must be applied not to two favored lines or three, but to the whole body of our fleet to make it sound, enduring, and effective.

With the lapse of the two injudicious special Brazil and China contracts, United States ocean mail payments to American ships shrank from $750,295 in 1874 to $40,152 in 1878, and to $38,779 in 1880. It was in 1880 that our steam tonnage registered for foreign commerce fell to its lowest ebb. Before 1878 the United States had paid generous sums for ocean mail service to foreign steamship lines, but in 1878 it began the policy which continued to the end of this period in 1890, of paying a great deal more of ocean mail money to foreign than to American ships. Thus, in 1878, while American steamers received $40,152, foreign steamers received $159,827 from our government. In 1880 the figures were relatively $38,779 and $161,030; that is, four-fifths of the mail payments from the United

States Treasury went directly into the pockets of foreign shipowners, nearly all of whom were aided in their successful efforts to drive our flag from the high seas by large subsidies from their home governments. In this year, 1880, Great Britain was paying $3,873,130 to her steamship lines, and was following the rigid practice which she adheres to still, of giving not one letter and not one penny of mail pay to American steamships if it could be prevented.

The one auspicious event for the American merchant marine in the period between 1876 and 1890 was the laying of the keels of the first steel war cruisers of the United States in the Roach shipyard at Chester. At first it may seem that between the building of warships and the building of merchant ships there is very little logical connection, for the two classes of vessels are so widely different one from the other, but, after all, they are products of the same industry, wrought out of the same metal by the same tools. A yard that can create a cruiser or battleship is equipped for any kind of merchant construction, for the building of the warship is always the more difficult, and the government is the most exacting of customers.

Since the " Alert," the " Ranger," and one or two other small iron sloops-of-war were launched in 1875, the Navy Department had done nothing whatever to give to American shipbuilding that powerful encouragement that had been given year after year to British shipyards by the British Admiralty, which procured three-fourths of its immense tonnage from private yards. Steel shipbuilding abroad was still in an experimental stage. In 1879 only six per cent of the new British tonnage was of this material. The early steel cruisers in foreign services had been so unsatisfactory that some of our most progressive officers favored iron. Nevertheless, Congress wisely decided that the three new American cruisers and the despatch boat should be built of steel of domestic manufacture. This was the genesis of our present superb fighting navy: its four pioneer ships, authorized by the Act of March 3, 1883, were the "Chicago," the Boston," the "Atlanta," and the "Dolphin." The contract for them was secured by Mr. Roach, then the largest and most active shipbuilder in the United States.

The " Chicago," " Boston," " Atlanta," and " Dolphin " have now been tried by many years of service, and they have proved themselves to be among the best steel steamships ever built. The " Boston," fourteen years after her launching, helped to win the victory of Manila Bay, where she held the left of the line with the heaviest battery for her tonnage in the squadron. The high quality of these first American steel cruisers shows convincingly that it was not a lack of technical skill, resource, or ambition among American shipbuilders which prevented the growth of the American steam marine. At the very first attempt an American shipyard had produced a steel squadron which ranked with the best that Europe had been able to develop after long years of experiment.

Swifter cruisers followed the " Chicago " and her sisters, and then came the first of our steel battleships. By the year 1890 the impetus given to our steel shipyards by the demands of naval construction began to be manifest in the merchant marine. Some fine steel steamers were built for the coastwise service, and for our few American lines in the foreign trade. Our steam tonnage registered for deep-sea carrying increased 21,000 tons between 1886 and 1890, but at the same time our registered sailing tonnage fell off about one hundred thousand tons.

Here is the record of the total registered tonnage of the United States, the total foreign commerce, and the proportion of this commerce carried by American ships in the fifteen years from 1876 to 1890, inclusive: —

TONNAGE AND FOREIGN TRADE. 1876–90.

| Year. | Shipping Tons. | Total Foreign Commerce. | Proportion carried in American Ships. | | |
			Imports.	Exports.	Combined Imports and Exports.
1876	1,553,705	$1,001,125,861	30.8	25.4	27.7
1877	1,570,600	1,053,798,346	31.5	23.7	26.9
1878	1,589,348	1,131,917,298	32.2	22.6	26.3
1879	1,451,505	1,156,217,216	32.6	17.6	23.0
1880	1,314,402	1,503,593,404	22.0	13.0	17.6
1881	1,297,035	1,545,041,974	19.9	13.3	16.2
1882	1,259,492	1,475,181,831	19.2	12.8	16.0
1883	1,269,681	1,547,020,316	20.7	13.4	17.0
1884	1,276,972	1,408,211,302	22.4	14.4	18.4
1885	1,262,814	1,319,717,084	21.3	13.7	17.0
1886	1,088,041	1,314,960,966	20.0	13.6	16.8
1887	989,412	1,408,502,979	18.6	12.2	15.4
1888	919,302	1,419,911,621	18.5	11.7	15.1
1889	999,619	1,487,533,027	17.0	11.6	14.3
1890	928,062	1,647,139,093	16.6	9.0	12.8

CHAPTER XVII

THE GREAT LAKE FLEET

One-Fourth of our Whole Marine — Protected by Law and Nature —
Early Lake Carriers — Fine Passenger Craft before the War —
Deepening of the Canals, and Wonderful Growth of Lake Steam
Tonnage — Chief Traffic, Iron Ore, Lumber, Grain, and Coal —
Admirable Cargo Steamships — Lake Rigs and Models in Gen-
eral — Skilful Seamanship of the Lake Fleet — Great Size and
Efficiency of the Modern Carriers — A Threefold Increase of Lake
Tonnage in a Quarter of a Century

THE great inland seas of North America, stretching
twelve hundred miles in a mighty chain and binding
together New York and Minnesota, bear the richest fresh-
water commerce in the world. More than one-fourth [1] of
the merchant tonnage of the United States is now employed
in this interesting traffic. Of all our marine it is the lake
fleet which has made the swiftest and most wonderful increase. Nature and protective laws have combined to hold
the lake-carrying trade in American control, while our unprotected foreign carrying has languished. Nine-tenths
of the lake commerce is from one American port to another,
and therefore reserved by ancient Federal statute to American vessels. Nine out of every ten lake ships fly the stars
and stripes. The traveller who yearns on the North
Atlantic for one glimpse of his country's flag can voyage
from Erie to Superior and back again and scarcely see
another color than the beloved red, white, and blue.

Two flags before ours have waved over the Great Lakes.
One has utterly vanished; the other, the "meteor flag" of

[1] The exact figures are 1,706,294 tons out of a total of 5,524,218.
Report of the Commissioner of Navigation for 1901.

England, streams only above some chance Canadian coaster.
It was a gallant Frenchman, René Robert Cavelier, Sieur
de la Salle, who launched the first ship upon the broad
waters above the Falls of Niagara. This was in 1679.
La Salle was bound westward toward the Mississippi,
which Joliet and Marquette had discovered six years before.
La Salle's bark, the "Griffin," so called from the armorial
bearings of his friend and patron, Frontenac, was built upon
the Niagara River, probably at the stream now known as
Cayuga Creek, two leagues above the cataract. The
"Griffin" was a petty vessel of only forty-five tons, but
she had a fierce figure-head and a battery of five small
cannon. A "floating fort," the astonished Indians styled
her, and Parkman speaks [1] of her as lying among a hundred
Indian canoes at Michilimackinac "like a Triton among
minnows." But the adventurous "Griffin" was not long
the wonder of the lakes. Her first voyage was her last one.
La Salle sent her back from the head of Lake Michigan
with a lading of furs for Niagara. The waters of Erie
never again beheld her white sails. Whether the "Griffin"
foundered in a storm with all on board, or was seized and
destroyed by the savages, La Salle was never able to ascer-
tain, and her fate remains to-day a mere conjecture of the
historians.

Like that iron-hearted pioneer, her builder, the "Griffin"
was many, many years ahead of her time. For a century
after her tragic disappearance, the blue horizon of the upper
lakes was flecked by nothing but the bateaux of the Canadian voyageurs or the bark canoes of the Indians. In the
course of events the sceptre of the North passed from
the French into the hands of a bolder maritime people. As
the fur trade grew in profit and the frontier posts changed
from mere sentinel blockhouses into important garrisons,
open boats no longer sufficed to transport supplies and men
over the hundreds of miles that lay between Niagara,

[1] "La Salle and the Discovery of the Great West," by Francis Parkman.

Detroit, and Mackinac. Small brigs were built for this service, and for a long time this rig remained a favorite with lake navigators. The "Gladwin" of eighty tons was plying on Lakes Huron and Michigan in 1783. The first American vessel on Lake Erie is said to have borne the good name of "Washington," and to have been launched near Erie, Pa., in 1797. The War of 1812 closed the lakes as with the winter's ice embargo, until Perry's victory freed them. There followed a lively period of shipbuilding.[1] In 1817, 1818, and 1819 the enrolled and licensed vessels of the Customs District of Buffalo Creek included a brig of 104 tons, another of 96 tons, several schooners from 132 tons downward, and the steamer "Walk-in-the-Water." The 96-ton brig, built in 1814, had been laid up soon afterward "for the reason, as alleged, of being too large to do business." The picturesquely named first steamer on the lakes above Niagara was constructed at Black Rock near Buffalo in 1819. She was an ambitious vessel for the time and place, of 338 tons' burden, and rigged with two masts and sails to help her crude machinery. The "Walk-in-the-Water" was designed for service to Detroit and the upper lakes. She was such a novel craft that it was thought necessary to bring a captain up from the North River. The story goes that this saline mariner was glad to resign his berth after he had encountered the short, vicious seas of one southwesterly gale on Lake Erie, and a lake sailor was promptly placed in command. Early and melancholy was the end of the "Walk-in-the-Water." She braved the November tempests of 1821. Her tea-kettle engines failed to hold her up in the teeth of a fierce southwester. She drove ashore and was lost. But her machinery survived the shipwreck, and went into another steamer, the "Superior," built in 1821–22.

The great westward migration which followed the peace

[1] "The History of Our Lake Commerce," by E. P. Dore, Esq., Buffalo Historical Society.

of 1815 soon began to send eastward a golden stream of
grain. Water carriage was cheap and easy. In 1836 the
first shipment came into Buffalo from the upper lakes, —
three thousand bushels of wheat in the brig " John Kenzie."
In 1842–43 the first Buffalo elevator was built. The lake
fleet now began to grow like magic.

Not all of its increase was in sail tonnage. In 1833 the
Canadians opened their Welland Canal between Lake
Ontario and Lake Erie. This gave the upper lakes access
to the lowest one, and access to the St. Lawrence River.
It also had an important influence on lake shipbuilding.
The smallest locks of the original Welland Canal were
only 110 feet long and 22 feet wide, with a draught of
eight feet. A four-hundred-ton vessel would have these
general dimensions. The steamers built to navigate
Ontario soon came to approximate to the canal-boat type.
They were bluff of bow and stern, straight of side, and flat
of bottom. They were thus able to carry the very largest
cargoes which could be hurried through the box-like locks
of the canal. The impress of the Welland Canal of
seventy years ago is still visible on almost every wooden
craft now afloat in lake navigation.

The early lake steamboats were sidewheelers, like the
first coasting and ocean steamships. They ventured at
first no farther westward than Detroit, but steamboats [1]
were running regularly to Chicago in 1830. They were
vessels of from 200 tons to 600, — of respectable capacity
and power. Railroads had not yet spread along the lakes.
The steamer was larger and more comfortable than the
stagecoach. The passenger traffic of the lakes grew and
prospered. Really large ships began to appear. In 1844
the " Empire," of 1,136 tons, was launched at Cleveland, and
next year the " Niagara," of 1,084 tons, was launched at
Buffalo. These great steamers were not intended for the

---

[1] "Shipbuilding Industry of the United States," by Henry Hall.

Welland Canal, which had now lengthened its locks to 150 feet. They were built wholly for the American passenger trade from Buffalo. They were fast ships for the day and luxurious, and many a successful man of business remembers how these old lake passenger steamers gave him as a lad his first glimpse of the splendors of the busy world. In 1848 several large passenger liners of from 1,000 to 1,200 tons were built, and one monster of 1,700 tons. In 1854 the old lake passenger trade reached its climax in the " Plymouth Rock," the " City of Buffalo, " and the " Western Metropolis," — noble vessels, more than three hundred feet long and sixty feet wide across the guards.

These great steamers were very fine ships. They were far stouter and stancher than the Mississippi River steamboats of the same era, — as they needed to be, for they faced fierce gales and sailed through rough waters. Their timbers and planking were well " salted," after the manner of the good ships of the ocean, and these lake steamers with their oak hulls lived long and profitable lives. But the iron horse, their relentless enemy, gradually overpowered them. The steam trains of the east and west railroads could run throughout the year. They were not blocked by ice or tempest. They were swifter than the swiftest of the splendid lake ships. More and more the railroads monopolized the high-class passenger traffic and left to the sidewheelers only immigrants and a little way freight. One by one the great passenger steamers that had been the pride of the lakes were dismantled or converted into sailing vessels or barges. For many years the passenger business of the lake shipping, save the summer excursion trade or runs between such points as Buffalo, or Cleveland, and Detroit, where the railway makes a détour and its mileage becomes great, was almost insignificant. Of late, however, with the improved efficiency and economy of marine engines, there has come an unmistakable revival of this lucrative branch of lake-carrying. The new lake passenger steamers are as commodious and beautiful as the famous vessels which ply the waters of Long Island Sound.

It is stated that the first propeller on the Northern lakes was the "Vandalia," built at Oswego on Lake Ontario in 1841. She is described as a bluff-bowed craft with a bowsprit, one mast set well forward, and one smokestack set near the stern, — for the machinery was in the after section. The "Vandalia's" general model was rigidly followed for years afterward. Even now the surviving wooden steamers on the lakes have her main characteristics. The "Vandalia" was of 138 tons, but the Welland Canal locks would pass a larger vessel. About 350 tons [1] was the average size of the early lake propellers, and it is said of them that "they have a strong resemblance to fast Erie canal boats fitted up for lake navigation."

There were enrolled at Buffalo, the chief lake port, in 1849, twenty-nine sidewheel steamers, eighteen of them ranging from 500 to 1,500 tons, ten propeller steamers, all of less than 500 tons, thirty-two brigs of from 129 to 316 tons, and eighty-five schooners, many of over 200 and the largest of 353 tons. On January 1, 1862, there were on the Great Lakes 147 sidewheel steamers of 64,669 tons, 203 propeller steamers of 60,951 tons, 62 barks of 25,118 tons, 86 brigs of 24,781 tons, and 989 schooners of 204,900 tons.[2]

This was a great fleet, but 1862 was a day of small things compared with what has followed. The Federal government has been liberal to the lakes. It has granted large and regular appropriations for extending harbors and deepening channels. Half a century ago there was begun the important work of making an adequate, navigable waterway between Lakes Huron and Michigan, and Lake Superior. Between this westernmost lake, the greatest of the inland seas, and its broad neighbors to the southward and eastward, there is a sharp difference in level. The

[1] "Shipbuilding Industry of the United States," by Henry Hall.
[2] Records of Board of Lake Underwriters.

St. Mary's River, through which Superior pours 90,000 cubic feet of water a second down into Lakes Huron and Michigan, falls twenty-one feet in fifty miles. Eighteen feet of this is at the rapids of Sault Ste. Marie, where the river rushes over a mile-long bed of rocks, and is navigable in its eddies only for the bark canoes of the Indian guides.

Alongside of these rapids in 1855 was constructed a lock with two chambers, each 350 feet long and 70 feet wide, admitting vessels with a draught of $11\frac{1}{2}$ feet of water. This gave Chicago, Detroit, Cleveland, and Buffalo direct access in ships of considerable size to the wheat fields and mines of Lake Superior. The first year's traffic was 106,296 tons (registered). This had increased[1] in 1873 to 1,204,446 tons (registered). In 1881 a new lock 515 feet long, 80 feet wide, and 17 feet deep over the mitre-sill was opened. In that year there passed through the canal 1,706 sailing vessels and 2,117 steamers, of a total registered tonnage of 2,092,757. Five years later, in 1886, the shipping of the St. Mary's Falls Canal had increased to 4,219,397 tons. This prodigious growth was due not only to the enlarged lock, but to the magical development of the valuable iron ranges of Lake Superior. In 1880 only 677,073 tons of iron ore were moved. But in 1895 the vast quantity of 8,000,000 tons passed through St. Mary's Falls lock eastward bound to the furnaces of Lakes Michigan and Erie. The tonnage[2] of the two canals —for in 1895 a new canal was opened on the Canadian side of the falls — reached in 1900 the stupendous figure of 22,315,834. A still greater American lock has meanwhile been constructed at the "Soo," — 800 feet long and 100 feet wide, with a navigable depth of 20 feet or over.

Another obstacle to the expansion of the lake-carrying trade for many years was the Detroit and St. Clair rivers

[1] Report of General Superintendent Wheeler.
[2] Annual Report for 1900 of Charles H. Keep, Secretary of the Buffalo Merchants' Exchange.

and the relatively shallow Lake St. Clair between Lakes
Erie and Huron. Here also the natural channel has been
dredged and straightened by the national government,[1] until
a draught of nearly twenty feet has been secured, and the
crowded waterway has been elaborately lighted and buoyed.
Not all of the ships which pass the " Soo " Canal — our Yankee simplifying of the old Jesuit Sault Ste. Marie — traverse
the Detroit River. Some of these vessels are bound to
or from ports on Lake Michigan or Huron. Moreover,
many vessels passing up or down the Detroit River never
approach St. Mary's. The commerce of the two great lake
waterways is therefore only partially the same. But both
are crowded maritime thoroughfares. The tonnage of each
channel far exceeds that of Suez[2] or the great ports of
Liverpool or London.

Railroads so gridiron the country all about the great
lakes that at first glance the swift and majestic increase of
this waterborne commerce is incomprehensible. The truth
is that most of the lake carrying is of cargoes of great bulk
and low price.

Three commodities[3] — iron ore, lumber, and coal — have

[1] " By every foot that this depth of water [in the lake channels] has been
increased, the distance between Duluth and Cleveland has been virtually
shortened by one hundred miles, so that in the forty years in which the depth
of water on the St. Clair flats has been doubled and a navigable depth of
twenty feet has been established in the St. Mary's Falls Canal, the cost of
transporting a ton of ore on the lakes has come down from four mills to six-
tenths of a mill per mile." John Foord, " North American Review," 1898.

[2] In 1897, 17,171 vessels, of 17,619,933 tons, passed through the St. Mary's
Falls Canals, and 2,986 vessels, of 7,899,374 tons, through the Suez Canal.
In 1898, the figures were 17,761 vessels, of 18,622,734 tons, for St. Mary's,
and 3,464 vessels, of 9,186,912 tons, for Suez. In 1899, the figures were
20,255 vessels, of 21,958,347 tons, for St. Mary's, and 3,607 vessels, of 9,895,-
630 tons for Suez. The St. Mary's vessels, of course, were bound on shorter
voyages. But the St. Mary's Falls Canals in the icy north are open to navigation only 225 days of the 365 ; the Suez Canal is always unobstructed. (Blue
Book of American Shipping, Cleveland, Ohio.)

[3] A report to the Treasury Bureau of Statistics on Lake Commerce, by
George G. Tunell of Chicago, 1898.

made up three-fourths of the tonnage of the lakes, and grain and mill products most of the remainder. Nearly all of these heavy cargoes are carried from one end of the lakes to the other. Four-fifths [1] of the Lake Superior iron ore goes to Lake Erie ports; most of the grain and flour sent out from Duluth, West Superior, or Ashland, at the western end of Lake Superior, and Chicago or Milwaukee on Lake Michigan, is destined for the capacious elevators of Buffalo. Lumber also usually is a long-distance lading. Coal, the chief westward freight, goes mainly from the railroad terminals on Lake Erie to Michigan and Superior.

This immense traffic in heavy merchandise demands the swift movement of an immense tonnage during the seven or eight months of each year in which the lake channels are free from icy bondage. Lake cargo steamships of the newer type are, as a rule, faster than ocean cargo carriers. A score of years ago lake shipowners were satisfied with fifteen or sixteen round trips between Lake Superior and Lake Erie in a single season, but they now expect twenty-two or more, and deepened channels and improved marine machinery have made this possible.

The increased size of lake vessels has been a factor in the steadily increased efficiency and steadily lowered cost of lake-carrying. In 1868 [2] the average size of the sailing vessels was 158 gross tons; in 1890, 258 tons; in 1897, 336 tons. The average tonnage of steamers has advanced from 231 tons in 1868 to 427 tons in 1890, and 551 in 1897. In this last year the average tonnage of newly built steamers was 1,436.

The great and heavy lake trade has developed some very interesting types of cargo steamships. Several years ago the "whalebacks" of Captain MacDougall were much in

---

[1] General Superintendent Wheeler states that the average distance that the 16,239,061 tons of St. Mary's Canal freight was carried in 1896 was 836 miles.

[2] Statistics of Lake Commerce, by George G. Tunell.

vogue, but the more recent tendency has been to produce
ships of an ocean model. In 1886 there were only six steel
vessels of a net tonnage of 6,459 afloat on the lakes. Now
lake shipbuilding in everything except small craft is almost
entirely of steel. There were 156,762 tons of shipping
launched on the lakes in the fiscal year 1901; 147,548 tons
of this represented iron or steel vessels, and 145,417 tons
of it steamers.

The steel shipyards of the lakes are blessed with cheap
and accessible fuel and materials, and a strong demand for
good cargo carriers. They are not harassed by foreign competition. A few European steamers have been run through
the Canadian canals into the lakes as an experiment, but
they have proved to be less adaptable to the work than the
lake-built vessels. On the other hand, many lake craft
have been sent down into the Atlantic Ocean, but this,
too, is still an experiment of dubious value to its promoters.
In the summer of 1901 Chicago was seized with an ambition to export its own grain and provisions direct to Europe.
Four or five rather small steamers, built especially for the
St. Lawrence traffic, were sent out, but it is understood
that the net result was not encouraging.

Yet lake steamers are undeniably good vessels. The
difficulty is that they are designed for one kind of service
and ocean vessels for another. One who knows both lake
and ocean craft, and can speak with exact technical authority, says [1]: —

"As to structural strength, it is true that there are a few
light vessels on the lakes, and, maybe, one or two weak
ones, but there are none so weak as many steamers that
were turned out from European shipyards about the year
1870. The modern lake steamer is quite as heavy and
fully as strong as the best type of ocean cargo boat, and
the upper bottoms of the latest fresh-water steamers are

[1] Mr. Joseph B. Oldham in "Cassier's Magazine" for 1897.

superior in arrangement and strength to those of any other class of cargo steamers."

Much of the lake tonnage is controlled by mighty railroad corporations, or coal or iron kings. The best-known single fleets are those of the Carnegie and Rockefeller interests. But a great many large modern freighters are managed by individual shipowners, and there need be no fear that the enormous lake-carrying trade will become a hard-and-fast monopoly. The nation has not lost, but gained, by excluding foreign competition from this distinctively American commerce. The laws of the United States have always properly treated as coastwise traffic a voyage from Buffalo to Duluth or Chicago to Cleveland. No foreign vessel can convey a single ton of freight from one port to the other. A foreign vessel can bring a load of barley from Canada across the lakes to Milwaukee or Toledo, because that is a foreign voyage. But it happens that the chief ports of the whole lake region are on the American side, and that the really great and lucrative trade is American in both origin and destination. A recent report of the British Vice-Consul at Chicago mourns: "That British shipping does not have its proper share of this trade is shown by the fact that while there were one hundred and sixty-one vessels entered at Chicago and South Chicago in 1899 from Canada, only twelve of these were British, the rest being American." But this British official handsomely acknowledges the high efficiency of the thoroughly Yankee craft which do all of our own and part of Canada's business. "The amount of work that can be got out of one of these lake steamers," he says, "is shown by the fact that the 'Andrew Carnegie' travelled in the year of 240 days a distance of 42,207 miles."

The sailing vessel, pure and simple, has disappeared much more completely from the lakes than from the ocean. Square-riggers have practically all gone. Schooner-rigged vessels are still numerous, but most of them are less sailing craft than barges. Though they retain their spars and rigging and can show considerable canvas to a fair wind, they are towed by steam consorts, one or more in a line. Of independent sailing vessels on the chief routes of lake commerce there are so few that the sight of one is unusual. Schooners are still used, however, for traffic between minor ports alongshore, so that the great expanse of the lakes is by no means sailless.

The lake schooner of wood does not compare favorably in model with her new, powerful, and symmetrical sisters of the Atlantic and Pacific seaboard. She has too many suggestions in her straight up-and-down sides and blunt ends of the river scow or the canal-boat. Her model is flat-bottomed; her light draught requires a centreboard. The two-masted lake schooner has her masts set very near bow and stern, and spreads more canvas in her foresail and less proportionately in her mainsail than does the two-master of the ocean. This large space between the masts leaves larger main hatches and facilitates loading and unloading. But it is at the expense of "looks" and, still more important, of speed and stanchness. The masts of lake schooners are not so carefully "stayed" as those of ocean craft. There is not the same neatness and precision observable in their whole rig and the set of their canvas. Their sails as a rule are grimy, because of the soft coal almost universally used on the lakes. The only real "white wings" ever observable on the lake horizon are those of pleasure yachts, — more numerous, swift, and beautiful than salt-water yachtsmen imagine.

But the lake schooners and the wooden tow-barges represent an old and dwindling class. Steel enters far more into lake than it does into coast construction. The typical lake freighter of to-day is a steel steamship. The number of these steamers is astonishing. There is actually a larger American steel steam tonnage on the lakes than on the ocean.[1] The lake steel steamers built between 1891 and

[1] Report of Commissioner of Navigation.

1900 amount to 450,089 tons; the Atlantic and Pacific steel steamers together to 292,741.

Many wooden steamers are still left on the lakes. They are, as a rule, of moderate dimensions. They are nearly all propellers. The sidewheel lingers chiefly in the passenger or excursion trade. Most of the wooden lake steam freighters have a high bow, crowned by the pilot-house, which in lake craft generally is much farther forward than in ocean vessels. Sometimes this pilot-house is literally "in the eyes" of the ship. This location of the wheel is of very great advantage to the steersmen in passing through locks, going alongside wharves, or threading narrow channels. The steady tendency has been to bring the pilot-house farther forward even on ocean steamships. It is undeniably sound sense in lake navigation, although it always detracts from the beauty of a steamer.

While the pilot-house is forward, the boilers and machinery are as far aft. Even in most of the newer lake vessels the boiler and engine rooms are in the aftermost compartments, leaving the whole body of the ship where she is widest and fullest for the cargo. This practice makes it possible to shorten the all-important but vulnerable propeller shafting, and by the use of water ballast tanks the ship can be "trimmed" to the desired lines when empty. Of course, with the machinery far aft, the smokestack or stacks are far aft also. This is another marked peculiarity of lake construction. It gives the newest and best ships an odd look, but these lake designers and builders have worked not for appearance but for utility. There are some vessels on the lakes which were constructed on ocean designs, except in their depth and draught of water.

The masts of lake steamers as a rule are mere flagstaffs. Sails, even scant trysails, are seldom used on steam vessels. In the new ships the masts are set far apart, and are lightly stayed and very slender. The heavy derrick-gear of ocean steamships is seldom carried. The hoisting apparatus is usually on the piers of lake ports.

Another peculiarity of lake ships is the number and extent of their cargo hatches. Between the high bow and the high stern, with their pilot-house, smokestack, and deckhouses, there stretches a long range of deck, often without bulwarks, having only light hand rails, over which the seas can easily wash. Here there is hatch after hatch, narrow, rather than broad, reaching almost to the sides of the vessel and leaving only a footway of solid deck fore and aft. These many large openings undoubtedly tend to weaken the upper hulls of lake vessels, though they can be and often are counterbalanced by the use of heavier materials of construction. Speed in loading and unloading is a most important consideration in lake commerce, and to this the large hatches and many of them are indispensable.

The large lake steamers have the beams for several decks, but below the upper deck these are often not covered with planks or plating, leaving only the deck beams stretching from side to side across the cavernous holds. This practice increases the carrying capacity of these vessels, but many of them are so large that they cannot load to their full capacity, or they would have too great a draught for the twenty feet of the locks of the "Soo" canal or the St. Clair Flats, which mark the limit of interlake navigation. Lake carriers look forward confidently to the time when this depth will be increased, and they can go up and down the lakes with the draught of ocean steamers.

The passage of canal locks and many narrow channels by these long and heavy craft calls for skilful helmsmen, stout and sure rudder gear, fine, accurate eyes, steady nerves, and a high order of seamanship. It amazes salt-water observers to note the ease and quickness with which these four-hundred-foot monsters, bearing four or five thousand dead-weight tons of iron ore for the Cleveland

and Pittsburg furnaces or of Northwest grain for hungry Europe, come pushing down the devious " Soo," meeting and passing all manner of craft, seldom slackening speed, and yet escaping every peril of reef or sandbar or collision. It is enough to turn white the hair of a salt-water seaman, whose pilot takes him away from his dock and down the tidal channel to the open sea.

These lake sailors look the men they are.   Tall and massive Northern Vikings, clear-eyed, tanned with sun and sleet, they stand imperturbable at the faithful wheel, or on the lofty bridge, while the thousand miles of lake panorama unroll before them.   Now and then, as they meet some known craft or friendly face, they lift their peaked caps or wave a brown hand across the water, or shout a deep-toned greeting.   But their look is ever onward, and even in the narrowest channels these lake leviathans move so fast that there is chance only for a gesture or a word, and five thousand tons of ore or wheat are shrinking to a smoky dot on the horizon.

Let nobody imagine that there is no peril on the " unsalted seas."   Lake weather is forever capricious.   A keen ozone-fraught northwester may change in the night to a vicious southeast gale, with an icy mist and foam-crowned, slate-dark surges, when the voyager on Huron or Superior may easily believe that he is battling the restless North Atlantic.   On Lake Erie, which is relatively shallow and swept by fierce winds, the waves raised by a gale are peculiarly short, steep, and dangerous.   Moreover, the lake is so narrow that there is always a lee shore near at hand. On the upper lakes, Huron, Michigan, and Superior, the sea room is greater, and so is the depth of water, but the winds have a wider expanse in which to marshal all their fury, and the mountainous rollers which sweep up or down four-hundred-mile-long Superior would test the stanchness of any ship that ever lived.

The passenger trade on the lakes is increasing in spite

of railroad competition. In recent years many noble vessels have been built for this specific purpose. The "North Land" and "Northwest" of the Northern Steamship Company, a part of the Great Northern system, are the most famous as they are the most luxurious of lake passenger ships, and their thousand-mile voyage is accomplished with all the exact discipline and ordered comfort of the best of the Atlantic liners. Many steamboats of new, swift, and powerful types ply from port to port in passenger service along the chain of lakes. The seaboard observer who came to scoff at lake models and lake seamanship finds himself full of admiration for the skill and liberality of fresh-water steam construction.

A mode of carrying which the ocean has tardily and partially borrowed from the lakes is the towing of barges by tugs or steamships. This method was brought to great perfection on the lakes before ocean shipowners plucked, up courage to attempt it. Barge-towing on the lakes began in the days of wooden vessels, but it has come to its highest development in the four-hundred-foot steel steamer, drawing after it a barge-consort of equal tonnage, the two moving between them eight or ten thousand tons of coal or ore. These huge vessels thread the narrow waterways of the Soo and St. Clair and deliver their cargoes safely at Chicago, Cleveland, or Buffalo, thereby making one set of engines perform double service. But the greater number of the very modern steamers work independently, thus achieving their voyages with greater promptness and ease.

The swift development of the splendid lake steam freight ships cannot be more vividly illustrated than by comparing the "Matoa," a large vessel of 1890, with the "John W. Gates" of 1900.[1] The "Matoa" is 290 feet long, 40 feet wide, and 21 feet deep. The "Gates" is 500 feet long, 52 feet wide, and 30 feet deep. The registered tonnage of the ship of 1890 is 2,311; of the ship of 1900

[1] Blue Book of American Shipping, Cleveland, O.

5,085. The "Matoa" carries an average cargo of 2,500 gross tons; the "Gates" of 7,000 tons. Yet so wonderful is the modern lake cargo handling apparatus that while the 2,500 tons of the "Matoa" require fifteen hours for loading, the 7,000 tons of the "Gates" require only twenty hours on the average. The unloading time for the old and small ship is thirty-six hours; for the new and great ship forty-three. Nor is the "Gates" an exceptional craft. She is owned by the United States Steel Corporation, which controls a dozen or more vessels, of equal or almost equal dimensions. The fleet is designed especially for the iron ore trade of Lake Superior. It is believed to be the most economical and efficient group of heavy cargo steamers in the world.

The following table, drawn from the official figures of the United States Bureau of Navigation, shows the tonnage of the Great Lakes within the past twenty-six years, the era of the notable development of fresh-water commerce. Sailing tonnage and steam tonnage are enumerated in separate columns, but the tonnage of the unrigged craft is included in the total. It should be explained, moreover, that the classification of "sailing tonnage" is somewhat misleading. Under this head the Treasury Department places tow-barges which do have masts and sails, indeed, but are dependent in the main upon the faithful engines of their steamer-consorts. Independent sail-vessels, as has been said, are fast disappearing from the lakes. They have almost entirely vanished from Lake Superior.

MERCHANT MARINE, GREAT LAKES, 1876–1901.

Year.	Sailing Tonnage.	Steam Tonnage.	Total Tonnage.	New Tonnage Built.
1876	331,498	201,742	613,211	16,124
1877	324,394	201,085	610,160	8,903
1878	315,908	201,550	604,656	11,438
1879	307,078	203,298	597,376	15,135
1880	304,933	212,045	605,102	22,899

Year.	Sailing Tonnage.	Steam Tonnage.	Total Tonnage.	New Tonnage Built.
1881	306,436	260,114	663,382	73,504
1882	313,651	292,257	711,269	58,369
1883	310,454	304,641	723,911	28,638
1884	307,933	322,456	733,069	30,431
1885	313,129	335,859	749,948	26,826
1886	282,319	381,907	762,560	20,400
1887	315,079	390,397	783,721	56,488
1888	314,765	480,138	874,102	101,103
1889	325,083	575,307	972,271	107,080
1890	328,656	652,923	1,063,063	108,526
1891	325,131	736,752	1,154,870	111,856
1892	319,618	763,063	1,183,582	45,969
1893	317,789	828,702	1,261,067	99,271
1894	302,985	843,240	1,227,400	41,985
1895	300,642	857,735	1,241,459	36,353
1896	309,152	924,631	1,324,067	108,782
1897	334,104	977,235	1,410,102	116,937
1898	333,704	993,644	1,437,500	54,084
1899	318,175	1,014,561	1,446,348	80,366
1900	335,183	1,110,565	1,565,587	130,611
1901	332,289	1,231,879	1,706,294	169,085

CHAPTER XVIII

A DECADE OF GAIN AND LOSS. 1891-1901

Congress turns again to Protectionism — Ocean Mail Act of 1891 — Inadequate but Beneficial — Our New Line to Europe — How the Inman Ships became American — British Subsidy withdrawn from American Owners — "City of Paris " and "City of New York" admitted to Registry, "St. Louis " and "St. Paul " built — Success of the New American Line — Splendid Service of our "Merchant Cruisers " in the Spanish War — "St. Louis " and "St. Paul " in Action with the Enemy — Auxiliary Navy and Merchant Marine — A Boom in Shipbuilding, but not for Deep-Sea Commerce — Coasting Craft and Men-of-War — Only a Few New Ships for Foreign Voyaging — Owners desire Further Protective Legislation — Shipping Bill of Fifty-Seventh Congress — Subsidies Important but not Omnipotent — The Morgan Combination — Capital Ready if Fair Play is guaranteed — Tonnage Record of a Decade — Revival of the Merchant Marine awaits only the Word of the American People

THE last decade of the nineteenth century brought here and there a rift in the dark storm-clouds that had long overhung American shipping. It is true that, between 1891 and 1901, there was a loss of more than a hundred thousand tons in the American fleet registered for foreign commerce, but this was due to the disappearance of sailing ships, for there was an increase of more than a hundred thousand tons in our registered steam tonnage. The American proportion of our deep-sea carrying, however, steadily lessened. It was 12.5 per cent in 1891 and 8.2 in 1901, — the very smallest figure in our history.

There had come in the mean time a feeble and partial return to the old national policy of maritime protection-

ism.   The idea that inspired the Ocean Mail Act of 1891
was exactly the same idea that had moved Washington,
Adams, Jefferson, and Madison, in the last decade of the
eighteenth century, to give our shipowners and seamen
the encouragement of discriminating customs duties and
tonnage dues.   These ancient methods had grown obsolete.
The practice of the nations and the terms of more than a
score of treaties of maritime reciprocity made a renewal of
the old discriminations impossible, but the United States
sought the same end in a different and modern way.   It
tardily followed the European example of offering subventions out of the National Treasury.

Two distinct bills were prepared for the consideration
of Congress.   One related to mail-carrying steamships;
the other, to cargo steamships and sailing ships.   Both
measures passed the Senate, but the House reduced the
rate of subsidy of the Mail Ship Bill, and rejected altogether, though by a very narrow vote, the Cargo Ship Bill
with its graduated subsidy based on mileage and tonnage.
The bill which was enacted is known as the Postal Aid
Law of March 3, 1891.   It was a well-drawn, comprehen-
sive measure; and if it had passed in its original form it
would have created a large fleet of high-class American
merchant steamships.   Unfortunately the House, in the
rush of the closing session, cut off one-third of the re-
muneration provided for the swiftest and most valuable
ocean liners.   Senator William P. Frye, of Maine, the
chief author of both of the shipping bills, had made a careful study of steam navigation, and had offered an amount
of mail pay that would offset foreign subsidies and low
wages sufficiently to insure the immediate creation of
an American steamship service to Europe and to South
America.   The hurried action of the House fatally de-
ranged these calculations.   Reduced one-third, the mail
pay was inadequate to meet the European subsidies and
smaller cost of operation.

As enacted, the Postal Aid Law divided American mail-carrying steamships into four classes. The first was limited to iron or steel screw steamships, capable of maintaining a speed of 20 knots an hour at sea in ordinary weather, and of a gross registered tonnage of not less than 8,000 tons. None but ships of this first class were eligible to carry the mails between the United States and Great Britain. A speed of 20 knots an hour in 1891 was a very high requirement. The second class was to consist of iron or steel steamships, capable of maintaining a speed of 16 knots an hour at sea in ordinary weather, and of a gross registered tonnage of at least 5,000 tons. It was believed that ships of this class would be available for a service to South America and China and Japan. The third class was to include iron or steel steamships, capable of maintaining a speed of 14 knots an hour at sea in ordinary weather, and of a gross registered tonnage of at least 2,500 tons. The fourth class was to be made up of iron, steel, or wooden steamships, capable of maintaining a speed of 12 knots an hour at sea in ordinary weather, and of a gross registered tonnage of not less than 1,500 tons.

For ships of the first class the mail pay or subsidy was set at $4 for every mile traversed on the outward voyage, — in Senator Frye's original bill, as the Senate passed it, the rate had been $6. For ships of the second class, the subsidy was $2 a mile on the outward voyage; for ships of the third class, $1; for ships of the fourth class, 66⅔ cents. Under this new subsidy law, ocean mail contracts were made with the Pacific Mail Company for a service between New York and Colon, and between Panama and San Francisco, thus giving the United States regular communication with Central and the northern part of South America. Another contract with the Pacific Mail Company covered the service across the Pacific from San Francisco to Yokohama and Hong Kong. The Pacific Mail ships were accepted as of the third and fourth class, though most of them were very much larger than the required tonnage. A contract was made with Boulton, Bliss & Dallett ("Red D" line) for a service between New York and Venezuela in steamships of the third class. Another contract with the New York & Cuba Mail Steamship Company (Ward Line) provided for a service between New York, Havana, and Mexico, also in steamships of the third class. An arrangement was subsequently made with the Oceanic Steamship Company, applicable to the two American steamships of its line from San Francisco to Hawaii and Australia.

In every case these contracts were formed with lines already existing. It was only those American shipowners with an established trade who felt that they could afford to bid for mail-carrying under the severe requirements of the Postal Aid Law, with its naval inspection, its penalties, and its sharply reduced compensation. A year or two after the enactment of the Postal Aid Law, the struggling American steam line to Brazil was abandoned. The new legislation came too late to save it. Anticipating the enactment of the Tonnage Subsidy Bill, the company had built, in 1890, two very large steel steamships, the "Vigilancia" and "Seguranca," of four thousand tons. They were such vessels as only the subsidized European mail lines could maintain in the South American trade. Under the Tonnage Subsidy Bill they could have been successfully operated, but under the Postal Aid Law they could not. They were transferred, when the Brazil line was withdrawn, to the New York & Cuba Mail Steamship Company, which carried a great many passengers to the West Indies and Mexico.

This Postal Aid Law of 1891 created at first no new line of American steamships. But it was of unquestionable value in improving the character of the American fleet. The influence of even the inadequate mail subsidies became manifest in the appearance, in the West Indies and the Pacific, of a group of high-class steel steamships of the Ward Line and the Pacific Mail Company. Some of these vessels were built in anticipation of the law; some, after its enactment. Thus, in spite of the shortsightedness of the National House, the ocean mail legislation of 1891 did add to the size and prosperity of the United States steam marine. Some of the American mail lines were being pressed by very severe foreign competition when this measure came to their relief.

Nobody came forward to undertake a North Atlantic mail service with steamships of at least eight thousand tons capable of twenty knots an hour. This mail service continued to be monopolized by the fast British, French, and German liners, and it looked as if the Postal Aid Law, as razeed by Congress, would fail of the prime purpose of this legislation, which was to gain for the United States some participation in the noblest sea-borne commerce of the world. The proffered subsidy of four dollars a mile for the outward voyage, or $12,000 for every round trip to and from Liverpool, was not sufficient, as Senator Frye had foreseen, to persuade capitalists to build an entirely new and costly fleet of American ocean greyhounds.

There were, however, keen and ambitious men in the shipping trade, who believed that they saw their way clear to create a first-class American line if they were given a little more encouragement. Many years before, in 1873, the International Navigation Company, a Philadelphia concern, had started a line of three steamers, under the Belgian flag, from Philadelphia to Antwerp. This company was made up almost wholly of American citizens, and they naturally desired to use American steamships. But they found, upon investigation, that it would cost so much more to build steamers in this country, and to officer and man them after they were completed, that the thing could not possibly be done in the face of cheap-wage or subsidized European competition.

27

They knew, moreover, that the United States would not give them any protection or encouragement. So these American gentlemen reluctantly organized a Belgian company to own their three new ships, retaining themselves all of the stock except enough to qualify the resident Belgian directors. Much to the gratification of these Americans, the Belgian government, more alert and liberal than their own, now offered a mail subvention of $100,000 for ten years with port privileges and wharfage worth $30,000 more, for a line of fourteen-day steamships between New York and Antwerp. This proposition was gratefully accepted. It marked the beginning of what has come to be the Red Star line of passenger and freight steamships, owned by American capital, and very successfully handled by American managers.

In 1886, the celebrated Inman line of British mail steamers, whose founder, Mr. William Inman, had died, was brought to the attention of the International Navigation Company. This was one of the three British subsidized steamship companies — the others were the White Star and Cunard lines — which were performing the tri-weekly New York mail service from Liverpool. The Inman directors desired to sell the property. The International Navigation Company purchased it, and, with true Yankee enterprise, began the building of two larger, swifter, and more seaworthy steamers than the world had ever seen. As subsidized British mail carriers, they were necessarily constructed in a British yard. Besides, no steamers of the modern Atlantic greyhound class had ever yet been launched in America.

These two new Inman liners were the famous "City of Paris" and "City of New York." When they were well along toward completion, it happened that the mail contract of the British government with the Inman, Cunard, and White Star lines expired. One day the American owners of the Inman line were astonished to receive a curt notification from the British Post-Office Department that the government had been considering the matter, and had concluded that three mails from Great Britain to the United States were not necessary — that two were enough — and that the services of the Inman line would be dispensed with. This was the official explanation, but the Inman managers [1] "were afterward told unofficially that the English government did not feel that a company owned entirely by American capital should receive mail pay from the British government." At that time the United States was giving to the Cunard, the White Star, and the German steamship companies several hundred thousand dollars a year.

The American purchasers of the Inman line now found themselves in a "serious predicament." The "City of New York" and "City of Paris," now nearly finished on the Clyde, could not be run without the help of the British postal and Admiralty subsidies. The two vessels were very much superior in speed and power to the older mail steamers of the British lines. In fact, they marked a revolution in marine architecture. They were the first twin screw ships, the first unsinkable ships, the most luxurious and costly passenger steamers that had been constructed. Fortunately, Senator Frye's Postal Aid Bill in its reduced form had now been enacted in the United States, and the American owners of the Inman ships made a frank appeal to Congress, explaining how they had been treated by the British government, and asking that the "City of Paris" and the "City of New York" be admitted to American registry, and made eligible for American mail pay, on condition that two similar ships be built by the International Company in American shipyards.

[1] Statement of President Clement A. Griscom of the International Navigation Company, before the Senate Committee on Commerce, Fifty-sixth Congress, First Session. Senate Document 149.

This proposition commended itself at once to Congress. An Act of May 10, 1892, granted the desired privilege. The International Navigation Company promptly ordered two new steamships from the William Cramp & Son's Ship and Engine Building Company, of Philadelphia, an old, well-established concern, that had been launching vessels on the Delaware for two generations. It was the Cramp yard which had built the celebrated "New Ironsides," the first American broadside armor-clad, and the most powerful vessel in the Union Navy in the Civil War. After the war the Cramps had constructed the steam frigate "Chattanooga," a fine-lined cruiser of high speed, the four large iron steamers of the American line from Philadelphia to Liverpool, many excellent coastwise steamers, and one or two successful warships for foreign governments. But the Cramp yard had won its chief renown in the creation of the new steel navy to which it had contributed the gunboat "Yorktown," the protected cruisers "Baltimore" and "Philadelphia," the flying commerce-destroyer "Columbia," and the armored cruiser "New York." It was now (1893) constructing the first-class battleships "Indiana," "Massachusetts," and "Iowa," the commerce-destroyer "Minneapolis" and the armored cruiser "Brooklyn." These naval contracts had enabled the Cramp Company to strengthen its mechanical resources, gather an army of skilled workmen, and organize what was probably the most effective shipyard in the world. Such was the result, in America, of a single decade of national encouragement of steamship building, — a policy which had been steadily enforced in Great Britain for more than fifty years. Three-fourths of the enormous steam fleet of the British navy had been launched from private British shipyards which had thus been powerfully assisted in acquiring the costly machinery essential for the best work of the merchant marine.

The first of the new American liners was launched on

Nov. 12, 1894, in the presence of twenty-five thousand people. The event was regarded as of national significance. President Cleveland was the especial guest of honor, and Mrs. Cleveland christened the ship "St. Louis," as the greatest vessel ever constructed on this Continent rode down the ways into the Delaware. On April 10, 1895, her sister ship, the "St. Paul," was launched, and the International Navigation Company now possessed the finest fleet of greyhounds in the North Atlantic service.

The company had been better than its word. It had made its two American-built steamships even larger than the "New York" and "Paris," safer, swifter, and more luxurious. The two new vessels were not meant to be record-breakers. President Griscom declared, in an address at the launching of the "St. Paul," that the aim of the American line was not to cut down the ocean record by one hour, but rather to produce steamers that should be trustworthy and comfortable in all winds and weathers, departing and arriving on regular schedule time.

Both the "St. Louis" and the "St. Paul" are thoroughly American in design as well as in construction. The trained eye of the seaman would recognize them as Yankee vessels a dozen miles away. In their external aspect they are like our splendid American coastwise steamships magnified. They have the straight bow, curving slightly away at the water-line, the long, fine Yankee sheer, the graceful stern, the wholesome freeboard, and the bridge and pilot house forward, where the steersmen can hold the ship well in hand, — all the salient characteristics of the modern seagoing steam merchantman of the United States. They have even the two clean taper schooner masts, which American naval architects adopted years ago as the best rig for steamers, while foreign craft were still dragging about the cumbersome square yards and canvas, now everywhere abandoned.

The "Paris" and "New York" are of 10,600 tons gross register.   The "St. Louis" and "St. Paul" are of 11,600 tons.   The two American-built ships are 554 feet long over all, 63 feet wide, and 51 feet deep, with five decks, and a very thorough system of water-tight compartments. Many a good ship has been lost because the doors of these compartments were not closed at the fateful moment of collision or grounding.   But in these two American liners, the unusual precaution was adopted of having no doors or other openings in the steel bulkheads below the main deck, thus making the vessels practically unsinkable. Added strength and security were provided by the naval requirements of the Ocean Mail contract, under which the two ships were built, that they should be adapted for service as auxiliary cruisers in time of war, and be capable of mounting powerful batteries of rifled cannon.

Both the "St. Louis" and "St. Paul" have proved to be very successful ships in the transatlantic service. Their American nationality commended them to the best passenger trade, and the favor thus won they have held by the swiftness and regularity of their voyages.   Their route has been to Southampton, not to Queenstown and Liverpool; and they have necessarily had longer passages than the Liverpool ships because they traverse greater distances.   But the two new American liners easily gained the Southampton record and held it for several years, until the "Kaiser Wilhelm der Grosse," a very much larger vessel, was constructed.   In August, 1896, the "St. Paul" established a record of 6 days, 31 minutes, from Southampton to New York, and in September, 1897, the "St. Louis" made a record of 6 days, 10 hours, and 41 minutes from New York to Southampton, — an average of more than twenty knots an hour from land to land, and a passage several hours shorter than the best of the British-built "New York" and "Paris."

Under the terms of the present postal contract with the

United States, the International Navigation Company receives approximately $12,000 for every weekly voyage outward from New York to Southampton. In the fiscal year 1900, the compensation actually paid to the American line was $647,278, and in 1901 it was $528,537. But the one American line does not monopolize the carrying of the United States mails to Europe. The American vessels take the mails that are ready in the New York Post-Office on the day of their departure. The mails that happen to be ready on the sailing days of the foreign lines are sent by foreign vessels, though at a lower rate of compensation. Thus, in 1901, the United States paid for mail service $213,103 to the Cunard (British) steamers; $91,591 to the White Star (British) steamers; $80,141 to the North German Lloyd steamers; $52,750 to the Hamburg American (German) steamers; $24,842 to the General Transatlantic (French) steamers, and smaller sums to other foreign lines. The American line received $528,537 out of a total of $994,344 expended by the United States for its transatlantic mail service. In other words, even under the Postal Aid Law, nearly one-half of the transatlantic mail pay of the United States went to European corporations, most of them generously subsidized by their own governments.

The general navigation laws of the United States require that all the officers of an American ship shall be American citizens. The Postal Aid Law of 1891 went beyond this, and stipulated that a certain proportion of the crews of subsidized mail steamers should be Americans, — one-fourth during the first two years of a mail contract, one-third during the next three years, and at least one-half during the remainder of the contract. When the "New York" and "Paris" were brought under our flag, it therefore became necessary to replace many of their alien sailors and firemen with citizens of the United States, who demanded and received, of course, the ruling

American rates of wages. On this point, the United States Commissioner of Navigation says in one of his annual reports : —

"The requirement that an increasing percentage of the crews of American transatlantic mail steamships shall be American citizens involves an annual expense for increased wages of about $60,000 a year, at the present time, at the end of five years amounting annually to about $120,000, which must be paid by the contracting corporation."

This requirement that the officers, and at least a large part of the crews of mail liners should owe allegiance to the flag beneath which they sail is a just economic policy and an essential military precaution. The United States received abundant proof of that fact in the Spanish War. Many of the foreign sailors and firemen, in the service of the American line, quit that service when the ships were armed and sent to sea to look for the elusive squadron of Admiral Cervera. They were not cowards, but they refused to risk their lives in a war in which they had no patriotic interest. The government had the same enlightening experience with the foreign steamships which it chartered for transports and colliers. Their officers, engineers, seamen, and firemen, in a great many instances, declined to go with their ships, and the Navy, or the War Department, was forced to fill their places with native or naturalized Americans before the vessels could be utilized.

This Spanish War brought a vivid demonstration of both the strength and the weakness of the American merchant marine of 1898. The war suddenly threw the nation back upon its own resources for the immediate creation of a naval reserve. A few foreign vessels, including one cruiser and one gunboat, were hastily bought before the outbreak of hostilities. Then the obligations of neutrality shut our government out of the European ship market. There were two distinct purposes for which merchant steamers were sought, — for the auxiliary navy and for the transport fleet. For the former service only American-owned ships were taken. Foremost among these, of course, were the four great steamers of the American Transatlantic line. The "St. Paul" was secured by the Navy Department on April 17, 1898, eight days before the declaration of war. The "St. Louis" was chartered immediately afterward. The "New York" and "Paris" followed, their names being transformed for the time to "Harvard" and "Yale." All four ships were hastily armed with light, rapid-fire guns, and sent southward to scout for Cervera's cruisers, which were stealing overseas, — whether bound for Cuba or our own long, vulnerable seaboard, no one knew. Next in importance after the four American liners, came the four ships of the Southern Pacific or Morgan line, between New York and New Orleans. These were "El Norte," "El Rio," "El Sol," and "El Sud," and they were renamed by the Navy Department "Yankee," "Dixie," "Prairie," and "Yosemite," — words which figure conspicuously in the records of the war. The four Southern Pacific liners were much smaller than the "St. Paul" and her sisters, but they were still notably large ships of a gross tonnage of 4,600 and nearly 400 feet long, with single-screw triple expansion engines, and a speed of from 14.5 to 16 knots an hour. They were manned by the naval militia, armed with five and six-inch rapid-fire guns, and kept constantly in service to the end of the war. Three of these ships were selected as a part of the Eastern Squadron, that was ordered to attack the coast of Spain as a counterstroke to Admiral Camara's futile expedition against Manila. But Camara got no farther on his way than Suez, a peace protocol closed the hundred days' war, and the bold cruise of the Eastern Squadron was abandoned.

Before the spring of 1898, many naval officers were sceptical as to the military value of merchant steamers lacking the protective decks and the fine watertight subdivision of regularly built men-of-war. But it is significant that these officers ceased to be troubled by such scruples in the actual presence of an enemy. At first, the auxiliaries "Yankee," "Prairie," "Dixie," and "Yosemite" were assigned to the relatively safe and quiet service of the northern patrol squadron, guarding the Atlantic coast north of the Capes of Delaware. There they proved to be such thoroughly efficient and reliable ships that they were all finally sent south to West Indian waters, and all came under the fire of the foe.

Three more fine merchant cruisers were purchased and armed at the outbreak of the Spanish War, — the "Yumuri" of the Ward line, renamed the "Badger," the "Venezuela" of the Red D line, renamed the "Panther," and the "Yorktown" of the Old Dominion line, renamed the "Resolute." These three ships all did good fighting service on the coast of Cuba. They were strong enough to carry batteries of four and five inch guns, and large enough to steam long distances without recoaling. Toward the end of the war a fifth Morgan liner, the "Nictheroy," was purchased from Brazil. This ship had had a remarkable career. She had been sent out from New York several years before to Rio Janeiro, fitted with a dynamite thrower and several other guns, and had played a part in subduing the monarchist insurrection. Thus, altogether, twelve steamships of the merchant marine were added to the fighting navy of the United States in the war with Spain. The four great American liners were chartered, and were returned to their owners in the autumn of 1898. The eight other ships were bought outright, and at the end of the war they remained in the naval service.

It was the fortune of the "St. Louis" and "St. Paul" to achieve some really brilliant exploits. They were sent off with their sisters, the "Harvard" and "Yale," and the swift commerce-destroyers, "Columbia" and "Minneapolis," at the very outset of the war, to scout along the islands that edge the eastern border of the Caribbean. Great was the satisfaction of the country when it became known that this superb squadron of lookouts was at sea. On May 18, 1898, the "St. Louis," commanded by Captain Caspar F. Goodrich of the regular navy, grappled and cut, off Santiago, the cable to Jamaica, which gave Captain-General Blanco communication with Madrid. This cable was brought up from deep water within 2,500 to 3,000 yards of Morro Castle, while the Spanish gun and mortar batteries were playing fiercely upon the immense unarmored merchantman. The "St. Louis" then had only a few six-pounders — mere popguns — to reply, and her only consort was the armed tug "Wompatuck." Two weeks afterward, when Admiral Schley made his first attack upon Santiago and the "Colon," lying in the harbor mouth, he fought with his heavy armor-clads circling at a range of seven to nine thousand yards.

The deed of the "St. Louis" was bold to the verge of rashness. A few hours after she left Santiago, Cervera's four great cruisers and his two destroyers arrived from Spain, and slipped into the harbor unobserved by American eyes. The "St. Louis" was then grappling for the French cable off Guantanamo forty miles to the eastward. This cable was finally found and cut by Captain Goodrich at its other end, on the coast of Hayti. The "St. Louis" subsequently took part in General Miles's expedition to Porto Rico, and handsomely performed every duty assigned to her as cruiser or transport.

It was the distinction of the "St. Paul" to figure brilliantly in one of the most exciting actions of the war. On June 22, 1898, she was attacked off San Juan, Porto Rico, by the Spanish cruiser "Infanta Isabel," and the thirty-knot torpedo boat destroyer "Terror" which had parted company off Martinique, a month before, with Admiral Cervera's squadron. The Spanish vessels came out about midday under the protection of the heavy guns of the shore batteries. The huge American liner, towering high out of the water for the nearly six hundred feet of her majestic length, was a superb target for the shells of the Spanish artillerists and the thunderbolts of the destroyer. The "Terror" drove straight at the "St. Paul" to blow her up. It was the first time in naval history that a destroyer had been brought into action. Swift as the "St. Paul" was, her officers and crew knew that the Scotch-built Spaniard was swifter, and that their only salvation lay in the power and accuracy of their guns. Captain Charles D. Sigsbee, of the lost "Maine," who commanded the "St. Paul," opened with his five-inch rifles at fifty-four hundred yards at the narrow snake-like "Terror" now rushing onward with her utmost speed. A few shots gave the Yankee gunners the exact range, and then a storm of fifty-pound shells fell upon the "Terror," crushing her machinery, killing her chief engineer and several of his men, and piercing the steel hull below the water-line. The shattered destroyer swerved from her course, gave up the fight, and fled for the shelter of the Spanish batteries. She was hurried into the harbor and dragged upon the beach to save the torn hull from foundering.

Another merchant cruiser, the "Yosemite" (the Morgan liner, "El Sud"), Captain William H. Emory, had a lively fight off San Juan six days later.[1] She was blockading the port when the Spanish transport "Antonio Lopez" attempted to run in under cover of a rain squall. The five-inch guns of the "Yosemite" promptly drove the Spanish craft ashore, and when several gunboats came out to the rescue, the "Yosemite" fell upon them and forced them to scurry back to the harbor. Then the plucky Yankee merchantman, manned by the boys of the Michigan naval militia, shelled the stranded transport until she was destroyed, although the great guns of the Morro

[1] "Our Navy in the War with Spain," by John R. Spears.

and the other San Juan forts were keeping up a furious fire of remonstrance.

The "Yosemite's" sister "Yankee," Captain William H. Brownson, besides holding her place in the line in one of Admiral Sampson's bombardments of Santiago, fought a Spanish gunboat and battery off Cienfuegos. The "Prairie," Captain C. J. Train, manned by the Massachusetts naval militia, another of the Morgan liners, helped to chase and destroy the powerfully armed Spanish transport "Alfonso XII.," at Mariel, near Havana. The "Dixie," Captain Charles H. Davis, fourth of the Morgan ships, bore an active part in the Porto Rico expedition. Captain Davis received the surrender of Ponce, on the southern coast, which became the main base of General Miles's advance on San Juan. Altogether these Morgan liners proved a handsome investment for the nation. The "Badger" (formerly the "Yumuri") aided in the attack on the "Alfonso XII.," at Mariel. The "Panther" (formerly the "Venezuela") took Colonel Huntington's marines to Guantanamo, where their gallant battle made this fine harbor secure as the naval base and coaling station of the Santiago blockade. When the war ended the navy and the country knew that good, strong, swift merchant steamers, of the modern steel and iron type, were an indispensable reserve of a fighting fleet, and that they could themselves fight well if they were bravely and skilfully handled.

But these auxiliary cruisers were by no means the only vessels which the government in its time of need drew from the merchant marine. The naval hospital ship "Solace," the most perfect vessel of her type afloat, the army hospital ship "Relief," and the navy repair ship "Vulcan" were purchased from the coastwise service. A great fleet of more than fifty merchant steamers, chartered or bought as transports, bore the United States troops to Cuba, Porto Rico, and the Philippines. More than half of these vessels were American built and owned, but when the government had secured all the American ships available, it required still more, and it was compelled to buy outright at a high price a considerable number of foreign steamers. The most important of these alien craft were the large passenger and freight ships of the Atlantic Transport line between New York and London, — a concern operating under the British flag but controlled by American capital.

The war with Spain, therefore, proved that the merchant marine of the United States in 1898 was not sufficient to provide the indispensable naval reserve for even a brief conflict with a third-rate Power. One of the familiar arguments with which legislation for the upbuilding of the merchant marine had been opposed before 1898 was that under modern naval conditions the merchant steamship had no military value whatsoever. It had even been insisted that the fast ships of the American line could not be successfully utilized as cruisers. The war brought a wholesome awakening. The military value of ocean-going merchant steamers has risen and not shrunk with the lapse of time.

The United States auxiliary navy in the Spanish War consisted of one hundred and twenty-three steamers, including yachts, tugs, and revenue cutters, or a fleet almost equal in numbers and tonnage, all told, to that of the regular service. Besides the nineteen navy colliers — all but two of them, by the way, foreign-built — which were purchased for use in the war, the Department found that it required many vessels for miscellaneous work, — distilling ships, supply ships, refrigerator ships, etc. Most of these craft, like the colliers, had to be hastily purchased from European owners before the actual outbreak of hostilities. Many of them proved to be grotesquely unfit for the purposes for which they were secured. The Navy Department might have been gravely handicapped by a lack of these essential auxiliaries if the war had been prolonged. The coastwise steamers were excellent ships, but because they were cleaner and swifter, with cabin accommodations for officers, they were drafted into the transport fleet of the War Department. Moreover, the navy for its collier and supply work needed vessels of greater tonnage. That is why so many purchases were made of foreign " tramps."

It is gratifying to remember, however, that the fighting merchant cruisers of the war with Spain were all American. The war found us with a small steam merchant fleet, but a fleet of admirable quality. A very large proportion of these American steamers were unusually fast and strong, fit to carry modern high-power guns and able to take hard knocks as well as to give them. Where the merchant fleet was deficient was in the relatively slow but capacious vessels of the ordinary " tramp " or cargo type. It was not high-class merchant cruisers but coal craft and the like that had to be procured from foreign services.

In the Pacific the American merchant marine happened to be relatively larger than in the Atlantic. The ships of the Pacific Mail and the Oceanic companies made excellent transports for the regiments that were hurried forward to reinforce Admiral Dewey in the Philippines. The distances were so great that all the American steamers that could be bought or chartered were not enough, and as the war summer advanced, many Pacific traders under foreign flags were pressed into the United States service. Later the large ships of the War Department that could be spared from Cuba were sent out to the Pacific, but the transport system between our Western coast and the Orient never was thoroughly efficient, or worthy of the government of the United States.

The war with Spain caused no direct loss to American merchant shipping, in spite of the Spanish threat to send privateers to harry our commerce. The cruisers of the United States, however, captured twenty or thirty important merchant vessels of the enemy, and many smaller craft. Most of these prizes were taken off the coast of Cuba.

It would be gratifying to close a history of the American merchant marine with a roseate picture of renewed, triumphant prosperity after more than forty long years of decline and discouragement. But that is not the honest meaning of the present clangor in our shipyards. Tugboats, yachts, men-of-war, coasting vessels, here and there a fine, stately steamship for one of the half-dozen corporations carrying the United States mails, — this is a handsome tonnage so far as it goes, but it does not constitute a great merchant navy. It is a sobering fact [1] that more than half of the steel shipping now under construction on both seaboards is composed of battleships, cruisers, monitors, and torpedo craft building to the order of the national government. These fighting vessels are all needed; there may be work for them to do. But it would be a costly delusion for the American people to fall into the idea that their deepsea carrying trade is coming back to them because this country launched a greater amount of shipping in 1901 than since the flood-tide year of 1855. Many ships were built in 1901, but few, very few, of them were for the purposes of ocean commerce.

For several years the subsidy question has been once more pressing forward in Washington, and early in the first session of the Fifty-Seventh Congress, opening in December, 1901, Senator William P. Frye, of Maine, Chairman of the Committee on Commerce, reintroduced the Shipping Subsidy Bill in an amended form. The new bill offered to mail-carrying steamships a subsidy based upon both speed and tonnage, which restored, in the main, the original rates of compensation of the Postal Aid Law of 1891, of which Senator Frye was also the author. It gave a fixed subsidy based upon tonnage to other steamships and to sailing vessels. But this protection was bestowed on only American vessels already registered, or those that may hereafter be built in the United States.

[1] The naval tonnage is 281,148; merchant, 273,865.

The later chapters of this history of the American merchant marine have had much to say, necessarily, of the policy of shipping subsidies. This is a factor of undeniable importance. It is the firm belief of the practical ship merchants of the United States that a subsidy in some form is indispensable to the prompt restoration of our almost lost trade of deep-sea carrying. It would, however, be a grave error to assume that because a subsidy policy is important, it is all-sufficient. It is at its best only one favorable influence, with which other favorable influences must coincide in order to make the upbuilding of our merchant marine quick and certain.

National aid to shipping by subsidy is potent, but it is not omnipotent. If it had not been withdrawn in 1858 by what was virtually a political crime, we should have saved our fine steam fleet on the North Atlantic even through the storm of the Civil War. If, however, a subsidy policy had been re-established in 1868 or 1870, after the lapse of a decade, it would undoubtedly have disappointed its sanguine champions. For the other essential factors in the problem were not favorable. It was (in 1870 and onward) an era of railroad building and not of shipbuilding. The energies and the money of the nation were absorbed by the urgent demands of home development. The American people had turned their eyes from the sea and were facing inward toward the marvellous riches of their empire of the West. No national legislation, however liberal or however strenuous, could have caused American shipping to spread and increase between 1865 and 1890. The most that could have been accomplished would have been to save it from the swift and terrible decline that was the heavy price of our actual national policy of neglect and discouragement.

Now, however, all the circumstances are far more propitious. The keynote of the present is no longer domestic development but commercial expansion. The eyes of the nation are once more turning outward to the sea. Our

28

railroads are built; our house is set in order. Enterprise
and wealth are available for that ocean adventure in which
the Americans of the first half of the nineteenth century so
conspicuously excelled the less bold and tenacious merchants
and mariners of Europe. It is profoundly significant that
the greatest shipping enterprise which the world has ever
known is the work of American capital. Mr. J. Pierpont
Morgan's purchase of the Leyland line of Atlantic steamers,
and then his startling combination of this and several other
British concerns with the International Navigation Company, has shocked Europe almost like a declaration of war.
Yet this mighty stroke of financial statesmanship has had
no immediate effect in increasing American tonnage. Only
four of the hundred or more vessels in the Morgan combination hold a United States registry, — the four American
transatlantic liners, "St. Louis," "St. Paul," "New York,"
and "Philadelphia." The others fly a foreign flag and are
at the beck and call of a foreign government. The American people are interested in and delighted by Mr. Morgan's
vast undertaking, but they are not satisfied that American
money and financial skill should thus go merely to the
upbuilding of alien sea-power. Nor in all probability are
Mr. Morgan himself and his associates. It is likely that
their full plan, their final purpose, has not yet been disclosed.

Following is the official record of the tonnage and foreign
commerce of the United States, and the proportion carried
in American vessels from 1891 to the present time : —

TONNAGE AND FOREIGN TRADE, 1891–1901.

Year.	Shipping Tons.	Total Foreign Commerce.	Proportion carried in American Ships.		
			Imports.	Exports.	Combined Imports and Exports.
1891	988,719	$1,656,540,812	15.9	9.3	12.5
1892	977,624	1,784,732,543	17.7	8.1	12.3
1893	883,199	1,626,082,075	15.5	8.8	12.2
1894	899,698	1,468,290,672	19.4	8.7	13.3
1895	822,347	1,456,403,388	15.5	8.2	11.7

Year.	Shipping Tons.	Total Foreign Commerce.	Proportion carried in American Ships.		
			Imports.	Exports.	Combined Imports and Exports.
1896	829,833	1,565,665,408	15.7	8.5	12.0
1897	792,870	1,714,829,043	15.0	8.1	11.0
1898	726,213	1,743,820,496	16.0	5.9	9.3
1899	837,229	1,806,876,063	12.4	6.9	8.9
1900	816,795	2,089,528,616	12.9	7.1	9.3
1901	879,595	2,151,935,411			8.2

Not by large American investment in European ship-yards or in foreign steamship lines is the American merchant marine to be re-created. That was not the policy of the fathers; it cannot be the policy of the sons. The preceding pages have shown that the great, prosperous, and glorious commercial fleet of the first half-century of the republic owed its birth and growth to the utilization of native ingenuity and enterprise. The famous Yankee packets, the clippers, and the mail ships were American through and through. When the United States launches its new fleet and reaches out for the mastery of the sea which is its rightful destiny and heritage, its new ships will surely be found to be distinctively American in design and in construction. Here and there expediency may justify the naturalization of another Paris or New York, but the shrewd American mind will always insist that this shall be the exception and not the rule, — recognizing that every merchant vessel built by our own mechanics of our own materials in our own yards means a strengthening of the productive power of this nation and a lessening of the cost of American tonnage, while every merchant vessel purchased abroad means a gain to the shipyard capacity and efficiency of our antagonist.

The American merchant marine in foreign commerce will revive when the American people demand it. Economic conditions are quietly shaping themselves now to make this revival easy and certain, but it can be hastened by an aroused patriotic sentiment, and postponed by a lack of it. Germany has lately given to the world a noble example of the swift creation of maritime power in response to an ardent national aspiration, — and Germany has a scant foothold on the deep sea, and none of the splendid nautical traditions of America. What the empire has done, the republic can do more readily, if it will. The same indomitable spirit which wrought our great railway system, subdued the Western wilderness, and is now driving the surplus output of our industries into all the markets of the world, can win supremacy on the ocean for the United States just as soon as it learns that it is worth while to make the endeavor.

The present exclusion of America from the deep sea is only for a time, and now for a brief time. No race like ours with a grasp upon two oceans and the mingled blood of Viking and pioneer can long be cheated of its birthright.

THE END

INDEX

INDEX